THE NATIONAL

The Story of a Pioneer College

SEMPER · FIDELIS

THE NATIONAL

The Story of a Pioneer College

THE NATIONAL TRAINING COLLEGE
OF DOMESTIC SUBJECTS

DOROTHY STONE

LONDON
ROBERT HALE & COMPANY

ISBN 0 7091 5774 6

Robert Hale & Company
Clerkenwell House
Clerkenwell Green
London EC1R 0HT

Printed and bound in Great Britain by
REDWOOD BURN LIMITED
Trowbridge & Esher

PREFACE

THIS HISTORY has been written by my wife Dorothy Stone. We have shared the research, as we have the whole venture. When the College closed in 1962, the Executive Committee handed over the remaining records to the Liquidator, who placed at the disposal of the National Training College of Domestic Subjects Trust the Minute Books with other records and some slight correspondence.

It was possible to supplement some of the earlier records by consulting the Commissioners for the Exhibition of 1851, whose office still remains on the edge of the original site of the National Training School of Cookery; the British Museum; the Deputy Head Archivist of the Greater London Council, covering both London and Middlesex; the Department of Education and Science; and the Ministry of Defence in which the Admiralty and the War Office are now merged. To these authorities we extend our thanks for willing help and for allowing us facilities for research.

Everything in this book which is between quote marks is a direct quotation from an authentic source, mainly from the Minute Books, the *Guild Magazine* and personal reminiscences. Interesting information has been gained from the study of contemporary newspapers and magazines, in particular *Punch*, to whose owners we are greatly indebted for permission to reproduce several cartoons. We thank the Countess of Longford and her publishers George Weidenfeld and Nicolson for the privilege of recording a sentence from page 417 of *Victoria R.I.*; Mr Jack Lindsay, author of *George Meredith – His Life and Work* and his

v

publishers The Bodley Head, for allowing us to refer to passages in the early part of that book; Methuen Ltd the publishers of *A History of the Teaching of Domestic Subjects* by the late Miss Helen Sillitoe for permission to quote some references to her close association with the College; and finally for allowing reference to some of his remarks and information about Thomas Love Peacock and for his kindly interest, the late Mr Felix Felton who alas cannot now read this acknowledgment. We also thank the Photographic Librarians of Fox Photos, the Associated Press, London News Agency Photos and the Keystone Press Agency for permission to reproduce without fee some of the press photographs taken at the College during its life.

In addition, many who have had long and intimate connections with the National have contributed personal recollections and been able to verify facts and dates. Among all these, we thank in particular Miss K. J. Lough, who shared so readily her own memories and those which she sought from a wide range of others, thus filling many gaps in our knowledge. Our typists have greatly eased our task and to Mrs Hasernik and Mrs Kirkby-Bott, who helped at the beginning, and to Mrs Pasley who came to our rescue towards the end, we are most grateful. The bulk of the book has been the responsibility of Mrs Jean Dyson, whose kindness and faultless help are beyond praise.

We would like to give special thanks to those of our friends who have borne the brunt of preoccupation and seeming neglect, and also those who have heartened us throughout the whole enterprise. Among the latter, we should like to include the name of Professor John Burnett, from whose knowledge and experience we have had kind and constructive help.

We thank Mr Grant Uden and Mr Charles L. Pickering for originally introducing us to Mr R. T. Cowern, Principal of the Brighton College of Art, now Brighton Polytechnic, which led to the ready co-operation of the Director, Mr G. R. Hall, and the Director of the Brighton Museums, Mr Christopher Morley, resulting in the printing of this book.

Finally we owe a particular debt to the Head of the Department of Printing, Mr J. A. P. Evans, for his encouragement and understanding. Without his interest, knowledge and professional skill and the scrupulous expertise of his technical staff this book could never have been completed. To him especially we express our personal pleasure in this collaboration, as well as the appreciation of the Trust.

We have tried to select those facts and aspects which would best illustrate the history of the College. The choice was not easy. For the inevitable omissions we ask forbearance, but we believe what has been written to be both objective and truthful.

B. G. STONE

May 1973

I identify myself with all my husband has written. I would like to add my meed of praise to him for his unending patience, and also to Mr John Evans. Both have shown such understanding that crises have dissolved, and the chief memory for us all is of hard work, tremendous interest and great enjoyment.

D. K. S.

May 1973

CONTENTS

FOREWORD

I have read with delight and fascination this vivid portrayal of the life story of 'The National,' beginning with its difficult birth in 1873 as 'The National Training School of Cookery,' through its turbulent pioneering years of growth when it became 'The National Training College of Domestic Subjects,' until its sad closure for lack of money in 1962. But the story does not end there, for such was the zest of the old students that a remarkable epilogue follows, which describes how they seized the initiative and formed a Trust whose final achievement in inaugurating with the University of Surrey an honours degree in Home Economics has set a lead yet again in this country. The book will have a wide appeal. It gives a stirring account of the struggles of a small College at the forefront of new ideas in its field. Old students and members of staff will find it enthralling, a thing of joy to be treasured and read time after time. Those who are interested in what we now call 'Home Economics' will find it a rewarding account. And everyone who takes an interest in social history will find this a valuable record of one of the most important transformations in our modern society – the changing status of women. Such is the blend of vitality and sound scholarship that distinguishes this book that it can serve all these differing interests worthily: it is indeed a fitting publication to mark the centenary of the founding of 'The National.'

The College was started by a small group of enthusiasts and built up, as so often with institutions at that time, by an indomitable Principal, Mrs Clarke. She steadfastly overcame innumerable vicissitudes, was haunted continually by financial crises, yet never missed an opportunity to press ahead with her aspirations, which always showed as much concern for human values as for excellence in craft skills. She in turn was followed by her daughter, another outstanding personality. They gathered around themselves a faithful team, who developed a tremendous loyalty to the aims and the high standards of the College. Another aspect of their strong individuality, and their determination to preserve their freedom to develop new ideas, was the long struggle to avoid being enmeshed by the bureaucracy of the London County Council and the Board of Education. It was this determination that enabled them to pioneer so vigorously. One wonders whether it was the dimming of that same spirit that left them defenceless amid the rising costs after the second World War; or whether their determined resistance to becoming a part of the State system of advanced education left them too isolated. However that may be, the question remains in our minds how we can seek in the present age to give scope for the individual initiatives which the College portrayed so splendidly, and which seem to be needed more than ever now, to leaven a spreading bureaucracy.

From the early cookery lessons for ladies, attended by their cooks, the College set the highest standards in the practical skills of cookery, and also sought to develop a wider outlook on the related arts and sciences; and thus it was closely involved in the changing position of women in society. When in its later years the College became one of the large group of Training Colleges for Teachers associated with the Institute of Education of London University, it proposed that Domestic Science as a field of study should not be envisaged as a part of 'curriculum studies,' but as contributing to the development of the students' own education: not simply a skill, but a rich medium to educate them for personal maturity. As long as a quarter of a century ago, it was proposed that a student should make a special study from 'an aesthetic, scientific or social studies approach, and from this angle make an integrated study of some aspect of Needlework, Cookery or Home Management.' It was a similarly forward-looking approach that the Trustees embodied in their recent conception of an honours degree in Home Economics, which has been sponsored by Surrey University; for their proposal envisaged an interdisciplinary course drawing on the humanities, science and social sciences to provide a coherent education embodying intellectual rigour and the warmth of personal values. One hopes that this University, a vigorous new institution with responsibilities for research as well as teaching, and with the advantages which a measure of freedom

xii

from detailed control can bring, will carry forward the pioneering developments in the field that were so honourably performed by 'The National' in an earlier age, and that have recently been expressed in the acceptance of this degree.

As I have intimated already, this book makes a valuable contribution to the social history of the last hundred years, not only because of the importance of its subject, but because of the high level of scholarship that has been meticulously observed throughout it. When it is said that the sun shone at the opening of the Exhibition, the statement has been verified; and so have the facts that Peacock was there, and the little girl too – and they probably held hands, though that is not known for sure. To have kept so close to original sources, and to have brought together accounts from different places into a text that is balanced in judgment and a delight to read, is a fine achievement.

That prompts me to say in conclusion how the book came to be written. When the College was closed, the Guild of Students refused to fade quietly away, and it was their initiative that led to the setting up of the 'National Training College of Domestic Subjects (founded 1873) Trust,' as described in the latter part of the book, without any support from the Governors. The chairman of the Trust was Mr Bertram Stone, who first knew the National through his wife who was on the staff of 'The National' for six years before she became, after many years of married family life abroad and in England, one of Her Majesty's Inspectors of Schools responsible for Home Economics. When the Old Students decided that a record of the College, describing its achievements in spite of difficulties, and the proud traditions it had established, should be written, it was first suggested that Bertram and Dorothy should edit and collate material and reminiscences. By the time the large packing cases of the surviving records of the College reached their home, a variety of mishaps prevented this idea, and so Dorothy Stone found herself committed, somewhat reluctantly, to the task.

As so often in the past, 'The National' has shown right to the end its characteristic ability to draw persons of outstanding gifts to its service when the need arose. Bertram Stone has devoted the last ten years largely to the work of the Trust, taking advantage of his varied experience as classical scholar at Cambridge, colonial administrator in Africa, and later in charge of the Students

Department at the Colonial Office, planning courses for students at all universities in the United Kingdom. It is through his personal efforts and skill that the negotiations with Surrey University have been conducted successfully. Yet what has been achieved has been above all the fruit of their creative partnership. Dorothy, who had the chance of a career on the stage or in scholarship, devoted her talents instead to the development of Home Economics. It was her experience in this field, and her imaginative grasp of what should grow in the future, that sparked off the initiative when the Trust was formed, and that subsequently lay at the heart of the proposal for an honours degree. And three years ago she found herself of necessity a historian, being faced with the task of writing the record of the College.

At first the account was to be a modest pamphlet. But soon it became evident that there were large gaps in the records, and enquiries had to be pursued with archivists at the L.C.C., Middlesex, Department of Education and Science, Church and Civil Service Commissioners, Army, Navy, Prisons, Workhouses, contemporary magazines and newspapers, biographies etc., for such was the spread of relationships of 'The National.' After three years of intensive work, her scholarly research and literary flair have brought the story to life.

One crucial need remained: to find a suitable printer. They could not have been more fortunate than in gaining the co-operation of John Evans, Head of the Printing Department of Brighton College of Art. He has worked very closely with them, showing great skill and sensitivity in devising the attractive layout and in reproducing old photographs, and the result of his efforts will be widely admired. Certainly this book is a distinguished and worthy tribute to 'The National,' and is likely to be an enduring one, though it marks the end of a memorable era.

RICHARD D'AETH

May 1973

Professor R. D'Aeth A.M. Ph.D.
Department of Education
University of Exeter

xiv

DEDICATED TO
ALL FRIENDS OF THE NATIONAL

'The number of inhabitants which may be supported
in any country, upon its internal produce, depends as
much upon the state of the Art of Cookery as upon that
of Agriculture . . . but if Cookery be of so much
importance, it certainly deserves to be studied with
the greatest care. . . .

'Cookery and Agriculture are arts of civilized nations;
savages understand neither of them.'

COUNT RUMFORD
(Benjamin Thompson)
1753 – 1814

EARLY DAYS

CHAPTER I

THE SUN SHONE. A line of carriages, in which no social distinctions were observed, stretched from the City into Hyde Park.
Here was gathered a great throng of people, with cravats, crino-
lines, laces, gloves and parasols as well as the humbler versions
of bonnets and shawls, and excitement ran high as they turned
towards the great focus, the vast glittering dome of the Crystal
Palace. Twenty-five thousand people, with no selection of class,
were privileged, for the payment of two guineas each, to enter
the doors of Sir Joseph Paxton's spectacular structure at eleven
o'clock to await the royal arrival at mid-day. The less fortunate
watched more distantly from the ground, from others' shoulders,
or from the branches of the surrounding trees.

Among those with a good view was a little girl of six, with fair
hair brushed smoothly under a straw bonnet, a gay flounced
dress and long, frilly drawers above small neat boots, holding
tightly to the hand of a distinguished elderly gentleman with
commanding presence, handsome features and fine blue eyes –
Edith Nicolls and her grandfather Thomas Love Peacock, the
well-known author and Head of the India Office.

Twenty-five years later, this little girl had become Mrs Charles
Clarke, the Principal of the National Training School of
Cookery, a post which she held for forty-five years, to the end of
the First World War.

On this day, 1 May 1851, Her Majesty Queen Victoria came
in state with His Royal Highness Prince Albert and the oldest
royal children, for the opening ceremony of England's first International Exhibition, held in the Crystal Palace, Hyde Park,

1

London. She was accompanied by various royal dignitaries and representatives of foreign states, and attended by her own Court and Ministers. The day was the climax after months of controversy, and the Queen now paid open tribute to the imagination and faith of her husband in this colossal enterprise. She further publicly displayed both her support and her stamina, by making with her family, at the end of the hot and solemn opening ceremony, a grand tour of the whole ground floor filled with a richness and diversity of display.

The Great Exhibition of 1851 remained open for five and a half months, until 15 October, and during all this time its lure was irresistible. It was visited by six million people who came from abroad as well as all parts of the British Isles. Season tickets with varying conditions cost from three pounds to five shillings, 26 May being the first day of the popular shilling entry. The total profit amounted to nearly a quarter of a million pounds.

Queen Victoria visited the exhibition almost daily until she left for Osborne towards the end of July; Prince Albert went even more. He was constantly on the alert for future developments, and little escaped his notice. Did it ever cross his fertile mind that this first Great Exhibition, designed to stimulate the study of art and science in Victorian Britain, as well as economic relationships abroad, should lead to the first organised, systematic instruction in this country in the art and science of cookery? Yet the way from the Crystal Palace to the corrugated iron shed where the whole enterprise started was surprisingly direct.

Sir Henry Cole, K.C.B.

THE POUND AND THE SHILLING.

"Whoever Thought of Meeting You Here?"

EARLY DAYS

CHAPTER II

THE GREAT EXHIBITION of 1851 was organised by a Royal
Commission set up by the Society of Arts, who had been responsible for London's first contemporary exhibition in 1756. The
Society was granted a charter in 1847 under the Presidency of
the Prince Consort, who initiated the first international gathering of 1851. The overwhelming success encouraged the Society
to sponsor, in the following decades, a whole series of small
international exhibitions. They were held on a site in South
Kensington, now commemorated by the name of Exhibition
Road, and were all organised by the Royal Commissioners for
the Exhibition of 1851, who to this day administer their affairs
from an office on the original site.

In 1873 Henry Cole, a member of the Commission, was asked
to give personal supervision to the exhibition for that year and
decided to include the subject of food. A Committee appointed
to deal with this section, under the chairmanship of the Hon
E. F. Leveson-Gower, felt that a series of lecture-demonstrations
on cookery could best serve this purpose and decided to approach
Mr J. C. Buckmaster, a well-known and accomplished lecturer
on technical subjects. This colourful character, who came of
centuries of prosperous Buckinghamshire farming stock, left
home at an early age to fend for himself after his mother died
and his father fell on evil days. He joined the followers of John
Bright and Richard Cobden in the Anti-Corn Law League
demonstrations of the eighteen-forties, touring the country in
these campaigns. He studied and learnt with this group, and
with almost no schooling he became not only informed, but a

fluent and persuasive speaker. Impressed by his ability and drive, John Bright urged him to take up teaching as a career, and secured a place for him in his early twenties at one of the first regular teacher training courses in the newly established college at Battersea. After qualifying, he taught general subjects in London elementary schools for a few years, and then turned his attention to scientific and technical subjects to such effect, that with his gift as a speaker, he was much in demand as a lecturer at the Mechanics' Institutes. Henry Cole, who held him in repute, had also often invited him to give lectures at the Department of Science and Art, South Kensington; it was therefore unanimously agreed that he would be the perfect exponent of food and cookery at the 1873 International Exhibition.

Mr Buckmaster is said to have been reluctant to undertake the role of professional cook, but native wit, hard study and manual dexterity soon made him an acknowledged authority. At this first Exhibition, however, he confined his part to the actual lectures and arranged for these to be illustrated by a French chef aided by several assistants. The engraving reproduced on page 7 depicts him giving one of these lectures in the large room specially equipped for the purpose.

This 1873 Exhibition was visited by half a million people, and the cookery section, with its lectures, caught the public imagination. Her Majesty Queen Victoria herself attended one, although she does not seem to have relished it particularly, for it is recorded that 'while waiting unwillingly for a demonstration of how to cook an omelette she had to listen to "a rather tiresome lecture".' The final cookery takings amounted to £1,765, largely made up by the sale of recipes, since attendance was free – apart from a charge of 6*d* for a seat in the front row, with permission for tasting. History does not record whether Her Majesty availed herself of this extra privilege.

Henry Cole (later Sir Henry Cole, K.C.B.) was a man of considerable parts. He was just in his forties, after some twenty years successful work in the Records Office, when he became one of the leading members of the Royal Commission for the 1851 Exhibition. In 1853, he was appointed Secretary to the newly created Department of Science and Art. Under its auspices the South Kensington Museum, later renamed the Victoria and Albert Museum, was founded, and Henry Cole remained as Director, until 1873, when he retired from the post at the age of sixty-five. He also originated the scheme for the erection of the Royal Albert Hall, and for the training school for music which eventually became the Royal College of Music.

This versatile man, assessing the public response to the cookery lectures, realised that their success could well be exploited to the benefit of the nation. Accordingly he persuaded the Committee responsible for the lectures to back his idea of establishing a national training school for cookery. Not only did he succeed in getting this support, but the members gave tangible proof by agreeing to remain in being as the first provisional Executive Committee with the Hon E. F. Leveson-Gower as Chairman.

Mr J. C. Buckmaster
lecturing at the International Exhibition, 1873

The Committee had a wide circle of eminent friends, whose interest they now enlisted, and this group decided to put the proposal to the test. The Marquis of Westminster (shortly to be created the first Duke) lent his house, Grosvenor House, Park Lane, for a public meeting on Thursday, 17 July 1873. Great was their satisfaction when, by unanimous consent, it was formally agreed 'to establish a national training school for cookery.' The proceedings of this meeting and the ensuing action taken by the Executive Committee are set out in a prospectus which was issued in December 1873, shortly after the first two official meetings of the Executive Committee on the 6 and 22 November. As the prospectus succinctly states the whole position at that moment, it is quoted in full in Appendix A. The first Proposal in the Prospectus stated the intention of the Committee 'to commence the work of the National Training School of Cookery as soon as possible in Exhibition Road, South Kensington, in the building lately used for the International Exhibition School of Cookery, which the Commissioners have liberally placed at the disposal of the Executive Committee of the Training School of Cookery for a limited period.'

The meeting on 17 July 1873 underlined the importance of establishing a training school of cookery which would be in alliance with the School Boards and Training Schools throughout the country. These last three words declare Henry Cole's particular aim. The new school was not to fill any purely local need; it was not to be a 'South Kensington', nor even a 'London' school. It was to be a 'National' school in the sense that it was designed to pioneer a national effort for the recognition and teaching of cookery (and incidentally hygiene) as being vital to the interests and well being of the whole country.

This pioneer school took its responsibilities very seriously, and its purpose was incorporated in its name. On Thursday, 6 November 1873, within four months of the July resolutions, the official minute book records the first meeting of the Executive Committee of 'The National Training School for Cookery.'

So was born 'The National' – thus to be known colloquially and affectionately all its life.

EARLY DAYS

CHAPTER III

THE FOLLOWING SUMMER seemed propitious to establish the school in the eyes of the public. Sir Daniel Cooper, Bart. had joined the Committee as Honorary Treasurer in January 1874 (a post he was to hold for the next twenty-eight years) and considerable thought over policy and finances followed. There had been little response to an appeal made the previous December and it was agreed that support from a wider circle was essential. Accordingly, the Executive Committee invited public attendance at their first Annual General Meeting, at the Society of Arts on 21 May 1874. In a long agenda, two main resolutions were passed. The first, unanimously agreed, stated that 'This Association is formed for the purpose of establishing a National Training School of Cookery, and of promoting generally the diffusion of a knowledge of cookery amongst all classes of Her Majesty's subjects.' The second was presented as a natural corollary; money was obviously needed if the school were to be established on a permanent and efficient footing. As the Committee had previously decided that the sum of £8,000 would be required for this purpose, it was resolved that an immediate and urgent appeal to raise this sum was to be directed to corporations and charitable institutions as well as to the general public.

But there is no trace of any campaign. The actual sum raised in small donations during the following months was under £600.

All the omens would seem to have been favourable; an awakening interest in food and cookery; an appreciation of the nation-wide scope; a realisation of the need for qualified teachers; and already an acceptance of the value of the newly opened classes. The Committee, distinguished and influential, remained stable. Their plans were realistic, and official minutes record their determination to set the whole undertaking on a firm foundation and ensure a proper endowment.

Yet nothing happened. Among the leading members, the Chairman, the Hon E. F. Leveson-Gower, M.P. was a public figure of repute; Sir Daniel Cooper was recognised as a financier; and the instigator, Sir Henry Cole (knighted in 1875) has been variously described as indefatigable, masterful, ingenious, and driving everything before him.

Unaccountably the advantage was not pursued. This failure of achievement seems inexplicable, with the implication of a lack of vision, courage and determination. Yet the Committee possessed all these characteristics in full measure.

Looking back through the years, and in spite of the consistent success of the School, the National was henceforth to be forever haunted, at recurring intervals, by the spectre of insolvency.

EARLY DAYS

CHAPTER IV

THE MINUTES of November 1873 record that the Commissioners for the 1851 Exhibition had 'resolved that the Committee of the National Training School for Cookery should be allowed the temporary gratuitous use of the Exhibition School of Cookery, subject to one month's notice.' This was a small collection of corrugated iron buildings, erected with no thought of permanence, in part of which Mr Buckmaster had given his lecture-demonstrations, with the remainder chiefly used as storerooms. Their site is marked on a map in the 1878 Report of the Exhibition Commissioners, on the west side of Exhibition Road, 250 yards from its junction with Kensington Gore, and set back 20 yards from the pavement. This area is now occupied by the new buildings of the Imperial College of Science. (See map on page 13).

Assured only of inadequate quarters on a precarious basis, the Committee took its courage in both hands and accepted the proffered services of Lady Barker to get the School under way. She was officially appointed Lady Superintendent in January 1874, and these undaunted pioneers set to work to organise classes and engage a staff of cook-instructors. Either the novelty of the enterprise, or the prevailing conditions of ordinary domestic service, attracted over one hundred applicants for the four posts advertised.

By February, the Committee, at the instance of Mr Cole, had been lent all the equipment and utensils used by the Exhibition School, and on the auspicious day of 23 March 1874, the National opened. The first class comprised fourteen Learners, as they were called, whose instruction began with a series of practical demonstrations. 11

A few months later, in July, the Commissioners, seemingly happy about the promise of the School, offered the whole premises including an additional wooden packing shed on a two-year lease free of rent. The Committee now acted with vigour and discernment. Urgent repairs were needed throughout, and Henry Cole's son, Lieutenant Alan Cole of the Royal Engineers, was called in to make a survey. His advice over the essential requirements gave evidence of the qualities which stood the National in such good stead for many years when later he served the Committee as Honorary Treasurer.

He now arranged the speedy completion of the necessary repairs, and also persuaded the original suppliers of the equipment to the former Exhibition School not only to make a gift of the kitchen ranges, stoves, sinks and general fittings, but also in some cases to make cash donations.

In spite of this activity, the working conditions in the buildings must have been rigorous in the extreme. The Principal, Mrs Clarke, in her annual report several years later referred to the trials of 'these unsuitable premises, where there is neither larder nor storeroom,' and where they were 'exposed to every change of temperature, which gives rise to great complaints amongst the pupils and affects the health of the Staff.'

There was no proper ventilation, wind and weather beat noisily on the corrugated iron, and by this time the rain dripped through the leaky roof. Only enthusiasm and dogged determination carried them through.

The Learners' classes started by Lady Barker became extremely popular, and ladies were encouraged to bring their cooks with them. The fees were three guineas for a course lasting a fortnight, with a morning session from 10 am to noon on cleaning methods, management of ovens and flues, and basic cookery processes. From 2 – 4 pm a lecture demonstration was given on a variety of dishes. The regulations noted that 'Persons wishing to avoid this Instruction in Cleaning may do so on paying an extra fee of one guinea, but such persons are not considered eligible to obtain a certificate.'

On the first Saturday in each month, all who wished were 'given the privilege of attending,' at a charge of 2s 6d, a written examination in the theory and practice of cookery. This included

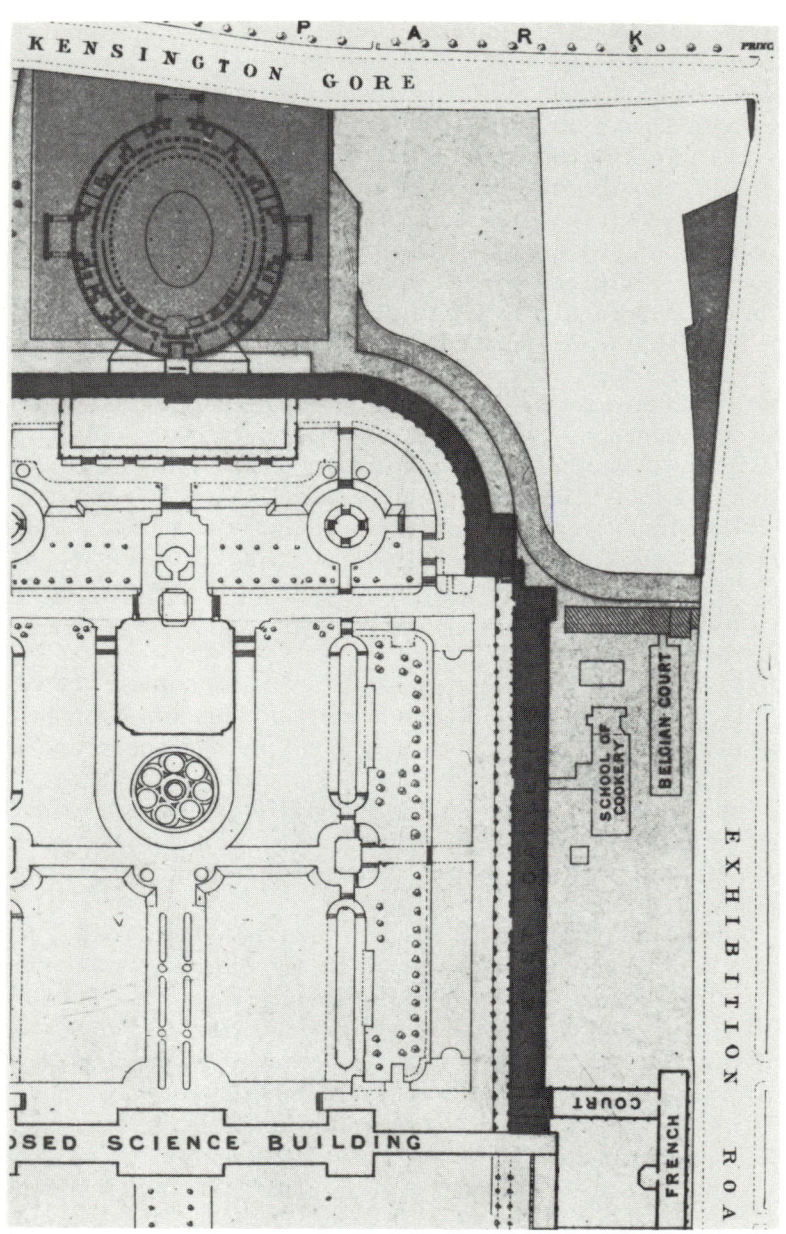

KENSINGTON GORE

P   A   R   K   PRINC

EXHIBITION ROA

SCHOOL OF COOKERY

BELGIAN COURT

FRENCH COURT

OSED SCIENCE BUILDING

a series of theoretical questions, with a maximum of 1,000 marks, to which were added practical marks (to include 'attendance') with a maximum of 680. The minimum pass mark was 40 per cent in both Theory and Practice. There were few failures.

Before taking the examination students were required to have studied the *Catalogue of the Food Museum* in Bethnal Green, and to have a theoretical knowledge of the first principles of cookery gained from such textbooks as Lady Barker's *First Principles of Cookery*, Buckmaster's *Cookery*, Soyer's *Cookery for the People* and Warne's *Shilling Cookery*.

In the first twelve months 176 students passed. Accompanying their mistresses, twenty-seven of these were cooks, whose status was indicated on the printed list by the omission of any prefix to their names!

By the Autumn of 1875 two further classes had been introduced. They are officially described as:

i) For Students or Cooks to practise Cookery under instructions (applicable to families who can spend from 20s to 100s weekly in the purchase of food to be cooked). Fee 4 guineas, unless Class A (i.e. Learners' class) has been previously attended, then only 3 guineas.

ii) For Students attending the kitchen where Cookery for Artisans is taught (for families who can spend from 7s to 20s weekly in the purchase of food to be cooked). Fee 3 guineas, unless Class A has been gone through, then only 2 guineas.

Each certificate could be taken separately. Success qualified for entry to the teachers' course, referred to by Sir Daniel Cooper, the Honorary Treasurer, as 'the chief aim and object of the School.'

Admission requirements for an intending teacher read: 'She should not be under twenty-one years of age. She must be sufficiently educated to be able to perform the duties of a teacher after the special training, to speak aloud, also to write from dictation and keep accounts.' The fees were 10 guineas. The original length of time of ten weeks was soon extended to twelve.

Details of the first course were printed under the heading: 'The following is an outline of the Course of Instruction for Persons wishing to qualify themselves to become "Teachers in Cookery",' and is given in Appendix B.

Mr J. C. Buckmaster

Practice in teaching was gained by lecturing for at least four weeks in the Learners' Kitchen. How enjoyable this exercise was to all parties is not known, but at this time all were at least studying the same subject. Some forty years later, an understandable plaint was registered by a Needlework student, that while doing her adult teaching practice in the National, the class consisted of Cookery students who 'did not relish being present, and regrettably, sometimes made it very difficult.'

By May 1875, three students had gained diplomas for teaching and were already spreading the gospel. At its annual general meeting in the same month the Committee, in reporting this landmark, stated that 'time must elapse before teachers can be produced in sufficient numbers to effect much reform in national cookery, and the process of producing them must be slow.'

But in fact the process snowballed rapidly. Two years later, by May 1877, teaching diplomas had been awarded to thirty-four students, and there were thirty-seven in training.

The aim of the school was established, and the National set on its course.

EARLY DAYS

AMONG THE SUCCESSFUL CANDIDATES in the examination on 1 July 1874 was Edith Nicolls, granddaughter of General Sir Edward Nicolls KCB, of the Royal Marines, who during a distinguished career fought in the Napoleonic Wars, helped to capture a French armed cutter at the age of twenty-four, and later became Governor of Ascension Island and Fernando Po.

Edith Nicolls' maternal grandfather, Thomas Love Peacock, novelist and poet, combined his writing with a full-time official career. From 1819 to 1856 he served in the East India Office, becoming its Head in 1836. In 1820 he married Jane Gryffydh, known as 'the Beauty of Caernarvonshire,' but this gay and dazzling girl became an acute melancholic.

Their eldest daughter Mary inherited her father's literary gifts and her mother's temperament – the brilliance and the instability. In January 1844, she married the young Lieutenant Edward Nicolls, RN, who two months later was tragically lost in a storm off the Irish coast near Kerry, while trying to save a drowning man.

Their daughter, Edith Nicolls, was born posthumously on 27 October 1844 at the home of her father's parents at Shrewsbury House, Shooter's Hill, Blackheath.

Bereft in her widowhood, Mary went to join her brother Ned Peacock in his Bloomsbury lodgings. Edith's life thus began under chequered conditions. She blessedly escaped the unstable streak in her inheritance, but her childhood would certainly have rested on shifting sands had it not been for the devotion of all her grandparents. She was always equally welcome in both

17

households and they did their utmost to compensate for her mother's somewhat erratic care. When still very young she went to France with her father's parents, and it is said that she spoke French before English. She grew up to be a staunch Anglican, but it was rumoured that her French nurse at that time had her secretly received into the Roman Catholic Church.

Meantime Mary had thrown herself feverishly into the artistic and intellectual life of the Bloomsbury circle. A beauty, 'with big eyes which could be vivacious or dreamy,' it was said of her that 'with a cultivated intelligence, she read Italian and French, and was accustomed to discuss freely all subjects, moral and political. She was a mixture of feminine grace and cavalier decision; sharp malice and blue-stockinged seriousness.'

The author George Meredith, another of the Bloomsbury set, fell completely under Mary's spell, and it is recorded that she inspired much of the passion and imagery in his poem *Love in a Valley*. Finally they married, on 9 August 1849, at St George's, Hanover Square, after he had reputedly proposed seven times. He was still only twenty-one, and she just twenty-eight. Shortly before, it is said that the four-year-old Edith, surprising a passionate embrace, declared roundly 'Mama, I don't like that man.' But George Meredith was charming and very kind to his little stepdaughter, and she later referred with great affection to the fun they had together.

Both husband and wife were now writing. Mary was inspired by her father's hedonistic delight in wine and good food to collaborate in an article on 'Gastronomy and Civilisation' for *Fraser's Magazine*. Peacock surveyed the subject with gusto and erudition, from the hospitality of ancient Greece to the iniquities of Victorian cookery, and Mary wrote it up. There is evident relish in their conclusion that even the most upright and abstemious people 'might well have been better men if they had moistened their throats with Madeira and enlarged their sympathies with grouse.'

But difficulties were arising. Meredith could find no market for his novels or his poems and Mary resented his refusal to consider any other work. Edith later portrayed their acid encounters in the telling phrase 'they sharpened their wits on one another.' Even after the birth of their son Arthur in 1853 matters were no better.

Thomas Love Peacock, aged 72

The climax came five years later, when Mary abandoned everyone and went off to Capri with the artist Henry Wallis. She returned the following year but apparently never saw again either George Meredith or her daughter Edith before she died in October 1861 at the age of forty.

Thomas Love Peacock's Mother

EARLY DAYS

CHAPTER VI

FOR SEVEN YEARS after the Great Exhibition of 1851, the little girl with the smooth hair and straw bonnet who had held her grandfather's hand among the press of people on that May morning, lived in the Bohemian literary world of her mother and stepfather, George Meredith. There were also many visits to paternal and maternal grandparents. They were all people of substance, belonging to high professional circles, with a wide range of cultured interests.

In 1858, when her mother went to Capri and broke up the home, Edith went to live with General Sir Edward and Lady Nicolls. She was thirteen years old, and in the following years, until Sir Edward's death in 1865, at the age of eighty-six, these grandparents lavished care and thought on her education. Lady Nicolls' knowledge of art and music, illustrated by constant visits together to galleries and concerts, helped to develop Edith's growing interest in these fields. Her informed grasp was reflected many years later with her own family, when she took her young daughters to concerts and taught them to appreciate different forms of music.

She continued to be closely connected with the literary world through her other grandfather, Thomas Peacock, to whom she was devoted. He became an increasing recluse, but Edith spent considerable time with him until he died, aged eighty, in 1866.

A few years later she was approached by Henry Cole, who had been an intimate family friend from the time when he entered the Records Office as a young boy of fifteen. He had always held Thomas Peacock in great affection and esteem, and he now proposed, as a tribute, to publish all Peacock's works. For this he wanted an authentic historical preface, and he appealed to Edith. She wrote the introductory 'Biographical Notice' for the first of the three volumes, which finally appeared in 1875. The *Encyclopaedia Britannica* referred to her contribution as an 'excellent memoir', thus ensuring her a niche in fame. At this time she had not even embarked on the totally different career which was to prove her life work and lasting claim to fame. It is tantalising that little other evidence of her literary inheritance has survived, though later the succinctness and clarity of her official reports reveal her understanding of the apt word and the concise phrase.

Edith's help over the writing and publication of her grandfather's works brought her into constant touch with Henry Cole, and strengthened the already close ties. By now he was also busily engaged on the founding of the new School of Cookery, and it was inevitable that she should share his absorbing interest in this project, so dear to his heart.

He knew that it was essential to enlist women of calibre for the venture; good administrators, able to appreciate a practical approach, but above all, with vision and a sincere interest in social service.

Possibly some of his enthusiasm brushed off on to Edith. Obviously he cherished a warm regard for her, admiring her character and capabilities, and with his shrewd judgment he may have felt from the beginning that she would prove a leader.

Probably he could not have found a better moment. Edith was temporarily free from close responsibilities; her grandparents had died; she was still unmarried; she had a good brain which needed something to bite on; she had artistic gifts and knowledge. She also had a strong conscientious streak, almost puritannical at times, certainly not inherited from her mother; possibly a reaction from this instability. Under thirty, she was ready for a vocation.

Nothing could be done, of course, unless she were qualified in this particular field. Clearly, too, until she gained an insight into the work, she could not satisfy herself as to her fitness or the wisdom of this choice. The first essential step was to take the training.

Thus it came about that Edith Nicolls entered the newly

Edith Nicolls, aged 30
(Mrs Charles Clarke)

opened National Training School of Cookery in April 1874, and gained her teaching diploma in July. Within weeks she was actively helping in the School and appointed to the panel of examiners. Her path was now marked out; it looked as if she were justifying Henry Cole's perception and faith in her.

Lady Barker was in charge, but was already pressed by home claims, and early in 1875 Edith was appointed to the newly created post of Lady Clerk, 'to relieve the Lady Superintendent of routine duties,' at a salary of £100 a year. Almost immediately Lady Barker tendered her resignation, as from 25 June, in order to join her husband in Natal, and Edith was empowered to act as Deputy Superintendent. On 3 July 1875, a year almost to the day after she had passed her examination, Edith Nicolls was offered, and accepted, the post of Lady Superintendent. The appointment was terminable by a quarter's notice on either side. The salary was £200 a year, although Lady Barker received £400. It was another twenty-four years before she reached this figure.

So began her reign as Principal of the National, which was to last for forty-five years.

Mary Nicolls, aged 37
Daughter of Thomas Peacock and mother of Edith Nicolls

EARLY DAYS

CHAPTER VII

INITIALLY EDITH NICOLLS was primarily concerned with the elementary principles of supply and demand. Demand could only be created by public recognition of both the present lack and the basic value of good cookery, with its implications of good food, health and happiness. This demand could then only be satisfied by an adequate supply of teachers. Both tasks were urgent, but resources were at hand. The Diploma course for training these teachers was already established, greatly helped by lectures, sets of recipes and cookery books, particularly from Mr J. C. Buckmaster, Miss Rose Cole and Miss Shaw Lefevre.

To Mr Buckmaster, however, should be given the main credit for rousing and inspiring the public, as he journeyed round the countryside as an evangelist in the cause of good food and cookery. Such was his stimulus that amid scenes of tremendous enthusiasm courses were planned as a follow-up to the immensely popular classes and lectures which he held everywhere, and which proved the forerunners of some of the future Schools of Cookery.

He added *Buckmaster's Cookery* to his series of little books on Chemistry, Physics, Geology and Science. It was described in the frontispiece as 'an abridgement of some of the lectures delivered in the Cookery School at the International Exhibition,' and included nearly four hundred recipes. He dedicated the book to H.R.H. Princess Louise, 'as an active patroness of the National Training School of Cookery and one who appreciates the importance of good cookery as an element of social and domestic happiness.' Indeed this was one of his most fervent beliefs, and

25

in his lectures he exhorted his audiences to share this view with all his powers of moral persuasion.

It is both a tribute and a measure of their joint success that, as Edith Nicolls wrote in her Report of April 1876: 'There have been schools opened for instruction in Cookery, taught by teachers trained at South Kensington, in Liverpool, Leeds, Oxford, Leamington, Shrewsbury, Birmingham, Edinburgh and Glasgow, and from all these satisfactory reports have been received; whilst other towns, such as Hereford, Bristol, Sheffield, Rugby, Dundee and Wickham will shortly have teachers sent to them to open schools in those towns also.' Small wonder that the Committee 'expressed satisfaction' at this achievement!

Eliza Youmans, in her Preface to the American edition of *The Official Handbook of the National Training School for Cookery*, published in New York in 1879, paid high tribute to Sir Henry Cole, by whose 'firm purpose and excellent judgment a novel experiment, surrounded by many difficulties, became a recognised success and a great national benefit,' and to his daughter Rose, who had compiled the lessons and recipes which constituted the first course of instruction in the School. Eliza Youmans wrote from personal experience. To use her own words 'I was a pupil there for several weeks and carefully observed its operations. The classes showed the most extraordinary mental and social diversity. There were cultivated ladies, the daughters of country gentlemen, old housekeepers, servants, cooks, and coloured girls from South Africa, together with a large proportion of intelligent young women who were preparing to become teachers.' Thus from the beginning the National welcomed all ranks and races; maybe the South African girls had been sponsored by Lady Barker in Natal.

But there was no thought of resting on their laurels. Edith Nicolls realised that if the success of this campaign were not to be a flash in the pan, there must be a genuine change of heart among housewives who must be convinced of the necessity for good food and cookery before they would bother to make what was bound to be an arduous effort. She faced the fact that very few of the present era were likely to be converted, and that the key lay in the hands of the rising generation, teaching the daughters to look further than their mothers. The campaign must therefore be strongly directed towards the elementary

NATIONAL TRAINING-SCHOOL OF COOKERY AT SOUTH KENSINGTON

MORNING—IN THE SCULLERY

AFTERNOON—LECTURE ON PRACTICAL COOKERY—"SEASONING FRICANDEAU OF VEAL"

schools. One of her earliest dictums was 'Our hope is in the children; our aim should be to reach them towards the end of their school period.' She also advocated the teaching of Cookery to boys, who, she said, 'made even more apt pupils than girls.'

A particular bone of contention was the grant of 4s a head for any girls in Standard IV and upwards, who passed an examination in two subjects, one of which had to be domestic economy. In the schools, the accent was placed almost entirely on needlework, to the detriment of cookery instruction, and it was vital that this grant should be allocated equally to both subjects. The teaching of practical cookery presented obvious problems and was therefore strongly resisted; the lack of teachers, proper premises and equipment all being cited in excuse.

At her instance, the Committee addressed a memorandum on this subject in March 1876 to the Education Department of the Privy Council, pleading for support in negotiation with School Boards 'that a special qualified Inspector should be appointed to look to the interests of Cookery and that Her Majesty's Inspectors generally should be instructed to look kindly on instruction in Cookery.'

That autumn saw Edith actively engaged in 'a scheme by which we could reach the working classes in the poorer districts of London and get at the school children to instruct them.' She reported this to the Committee in June 1877, as follows:

'I talked the matter over with our earliest supporter, the Rev Robert Gwynne, Vicar of St Mary's, Soho, and encouraged by his warm and hearty promise of help in his district, I determined to feel my way towards establishing classes in the midst of the people. Mr Gwynne lent me his schoolroom every Wednesday evening, and provided the gas needful for the lesson, and the gas stove. The expense of the pots and pans, the material to be cooked, the teacher's fee, the kitchen-maid's pay, and advertising, etc, were to come out of monies taken at the door and from the school mistresses and pupil teachers of the neighbouring schools, who took tickets for the course of lessons. This class succeeded well, and others have sprung from it in various parts of London and the suburbs. Up to the 31st March last we had realised £191 10s 2d profit on these local classes. Since then they have spread steadily and are well attended.'

The Committee decided that the National should start classes on these lines in London and the suburbs, wherever there was a promising opening, 'undertaking the entire management and the risk of loss or profit.' She was authorised to extend this to the Provinces as an experiment and arranged to begin in Shrewsbury and the neighbouring towns in October. It was agreed that the system would ensure continuous employment for an increasing number of good teachers; accordingly six posts of Staff Teachers were created 'on a higher scale of fee and a better standard of engagement, viz, £100 per annum with extra allowance for board and lodging when sent to reside out of London.'

At this same meeting, she reported 'Our receipts for the services of our teachers in the provinces have this year yielded £711 as against £373 for last year,' and also that the Society of Arts had given five scholarships of ten guineas each, the successful competitors being already in training for teachers. She was not satisfied with the present training, and asked leave to submit a paper proposing 'extension and improvement' to enable the Committee 'to decide upon the future teacher training course to be followed, to come into operation on the reopening of the School in the Autumn.' This was already June; no grass grew under her feet. In addition she reported that 'The class of Practical Cookery in Whitelands Training College, Chelsea (started in 1876), has from time to time been held during the last twelve months; it is greatly to be wished that other Training Colleges would follow this example.' Further, 'The Cooks Company have set a practical example to the other City Companies of London, in sending twelve girls from their Ward Schools to the National Training School twice a week for a lesson of three hours' duration in the Artisan Practice Kitchen. The instruction given was simple and useful in its character, our object being to teach the girls as clearly as possible the fundamental principles of cookery required by girls seeking situations as Scullery-maids, namely roasting, boiling, frying, cooking vegetables, etc. These lessons, part of the campaign to teach the children, proved a useful term's work.'

Contact with the Nursing profession began as early as July 1874, when Sir Daniel Cooper advocated Cookery classes for nurses 'for a fee that will give a profit and at the same time spread a knowledge of cookery amongst a body of women who are a necessity in all civilised communities.' A laconic correspondence between the Committee and Miss Florence Nightingale at the end of 1879 led to Cookery classes for hospital nurses being held during the holidays in August and September 1880. No regular tuition is recorded during the following years apart from the Naval and Military hospitals, but by 1893, classes were established at both Guy's and the London Hospital and another long tradition began.

It was borne in on the Committee that it was the Principal's personal drive which was rapidly establishing the National as a force to be reckoned with, and initiating the wide range of flourishing activities. Possibly conscious that her salary was only £200 a year, they gave her a gratuity of fifty guineas in appreciation, and raised her salary to £250 as from Christmas 1877.

*   *   *   *

Equally convinced of the urgency, and working tirelessly to establish cookery classes in Elementary schools, were Miss Fanny Calder of Liverpool and Mrs Buckton of Leeds, who with Edith Nicolls share the honours of pioneering this movement. Even with their combined indomitable tenacity it took six years to win approval for a separate grant of 4s a head for any girl over the age of twelve who attended a cookery class for not less than forty hours in the school year.

During 1876, a National tenet was established when the Committee gave a ruling that only students actually trained at the School should be allowed to hold its Diploma.

This decision was precipitated, in June, when the President of the Liverpool School of Cookery wrote on behalf of her school and the Yorkshire Training School, to enquire whether the National Committee, in view of the desirability of maintaining one standard of merit for teachers, would, 'for certain fees,' undertake local examinations in different towns, entitling the successful candidates to Diplomas issued by the National Training School of Cookery.

The Committee was unwilling to undertake this extra responsibility, but the rejection of the invitation effectively debarred the School from setting a national standard throughout the country.

Staff Teacher from National with her class and their Captain
Netley Military Hospital, 1885

The upshot was the formation of a Northern Union of Schools of Cookery, eventually incorporating the schools in Liverpool, Leeds, Leicester, Manchester, Edinburgh and Glasgow, as well as a number of smaller local schools. It was not until 1919, when the examinations for teachers' Diplomas came fully under the aegis of the Board of Education, that an accepted uniform standard was recognised.

Some Teaching and Domestic Staff with School Secretary, 1885

EARLY DAYS

CHAPTER VIII

AT THE PARISH CHURCH of Little Marlow in Buckinghamshire, on 22 August 1876, Edith Nicolls married Mr Charles Clarke of the India Office. She had another fifty years of life ahead, and although his span was shorter, they celebrated their silver wedding. He was a year her senior, and seems to have given her active support in her professional work, as well as sharing her artistic interests. He sketched the design for the official seal when the School was incorporated as a limited company in 1888, and this remained in use until the first change of name after his death. They had a family of three daughters, the eldest of whom, Edith Gladys, was born in August 1877, and was destined to follow her distinguished mother as Principal.

Each daughter was brought up with individual care and understanding. Music was an inherited interest and Gladys recalled that they were 'taken to hear the great singers of the day from the age of three.' She vividly remembered the musical preparation given by her mother before going with her to the opera as a small child, and that 'all the great parts were marked for me in her copy.' She marvelled how her mother 'contrived to give so much time to us. She taught me herself until I was six years old.'

Although Gladys's professional work lay in the Domestic Subjects world pioneered by Mrs Clarke, music remained a ruling passion. Her natural singing voice was well trained; all through her life she sang at College parties and her sister Elinora would recite. Elinora studied Speech and Drama as a career, and in later years she made an active contribution to the

33

life of the National, lecturing and coaching students in Voice Production both for teaching and dramatic purposes. These two sisters remained unmarried. The third became Mrs Hall Thorpe; who also shared much of the School life. There was a certain family likeness between the three sisters. Tall, somewhat pale with strong features, dark hair and fine hands, they all inherited their mother's compelling heavy-lidded eyes.

Original Seal of National Training School of Cookery, 1874

The upbringing of this family, developing their special talents, could well have been regarded as sufficient occupation for any mother, especially in those days when women, unless driven by circumstances, rarely undertook full-time work outside the home, but it was not so for Mrs Clarke. Admittedly her professional work was inextricably bound up with home life, but she was entering on an era when long and hard battles lay ahead for the emancipation and recognition of women, in which she took an active share.

She was a hard task master and a perfectionist, permitting nothing slipshod either of herself or of others and her high standards were reflected in everything she undertook. Her realisation of the importance of skilled craft was illustrated by her insistence on the mastery of technique; her understanding of the needs and claims of a family made her take practical steps to help the underprivileged. She brought her intellectual and artistic gifts and social conscience towards solving the problems of her day.

Miss Gladys Clarke as a child

THE·NATIONAL·TRAINING·SCHOOL
FOR
COOKERY,
Buckingham Palace Road

DIPLOMA
FOR PLAIN COOKERY

Awarded to

CHAIRMAN.   LADY SUPERINTENDENT.

Original Diploma, 1874

EARLY DAYS

CHAPTER IX

THE NATIONAL was already beginning to make its mark, but continuing success depended on finances. In 1877 it benefited by a grant of £500 from the Exhibition Commissioners, but in 1880 suffered a set-back with the rest of the country from the general depression in trade and agriculture. This was aggravated by two exceptionally severe winters during which the Thames was frozen over, communications were disrupted, and Mrs Clarke reported 'our building is of a temporary character, we are consequently dependent upon the weather, our Kitchens being emptied by extremes of heat and cold.' Attendances dropped alarmingly, and the bank balance sank to £37.

In addition, the Committee was in a quandary over the premises, as part of the site was now needed by the Commissioners to build a Technical Institute for the City and Guilds of London. The National was therefore required to transfer some kitchens to an adjoining building, which obviously entailed considerable expense. Estimates of £325 finally amounted to £500. Sir Daniel Cooper arranged a bank advance, guaranteed by the Committee, and for the moment the breach was filled. But the loan had to be repaid, the makeshift premises were still unsatisfactory, and the School was in trouble.

In this context, Mrs Clarke made a plea in her annual report to the Committee in June 1881: 'It would be of considerable advantage to the efficiency of this School if we had a reserve fund upon which to fall back, over and above what we can realise. In a good season with the greatest care in all matters of detail, I believe it is possible to carry on the work upon the receipts; but we are subject to many fluctuations. I cannot reduce the Staff in proportion to the Pupils, or when the Kitchens are full I should often be at a loss for good Teachers who are experienced. Many improvements suggest themselves to my mind which I cannot carry out thoroughly for fear of the expense.

'There is plenty to be done; the lower we can place our fees the more we increase our work, and keep in view the original object to reach the people, and to insure to the working man a wholesome meal, which will supply the nourishment that he requires to enable him to do a hard day's work. The lassitude produced by bad food and hard work is a constant source of the craving for drink which drives the working man to the public house.'

One of her great obsessions was the evils of drink, and she never failed to drive home her belief in good food as a sovereign remedy. She continued 'Experience has certainly taught me that it is nearly hopeless to try and teach the wives of the Artisans how to improve their cooking; they are utterly indifferent. Once again, her plea lay in recognition of practical cookery for the children.

In spite of the upheavals, students returned as the weather improved, and the School kept its head above water. But the summer was hard. In April 1882 Sir Henry Cole died and Mrs Clarke was bereft. He had been guide, philosopher and friend all her life and the prime mover in the whole enterprise of the School. She was at a low ebb when in the autumn the Exhibition Commissioners, who had at Sir Henry's instigation brought the National into being in 1873, now offered a life line which was to found its eventual success. Throughout the intervening years the Commissioners had continued to arrange exhibitions, and with their decision to hold a Fisheries Exhibition in 1883 came the turn of the tide. A deputation from the Commissioners waited upon Mrs Clarke in the autumn of 1882 to ask if she would arrange for lessons in the cooking of cheap fish to be given during the Exhibition. The Committee seized this heaven-sent chance and the Chairman, Mr Leveson-Gower, talked over with Lord Hamilton, Chairman of the Exhibition Committee, what the School might do.

It was decided that the School should be responsible for giving each day three demonstrations of fish dishes from noon to 1 pm, 4 to 5 pm, and 6 to 7 pm, and also for providing cheap fish dinners

Staff at Fisheries Exhibition, 1883

at 6d and 1s a head, from 1 to 3 pm and 7 to 9 pm. Respective responsibilities concerning supplies and staff, both for kitchens and dining rooms, were clearly defined. The one note of discord arose over the dresses of the waitresses. Possibly in the fear of somewhat bizarre attire, the School declared very firmly that 'it would be dangerous to be mixed up with fancy costumes of any sort; it would be impossible to make the public understand that the School has nothing to do with the costumes of the waitresses, and it would very probably interfere with young ladies joining the School in future.' The proprieties were observed by final agreement for the waitresses to be 'dressed in black with white caps and aprons, all as neat and tidy as possible.' See illustration on page 39.

Both the demonstrations and the dining rooms were thronged. Their popularity inspired *Punch* to burlesque Mrs Clarke's fervent campaign against the evils of drink by illustrating a drunken husband defending his indulgence with the words 'Fish dinners very cheap, but make you uncommonly thirsty.' See cartoon on page 43.

The agreed fee to be paid to the National was £500. In addition a book of Fish Recipes was prepared by Mrs Clarke and an edition of 10,000, printed by William Clowes and Sons, was sold at 3d a copy. The profit of approximately £180 was divided equally between the Exhibition authorities and the National. The Committee, in token of gratitude for her work, gave half of this share to Mrs Clarke.

Small as was this total profit, the resounding success of the enterprise proved the value of the School. The Fisheries was the first of a series of International Exhibitions, following hard on each other's heels, which kept the National in the public eye and laid the basis of its fortunes. Few could have imagined that before the end of the decade the debts would be paid, the dilapidated corrugated iron huts thankfully abandoned, and the School established in the fine building which was to be its home to the end of its days.

The National was brought into the life of the Health Exhibition which followed in 1884, by again undertaking the responsibility for demonstrations and dinners at the same price of 6d and 1s a head. The School was asked particularly to illustrate the best methods of preparing the ordinary food used in the daily

OUR INSANE-ITARY GUIDE TO THE HEALTH EXHIBITION.

"OBJECTS OF INTEREST" AT THE HEALTHERIES—AND OTHERS!

life of the country, and to make a feature of canned and frozen goods from the Colonies (Australia, Canada and New Zealand), chiefly to encourage trade with these countries by persuading the public to overcome their prejudice against food of this type. The success of the advertising campaign was largely instrumental in promoting the Colonial and Indian Exhibition of 1886. Both here and at the Inventions Exhibition in the intervening year of 1885, the National played its now accepted role. The price for the best dinners rose to 2*s* 6*d*.

The popularity of the dinners brought social fame. Articles, references and illustrations in society columns and the fashionable magazines of the day were highlighted when *Punch* again satirised the whole affair in a series of articles and delightful cartoons.

Their star was in the ascendant, and in December 1883, the accolade was given when H.R.H. the Prince of Wales consented to become Patron of the National Training School of Cookery. This honour of Royal patronage, always a matter of especial and personal pride to everyone connected with the National, was to continue unbroken all through its life.

The Prince of Wales himself instructed Sir Philip Cunliffe Owen to write to Mrs Clarke on 19 May 1887, to thank her for the admirable manner in which she had carried out the work of the School in connection with the Colonial and Indian Exhibition. The Committee was pleased to endorse this Royal recognition which it 'considered she had fully earned.' The Exhibition activities had occupied a major part of her time and energy. But the enterprise had been very profitable. The National was allowed to keep the difference between the takings in the dining rooms and the actual cost to the Exhibition authorities of providing the services. The result was a total accession of £5,000 to the funds of the School. In accordance with a previous agreement Mrs Clarke was given an honorarium of 100 guineas, and also a share of the profits amounting to £687. Never again was she to receive from the Committee so handsome a sum; never again were their profits so high.

Lovers of statistics may care to note that during the four exhibitions over one and a half million dinners were served (the exact figure being 1,624,722); the quantity of food consumed was 188 tons of fish, over 58 tons of beef, and nearly 4,000 sheep.

Little Wife (*indignant. She had just let him in,* 12·30 *Midnight*). "I CAN'T UNDERSTAND WHY YOU GAVE ME THE SLIP TO-DAY, YOU UNMANLY WRETCH!"

He. "SUSH A PLACE THAT FISH'RIESH-EXSH'BISH'L, MY DEAR! SHIMPLY COULDL'T FIND YER. WENT SHIBERIA, 'N SHINA—NOT THERE,—SHPAIN—NOT THERE! LIFE-BOASH—'FRESH-MENSH'"—(*this seems to remind him*)—"FISH-DILLER VER' SHEAP—BUT MAKESH Y ULCOM LY SHIRSHTY!!"

The National Training School of Cookery in 1889
72–8 Buckingham Palace Road, London S.W.1

THE NEW BUILDING

CHAPTER X

THE PATRONAGE OF H.R.H. THE PRINCE OF WALES in 1883 and the windfall from the International Exhibitions materially influenced the immediate future. Sadly, Sir Henry Cole did not live to savour the School's triumph in the exhausting round of demonstrations and dinners which he had done so much to promote. When it resumed its normal life the Committee sat back and took stock. Good premises were clearly the immediate priority. Accordingly in November 1886 the Exhibition Commissioners were approached, requesting 'a grant of the land upon which the temporary School buildings now stand, and permission to erect thereon a new building.' The Commissioners, sympathetic, nevertheless made it clear that the site had been earmarked for other purposes. But they offered an alternative in Jay Mews, Kensington Gore, on the west side of the Royal Albert Hall, which the Committee accepted early in December.

Had this gone through, the National would have risen in this magnificent position, in the heart of cosmopolitan culture, one of the famous company of the Schools of Music, Art, Drama, Science, the Imperial Institute and the Victoria and Albert Museum. Would the concept and the subsequent national image of Cookery have been quite different?

Negotiations, however, hung fire, and when no decision had been reached during the next six months, the Duke of Westminster, the President of the School, in June 1887 put forward an alternative proposition. He offered a leasehold site on his Grosvenor estate in Buckingham Palace Road. He also promised, if the Committee were interested, to consult his own architect

45

about a suitable building, to help with the ground rent, and to sponsor an appeal for funds. The Committee, relieved, gratefully closed with this offer.

A ninety years' lease was agreed, to date from Michaelmas 1887, although it was not actually signed and sealed until December 1888. The annual ground rent was fixed at £210. The Duke promised to forego the latter for the first two years, which proved to be exactly the period before classes started in the new building.

The preparation of plans for the new School was entrusted to Mr Caspar Purdon Clarke, Architect and Keeper on the staff of the South Kensington Museum, who had worked under Sir Henry Cole, and later – as Sir Caspar – followed in his footsteps as Director.

The lowest tender, from the firm of Mowlem, for £8,227 was accepted, and building began in July 1888. It was estimated that fittings and equipment would cost a further £2,000.

The nest egg of £5,000 capital accrued from the Exhibitions covered half the cost of the enterprise. To meet the balance, the Trustees of the Berridge Estate (who subsequently provided funds for the National Society's Training College known as Berridge House, in Hampstead) lent £5,000 on mortgage at five per cent interest, generously converting this into a free gift two years later.

The legal position of the School now had to be settled. Approval was given at the Annual General Meeting on 22 February 1888, 'to incorporate the School as a Company under the Joint Stock Acts and to draw up suitable Articles of Association.' The latter, together with the names of the original guarantors are set out in Appendix C. This registration was an assurance of stability. The distinguished array of guarantors proved their support by underwriting the enterprise.

The Baroness Burdett-Coutts had lent her Piccadilly house for this meeting. She lavished much of her time and considerable fortune on a variety of religious and educational projects, and her husband, Mr William Burdett-Coutts, M.P., had been a member of the Committee since 1883. In acknowledging the vote of thanks the Baroness referred to her 'deep interest in the School,' and continued that she 'highly approved of the action which the Committee intended to take, particularly in reference

'I promise to eat all you cook! . . .'
Cartoon from *Punch*, 9 December 1884

to providing rooms for students in training.' This was the beginning of a long and at times uneasy relationship between the National and this wealthy patron of good works.

Mrs Clarke could now feel that the School was firmly on its feet. In the fifteen years since the classes began, over 40,000 students had received instruction, including 327 who had gained the full teaching Diploma. The venture had proved itself.

With the move into the new building came the need and the opportunity for complete reorganisation. In Mr Purdon Clarke's plans, as well as better space for the present courses, there were additional kitchens for training 'good plain cooks – domestics apparently extinct,' as the Report of 1887 states! A limited number of these servants could live in the building and there would also be rooms for 'some of the Pupils and Teachers in training.'

In the eleven years up to 1900, 340 cooks were awarded certificates; 200 for Plain Cookery and 140 for High Class. By the next survey in 1912, successful numbers had risen by 50 per cent to give 309 Plain and 202 High Class certificates.

In South Kensington finances had been considerably hampered because of the difficulty of disposing of the dishes cooked, especially the most expensive entrees and soups. In order both to combat this loss, and also to make a profit, the Committee now proposed to have a 'Restaurant open to the public, at one end of the School, and with an entrance quite apart from the rest of the building.' Everyone was so confident of its success that it was arranged to lower the School fees as soon as the project was established.

Speed was of the essence. On 21 May 1889, only ten months after the signing of the contract the Executive Committee actually met in the new building. It was decided to move the School in August, in readiness for the Autumn Term. The removal in its entirety cost £12 10s. It was a hectic summer for Mrs Clarke and her staff, who swept all difficulties aside in the excitement of this momentous undertaking.

They had staked all, when on Monday, 16 September 1889, the National opened its doors to begin the new era. An imposing red brick façade incorporated the equivalent of four houses, numbers 72 – 78 Buckingham Palace Road, S.W.1. From the pavement, under an arch of wrought iron, bearing the name

National Training School of Cookery, a shallow flight of five steps led to an entrance of double doors. The frontage, apart from an additional floor largely hidden by the parapet, has remained virtually unchanged to the end of its days.

Mrs Clarke now had her long sought opportunity to revolutionise the syllabus which she had been struggling to improve ever since her appeal to the Committee in 1877. On her initiative, separate courses were formed for Plain and High Class Cookery, each to last twenty weeks, leading to the award of First and Second class Diplomas. Comprehensive knowledge and exacting skills were increasingly demanded, and the aspiring teachers were most carefully chosen. The School sought mature young women, in their late twenties or early thirties, of good background, who already had some experience of home and social duties.

In the training, as it developed, there were three main courses which dealt with different standards of cookery. Household Cookery, broadly speaking, catered for the professional classes, and Artisan Cookery for the homes of manual workers and the children in the elementary schools. It was emphasised that High Class Cookery differed not only in variety and cost, but also in the manipulative skill, theoretical knowledge and aesthetic appreciation required to produce complicated dishes, and elaborate meals.

To obtain a full Diploma, students had to pass a practical and a theoretical test, of two and three hours respectively in each of the three branches. This qualified them to teach in every type of class and school. Those who were unwilling, or unable, to take the full course, could omit High Class Cookery and gain a Diploma in Household and Artisan Cookery. This entitled them to teach Cookery in elementary and continuation schools only. In either case, a First-class Diploma required a mark of 80 per cent, and a Second-class 60 per cent in each section taken.

Most students preferred to take the full Diploma, especially as the demand for teachers was so great. Few seem to have fallen by the wayside; the policy of training hand-picked students to a high degree of skill was rewarded by the calibre of these pioneer teachers. Records show them undaunted and unflagging, constantly involved in long days of almost non-stop toil. Up and down the country they preached the gospel, often travelling in bitter discomfort, on salaries rarely exceeding £80 a year, with undiminished zeal and dedication.

One of the first concerns was with the public restaurant which opened in May 1891. In connection with this, Mrs Clarke bought an unknown quantity of knives at a cost of £21 12s 2d, and twenty-four dozen table napkins, for which, unfortunately no price is recorded. She was also authorised to buy two clocks at a total cost of not more than £8.

To their amazement and dismay, the restaurant did not succeed. There proved small response from the public, and in less than a year, the anticipated profit turned into a loss of over £5 a week.

The Committee had placed too much faith on carrying on the tradition of the Exhibitions where the meals served by the National had been universally popular. But in the new district, there was no tradition, the School was still unknown and there was as yet nothing to draw the public.

It was a sad day when, in May 1891, the Committee faced the decision to cut its losses. With it went many confident hopes and plans. The vaunted restaurant, which could have prevented many later financial troubles, was diverted to children's classes. Later, when the National was well established and acclaimed, a restaurant could well have repaid them, but by then all the rooms were in full use for other purposes, and the Committee, once bitten, twice shy, was not prepared to take the risk until forced to do so in the First World War.

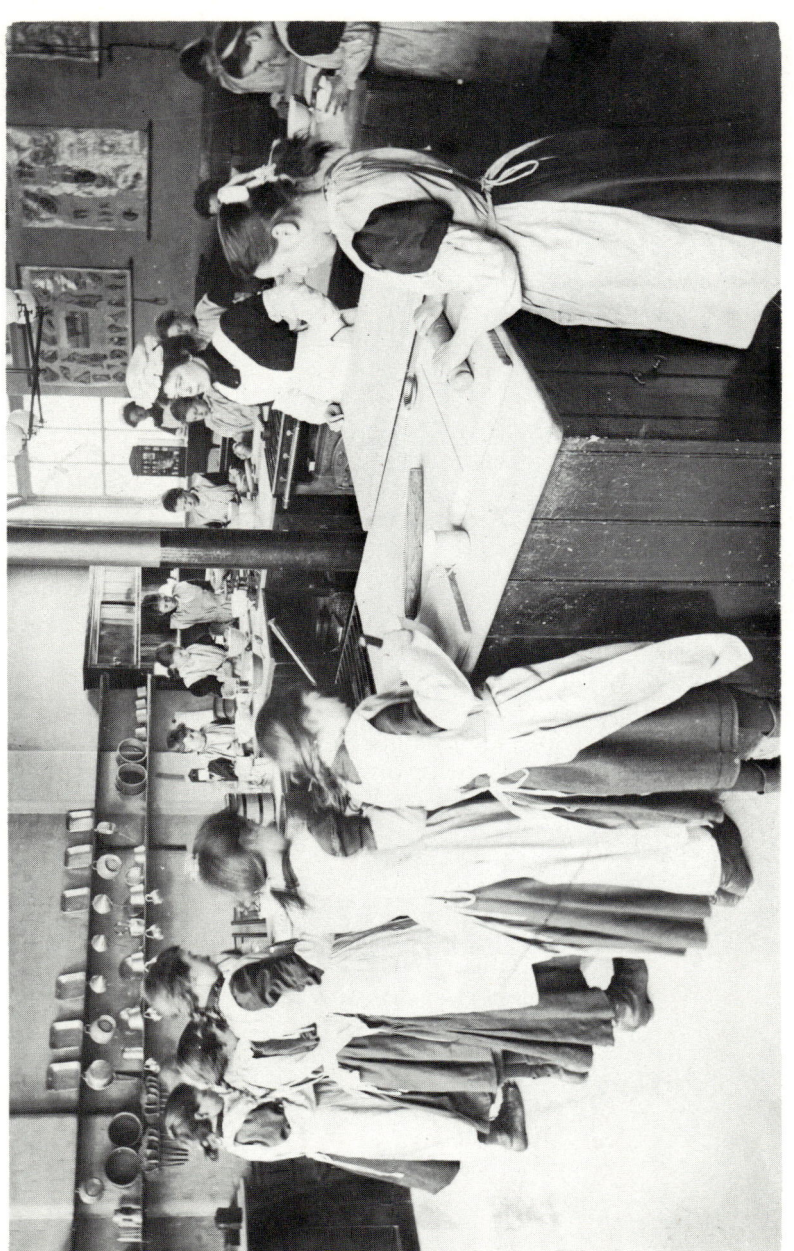

Children's Cookery Class, 1892

Children's Laundrywork Class, 1895

THE NEW BUILDING

CHAPTER XI

MRS CLARKE had received a welcome and well-deserved honorarium for her gruelling four years' work at the International Exhibitions; nevertheless her salary still remained at the £250 approved fifteen years earlier. It was not a propitious moment, however, to raise this question, for after the short breathing space when the School was temporarily in funds, the Committee was forced to devote most of the two meetings in October and November 1889, when barely settled in the new premises, to drafting a leaflet appealing for public support.

She therefore wrote to the Chairman in December 1889, suggesting that in lieu of the increase to which she felt entitled, she might be allowed to live for a further year in the rooms on the top floor which she and her family at present temporarily occupied. The Committee unanimously rejected this proposal; members preferred a salary increase 'if funds permitted.' Evidently they felt that something should be done quickly as they approved a further £100 a year in January 1890. Mrs Clarke now quixotically refused to accept more than half, 'until finances were on a surer basis.' It was another three years before in 1893 the remaining £50 was added to her salary, to bring the total to £350, 'in acknowledgement of the able manner in which she had carried out the work of the School.'

Nearly a quarter of a century's service was given before, in March 1899, she received £400, the equivalent salary enjoyed by her predecessor who had briefly held the reins during the School's first year.

Financial stringency now led to the first of many subsequent approaches to the London County Council. The National's work, both in instigating and promoting children's classes, was held by the Committee to justify an annual grant. The Schools Sub-Committee of the London County Council agreed, and recommended £500 a year, but as the full Council were not in favour, no help was forthcoming from this quarter, and the children's classes were to become a recurring drain on the funds.

The bogey of a deficit, however, was offset to some extent by the enormous popularity of the School, which flourished in the congenial surroundings. Students flocked to join the classes, where the already high standards of work became even higher under the direction of able teachers.

This was the era when famous chefs were increasingly esteemed. Alexis Soyer, in his brief life of less than fifty years, had blazed the trail when he went from Paris to London, where he was honoured in great houses and as chef of the Reform Club. At the Government's request he set up kitchens in Dublin during the Irish famine; finally he advised in the Crimea on cooking for the Army and on his return reformed military hospital diets. It was in these particular fields that Mrs Clarke followed directly in his footsteps when she took up the cudgels during the Boer War. But at present her energies were concentrated nearer home. From the outset she had determined that the Cookery at the School should merit renown, and already in 1890, in order to gain an insight into highly professional expertise, the idea was mooted of inviting certain personally recommended chefs to give their advice. Further discussion, however, decided the Committee to procure the regular services of a recognised expert, and in June 1892, Mr Herman Senn, a Swiss chef of repute, who had founded the Cookery and Food Association in 1885, was appointed as Lecturer and Inspecting Chef, at a salary of £110 a year, thus taking the first official step towards the prestige attached to the art of the master-craftsman. Herman Senn took all in his stride; eventually in fact this is precisely what he made a bid for. Short and thick set, with temper matching his fiery hair, and dark eyes hidden behind thick spectacles, he was both a brilliantly creative chef and a gifted demonstrator. This formidable character, who brooked no interference, inspired the School as never before. His volcanic energy was like a flaming sword, and under the pressure of his uncompromising standards the staff rose to undreamt of heights of skill.

It was during this last decade of the century that the National's prowess in cookery securely established a reputation which mounted steadily to become deservedly acclaimed and zealously maintained.

Children's Laundrywork Class, 1908

Illuminated Address to Mrs Clarke, 1899

THE NEW BUILDING

CHAPTER XII

THE PUBLICITY attendant on the rising reputation of the School kept Mrs Clarke's name to the fore and she was consulted as an acknowledged authority on educational matters concerning food, diet and hygiene.

One of the first official approaches came from the War Office with whom, as early as 1883, Mrs Clarke had forged a link after she had complied with a request from the R.A.M.C. to send teachers from the National to instruct Army staff in the military hospitals at Aldershot, Netley and Woolwich. Now, in March 1891, Colonel E. H. Hutton, who was responsible to Lieut-General Sir Evelyn Wood for the conduct of the Army School of Cookery at Aldershot, consulted Mrs Clarke about raising the standard of instruction and reorganising their School, with the wider object of improving the cooking generally throughout the Army. He emphasised that Sir Evelyn 'earnestly wished to achieve three main objectives:

i) To improve the diet and to economise in the outlay on food for the ordinary soldier.

ii) To teach cookery suitable for a hospital.

iii) To assist the learner cooks towards lucrative employment after leaving the Army, by imparting a higher degree of instruction in cooking.'

Their proper concern for the future welfare of the troops thus adroitly included a recruitment bait.

Colonel Hutton asked that, as a preliminary, the Warrant Officer in charge of the Army School might be permitted to attend Plain Cookery demonstrations in the morning, and Plain

Cookery practice classes in the afternoon, for a period of fourteen days, assuring her that 'Sergeant-Major Thompson, late
Scots Greys, is a very highly educated and excellent man,' who
would consider any assistance 'as a great boon.' He further
requested both the formation of a class for a group of instructors
for fourteen days in the following July, and also that an experienced lecturer from the National should visit Aldershot for
a couple of days in April, to give instruction in Plain and Sick-
room Cookery.

Colonel Hutton's original letter, with thick pen strokes, sur-
vives, and on it Mrs Clarke has herself noted and initialled in
somewhat paler ink '10 Dems. 4/6. 10 Practice £2 2s, 3 – 5 pm.
Teachers to Aldershot to stand over.' Proving by the latter
decision she did not rush to grant all his wishes.

All the same, she quickly realised the significance of these requests and immediately made plans for special lessons for the
Sergeant Major. That the Army valued her efforts is shown by
an April letter presenting, with Sir Evelyn's personal thanks, his
desire that his 'appreciation of the kind goodwill of all concerned
be conveyed to the Chairman and Committee,' followed in May
by another, rather heavily blotted, from Colonel Hutton beginning: 'I can't say how much we are indebted to you for the help
you gave us with our Sergeant Major,' and asking if they might
now send Sergeant Dalton, (also 'an excellent man in every
respect – he was in the Third Hussars') for exactly similar
tuition.

At the same time Colonel Hutton sent Mrs Clarke the newly
printed *Memoranda on the Messing of the Soldier,* which 'is now
being acted upon among the troops in Aldershot,' stating that it
was the outcome of the last few months' work. The slim nine-
page booklet ends with the aphorism 'The principles involved by
the culinary motto of "Skim, Simmer and Scour" are the foundations of any system of good and economical cooking,' followed
by a recipe for making 40 lb brawn at a cost of five shillings.

In an interview to the magazine *Hearth and Home* in February
1892, Mrs Clarke is quoted as hoping that much would result
from the interest taken by the Army in the subject of cookery for
soldiers; nevertheless adding the sardonic, and (in view of her
recent experience) singular comment that 'military red-tapeism

is so obstructive that it requires quite six months' negotiation before a spoonful of flour, more or less, is permitted to take the place of the established dietary!'

A year after Colonel Hutton's first letter, in March 1892, Mrs Clarke suggested to the Aldershot School of Cookery that they should give demonstrations at an Exhibition arranged by Mr Herman Senn on behalf of his Cookery and Food Association, to be held in London in May. This was a revolutionary idea, and at first strongly resisted. 'I confess,' wrote Colonel Hutton, 'that I do not see how we can reasonably help. . . . It would not be possible for us to illustrate our simple and practical expedients (to ensure economy and sound food) alongside the productions of Chefs and other masters of the Culinary Arts who compete in the excellence of certain dishes.' Mrs Clarke has left a cryptic note to the effect that she 'wanted the soldiers to give Demonstration lessons, not to compete.' She won them over. In May, Colonel Hutton wrote to say that 'Our School is indebted to you for proposing that we should take part in this Exhibition, as it has been of great benefit to our Staff,' and hoping that Mrs Clarke was 'satisfied with our efforts.'

Such was their success that this proved the beginning of a series of practical demonstrations given by the Army School at the Cookery and Food Exhibitions in London extending over many years. It also brought them to the notice of the Baroness Burdett-Coutts. In September 1892, Colonel Hutton wrote rather apologetically to Mrs Clarke to reveal that the Baroness had approached him to know if his School could undertake weekly lectures and demonstrations at her Westminster Technical Institute, in 'teaching the fundamental principles of economical cookery'; he had the grace to add 'it would be really the resumé of work and experiments at Aldershot.' He also wished to assure her that it would not affect the technical lessons already being given by 'your nominee from the National School,' who 'would deal in the details of cookery (more in the way of your School) rather than the main principles.' This last statement must have been galling; alas, there is no record of her reply.

Colonel Hutton had now left Aldershot, and the little bundle of friendly letters ceases on this clouded note. It is clear that up to this time relationships were always cordial, and that the

Army valued the National's tuition and advice. But the Army School was learning its Cookery lessons, and no longer felt the need to be sponsored by Mrs Clarke in the world of contemporary Cookery. Another twelve years were to pass before the Army School of Cookery was driven back to the National to seek their aid. Meantime, Mrs Clarke took a realistic view and helped whenever asked, providing tuition in London and Aldershot, and advising on Army publications. But the contacts were never again so close.

Dressmaking Class, 1905

THE NEW BUILDING

CHAPTER XIII

ALTHOUGH COLONEL HUTTON had written in June 1891 that 'through the assistance of the National School of Cookery we have already raised the standard of army cooking in a most surprising manner,' there was bitter public outcry over the feeding of the sick and wounded in the Boer War. Mrs Clarke was touched on the raw. The double cause of humanitarianism and good cookery brought the following letter, published in *The Times* and other newspapers:

COOKING AND THE WAR

Sir – May I ask if in all that has been done for the help and comfort of the sick and wounded in South Africa, any steps have been taken by the Government or various nursing societies to provide suitable cooking for them? If not, surely some trained ladies holding cookery diplomas should be sent out with all despatch. . . . I have seen that doctors, trained nurses, and all sorts of appliances have been sent out, but I have seen no mention of trained cooks. We all know the danger to people in health of badly cooked food. How much more serious must the consequences be to those exhausted by hard fighting, wounds, and sickness? Out of all the funds that are being so generously subscribed for the help of our men and their families, surely some conld be devoted to sending out ladies who, by their knowledge of invalid cookery, would help the nurses and doctors to save many a valuable life – I am Sir, Your obedient servant,

EDITH CLARKE
National Training School of Cookery
Buckingham Palace Road, 7 December 1899.

This fervent appeal to patriotic duty brought publicity in a spate of correspondence in the daily newspapers, ranging from the virtues of arrowroot to the beneficent effect of wars on cookery!

Among those who rallied to her call was Baroness Burdett-Coutts, who subsidised, not a corps of lady cooks, but free cook– ery lessons at the National for the wives of reservists and others who had already gone out to S. Africa. The fees paid were not high. The Committee also decided to reduce the fees for the Queen's Jubilee Nurses to 15s a head for a course of ten lessons. Both these efforts helped the School's status, but not its finances.

The Admiralty had not been slow to follow the example of the Army in seeking the services of the National. In response to an official request in April 1894, the Committee agreed to send a member of staff with Mr Senn to Portsmouth, to inspect and report on the system of cookery on board H.M. ships. There were many matters to thrash out, and it was twelve months before it was decided that proper lessons should be given to the cooks of the Officers' Mess on H.M. Flagships stationed in home waters, and that instruction in sickroom diets and cookery should be provided at the naval hospitals at Haslar and Ply- mouth. The somewhat desultory contacts over the next ten years did not augur any particular connections in the future; nevertheless it was above all with the Royal Navy that eventu- ally there was a life long relationship.

Much water was to flow under the bridge before then, how- ever, and less glamorous contacts were afoot.

In April 1899, the Prisons Commission enlisted Mrs Clarke's help in the inspection of the kitchens at Wormwood Scrubs Prison and advice on the equipment and methods of instruction, expressing concern over the capabilities of the catering officers responsible. This resulted in some of the Chief Warders attending classes at the National. Also, at the authorised fee of one guinea plus travelling expenses, Mrs Clarke agreed to carry out a series of inspection visits, which her Report in 1906 records as still continuing year by year.

At the same time, the National was consulted by the Local Government Board about the cost and quality of the food sup- plied to inmates of workhouses throughout the country. Investigation revealed that at best the meals could hardly be termed appetising, and dietary values fared ill as against cost. Cheese paring was the general order of the day, but with this often went appalling waste, and the cooks' 'perks' of selling fat, dripping and bones held good here as in other institutions. The Inspectors of the Board sought in particular the collaboration of Mrs Clarke in the trial and preparation of recipes, at a fee of five shillings each.

Mrs Clarke set both herself and her staff to work and tackled the problem with her accustomed vigour. The work continued for two years, when at the Board's request, the Committee undertook to compile and publish in 1901 a *Manual of Workhouse Cookery* – the copyright to remain with the School. It was agreed to authorise William Clowes & Son to print 2,000 copies at a cost of £20 16s 8d. The Board distributed 1,500 to workhouses at 3d a copy, and the remaining 500 were on sale at the School at 4d a copy. There most of them remained. Understandably, they had no particular appeal to the general public.

Hon. E. F. Levison-Gower

THE NEW BUILDING

CHAPTER XIV

THE BELLS RANG IN the New Year of 1900. But the turn of the century was no more auspicious for the National than for the country as a whole, sunk in gloom over the bad news from South Africa. The depression engendered by the major reverses before Christmas seemed as black as the widespread bitter weather and impenetrable fogs.

The great Victorian age was closing; the National had completed its first quarter of a century and within three years it faced personal losses which in truth reflected the end of an era. However resolute in purpose, it meant putting on a brave face for a long time before the clouds lifted to usher in the brief bright Edwardian days.

In 1899, the death of their influential President, the first Duke of Westminster, removed a source of strength on which the School had come to rely. He had been instrumental in giving them their niche in Buckingham Palace Road and also in history. His role was never filled again. Thirty years later the lack of his attentive ear and readiness to help deprived the National of sympathetic action in a crisis which proved to be a turning point in its life.

The year 1902 took further toll. Mrs Clarke's husband Charles died in January; Sir Daniel Cooper, who had been the Honorary Treasurer for twenty-eight years, a few months later. At the Annual General Meeting in November, the Hon Frederick Leveson-Gower resigned from the Chair which he had occupied at almost every meeting of the Executive Committee since 1873, but he remained as Vice-President until his death in 1907.

In her personal loss, Mrs Clarke was supported by her three daughters; Gladys, the eldest, being already on the School staff. But on the professional side, the National was the poorer for the loss of the Duke and his colleagues, these eminent men who had borne the heat and burden of the day and guided the School from its inception.

Happily, however, a new and valuable link was now to be forged in the National's long chain of faithful relationships. Mr Alan Cole, son of Sir Henry and brother of Rose, had maintained the family connection when he joined the Committee in 1900. Already, as a young man, he had advised the Committee cver building problems at South Kensington in 1874, and now, in the hour of need, he agreed in November 1902 to take over the Honorary Treasurership. Throughout the succeeding years he gave unstinted devotion to the National, staving off crisis after crisis with consummate skill. The new Chairman was the Duke of Abercorn, with Mr (later Sir) Almeric FitzRoy, Clerk to the Privy Council, as Vice-Chairman.

The new Honorary Treasurer was a tower of strength, but even he could not make bricks without straw. A mortgage of £1,000 raised on the building in 1900 enabled the bank loan to be redeemed, but the balance was fast dwindling. In the immediacy of this stress, the Committee was open to any suggestions.

At this point Mr Herman Senn entered the arena. He approached Mrs Clarke with a proposition for reorganisation designed to put the School's finances on a stable basis. He offered his services, so he said, 'without prejudice to the School's independence or to Mrs Clarke's position as Principal.'

Almost at her wits' end, Mrs Clarke agreed that his ideas should be put to the Committee, and on 13 December 1904 he submitted a long memorandum. He represented that in his desire to assist the National he was prepared to leave in abeyance the establishment of a College of Cookery now planned by the Cookery and Food Association of which he was Chairman. Instead he would devote all his energies to developing the School where, with the aid of his own circle of distinguished fellow chefs, he would concentrate on the teaching of High-class Cookery.

Under this apparent altruism lay the pistol at their heads, for he further required formal authority 'to reorganise the system of supplies from tradesmen and the sale of cooked dishes; to appoint a maître chef-de-cuisine to work with the examiners in the syllabus for the teachers' course'; and finally 'to be responsible for the programme of public demonstrations.' All this hardly fitted his protestations as to the inviolability of Mrs Clarke's position.

It is a measure of the Committee's anxiety over the financial position that they acquiesced in these arbitrary proposals, only stipulating an experimental period of six months. The following day, 14 December 1904, Mr Senn was authorised to proceed, as from 1 January 1905.

That all his confident hopes were not fulfilled is evident from the bald statement which he sent to the Committee on 25 January 1905, that he 'preferred to leave the matter of the tradesmen as it was formerly.' At the following Committee on 1 March, it was briefly recorded that 'Mr Senn's resignation be accepted with regret.'

The scheme had come to naught. In Mrs Clarke he met his match; she had no intention of abdicating or playing second fiddle.

Apart from his gift for creating storms, the main rock on which Herman Senn foundered was his endeavour to gain control of the teachers' course. Perhaps by now, also, he realised that the National would not prove a gold mine, and that his particular interests would be better served in other directions. Four years later, in June 1909, the Cookery and Food Association opened the 'International College of Cookery' in Vauxhall Bridge Road. Both the proximity and similarity of title to the National gave concern to the Committee who feared confusion in the public mind. Eventually, however, it was decided to ignore it.

Meantime the bank balance was only £200 and Mrs Clarke herself stepped into the breach. Acutely aware that they were on the brink of a precipice and devoutly thankful to be rid of Mr Senn's schemes, she offered to the School a personal loan of £500 at 4 per cent interest. The Committee accepted without demur this large slice of her slender savings; half was repaid in instalments over the next three years until she received the remaining £250 in a lump sum in May 1908.

Relations with Herman Senn were understandably strained

for a time. In spite of an agreement the following October 1905 that he should give a series of demonstrations for a period of six months at a cost not to exceed £50, the state of armed neutrality may be judged from Mrs Clarke's 'Addition to the Preface' in the tenth edition of her *High Class Cookery* in 1906. She referred to 'the valuable help I have received from Mr Herman Senn who was, as late Consulting Chef de Cuisine to the National Training School of Cookery, at one time associated with my work for eight or ten years, and to whom I am indebted for the notes from which some of these recipes are written,' thus blandly ignoring his close and constant work at the School for the past fourteen years. Possibly this was her retaliation for the reference to Mr Senn in the latest edition of *Mrs Beeton*, as Head of the National Training School of Cookery. This matter was taken up with the publishers who, obviously in a quandary with the book already in print, showed such 'an unaccommodating spirit' that the Committee felt it not worth while to pursue it.

GREAT DAYS

ONE OF THE MOMENTOUS HAPPENINGS of the early years of the century proved to be the arrival of Miss Alice Caddow, who created for herself an unchallenged place in the annals of the National and remained supreme in her own right. Diminutive and trim, bright and bird-like, she had both irrepressible gaiety and tireless energy.

She came to teach Dressmaking and Millinery, but her gifts lay in many fields. At first resident in the building, she became Students' Warden and Housekeeper, but within a short time she was also helping in the Office, and established as personal assistant to Mrs Clarke. By 1906 she was School Secretary, and so successful in all her contacts that it came as no surprise when in 1908 the Committee appointed her 'Secretary and Deputy.'

She had incomparable charm and a prodigious memory. Not only in Committee, recollecting with accuracy discussions and decisions, did this prove invaluable; her immediate joyous greeting of a middle-aged matron, perhaps not seen for twenty odd years, would evoke delighted merriment as she unerringly recalled the year, the course, the group, and some racy anecdote connected with them.

Every year, in the *Guild Magazine*, as she recounted the news of staff and school, her inimitable account was eagerly seized on, and read with avidity. Bland and imperturbable, trouble flowed away before her; her responsibilities never wore her down.

When Miss Gladys Clarke succeeded her mother as Principal in 1919, Miss Caddow was appointed Vice-Principal, holding this post until retirement regulations forced her to relinquish it in 1931. She then remained as College Warden until after Miss Clarke's death, retiring in 1937 at the age of seventy-three.

She was a recognised member of the family hierarchy, and knew, as probably did no one else, the inner history of the National up to the Second World War. She always lived in the building, and she had an intimate knowledge of all the personalities, the motives and the implications in the tangled threads of problems and negotiations connected with every single enterprise. She was at the hub, sharing Miss Clarke's personal interests and she saw through to its end the proud era of the 'family régime' with its triumphs and near defeats, which covered more than two-thirds of the life of the College.

Miss Caddow was a trusted confidante; letters, papers and unique memories remained untold secrets when she died aged nearly ninety in 1954. It was said of her 'Thy sky is ever clear; thou hast no sorrow in thy song, no winter in thy year.'

Miss Caddow, Mrs Clarke, Miss Gladys Clarke

GREAT DAYS

CHAPTER XVI

A VERITABLE SWORD OF DAMOCLES now hung over the National. Money was still tight, and some members of the Committee had become inured to welcome any means towards financial stability, however irksome to the School's independence. It can have been no coincidence that in October 1906 Mrs Clarke was visited by the Chairman of the London County Council; he came to ask her privately if she would confer with their Education Officer as to 'possible development of the School.' A letter followed just before Christmas enquiring 'the terms upon which the authorities of the School would be prepared to transfer it to the County Council.' This was a direct take-over bid. The Committee members noted its receipt, suavely stating that any decision must be deferred until their next meeting on 31 March 1907.

In the intervening three months they desperately cast round for means of escape. They found none; equally they postponed their answer.

In this dilemma they perforce reported the position to the Annual General Meeting in May 1907. They reminded their audience of the nation-wide standing of the School, emphasising that it drew students from the whole country and was not just a local London institution. Nevertheless, such was the financial predicament that the outcome was agreement by the meeting that the National should 'bear in mind in future negotiations' the resolution which the Committee itself had framed in its duress – namely 'the possibility of ultimately transferring the School to the Council.' The Committee was on the spot. But

71

there were stout hearts among them who had no intention of hoisting the white flag.

Mrs Clarke was also full of sound sense, never harbouring resentment to the detriment of her interests. Over Herman Senn's proposals she had made her point and won the day, albeit at some personal expense. She now critically and dispassionately reviewed the School's position.

There was no question but that the training of teachers must go on, though there was no money to be made here. All the same, even at the point of the bayonet, she had not the faintest intention of handing over to the London County Council. Another way out must be found.

It struck her that this already lay at hand if she could couple the present vogue for elaborate luncheon and dinner parties with the superb technical skill of some of her staff, exploiting the fashion by stimulating and then meeting a demand for High Class cookery instruction. She was confident of being able to satisfy the public, but to attract them she must have a draw, a name recognised in the world of Cookery. Outstandingly able as were some of her staff, none were public figures. Herman Senn was the answer; his demonstrations in 1905 and 1906 had been extremely successful. Mrs Clarke decided to let bygones be bygones and carried her Committee, who invited Mr Senn to plan and personally conduct a series of Public Demonstrations at Buckingham Palace Road with the assistance of the staff.

All was grist to his mill. The famous M. Escoffier was now everywhere lauded as Chef at the Carlton Hotel, and the chance of a different limelight was acceptable to Mr Senn. He entered into the project with verve and spirit.

There now began, in the Autumn of 1907, a partnership which went down in the School's history. Miss Maud Rotheram was one of three gifted sisters who both trained and taught there, their combined span of service covering nearly forty years. She returned to the National in 1903, after being Head of the Cookery Department at Edinburgh; already a brilliant exponent of High Class cookery she perfected her skill as she worked with Herman Senn.

Together they gave a series of public demonstrations which were eulogised in the Press and Society periodicals, creating a wave of fashionable enthusiasm which rose to a furore.

NATIONAL TRAINING SCHOOL OF COOKERY

AND OTHER BRANCHES OF DOMESTIC ECONOMY.

SPECIAL DEMONSTRATION

OF

AN ENTIRE DINNER,

TUESDAY, JUNE 29th, 1909.

By MR. C. HERMAN SENN,

Assisted by MISS ROTHERAM,

Commencing at 11 a.m.

·····➤ Menu. ◄·····

Hors D'Œuvre :

Les Friandises du Gourmet.

Potage :

Le Consommé Pompadour.

Poisson :

Les Tranches de Saumon Jurassienne.

Entrée :

Les Epigrammes d'Agneau à la Chartreuse.
Les Croûstades à la Chambord.

Roti :

Les Cailles à la Mesina.
La Salade de Houblon à la Princesse.
Les Pommes de Terre en Brioche.

Entremets :

La Suprême de fruits à la Romanoff.
Les Sablets à la Vanille.

Les Fondues de Camembert.

Admission   ...   .   **10s. 6d.**

For tickets apply as early as possible to the Secretary,
National Training School of Cookery,
72-78 Buckingham Palace Road, S.W

NATIONAL TRAINING SCHOOL OF COOKERY

AND OTHER BRANCHES OF DOMESTIC ECONOMY.

SPECIAL DEMONSTRATION

ᴏꜰ

AN ENTIRE DINNER,

By MR. C. HERMAN SENN,

TUESDAY, OCTOBER 5th, 1909.

Attendance—11 to 1 and 2 to 4 p.m.

⤳ Diner de chasse. ⬿

Huitres à la Moscovite.

Potage Crème au Gumbo.

Turbot à la Tolstoi.

Côtes de Mouton, Parisienne.
Pommes de Terre en Grappe.

Selle de Lièvre à l'Ardenaise.
Artichauts farcis au céleri.

Faisan rôti en casserole.
Salade Henriette.

Mousse aux pêches à la Châtelaine.

Profiteroles gratinés.

Admission ... ... **10s. 6d.**

For tickets apply as early as possible to the Secretary,
National Training School of Cookery,
72-78 Buckingham Palace Road, S W.

The volatile Herman Senn, adroitly performing culinary feats with inimitable slight of hand, carried all before him. Tempestuous and domineering, he had the perfect foil in Miss Rotheram. Cool, slender and immaculate, working with dexterity and precision of manipulation, she revealed a delicacy of touch and flashes of pointed wit to make the partnership irresistible.

The Demonstrations were crowded out; the leading periodicals continued fulsome in almost hysterical acclaim and the public were insatiable. No one demurred at the charge of half a guinea; indeed, they vied to get in!

The ingredients used were costly, as may be seen from the two menus shown.

During all the Edwardian period, teachers of outstanding skill and personality worked as members of the School staff in this heightened atmosphere. As with the early pioneers, much was demanded, and much was given, in spite of small financial return. Some of these teachers were at the beginning of their careers and remained at the School for another twenty-five years, carrying on the standards imbued in them at this time. They were perfectionists, and all their lives, in the face of changing values, nothing less was acceptable.

An example of the technical skill achieved was long cherished in the annals. The School was graciously permitted to make a cake, in May 1912, on the occasion of the birthday of Her Late Majesty Queen Mary, and decided to illustrate its devotion to 'Princess May,' as she had long been affectionately known. A white iced cake, a yard in diameter, circled by an inch deep trellis of white icing, was decorated by laying across it a great branch of may flowers, modelled in sugar. A student who actually took part has recalled that everyone in the High Class Cookery kitchen worked at it; under expert tuition each twig and leaf and petal and stamen was made and coloured, and at last the exquisite bough was created. The superb cake was delivered at Buckingham Palace, and there a chef gave his verdict. Scathingly he remarked that anyone could pick a branch from a hawthorn tree and lay it on a cake. The illusion was complete – praise could go no higher!

The great tradition of Cookery remained. Other departments rose to maturity and acknowledged excellence, but the impact of the original subject never lost its force. To the end of its days, the name of the National was synonymous with that of Cookery.

In 1895 classes had also been started in Needlework, Dressmaking and Laundrywork, followed by Housewifery, Millinery and Tailoring, and finally in September 1900, the Cordon Bleu training began. To give official recognition to these extra subjects, legal steps were taken at a Special Meeting in November 1902, to change the title to 'The National Training School of Cookery and Other Branches of Domestic Economy.'

Royal permission was given to incorporate a crown into the design for the new Seal. The original name remained on the wrought iron arch. Later, the new title was printed in large gold letters on a dark blue board which stretched across the face of the building.

Particularly in demand were courses in Needlework and Dressmaking, led by two revered teachers for over twenty years. The 'debs' of those years also flocked to various special classes, and another student of that era recalls that great interest was evinced in 'the smart carriages, often with footmen, in which they drew up at the doors.'

The School revelled in its acknowledged privilege of lining the road when Royalty received distinguished guests at Victoria station. The consciousness of this proximity to the Royal Family was an integral part of daily life, and at times of processions the School identified itself with the glamour and the pageantry. The spectacle of the Guards as they marched to and from the Palace every morning never palled; it was a trumpet call to one and all, and they were lucky students who were working in rooms overlooking the road and so could throng the windows, and thrill to the band with its reverberating drums.

GREAT DAYS

CHAPTER XVII

THE PROFITS from the Public Demonstrations put the National temporarily on its feet, and within a year, by May 1908, the horizon had brightened to the extent of a balanced budget with £250 surplus. With the promise of increasing surpluses to come – a confidence later completely justified – the negotiations with the London County Council were thankfully allowed to lapse.

The Committee now felt able to salve its conscience by attending to the revision of staff salaries, 'as a matter of equity that had been unfortunately postponed through stress of circumstances,' and appointed a sub-committee including Mrs Bridgeman, Mrs Clarke and Mr Cole, who reported to the meeting on 17 June 1908. They recommended a new scale which was unanimously adopted by the full Committee, and the accepted remuneration of that time is a striking commentary on the changed value of money.

The members of the teaching staff, numbering eighteen in all, were grouped in three classes.

Class A was composed of the Head Teachers in charge of Departments for both the Diploma and Technical students. For the Diploma students, Mrs Wilson, Head of Cookery with a salary of £130, was about to retire and to be succeeded by her chief assistant Miss Gladys Clarke on a salary of £100. The Head of Laundrywork was Miss Marsh, and of Housewifery Miss Jefferys, both also receiving £100 a year.

On the Technical side, Miss Rivers in charge of Cookery received £150; Miss Thorpe, also Cookery, £90; and Miss Rotheram (Demonstrator) £110. It was agreed to ignore all existing distinctions and to place Heads of Departments on a new scale starting at £125, rising by £5 a year to a maximum of £150.

All, irrespective of age, service or responsibility, were bracketed together on the lowest rung, to mount the ladder equally. Only Miss Rivers was exempt, and allowed to retain her £150. Welcome as were the increases, there was grievance over the levelling of status.

Class B grouped five teachers next in seniority. Miss Dabbs was in charge of the London County Council Children's classes and received £125 for this post of special responsibility. Of the other four, for Cookery Miss Bussell received £100 and Miss Fitzgerald £93; for Upholstery Miss Eckford £93; and for Dressmaking Miss Cookes £88. The new scale raised the starting salary to a basic £105, rising by £5 a year to £130.

The consequent adjustments, on the face of it, seem somewhat irrational. Miss Dabbs was immediately promoted to the maximum of the scale, £130, Miss Eckford and Miss Fitzgerald to the £105 minimum, while Miss Bussell and Miss Cookes each received £115.

Class C comprised six teachers of recent service receiving appropriately meagre salaries. Five of them taught Cookery, Miss Byatt and Miss Underhill receiving £87, Miss Broderick £78, Miss Senn (daughter of Herman Senn) £66 and Miss Janie Clark £52. Miss Ironside, teaching Laundrywork, received £73.

The new scale ranged from £75, by £5 a year, to £100. Now the salaries of Miss Byatt and Miss Underhill became £90, Miss Broderick £85, Miss Ironside £80 and Miss Janie Clark the minimum £75. Miss Senn, who seems to have been part time, had £70.

Miss Caddow, who had been appointed School Secretary in 1906, now became officially 'Secretary and Deputy.' As always, she was in a class apart. Her salary was raised from £100 to £115 a year, to rise to a maximum of £160. In addition, she was to continue 'to receive board and lodging.'

The new scales, with the appropriate increases, were made effective from 1 August 1908, and the Committee stressed that there should be no differentiation between the salaries for the teachers of Diploma and Technical students, thus firmly supporting Mrs Clarke in her conviction that students in both courses should be taught together.

Mrs Clarke herself reached her maximum salary. She now received £450 a year, never to be increased in spite of expanding work and mounting problems, including the tensions of the coming War.

In April 1912, the salary structure was simplified by reducing it to two classes:

A. Heads of Departments, £130, rising by £5 a year, to £150.

B. Assistant Teachers, £90, rising by £5 a year, to £125.

These rates held good until March 1919, when they were revised at the end of the First World War.

London County Council Cookery Scholars, 1905

Sheldrake, with Peter

GREAT DAYS

CHAPTER XVIII

IN NO QUARTER did the spirit and tradition of the National evoke more unquestioned devotion than amongst the domestic and house staff. Queen in her own sphere was Mrs Christie, always known as Louisa, who was with Mrs Clarke in the early days and watched the family growing up. She dominated all who entered the dining room, everyone quailing under her imperious blue eyes. She had strong likes and dislikes which she made no effort to disguise, and with her high curled hair and wasp waist, she was uniquely privileged. Only she would ever have dared to lay down the law to Miss Gladys Clarke, even when she was the Principal. With *sangfroid* she would snatch a succulent morsel from one who had incurred her displeasure, no matter how senior, and bear it off to a favourite. No one reprimanded her. But then, as she used to claim, she and Mrs Clarke 'started this School.'

Under pressure Louisa retired in 1934; deprived of her despotic rule, her tyranny and her unswerving loyalty, the National lost one of its inimitable characters. Living with her devoted daughter, she died, eighteen years later, in her ninety-third year, relishing to the end any news of the 'dear old School.'

Sheldrake was described by Miss Caddow as 'our beloved and honoured Commissionaire.' Upright, dignified and handsome, he came in 1896 after serving in the King's Royal Rifles. His hair and long moustaches shone like white silk; he wore his uniform and row of medals with an air of distinction, and as if still on parade. In the Afghan Wars he had been on the march to Kandahar. It was recalled that one day Lord Roberts came in to see a daughter who was taking lessons, and to Sheldrake's undying pride, hailed him as an old comrade.

Sheldrake himself never forgot a face. Through long hours in the draughty hall, usually with Peter, the small brown dog of mixed breed and uncertain temper, he was ready with unfailing courtesy to attend to all who entered. He noted and assessed everyone, whether a visiting Duchess or the humblest, newest student. He was never fooled. Beneath his gentle mien, he was shrewd, astute, utterly reliable and the soul of discretion. His pride in the School made him an unbending critic, but there was no disguising his innate kindness and readiness to help. Many an anxious heart must have been soothed by Sheldrake coming unobtrusively to the rescue, dealing faithfully and tactfully with those distracted by their fears or follies, including the calls of romance. As for the latter, once a young man had braved the portals and received the seal of approval, all was safe in Sheldrake's hands.

In 1928, aged seventy-five, reluctantly he retired, but as a member of staff wrote later, 'he missed his work as much as we missed him, so Miss Clarke asked him to come back to us for three days a week – and we welcomed him gladly.' So did Peter, who was 'Sheldrake's shadow.'

He stayed with the National, to the pleasure of all, till his death, after a few days' illness, at the age of eighty-three in 1936. A final tribute to Edwin Sheldrake recorded that 'he was a most faithful and loyal friend for over forty years, and everybody loved him. He was a perfect gentleman.'

The domestic staff were long serving and often long suffering, but their welfare was a matter of personal concern. Judged by the prevailing practice of the times, the early Committees were very fair and even generous to those who proved trustworthy.

Mrs Crockett came in 1874 and was promoted, 'to have care of the household staff,' and to live on the premises when the School moved in 1889. She was evidently a person of calibre, for in 1890 it was decided 'to receive three or four cooks to pay £1 each per week' to be trained under Mrs Crockett and to assist her in the Demonstration room; in 1893, she enjoyed a gratuity of £10 from Indian funds for helping to teach two members of the Gaekwar of Baroda's staff, who attended the School for twelve months. When she remarried in 1897, the Committee presented her with a

Dining Room, 1921 (with Louisa on right)

silver salver which cost £16, suitably inscribed to record their appreciation of twenty-three years' service.

Other instances of benefaction include an ailing kitchen maid who was retained on half-pay for several months before she was able to resume her duties; another was given a pension of 5s a week, seemingly in perpetuity.

Recognition of actions like these helped to found a reciprocal loyalty. In much later years, it was typical that Mrs Lapwood and Ethel, even when off-duty in their dark basement sitting-room, would respond to every beck and call.

After the Second World War, when drastic changes in world conditions made the same dedication virtually impossible, still a few upheld the old tradition of service. Among these was Mrs Macgregor, the tall, forthright Scot with chiselled features and iron grey hair, who for years was a pillar of the Public Demonstrations, 'always ready,' it was said, 'with the perfectly flavoured sauce.' 'Mrs Mac' joined the domestic staff in 1919, remaining for about forty years until she was eighty. The National's superb collection of copper was her pride, and the gleam of the saucepans in her own kitchen warmed the dullest day – the final polish achieved by a dry soap powder rubbed on with her bare hands.

All the names of this army who toiled through the long years cannot be listed, though probably every student has a corner in her heart for at least one. But the memory of their devotion is imperishable.

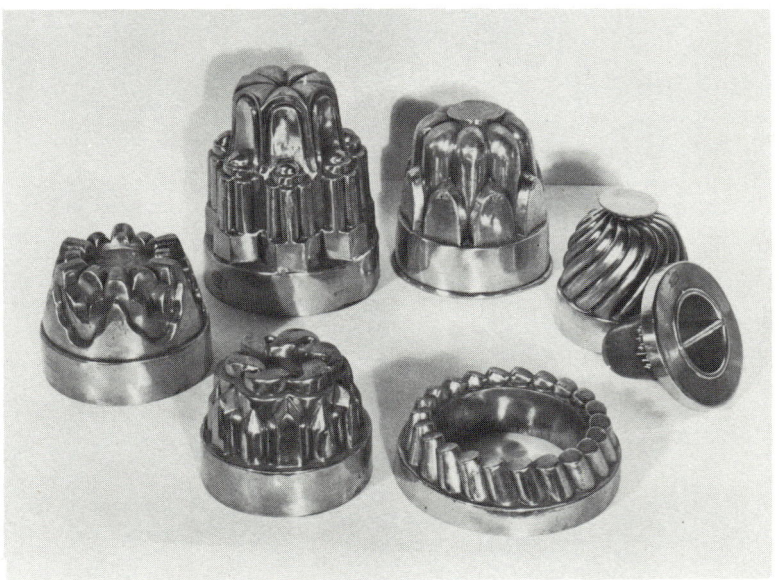

Selection of the National Copper (now in Brighton Pavilion)

Children's Cookery Class, 1908

GREAT DAYS

CHAPTER XIX

IN SPITE OF ALARUMS and excursions, the years from early in the century up to the First World War were in truth the heyday of the National.

Mrs Clarke, in her sixties the doyenne of Domestic Economy, her advice sought on all sides, led the School in a period of unparalleled vitality. Nothing escaped her; she had a finger on every pulse and in every pie, and an iron in every fire. She was on top of her form, alert, able and shrewd as ever.

The School was professionally secure with an unrivalled reputation for craft technique and a lively interest in modern thought. Mr Buckmaster had early inculcated the belief in a sound scientific basis, but the mounting speed of developments in Science demanded reappraisal of the provision on this side if the School were to keep abreast. At the same time, Mrs Clarke's inborn appreciation of the humanities in which she was nurtured called for a proper balance between the two cultures, and her sagacity prompted her to review the whole position and attempt to gauge future needs.

Authentic reminiscences of a year's course from September 1903 to July 1904 reveal that in the first term rigorous instruction in cleaning and scullery work was given by the domestic staff, followed by elementary Artisan cookery. Students were allowed to attend certain demonstrations and they prepared dishes under the supervision of a senior student, with a member of staff at hand.

In the second and third terms they graduated to 'Household' and 'Superior Household' cookery, some of the tuition being

given by Herman Senn himself. The final test, in which expensive
ingredients were used, was a seven course dinner, 'as in a first
class hotel' of that period. Throughout the course great stress
was laid on hygiene, food values, menu-planning and manipulative dexterity, with skill in decoration. Little consideration
was given to the cost or labour involved.

Occasional demonstrations were given by the students to
adults and to the children in the London County Council classes
held at the School. The theoretical background throughout the
course was provided by lectures given in Chemistry of Food and
Cookery, Physiology, Education and Method, and Speech Training. Of necessity, the time for these was limited.

The comparatively high fees restricted admission to those of
comfortable means who had been relatively sheltered. To a
certain extent this continued at the School for those who were
resident under the care of the Deputy Principal; a maid always
waited up if they went out in the evenings. At the same time it
was accepted that these slightly older students had a sense of
responsibility and they were allowed far more freedom than
their contemporaries in normal training colleges. Mrs Clarke
set great store by responsibility; these were to be the future
leaders, and she was determined that a course should be devised
worthy of their potential.

The first students had been hand picked to produce pioneer
teachers and leaders in the field of Domestic Economy, but
present trends pointed to an extension of outlook. Unless the
training provided opportunities for wider study, there would be
small chance of understanding or sharing in decisions of policy
which were the accepted prerogative of leading educationists.

This conclusion implied a more academic approach than
hitherto, but Mrs Clarke became as convinced of its importance
as she was aware of the dangers of narrow specialisation. It also
reinforced her belief in recruiting mature students of cultured
background rather than submitting to the Board's policy of
concentrating on young entrants.

With customary realism she faced that the necessary action
would entail complete reorganisation of the Training departments, undaunted by the prospect of the extensive changes
involved in curriculum, premises and equipment.

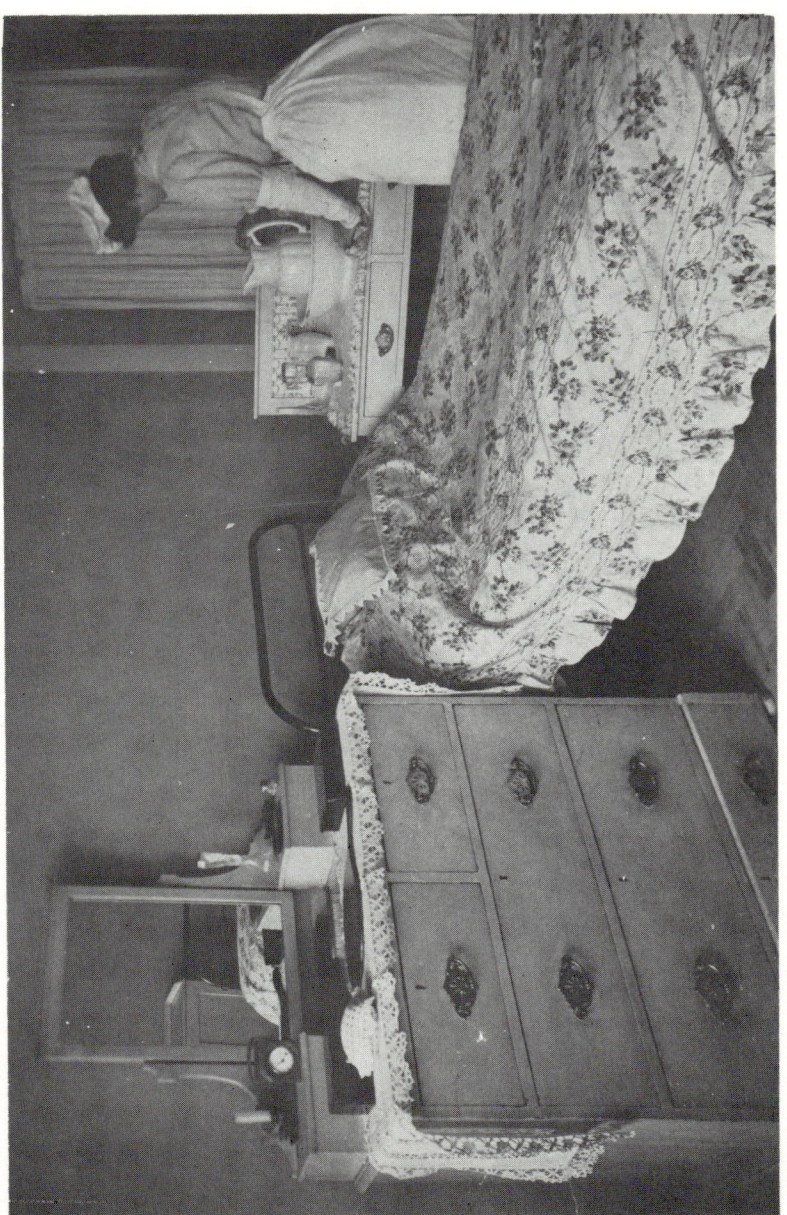

Home Management, 1905

Considerable discussion ensued, both with the Committee and with His Majesty's Inspector Miss Sillitoe, a Dresden china figure whose limpid blue eyes and velvet glove masked keen critical judgment and a firm grip. Through the years she proved a true friend to the National and to Mrs Clarke, where mutual respect often made it possible for them to agree to differ.

Empowered by the Committee, Mrs Clarke now tackled, simultaneously, the two major issues of Science and academic work. Not a whit did this deter her from dealing with the host of attendant details and other concerns, which she met with resilience. It seemed as if the labours of the first twenty-five years, which blossomed in the nineties, were now fully bearing fruit.

Mrs Clarke first consulted Dr J. A. Brincker, who had been appointed to the staff following Dr Pilley as full-time teacher of Science, at a salary of £150 a year in 1906. The revised Science course which he drew up at her instigation and submitted to the Board in March 1909, drew in reply suggestions for further developments involving not only the syllabus for Science but also for concomitant subjects.

A small sub-committee including Mr Cole, Miss Gladys Clarke and Miss Caddow, accordingly devised a comprehensive syllabus and detailed timetable for a two-year course with Science and the practical Domestic Subjects classes planned concurrently. A practical laboratory was felt to be essential and it was suggested that space for this would be available if some of the present residential accommodation were converted. The scheme, agreed by Dr Brincker and Dr Pilley (now the School Examiner) was approved by the Committee who, full of hope and confidence, sent it to the Board, adding a query as to possible help towards the cost of the laboratory. The Board gave its blessing, sanctioned the appointment of a full-time Science Mistress at a salary of £100 a year, but offered no financial support.

The School was left to find the money. In the event, as usual, it could afford very little. The ensuing frustrations may perhaps throw some light on the new teacher's resignation (for reasons unstated) twelve months later.

The Committee agreed in February 1910 to equip the kitchen then used as a London County Council classroom 'with counters and troughs suitable for use as a Chemistry laboratory, in such a way that the room can also be used as a Practice Kitchen when not required for Science.' The conversion was to be put in hand during the Easter holidays at a cost of £79. At best it was a compromise. At this same time, complicated negotiations were in train with both the London County Council and the Board of Education and nobody felt able or willing to produce the essential commodity – money.

But all these efforts were not in vain. The outcome of Mrs Clarke's initiative was an appraisal of the School's position and purpose, leading to complete revision of the main courses. For this, work towards building up academic strength on which she was simultaneously engaged, greatly influenced the proposals. Lack of immediate provision prevented these from being put into effect, but was proved to be only postponement. The foundation work towards study in depth was laid at this time and used as a basis for the new plans drawn up in 1912, just three years later. By then the suggested conversion of bedrooms had resulted in two classrooms and a laboratory. The latter was too small (noted by the Board at their Full Inspection, without comment) but at least it was a beginning.

Robbed of the real target, the School could nevertheless instal and illustrate the use of the latest equipment. Mrs Clarke set about the necessary investigations. Her genius for reconciling progress with the dictates of the bank balance had always been evident in the choice of fuel and equipment for the kitchens. In the early days of the National there was no practicable alternative to the coal range, but already by 1882 the official report of the Smoke Abatement Committee acknowledged 'the aid given by Mrs Clarke when carrying out experiments and tests with gas stoves.'

Gas was certainly used for much of the cooking in Buckingham Palace Road, and H.M.I. Miss Sillitoe's recorded belief that 'Mrs Clarke was the first person to adopt cooking by gas' was thought to refer also to some of the South Kensington Exhibition dinners and demonstrations prepared on the early stoves. In an interview given to the magazine *Hearth and Home* in February 1892, Mrs Clarke drew attention to the fact that 'only luminous gas is used, much to the disgust of the Gas Company, who would prefer the employment of atmospheric gas, which is however too creative of fumes.'

A visiting journalist from the magazine *Woman* in 1900 recorded that 'the gas ranges for cooking which you see at each table were carried out by a practical gas engineer who took up Mrs Clarke's own ideas.' One wonders what she would have made of North Sea gas!

But now in 1909 electricity was in the news, and Mrs Clarke was determined that the School should be among the first to demonstrate its use for practical purposes. Action was delayed almost more by lack of space than of money, and she had to wait until the conversion in 1912 provided a new classroom which was fitted with electrical equipment.

The Westminster Electric Supply Company then agreed to instal and provide lighting, heating and cooking facilities. Their bill, sanctioned by the Committee because it 'could benefit students in training to have instruction in the use of electricity,' was as follows:

	£	s	d
Wiring	30	0	0
2 convector heaters	8	8	0
1 cooking stove	12	12	0
3 electric irons	3	0	0
3 boiling rings	4	2	6
	£58	2	6

Running costs would be $5\frac{1}{2}d$ a unit for lighting and $1d$ a unit for cooking and heating. The company offered this equipment, on permanent loan and free of charge, as long as the consumption of electricity at $1d$ a unit amounted to at least £5 a quarter.

The boiling rings were intended for sweet-making, and the gentle heat of the convectors was said to be 'very suitable for coating chocolates.' This room was immediately dubbed the 'Electric Room' and the name stuck long after its purpose changed and most of the equipment had been removed.

It was a notable step, and in furtherance of this lead the Committee agreed in the following Summer of 1913 to instal a large electric cooker at a cost of £34 11s in the practice kitchen where the public also could share the benefits of instruction in this modern medium.

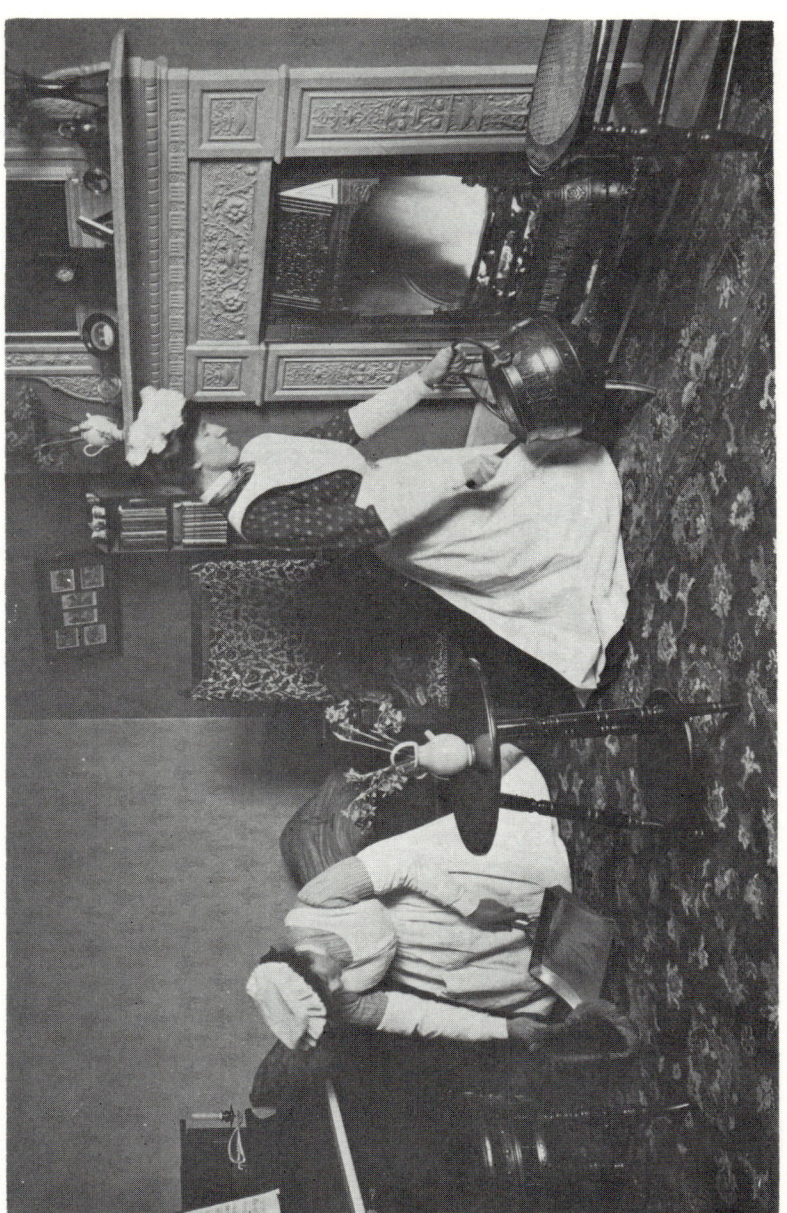

Home Management, 1908

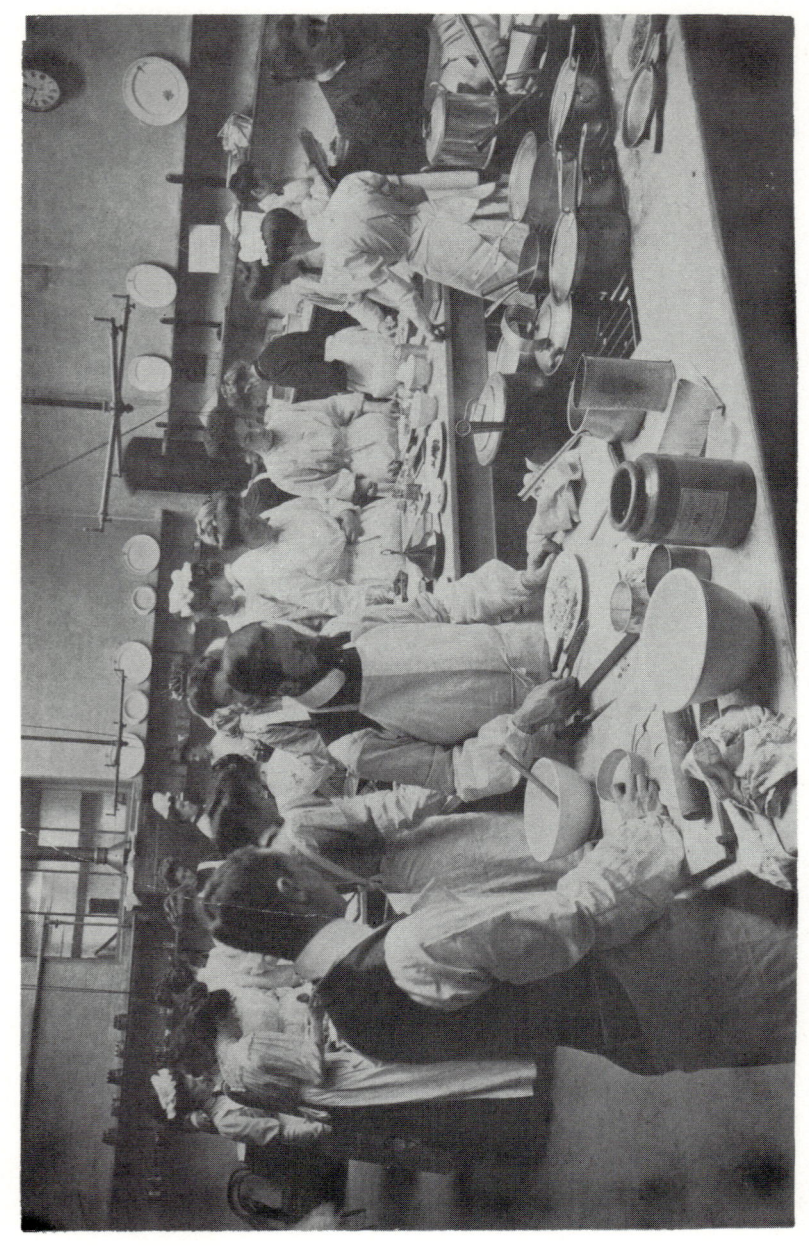

Naval Paymasters in High Class Cookery Kitchen, 1906

GREAT DAYS

CHAPTER XX

CONNECTIONS WITH THE SERVICES had been preserved, though at times on a somewhat tenuous basis. After the cordial relationship with Colonel Hutton in 1892, Army contacts lapsed until the Army School of Cookery was brought up with a round turn twelve years later.

The Army School meanwhile had continued to take part in the annual Exhibitions at the Royal Albert Hall arranged by the Cookery and Food Association under Herman Senn's chairmanship. Invitations to enter were much sought and there was keen competition for the awards. The National prized highly its own successes, including the Gold Medal of 1895 and the Challenge Shield of 1903. But the Army School was no longer even in the running. The standard of their cooks had deteriorated to such an extent that they were officially reprimanded by the Jurors of the Exhibition in 1904.

Herman Senn took up the matter. He was outraged by this fall from grace which it was agreed must be blamed on poor training. A remedial course, emphasising dietary values and the best use of Army rations was essential; and for this, who better than their original mentors at the National? He acted with his usual celerity and in February submitted a memorandum to the Committee, quoting the Jurors' strictures on 'waste of rhubarb, suet, pastry; throwing quantities of flour upon the boards, etc.' and asking for help. Magnanimously the Committee refrained from pointing the moral and simply offered their assistance to the War Office. The response was immediate, and by May teachers from the National were again giving lessons at the Military

Hospital at Netley and the camp at Aldershot. Four R.A.M.C. Warrant Officers were also accepted for training for the High Class Cookery Certificate. Relations were thus resumed. Honour was satisfied when the Army School obtained an Exhibition award only a few months later.

Herman Senn had turned the affair to good account and achieved several objects. The Jurors approved equally his treatment of the Army School, where sound training was restored, and his concern for the prestige of the Exhibition. He also put himself in a good light with the Committee members at the National, doubtless inclining them to attend more readily to his bold take-over bid later that year. He had incidentally done the School a good turn by drawing attention to the rewards of initiative, for after the War Office had welcomed their offers the Committee decided to approach the Admiralty to see if the School could be of further help in that quarter.

A link with the Royal Navy had been maintained through the teachers from the National attached to the naval hospitals near Portsmouth, and also by the presence on the Committee of a retired senior officer, Captain the Honourable John Manners Yorke, whose support added considerable weight to the letter which was now directed to the Admiralty.

Again, there was swift co-operation. By October 1904 discussions with the Cookery sub-committee of the Admiralty led directly to the organisation of cookery courses for Ships' Cook-Instructors, who were to attend at the School in small groups for six or eight weeks at a time, at intervals throughout the year. A special course of four weeks was arranged for Paymaster Commanders and Lieutenant-Commanders who were responsible for the messing arrangements on board His Majesty's ships. The importance which the Royal Navy attached to this may be judged by the large group of high ranking officers who came to the first experimental course, testing the value at first hand. All the courses were under way by February 1905. At Mrs Clarke's request the Admiralty appointed a senior naval officer, Fleet-Paymaster Silk, as liaison to discuss, assist and advise as necessary.

From then on, the Royal Navy was part of the National scene. In this field, Miss Janie Clark reigned supreme. Like a diminutive turkey cock, small, autocratic, *pince nez* on a long black ribbon, she barely touched a dish herself. Standing by a powerful naval Paymaster, she would indicate with a few words and slight gestures of her tiny hands, the exact finish required, and under this inspired direction his great hands would perform miracles of deft control.

Perhaps fittingly, there are few recorded communications from the Silent Service, but relationships always seemed to be friendly. In 1919, when the School was in low water with depleted classes and exhausted by War efforts, the Royal Navy, ever faithful, warmed hearts and restored spirits by sending another group of Paymasters for the time-honoured instruction. Miss Janie Clark was there to greet them. This tradition of training the Royal Navy in the art of Cookery remained almost unbroken until shortly after the Second World War.

One thing led to another. Both the Army and the Navy were now in recognised contact with the School, so it was natural that Mr Lloyd George, as President of the Board of Trade in 1906, should also turn to the National. He needed help to implement the provision in his Merchant Shipping Act that every British foreign-going ship of over 1,000 tons must carry a qualified cook, holding either the Certificate of the Board of Trade or of an approved Cookery School. It was immediately realised that the training should meet the particular conditions under which these men at sea would be working. To devise such a course presented no problem to Mrs Clarke, by now experienced in special naval needs. She was instrumental in organising the Schools of Nautical Cookery set up at all the major ports, and Mr Lloyd George wrote to the Committee to express his gratitude for her co-operation and initiative.

In July 1907, Mrs Clarke reported 'the satisfactory results of the training given to the men' and that she 'was considering a syllabus to be adopted by the Shipping Federation.' The success of this scheme spread far and wide. It aroused interest throughout the country, and was the subject of much favourable comment in the Press.

The improved diet in ships of both Royal and Merchant Navies during the early years of the century was the direct outcome of Mrs Clarke's personal work in co-operation with the Services concerned.

1914
June 29th:

Alexandra *Marlborough Hesse*

Marie *Empress of Russia*

Signatures of Her Majesty Queen Alexandra and her sister
Empress of all the Russias

June 14th
1916:

Mary R

Signature of Her Majesty Queen Mary during the First World War

GREAT DAYS

TWO MAIN ALTERNATIVES for strengthening the academic side were open – either development within the School or in co-operation with others, and the answer lay at hand.

In 1908, a three-year course in Home and Social Science had started in the Women's Department at King's College, incorporated in the University of London. University courses could lead to the award of a degree, a fact not lost upon Mrs Clarke in her quest for a training and qualification bestowing the right to talk to leaders of thought on an equal footing. In spite of adverse criticism of both the craft and the Science, the new course went ahead, and Mrs Clarke felt that here was the opportunity. Her unerring instinct for timing impelled her, at the precise moment when the sheer brilliance of the Public Demonstrations was focussing attention on perfection of craftsmanship, to make a bid for academic strength.

Her intuition served her well, for this golden age of prosperity was not to last. His Majesty King Edward's death curtailed the lavish hospitality which had sown the seeds of the School's rich harvest, and the fruits of luxury were garnered. With lack of demand, the vaunted Public Demonstrations dwindled and inevitably collapsed at the onset of the First World War. But in 1909, with a surplus in the accounts, and no obvious reason why it should diminish, Mrs Clarke nevertheless bent her mind and energies towards entry into the acedemic field.

Always punctilious in matters of etiquette, she made no direct approach to King's College, but sought elucidation at an interview in June 1909 with the Chief Woman Inspector, the Honourable Maude Lawrence, and with Mr Oppé, at the Board of Education. At just the same time the small sub-Committee, with Miss Gladys Clarke as a leading member, was at work on the revised training schemes for the School, where the approach was greatly influenced by Mrs Clarke's endeavours to penetrate the academic sphere. So she was doubly anxious to take part in the new venture.

She was assured that 'the Board was watching the new course' with its proposal to lead to a degree, but she was 'advised that the National should not approach King's College with a view to co-operation or combination.' She perceived that she was hamstrung. By this ruling she was debarred from any approach to King's College or any further official discussion of the subject. The target of a degree course, which her acumen and realism so clearly envisaged, had been moved to a much greater distance, and she had to reset her sights. The only way left open was to concentrate on academic work within the School, and in this she was upheld by her eldest daughter Gladys, herself an intellectual at heart. Before the end of June, she reported the position to the Committee, who supported her to the hilt.

The right climate of opinion was essential, and in view of the prevailing feeling that the attitude of King's College, reflected in the Press, tended to ignore the existing Schools of Domestic Science, the Committee agreed to institute a campaign drawing attention to the comprehensive quality of the work at the School, emphasising the theoretical and scientific sides so often overshadowed by the craft.

Articles in the *Pall Mall*, *Westminster* and *St James's* Gazettes were strengthened by one in the *Spectator* written by Dr Pilley, where he formulated the views already agreed with Mrs Clarke over the revision of the School's two-year course. As Acting Chairman, Mr Almeric FitzRoy proposed that 'when the suggestion of a degree in Home Science and Household Economy is brought forward by King's College, the National should approach London University and ask for recognition on the same lines.'

A year later, in July 1910, Mrs Clarke reported that she had 'made enquiries from someone connected with London University and had been advised that the whole question of a Science degree in Domestic Science was premature, and had not been promised to anybody.'

This same year saw the Women's Department of King's College receive the status of King's College for Women. In 1916, it moved to new buildings on Campden Hill, where in 1920 the University recognised the three-year course for the degree of B.Sc. in Household and Social Science.

Mrs Clarke's approach to the Board of Education in June 1909 had been followed in July by official approval in principle of the revised schemes of training submitted by the National. In December a visit from Dame Maude Lawrence and Mr Oppé, involving rigorous investigation, gave the opportunity to assess the potential for advanced academic work. Paying all due tribute to Mrs Clarke as pioneer and leader in the field of Domestic Science, it was nevertheless suggested that there was a tendency to in-breeding, and that the very excellence of the craft technique could limit horizons. The crucible, in fact, was in danger of becoming more important than the contents. This was exactly what Mrs Clarke herself felt, and it strengthened her hand in dealing with it. From that time all policy was directed towards academic strength and the sub-Committee pressed ahead. Their hard concentrated work enabled the School to submit specific proposals at the Full Inspection in 1912 – proposals which were to be embodied in the radically changed syllabus, which at the very moment of implementation was swept aside by the onslaught of the First World War.

Attention had been drawn by the Board of Education to a deficit in the preceding year of over £100 in the School funds, which was not helped when, due to some minor query, the Board's own grants were then withheld. The London County Council, hearing of this, chose to interpret it as showing a lack of confidence in the National, and in turn, decided to suspend their payment of the maintenance and scholarship fees which they paid under contract for their sponsored classes. Thereby a series of prolonged and irksome exchanges was set on foot between the Committee and the London County Council.

Meantime the School's financial position was undermined. The Board of Education had been able to help from 1907 onwards with grants of up to £12 a head for all students who completed the full two-year Diploma course. The grant due for 1910–1911 was £1,000, but the Board's conditions at this moment proved particularly onerous. Their stipulation that Diploma students should only be admitted at the beginning of a term was one thing to accept, but their rigid requirements in regard to the separation of diploma and technical students quite another. This decree struck a blow at both the School's finances and one of the tenets of Mrs Clarke's faith. She had always been convinced of the mutual benefit when students from these different courses worked together, and from the beginning, she had always insisted on this condition. But the Board found it unacceptable, thus necessitating differentiation in the teaching, involving more staff and more expense. Her indignation at this rejection of her beliefs was not lessened by the attendant loss to the School exchequer. The Board's policy aggravated the financial position of 1910, after the virtual loss of the money-spinning Public Demonstrations. It became imperative not only to search for fresh income, but again to study means of retrenchment within the School.

An event of great significance in the constitution of the Executive Committee had been the appointment in January 1905 of the first woman member, Mrs Ruth Homan, nominated by the London County Council to represent their Technical Education Board. Her balanced, sympathetic interest culminated in her able Chairmanship during the First World War.

She was joined on the Committee in October 1910, also as a London County Council representative, by Mr Isidore Salmon. This astute business man swiftly recognised the inherent weakness of the School's finances and pressed for immediate action. He urged a comprehensive review of costing, buying, and checking supplies, which, from his own specialised knowledge of catering contracts, he felt to be haphazard.

The National had always insisted on quality. They had no scruples in changing their suppliers, particularly their butchers, who were often in disgrace when goods were not considered up to standard. But individual judgments were accepted, and different tradespeople served different classes, resulting in several suppliers of the same products. Furthermore, there was no overall check of goods on arrival, as each kitchen dealt direct with its own orders. Mr Salmon was insistent on the necessity for bulk buying, proper co-ordination, and the appointment of a reliable store keeper who could both advise and supervise.

The Committee, thankful for this expert help, readily accepted the recommendations and agreed that the vital appointment of the first Store Keeper called for someone both professionally knowledgeable and conversant with the School. Thus it was that Miss Maud Rotheram, freed from the demands of the Public Demonstrations, took on the post in 1911. It proved no sinecure, but she justified the Committee's decision; costs were cut substantially and during her régime she set the pattern for future Store Keepers who, in a key position, kept watch over cost as well as quality.

Far reaching as were the effects of this reorganisation, they could not fill the economic gap. Immediate problems were made worse with the official grants, for no seemingly justifiable reason, still unpaid. Even so, regular sources of income were insufficient, and the Committee decided to review these. Examining the London County Council's remuneration, it became convinced that the School was considerably out of pocket, and provided a case for further substantial subsidy.

A sub-Committee, headed by the Vice-President, Lord Sheffield, was set up in January 1911, to go into the position and 'conduct possible negotiations.' But first the National pressed for payment of the overdue grant. Relations were strained when the London County Council implied continued dissatisfaction over certain practices, chiefly the suggestion that the children in their classes were taught by the students rather than the Staff teachers, and suffered in consequence. Indignant at this slur, but recognising the wisdom of amity, particularly in view of their impending plea for increased grants, the Committee swallowed its wrath and merely continued to press for its dues.

It was April 1911 before all the grants were paid. They included, in addition to the London County Council fees, grants for Diploma, Technical and Evening classes, and totalled £1,062. But by this time they were mortgaged, and funds were low.

It was also in April that Lord Sheffield, on behalf of the Committee, himself signed the letter to the Education Officer of the London County Council. In it he set out the work done by the

School for the Council, giving details of the cost in use of rooms, maintenance, equipment and teachers' salaries; on the evidence submitted he claimed that a subsidy of £600 a year was needed to cover expenses. He added that if this claim were agreed the National would be prepared to invite increased representation on its Committee. He then concluded, 'the Committee would be glad to consider any proposition of the London County Council tending in the direction of a still closer connection for the advancement of the work in which they both take such an interest.' This last sentence, open to various constructions, even to the extent of a possible take-over, is believed to have been dictated by Lord Sheffield's personal views, for he had come to be in sympathy with the idea of 'placing the School on a basis of public support.' Some apprehension was felt, particularly by Mrs Clarke, but the phrase was left and the letter despatched.

The Education Officer made no specific reply. But on 15 and 16 June four London County Council Inspectors, including the Chief Inspector, paid an exhaustive visit. They stated that there was no precedent for a subsidy to a Domestic Economy Training School, and emphasised that if the School would convert its residential accommodation on the top floors, thirty classes of elementary school children could be taught, instead of the present fourteen classes. The cost of this conversion they reckoned at £1,200, and an outside Hostel was advocated. There was no suggestion as to the manner of meeting these costs. Finally, they 'strongly advised that the Technical side of the work should be kept up,' an implication that the Council was concerning itself with the School as a whole, instead of confining itself to its own interests, which was not lost upon either Mrs Clarke or the Committee.

Their recommendations stirred up another tiresome issue. After the School had moved in 1889 and the Committee ruled that Mrs Clarke and her family should not occupy living accommodation on the top floors, quarters had been designed for a newly appointed Manager-cum-Secretary, and also for Mrs Crockett, in charge of the Domestic Staff at a salary of 25s a week. The scheme was short-lived. Within a year the former had left, and was replaced by a non-resident Secretary, and a resident Housekeeper with curtailed accommodation.

Living with Mrs Crockett, on wages of 5s a week, was her housemaid daughter. It would seem that the latter was a permanent member of a small group of resident maids kept for the purpose of implementing the Memorandum of Association of 1888 which stated that one of the objects of the School was 'to establish a servants' registry office for cooks and kitchenmaids.' Although this object never really matured, it proved useful to have a few such prospective maids working in the School and meanwhile living on the premises.

The remaining rooms were let to 'Ladies' or 'Cooks' attending the School. The latter paid 10s or 12s a week. The former were asked to pay £1 10s a week for a single, or £1 for a shared room; this residence proved attractive to students with homes at a distance, easing the minds of parents of hitherto sheltered daughters. By 1905 charges had been raised slightly, bringing in an additional £217 a year from the boarders who now numbered twenty-four. But with money tight, the thin edge of the wedge was driven. Classes brought in more than boarders, and in 1906 alterations to the top floors, to provide classrooms at a cost of £76, were approved by the Committee.

Mrs Clarke had viewed this decision with misgivings, but the financial gain added to her genuine interest in children had dictated acceptance. She still regarded these premises as ideal for residence yet now, in 1911, the London County Council's recommendation threatened further encroachment. Not wishing to precipitate a decision, it was agreed to sit tight and await a further move. It proved a long wait.

In March 1912 the Education Officer, on behalf of the Council, replied to Lord Sheffield's letter of the previous April. He simply reiterated their views as to an outside Hostel and the use of the top floors, and asked for an assurance that the National would be responsible for any necessary conversion should the Council decide in favour of an annual maintenance grant. A cold rejoinder from the National stated that this proposal would 'hamper the work for which the School had been founded'; to hand over so much space to the London County Council classes would 'alienate their own students' by the loss of classrooms and residential accommodation, all at considerable expense which could not be recouped. The National's concern for the children prompted it to offer to undertake responsibility for syllabus and teaching for the thirty classes required, if the Council would provide the premises; in which case the School would be prepared to waive its claim to a maintenance grant. Finally, the Committee 'wished to point out that during thirty-five years, the National had supplied over 75 per cent of the Cookery teachers for the London County Council, as well as of other Domestic Subjects.' The fat was in the fire.

The Education Officer contented himself with the remark that the principle of dual control of teachers might lead to problems in practice. But he offered to transfer the classes, if the School really desired it, 'to a building to be erected in Ranelagh Road, when ready.' Meantime, 'it would be a convenience if the pupils could be retained at the National Training School.' They were back to the old terms. In June 1912, after interminable discussion, the Committee reverted to its original request of April 1911, for an annual maintenance grant of £600, and an offer to convert the top floors (this time to take eighteen classes, instead of the present fourteen, which in no way approximated to the thirty classes requested), on condition that the Council would defray the cost, which 'would, we believe, be under £1,200,' the sum previously named by their Inspectors. The letter concluded by again urging the claims of the School, with the 'very large amount of practically unpaid work performed by it for the Council for many years at a heavy loss.' The offer of further representation on the Committee, or closer co-operation in any form, was not repeated. This letter was sent to the Education Officer on 25 June, with a covering note from Mrs Clarke asking for a personal interview. On 16 July she reported that this had been refused and the letter was now in the hands of the full Council. Their reply, brief and uncompromising, came in October, stating that 'having regard to all the circumstances,' they were unable to agree to the applications in the letter of 25 June.

Sir Almeric FitzRoy (now K.C.V.O.) in the Chair, read a letter from Mr Salmon in his absence, advocating another effort before closing negotiations. He suggested a meeting between deputations from both the National Executive Committee and the Council's Education Department, or alternatively a joint sitting of the two Committees in full.

The question then arose of 'the advisability of accepting help from the London County Council.' Finally the Minutes record the decision 'to let the whole matter drop for the present at all events.' The School had got nowhere; the wrangles had wasted time and energy and goodwill. The children's classes continued as before.

For the present the door was shut, and no one particularly wanted to open it. Fifty years later, it was open for ever.

Reproduction of signatures of Her Majesty The Queen of Denmark with her daughters the Princesses Alexandra and Thyra

March 15th Luncheon 15th March
Whitsunday:

Northcote —
Devonshire
Maurice [...]
Granville
Arthur Russell
Rudolstone
[...] Ellis.

Devonshire
[...]ley
J. [...]

Very well
cooked luncheon

Albert Edward P. and Luncheon Party, 15 March 1890

GREAT DAYS

MRS CLARKE'S INNATE REGARD for the proprieties on occasion warred with her Bohemian ancestry, but as Miss Eliza Youmans had realised as early as 1879, she had a strong sense of democracy and was ever a believer in mixing all ranks and races, sometimes with unusual results. An example lies in the official Visitors Book.

This massive volume, with thick pages and heavy leather spine and corners, begins in June with an array of impressive signatures, including Mr and Mrs Percy Wyndham, Lady Isabella Stewart, Sir Burke Clippage, the Earl of Longford and the Honourable Mrs A. Sartoris; while a medley of distinguished names crowd the following sheets. Besides their address many wrote laconic references to bread, or cakes, or soup or receipts. for the imposing book had now become a register of attendance at cookery classes or demonstrations.

Unexpectedly, in the midst of this record of somewhat humble activities, isolated on the handsome page only by wavering ink lines, comes the proud entry of 'Louisa, Queen of Denmark,' with 'Alexandra' and 'Thyra' beneath. It is the first recorded visit of Royalty to the School on 25 November 1875.

The same year ends with the names of a constant stream of visitors jostling on the pages, but the task of recording was unaccountably abandoned until May 1886, when a party of fifteen eminent Australians were entertained in May, and a dozen or so visitors came in June.

November 1889 takes up the tale of the classes once more, after the move to Buckingham Palace Road had obviously proved a great incentive to resume the annals. From then until March 1890, covering a hundred and fifteen pages, approximately 3,600 recurring personal signatures record, in heterogeneous order, attendances at Plain, High Class and Demonstration lessons, until, without any break, on the bottom half of a page, the long list is crowned by a most illustrious signature.

On 15 March 1890, under 'Lunch on 15 March,' is 'Albert Edward P.' dated, and with the comment also in his own hand of 'Very well cooked luncheon.' Beneath come the signatures of the ten Committee members who attended him. Unfortunately no record has survived of the dishes served at this delectable meal. His Royal Highness the Prince of Wales had become Patron of the School in 1883, and the honour conferred by this visit so soon after the move into the new building set the seal of Royal approval on the enterprise.

After this auspicious entry comes another long gap until 1903 when it can be seen that Miss Pankhurst was there on 3 April, and various members of the nobility in July.

The next highlight on 24 July 1907 is a bold 'Louise Auguste, Princess of Schleswig-Holstein,' more generally known as Her Highness Princess Marie Louise.

The ordinary entries now become more selective; no longer is the book used as an attendance register and the main lists are chiefly confined to educationists at home and from abroad; even so, there are long inexplicable omissions. In 1925 Lord Burnham, ex-President of the Board of Education, paid a highly appreciated visit with Lady Burnham, soon after consenting to become the President of the National. About thirty visitors signed in 1929, followed by sporadic entries which end in 1958.

Interspersed with these are treasured signatures recording honoured visits, by now accorded the deference of individual pages. On 27 June 1914, a striking 'Alexandra' with 'Marie Feodorovna' beneath recalls the excitement when Her Majesty Queen Alexandra, as Queen Mother, brought her sister, Her Imperial Highness, the Dowager Empress of all the Russias, to see the School.

At this moment, the National was desperately trying to raise money for a students'Hostel, for the double purpose of residence and practice house, for without the latter the new training

schemes could not be put into effect. It was decided to make an
appeal in memory of the late Chairman, the Honourable Frederick Leveson-Gower, and try to raise £5,000. At Christmas 1913,
it was agreed that the initial appeal should take the form of a
Bazaar in the following summer. A distinguished Committee,
including many members of the nobility headed by Lord Sheffield,
promised to direct proceedings, and Royal patronage was
secured.

The Bazaar was held in June 1914, and opened on the first day
26 June by Lady Howard de Walden and on the following day by
Lady Sheffield. All the tables, chairs and china were lent by
Mr Salmon; a uniformed policeman was on duty in the hall each
day at a cost of one guinea for eight hours.

It showed particular kindness for Her Majesty Queen Alexandra to sponsor this effort by her presence at the School. In
the current *Guild Magazine* Miss Caddow gives a vivid picture
of the occasion: 'We had notice in the morning of the intended
visit, and the staff and students, all arrayed in white, lined up
to meet the illustrious visitors. Surely nothing could have been
more charming than this unique reception of their Majesties,
who were met in the hall by Lord and Lady Sheffield and Mrs
Clarke, and conducted to the kitchens. They visited every stall,
and purchased something from each, Queen Alexandra specially
selecting a photograph of Mrs Clarke. She showed Her Majesty
Queen Alexandra the signatures of the Queen of Denmark,
Princess Thyra and her own, obtained on their visit to the old
School in 1875, and also His Majesty King Edward's signature
given at a later date. Queen Alexandra was much interested,
and she and the Dowager Empress both signed in the Visitors'
Book. . . . Their only regret was that there was no Cookery
going on.'

In the final event the funds raised were only £516, for within
six weeks of the great Bazaar, the outbreak of the First World
War put an end to any further appeals. None the less, the Hostel
Sub-Committee were given full powers to look for a Hostel and
report to the Executive Committee in October.

The National was indeed blessed by Royal kindness, for the
next signature is in the firm and flowing hand of Her Majesty
Queen Mary, when she strengthened everyone's morale on her

visit of 14 June 1916, at a particularly bad moment of the First World War.

In 1937 there was a renewed link with the past when the visit of Her Highness Princess Marie Louise in 1907 was followed thirty years later by that of her sister, Her Highness Princess Helena Victoria, on 7 December.

Deep as was the mingled affection and pride felt by the National for all its Royal visitors, the Patron whom it really took to its heart was Her Majesty Queen Elizabeth the Queen Mother. She paid three memorable visits during her twenty-five years as Patron, and the beautiful and distinguished signature of 'Elizabeth R' graces three pages.

Her Majesty came on her first two visits in 1943 and 1949 as reigning Queen,when her radiance and kindliness put everyone at ease and endeared her for ever. At the last sad visit of 5 June 1962, at the end of the National's life, her warmth and understanding brought balm to many sore hearts.

The now rather battered old Visitors' Book, with over a hundred pages still blank, which began so bravely in 1874, closes on 5 June 1962 with the best-loved signature, 'Elizabeth R.'

GREAT DAYS

THE IDEA of forming a Guild of Old Students took practical shape in the autumn of 1911, with the warm approval of the Executive Committee. Invitations to join were sent out to all National students who held a Teacher's Diploma or a Cordon Bleu medal, and the response brought two hundred to the Inaugural Meeting at the School on 17 February 1912. In a 'charming speech' Mrs Clarke expressed her wish that 'the Guild should become a great power and be a help to all its members,' a wish enthusiastically endorsed by her audience, described as being 'of all ranks and grades in the profession from Inspectors, Examiners, Heads of Training Schools down to the student just ready to leave the School.' On their behalf, Mrs Clarke was presented with a gold and blue enamel badge, in the centre of which the School monogram was raised in gold on a blue ground, with the motto *Semper Fidelis* beneath. It was adopted as the Guild badge, and by the following June it had been struck in silver and different coloured enamels – blue for Teachers of Cookery, Laundry and Housewifery; red for Needlework subjects; and green for Cordon Bleu members; at a cost of 2s each.

The inauguration of the Guild was celebrated by music, supper and dancing. A Committee had already been elected, and the Rules drawn up: these, printed with the programme of the evening, were given to every member. There was unanimous agreement both to the proposed Constitution and Rules and to the Committee of eleven, consisting of:

President and Chairman   The Principal (*ex-officio*)
Three Members of Staff   Miss Caddow

113

	Miss Gladys Clarke
	Miss FitzGerald
Treasurer	Miss Underhill
Secretaries for Cookery, Laundry & Housewifery Teachers	Miss Jefferys
	Miss Marsh
Secretary for Dressmaking, Needlework and Millinery Teachers	Miss Wallbank
Secretary for Cordon Bleu Teachers	Miss L. Thorpe
Three Outside Representatives for:	
(i) Cookery, Laundry and Housewifery Teachers	Miss Nash (*also Vice-Chairman of Committee*)
(ii) Dressmaking, Needlework and Millinery Teachers	Miss Roworth
(iii) Cordon Bleu Teachers	Miss Gillham

Members were to serve for two years and then to be eligible for re-election.

In 1913 it was agreed to add three members to the above; two more to represent Cookery, Laundrywork and Housewifery teachers, and an extra one for Needlework.

The original Aims and Privileges of the Guild were laid down as follows:

AIMS
1. To further good fellowship and public spirit amongst the members.
2. To prevent any slackness that may arise when a member has left the Training School for some time.
3. To keep the members of the Guild in touch with all developments connected with Domestic Subjects.
4. To enable members to hear of appointments and to be recommended for them.

PRIVILEGES
1. Free admission to lectures and demonstration lessons in the School, on application by letter, providing there is room in the class.
2. To ask advice and talk over difficulties with the Principal and the Staff of the Training School, by appointment.

3. An annual Social Reunion to be held on the first Saturday in October.
4. An annual Conference to be held in the Spring Term.
5. An annual Report to be sent out in January.
   The annual subscription to be 2s 6d.
   Membership soared. By the end of 1912, the numbers were 440; and in March 1913, at the time of the first Conference, they had risen to 520.
   It was evidently felt that some of the Aims might be more happily phrased; at the end of the first year they were revised to read:
1. To create a bond of fellowship between past and present students.
2. To keep the members of the Guild in touch with all developments connected with Domestic Subjects.
3. To approach Educational Bodies when advisable.
4. To enable members to hear of appointments and be recommended for them.
   The first issue of the Annual Report, immediately dubbed the *Guild Magazine*, at once established its popularity. Throughout the next fifty years the pattern hardly varied. The Principal's letter set the scene, followed by a racy survey of the affairs of the School and old students written by Miss Caddow with her customary felicitous turn of phrase. Further information of professional and personal interest, and special contributions, completed the picture.
   The Guild brought a new focus into the life of the School, binding the old students to it more firmly than ever before. Here they shared a common bond and common interests in an age when 'career' women regarded themselves as uncommonly emancipated. Enthusiastically they banded themselves together to pursue and project their calling, and in this spirit the first meetings of the Guild attracted large numbers to sit at the feet of the acknowledged experts. One of these was Mrs Pillow, the zealous Examiner of long standing, an active supporter both of the National and the Guild, and a power in the Domestic Subjects field for many years. On 1 March 1913, to an ardent audience, she delivered a long address, full of good sense and morals, which was printed in full in an early magazine for all to read her telling picture of the insidious dangers of slackness.

For the first two years the meetings under the Constitution were faithfully carried out. The Spring Conferences were planned a year ahead and the Debates were matters of moment. Among topics of the day, the Chairman of the A.T.D.S. spoke on the 'initiative, self-reliance and individuality of the pupil'; the redoubtable Mrs Pillow again on 'The Domestic Subjects Teacher as Reformer'; others on the 'History of the Drama', 'The Rise in the Cost of Living and its Social Effects', 'Should Fairy Tales be told to Children?' and a question hotly debated 'Speed *versus* Accuracy', where Speed carried the day, although Miss Amy K. Smith, the Needlework authority, considered that 'if efficient work is to be maintained, speed and accuracy must go hand-in-hand.'

At first not even the War disrupted their plans, though a debate arranged for 1915 proposing 'that the teaching of Domestic Subjects must necessarily be academic' gave place to a lecture on the Empire's share in the War.

At the first Guild Reunion of the War on 3 October 1914, a lecturer from the National Service League spoke on the events leading up to the War, and the duty before each citizen, which led directly to setting up the Guild War Relief Fund. The declared aims were to raise money to be used for the relief of need attributable to the War, after proper investigation had confirmed that the case could make no claim on any existing Relief Societies; to contribute to the Women's Emergency Corps, and to train men or women cooks. To this end each member was asked 'to put by 1*d* a week, more if possible.' By the end of October, in fact, £16 16*s* had been distributed.

There was also an appeal for knitted socks and helmets, and in December a large consignment of knitted comforts was sent to the British Expeditionary Force in France, as well as plum puddings hastily converted from the cakes awaiting Christmas icing.

As the four years of War went on, Guild members kept in touch whenever possible; they were found in a variety of activities, giving cookery lessons in camps and to members of the Red Cross; working for Belgian refugees and the Soldiers and Sailors Families Association; helping to staff Food Vans; catering and cooking in hospitals; and also organising concerts, the latter sometimes 'to counteract the attraction of the public house.'

The first two Reunions were thronged. They were held in the evening; musical and dramatic programmes were arranged, and the National's usual sumptuous refreshments were provided. The opportunity was taken for the Principal to speak on matters of importance. In 1913 the Guild Library was started and an old student returning to Cape Town opened a branch of the Guild in South Africa, where many Old Nationals were settled. A Sports Club suffered eclipse with the First World War.

There was no indulgence at the 1914 Reunion, but by the end of the War the austerity was not just self-imposed; food was short. It was 1919, even though there was still rationing, when the two hundred present on 18 October enjoyed a 'supper approaching those of pre-war days' and an hour's music.

The Reunion was preceded the night before by a Service at St Paul's, Knightsbridge. This practice had started in 1915, when a special service had been arranged for Guild members at St John's, Westminster, and in the following year at St Paul's. In 1917 when the Reunion was postponed for a week due to the risk of air raids at the time of the full moon, the Service was held for the first time at St Peter's, Eaton Square, where the number of uniforms worn illustrated the range of Old Students' war work. The practice of an annual Guild Service to precede the Reunion was now established, though it was not written into the Constitution for another fifty years. The year 1920 saw the beginning of the long, almost unbroken tradition to hold the Guild Service at St Peter's, Eaton Square.

The pinch was felt in some ways more sharply in 1919 than before. Miss Clarke wrote 'On account of the shortage of paper and difficulties of printing, I make my contribution to the Report as brief as possible.' The magazine, which had numbered 98 pages in 1917, had dropped to 33 in 1918, and now the 1919 issue was curtailed to 15 pages, the shortest of all time, apart from the gaps during the Second World War. Nevertheless, it was felt that conditions were sufficiently normal for the Guild to 'renew, enlarge and develop its pre-War activities.' It was decided to elect three more Committee members, to organise a Sports Club and to arrange for increased 'Socials and lectures.' The War Relief Fund was wound up.

The Guild Constitution thereafter remained virtually unchanged. In 1947 it was revised slightly, inserting 'an annual

College Service' to precede the Social Reunion in October. The Committee was officially confirmed as follows: The Principal to remain *ex officio* President and Chairman. The elected members to include a Vice-President, Treasurer, General Secretary, six Organising Secretaries, eight representatives of past students, two representatives of present students, one representative of present Staff, the Editor and Sub-Editor of the *Guild Report.*

Official recognition was now given to the name by which it had been hailed in 1912, and in 1948, the 'Annual Report of Students' Guild' became the *Guild Magazine.*

The decision to form the Old Students' Guild proved infinitely more far reaching than could have been foreseen. It was cemented by the challenge of the First World War, and developed into a strong body reflecting Old Student opinion. In the end it was the voice of the National itself.

GREAT DAYS

CHAPTER XXIV

MRS CLARKE'S DESIRE for a degree course evinced by her interview with Dame Maude Lawrence and Mr Oppé resulted in a concentrated effort towards a more academic approach, and paved the way for the Full Inspection by the Board of Education in 1912.

Work and discussions were hard and tough. Until the Board was convinced that the School was capable of advanced academic work it could not give the necessary support; evidence of this was consequently sought during November 1912 when four of His Majesty's Inspectors spent several days assessing development since 1910.

Their conclusions were somewhat tentative. They paid tribute to the excellent tone of the School, happy relationships, smooth, if over-complicated organisation, conscientious teaching and a high standard of craft, designating the Cookery as 'excellent' and appreciating that attention was given to underlying scientific principles. On the other hand, they queried the sequence in which the Craft subjects were taught, and felt that these should be more closely allied to the Science teaching. They commended 'some excellent lessons' in the childrens' classes, although doubting if these were sufficiently related to their capabilities or the needs of their homes, thus supporting the judgment of the London County Council in June 1911; but they verified their own temporary arrangement which allowed four-fifths of the teaching to be given by students. They pressed for proper co-ordination between the Theory of Education and these classes, advocating as an urgent priority the appointment of a full time 'Mistress of Method.'

119

They noted also some over-crowding of kitchens, inadequate cloakrooms, and the limitations of laboratory space to ten students at a time. The meagre provision of books, with no library, was criticised; it was agreed that students' writing showed little original thought. Finally they commended the National's endeavours to adapt itself to 'conditions demanding greater educational efficiency that promise well for its future progress' – a tribute to the sustained work of the preceding years by the small sub-Committee.

The National was now left to revise its scheme on the lines advocated by the Board, and generally to put its house in order. Much depended not only on the proper provision of premises, especially for Science, but also on an understanding between all the departments of the scope of the work and the essential cooperation. That the former was not always grasped was shown in a note to the Committee by the new Science mistress, to say that she considered the new laboratory would be 'suitable for the work, and the accommodation sufficient for the classes, for several years to come'. In the event, it had to suffice, but the need for expansion was evidenced when during the War, even in the troubles of the Autumn of 1915, another room was fitted up for practical work and an assistant teacher appointed.

To find the right 'Mistress of Method' proved more difficult, and it was only after war-time changes and vicissitudes that Miss Charlotte Morgan was appointed in January, 1919. The work was in a state of flux, and she set it on a new road. Married in 1922, as Mrs Hutchinson she led this Department with gentle determination for another fourteen years; her contribution fulfilled when she acted as Principal for a year after Miss Clarke's death, holding the fort until Miss Eland arrived.

As the Board of Education diversified its activities under the direction of Sir Robert Morant, so the volume of paper work mounted. Mrs Clarke, nearing her seventieth year, felt the need for an official deputy who could relieve her of much administrative routine as well as actively help with the planning. Naturally she wanted her own daughter, Gladys, who had the real interests of the School at heart, and had already given years of unremitting thought to the radical changes essential for the desired academic approach. She was also recognised as a good organiser, with wide cultural interests.

Mrs Clarke had been made an *ex officio* member of the Executive Committee in 1912, and at the Meeting on 18 February, 1913, she formally asked the Committee 'to create the post of Vice-Principal, such an office now being required owing to the continuous increase of the work.' Mr Alan Cole spoke to this and proposed that 'Miss Gladys Clarke should be appointed Vice-Principal, to assist Mrs Clarke and Miss Caddow, organise schemes of work, inspect classes inside and outside the School, and to be trained to succeed Mrs Clarke on her retirement.' Seconded by Mrs Homan, the proposal was unanimously carried. The salary was agreed at £175, rising by £15 to £250 a year, with the appointment to date from 1 April 1913. At one stroke Mrs Clarke had secured a cherished deputy and ensured the succession.

Miss Gladys Clarke had already embarked on the revision of the Teacher Training course as suggested at the Full Inspection. By March 1913 the amended proposals of the sub-Committee were submitted to the Board of Education for approval, with the additional requests that the rule against Technical and Teacher training students working together in the same kitchens should be relaxed, and also that an improved grant should be given for all classes of students. A special plea was added for grant-aid towards a new Hostel, at the same time providing the practice house recognised as essential for the proposed new course of training.

The main proposals were based on seven terms of thirteen weeks, thus lengthening the training by one term, with admittance each term. Lectures on Theory and Method of Education were to be given throughout the course, beginning in the first term. There was complete re-arrangement of subject teaching, basically with Laundrywork in the first two terms, Cookery in the following three, and Home Management, with elementary cleaning already covered, in the sixth term, with practice at the Hostel.

Pride of place was given to Cookery with 772 hours, reduced from 840. Home Management had just under half this time, with 368 hours; Laundrywork was allocated 480 and Science 143. In addition there were to be twelve Elocution lessons. The importance of Needlework was recognised by the suggestion that instead of training for two years and one term, students should enter for three years, to include Needlework and Millinery.

It was requested that Diplomas should be awarded upon Terms' and Examination marks in equal proportion, as the present system whereby the Examination claimed three fifths of the maximum was held to be unsatisfactory.

In the new final term, besides giving the opportunity to cover work unavoidably missed, the time was to be devoted to further teaching practice, management of the Hostel, marketing and work in a Crèche, including visits to connected artisan homes and schools for the mothers.

Already pairs of students attended a Notting Hill Crèche for a week at a time during their Home Management course. On 28 June, 1910, the Committee endorsed Mrs Clarke's view that it would be excellent training 'actually to handle babies for a week,' and offered the creche 10*s* a head for this purpose. Approved by the Board of Education 'as an Experiment' it became an integral part of the Home Management Course, and the long association thus begun with Notting Hill was maintained through another fifty years.

The close relationship led to a combined effort during the First World War. In 1916 the sudden increase in the demand for trained matrons for day nurseries, due to the thousands of mothers flocking to work in munitions, led to a special training agreed between the National and Notting Hill Day Nursery. The course, at one guinea a week, covered twelve weeks at the School, and twelve at Notting Hill.

The keystone of the National's new scheme lay in deeper knowledge of underlaying principles. This was illustrated by correlation with Science of every subject at all stages of the course; the teaching of children based on a sounder knowledge of psychology; appreciation of wider issues; and much more freedom of approach. In this connection, students were to be given opportunities for individual marketing, to practise Hostel management and 'occassionally to conduct classes entirely according to their own ideas,' subject to supervision.

Some of the innovations, such as the Elocution lessons, proved the thin end of the wedge. Justified by their value in teaching, they led to the inclusion of dramatic art and singing in the life of the School.

The Teaching Staff, 1912. Front row from left
Misses Thorpe, Rotheram, Caddow, Mrs Clarke, Misses G. Clarke, Marsh

In their reply of April 1913, the Board gave overall approval, while querying several of the proposals and underlining the problems of organisation arising from extension of the course to seven terms, with termly admissions. They felt unable to sanction the joint instruction of Technical and Teacher Training students, but were prepared to consider some adjustment 'in a period of transition.' Any change in the proportion of marks awarded for the Diploma was considered unsatisfactory, and it was decreed that the present practice of allowing 60 per cent to examinations and 40 per cent to records during training must be adhered to. They were not in a position to make any statement with regard to any increase in the grants, neither had they power 'to make any grant in aid of the establishment of the proposed Hostel.' But the final verdict was 'to give the scheme their general approval.'

The pattern thus set accentuated the importance of Teacher training at the expense of the Technical side. The Board of Education was obviously chiefly concerned to further the interests of the former, but there was apparently no query nor dissenting voice raised among the members of the Committee.

A highly important peak had been surmounted. The revised course was sanctioned, the need for a new Hostel recognised and a campaign to raise the necessary funds agreed. The great Bazaar, as the initial effort, was held under distinguished patronage and visited by Her Majesty Queen Alexandra herself.

In the summer of 1914, all seemed set fair.

WAR

THE VISIONS, the hard work, the high hopes were all dispelled at one fell stroke. Mrs Clarke was seventy. Without any repining she turned to face the challenge of unknown demands and the most testing years in the history of the School.

On 29 September 1914, under the Chairmanship of Mr Alan Cole, acting for Sir Almeric FitzRoy, an Emergency Committee Meeting was held to consider how the School could further the War effort. Major decisions were postponed for the regular Committee a few weeks hence. Meantime it was agreed to give courses for Voluntary Aid members of the Red Cross and to offer free instruction in Cookery to six men from the Army and six from the Navy every month. It was also decided to run a Soup Kitchen, although the Committee thought it was undesirable 'actually to feed the poor on the premises, but agreed that it would be excellent to prepare soups and stews from surplus food, and to dispose of this to well authenticated centres of distribution.'

At the Committee on 20 October, there was general belief that the War would soon be over. Most of the time was spent in clearing up outstanding items of minor importance. Mrs Clarke reported that the Board of Education had refused to confirm the appointment of a teacher who 'interests the students and gives an ideal lesson to children, but is dowdy and non-academic in language.' On the report of the Hostels Sub-Committee the latest proposal for a property in Warwick Square was abandoned owing to problems, including drains, and thus the chance of a practice house for students was again lost. The renting of an artisan house for this purpose was then suggested and at the Committee on 17 November it was referred back to the Sub-Committee. Another sub-committee reported on 15 December that 'risk from air bombs was held to be slight'; fire insurance for £15,000 for the School and contents was held to be sufficient. Somewhat reluctantly it was agreed to insure in addition against air damage provisionally for one year as long as the premium did not exceed £25. This was carried out the following day, 16 December, at a cost of £21 5s. It marks the striking difference both in risks and the value of money between the First and Second World Wars.

But there was little sense of urgency, and the year 1914 ended on a note of restrained optimism.

By the new year some inkling of the difficulties ahead was being driven home to Mrs Clarke. Records of these days reveal staff and students rallying to other calls, and with emptying classrooms, no means to replenish the coffers. Within the School a series of frustrations began. New regulations of the Board of Education decreed raised entrance standards and yearly admissions. Mrs Clarke sought latitude in both respects, supported by Mr Charles Buckmaster, who in June 1914 had retired from his combined positions as Assistant Secretary and Chief Inspector on the Board, and at the instigation of Mr Alan Cole had joined the Executive Committee. He attended for the first time on 16 February 1915, and from then on, until his great age forced him to retire in 1948, a year before his death at ninety-five years, his wisdom, kindliness and clear mind were at the complete disposal of the National. His intimate and longstanding connection with the Board made him an invaluable counsellor, and many thorny matters were smoothed by his advice.

Negotiations with the Board of Education covering a wide range of subjects continued endlessly with varying vicissitudes all through the War. An early ruling was welcomed when the Board decided to take over the examinations, and also agreed to two separate admissions in September 1915 and April 1916 instead of the yearly entry. But the Committee was looking still further ahead and Mrs Clarke, in her reply of 14 April 1915, set out the complicated organisation of the various departments, and asked for permission to admit students every alternate

term, beginning in January 1916. The response was not favourable; other Training Schools, in the same plight, sought a joint
interview. On 25 July 1916 the Board received a deputation from
Berridge House, Gloucester, Liverpool and the National and
conceded admissions each term for the duration of the War, on
condition that the Training Schools arranged their own examinations. In their relief it was generally felt that the former
concession largely compensated for the extra work imposed by
the latter condition.

This arrangement continued until the end of the War, but on
22 March 1917 the Board again received the Principals, who
were now seeking increased grant in view of the 'grave financial
position of all the Schools, with the decline in number of students
and rising maintenance costs.' Nothing came of this. It was
August 1918 before there was a substantial increase in the *per
capita* grant, raising it from £9 to £20 a year. By this time, it was
swallowed up in costs.

At least the School's telephone account would not break the
bank. No telephone had been installed until the autumn of 1906,
maybe merely by chance coinciding with the appointment of
Miss Caddow as Secretary. In March 1912 the London Telephone
Company offered unlimited service inclusive of all charges for
£17 a year; a rate which happily continued.

As classes diminished, the need to encourage students became
urgent. Distinguished patrons, however, did not desert them.
Lady Rosemary Leveson-Gower, sister of the Duchess of Suther-
land, who in 1915 went as cook in her mother's hospital at
Dunkirk, had taken her training at the National, after Lady de
Trafford and her daughter Violet had originated the idea of
these lessons. Others who joined were Countess Nada Torby,
later married to Prince George of Battenberg, Lady Mary
Hamilton, Lady Penrhyn and her daughter Lady Norreys, who
'all embarked with immense enthusiasm on a thoroughly practical course.' But such attendance was necessarily of short
duration, and it was therefore a great satisfaction when the
Ladies Field on 29 May 1915 featured the School in a special
article, drawing particular attention to the prospects after
training. It was recorded that after a three-year training in 'as
many domestic subjects as possible,' salaries varied according

to school and locality. The County Councils paid £80 – £85 a year, rising to £120, rather less than the salary of normal trained elementary school teachers, who were on a scale of £90 rising to £150, but 'the former work is pleasanter.' In Secondary, Technical and Training Schools, and in many High Schools and good private schools, Domestic Subjects teachers could receive the same as other qualified teachers, from £100 to £150.

The Cordon Bleu qualification led to appointments in a wide field. The best paid service in hospitals and nursing homes was £35 to £40, rising to £60, £80 or even £100 a year. Pay in tea rooms varied with experience; posts under public services were often daily engagements; cooks in City offices were prized, and could earn £75 to £100 a year.

The School by now was launched on a series of War efforts. The Committee offered the use of the School from 5.30 pm each day to the National Guard who met soldiers returning from the Front, to provide a resting place instead of weary waiting in stations or streets, before going on to their destinations. Patriotic duty dictated that no appeal ever went unanswered, and a depleted Staff coped with enterprises often quite outside their experience. Classes for the Services were already well within their competence, but in addition to these they had to demonstrate in a wider field the best possible use of every available scrap of material. This involved travelling all over the country and even to running a Food Demonstration Depot in the Old Kent Road for a short time in 1917. Here a friendly policeman, by actively encouraging the general public to attend, greatly supported the campaign for nutritive alternatives to 'anything fried.'

The growing concern over increasing shortages led to a Thrift Exhibition, the first of its kind in London, which was held at the National for three days in May 1916. The Lord Mayor opened the exhibition, which covered an enormous range of topics including fuel, food values and substitutes, utensils, contents of dustbins, laundrywork, clothing, upholstery, infant needs and welfare, exports and imports, cleaning materials, toys, carpentry, labour-saving devices, medicinal herbs, poultry and gardening. Appropriately, the care of money was highlighted. Among the series of lectures on the many different topics given by distinguished experts, the opportunity to promote the cause of temperance proved irrestible, and a fervent supporter quoted the rousing declaration, attributed to the Kaiser in 1910, 'In the next war the nation which drinks least alcohol will be the winner.'

During the Exhibition it was noted as a special feature that 'three women police were on duty to regulate the traffic and keep a watchful eye on the proceedings.'

The whole enterprise was undertaken by Miss Gladys Clarke, who as the Organising Secretary led a team of enthusiastic helpers. The immense success not only emphasised the war effort of the National, but also drew attention to Miss Clarke's marked organising ability. She was asked by the National War Savings Committee to take the entire exhibition to Knightsbridge, which was only prevented because the space available was too small. She then arranged for certain sections to be shown in various places, the Food Section drawing large audiences to the People's Palace to hear Miss Underhill's lectures on Economical Cookery.

This proved the beginning of many personal calls on Miss Clarke. She served on innumerable committees, some far-reaching decisions stemming from the Lord Mayor's Metropolitan Committee for War Savings. This was later affiliated to the Ministry of Food as an Advisory Committee, with sub-sections dealing with exhibitions, communal kitchens, propaganda and experimental work. Once again she was Chairman of the Association of Teachers of Domestic Subjects, helping to direct and guide early policy, and supervising the publication of several Wartime Leaflets in addition to the nine pamphlets published by the School at a cost of 10d post free, under the title of *Thrift for Troubled Times*.

Miss Clarke was serving her final apprenticeship under exceptionally difficult conditions for the exacting role of Principal, in succession to her mother. Unquestionably, she proved her ability, indefatigable tenacity and power of leadership.

Meantime the students in training dealt valiantly with increasing shortages of food and fuel and fabrics, with equipment becoming shabbier each year. At a most taxing time in 1916 the School was invigorated by an official visit in October from Her

The National

Majesty Queen Mary. It was said that 'every member of the staff and every student' appreciated this great event when each department was visited and 'nothing escaped her kindly notice with her interested questions and shrewd remarks.' Beyond any doubt this honour boosted morale and stimulated afresh the pride in tackling difficulties typified in one of the current songs of the period: 'Are we downhearted? No!'

It was behind the scenes that the battle inevitably lay. Mrs Clarke continually deployed her forces and fought every inch of the way. It was a battle against frustrated plans, loss of students, depleted staff, inadequate equipment, conflicting interests, official demands, red tape and above all, lack of money. Always there was this nightmare, haunting the Principal and the Committee.

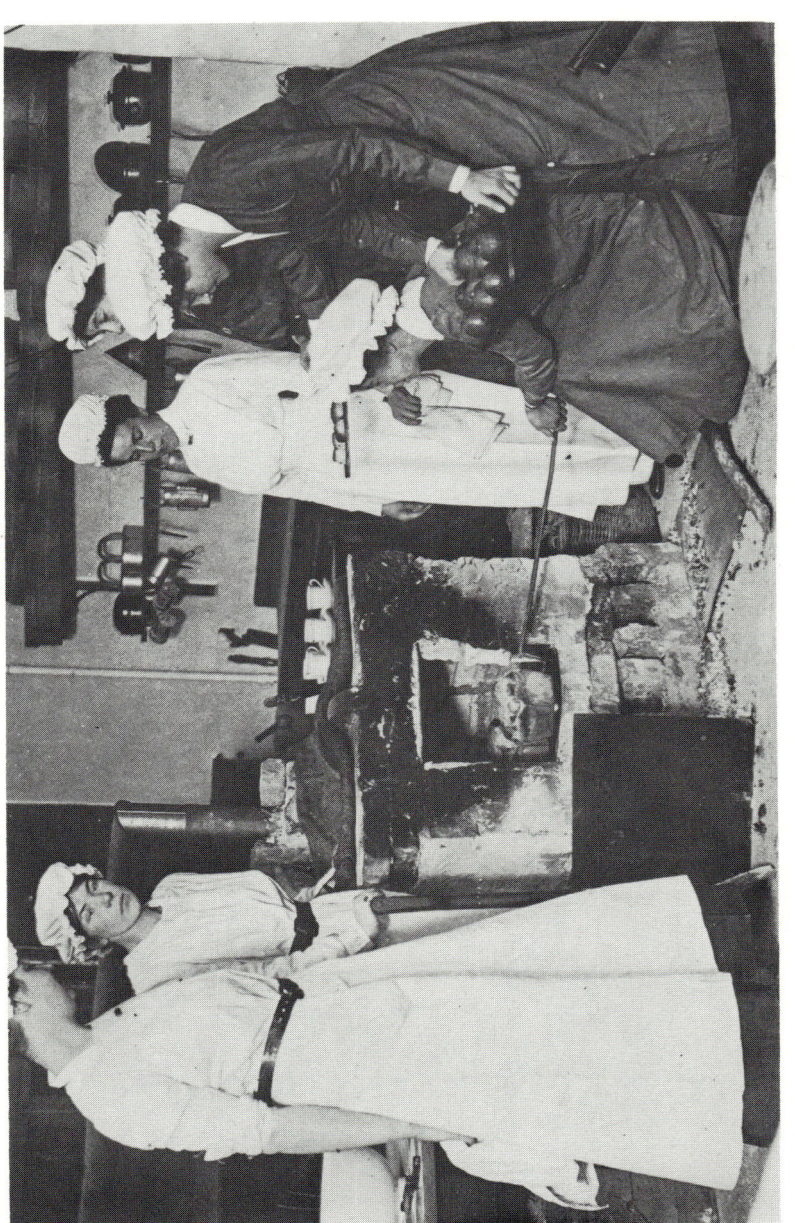

Field Kitchen, First World War

Public Restaurant, 1918

WAR

THE CRYING NEED for a Hostel combined with a practice house now came uppermost in the interests of the students. When in March 1915 there was still no satisfactory outcome of various propositions, Mrs Clarke offered Orchard House, which she had acquired in Porlock. Even though the distance between London and Somerset precluded easy communication and involved costs of maintenance and travel, the Committee gratefully accepted. By May 1915 a group of seventh term Housewifery students was already installed. The following December the Committee reviewed the situation and decided to pay Mrs Clarke £80 a year rent, but this did not last long. By July 1916, with depleted funds, alternatives were being raised, but nothing suitable appeared and in this dilemma Mrs Clarke offered to waive the rent; parents were also asked to pay half the railway fares.

The scheme prospered briefly for the students, but this respite in good air away from London pressure ceased in July 1917. It was reported that the end came 'not because it had not been a triumphal success, but because there was no Division of students ready to go there in the Autumn Term, and because the difficulties of ways and means made it advisable to forego the expense entailed.' Probably the key lay in the eternal question of expense, for by now the School was in deep water.

Shortly after the visit of Her Majesty Queen Mary in October 1916, Miss Caddow was warning in the *Guild Magazine* 'The finance of this School is causing great anxiety, and the most scrupulous economy must be practised in all sections to enable us to pay our way. Let us hope and pray that we shall weather the storm.'

Some time earlier there had been changes on the Executive Committee. Sir Almeric FitzRoy, K.C.V.O., K.C.B., with increasing claims on his time and energy, resigned in April 1915 from the Committee which he had joined in 1890. As Vice-Chairman and Chairman he had taken the Chair at almost every meeting from January 1903, and the loss of his able mind in this capacity was keenly felt. Lady Baring suggested that Lord Herschell, a Lord-in-waiting and a keen connoisseur of cookery, should be invited in Sir Almeric's place, but other duties absorbed him while the War lasted and Mrs Homan was reluctantly persuaded to act meantime. She had given unsparing thought since 1905, serving on the Committee as the London County Council representative, and she now began six arduous years of Chairmanship. In May 1916 when finances were at a low ebb, Mr Alan Cole, C.B. gave up the Honorary Treasurership which he had held since 1902 and resigned from the Committee. It was a sad day for the National. Sir Henry Cole and his children Rose and Alan had virtually brought the School into being. Thus two staunch, longstanding supporters had gone and left Mrs Clarke to feel their loss deeply. Mr Guy Sebright, a Committee member since February 1913 agreed to become Honorary Treasurer, taking over the mounting burdens which were so nearly to threaten extinction.

In April 1913 attention on finances had been sharply focussed when the mortgagee of the School sought either an increase on the interest payable, or repayment of part of the sum mortgaged, which since 1900 had remained at £3,000. Mr Cole and Mr Salmon took the opportunity to overhaul the various insurance policies, which included one for £13,000, to mature in 1978 on the expiration of the lease. To ensure the continuance of this particular policy it was decided to institute a Sinking Fund. The mortgage of £3,000 was then redeemed in full by a loan from the bank. The annual payments involved were comparatively small, but as war and rising costs took toll of the slender finances, even these became a burden.

Every effort was made to maintain a reserve of £1,000, but by the time Mr Sebright took over in June 1916, the total balance was reduced to £949, while the School faced an overdraft. A brief gleam of comfort followed a personal appeal by an ex-

Sheriff of the City, which led to a gift of £100. But it was a drop in the ocean.

By 17 July 1917, still with a £1,000 reserve, the overdraft had mounted to £502, and Mr Sebright took a grave view. 'We are walking into debt,' he said, and further stated that although willing to take almost any risks to keep the School going, if the liabilities should exceed the total assets by £200 he would feel compelled to advocate closure, possibly temporary, fully as he realised 'that it would be very bad to destroy its continuity and interfere with its history.'

In dire distress the Committee sought for a way out. It was suggested that the Government might run the School until times were better, or that some arrangement might be made with the London County Council. Even in this plight, Mrs Clarke recoiled, and the idea was vetoed. An appeal to old friends for gifts or guarantees was proposed, and also a scheme to cajole the Agents-General for Australia into persuading Australian girls to enrol at the National, and paying their fees. The danger of the journey on the high seas with the U-boat campaign at its worst was ignored, but doubtless contributed to the decision of the Agents-General to postpone consideration until after the War. The seed, however, had been sown and although the immediate need was not filled, forty Australian Nursing Sisters in the summer of 1919 'enjoyed a three-months course' under Miss Rotheram's tuition.

It was decided to repeat the plea for help to the Board of Education, and to remind the Admiralty and War Office of the National's continuous service. After its long period of unassailed glory, the School was *in extremis*.

Miss Gladys Clarke's widespread work on behalf of the different committees and campaigns was commended by the Executive Committee who stressed the goodwill thereby engendered towards the School. But there was no financial profit in it; official thanks did not pay the rent. Although the required £200 for this was comparatively modest, yet at this moment it assumed dizzy proportions. It was a further blow when an appeal to the Duke of Westminster, for temporary remission, failed.

The position worsened. By 31 July 1917 the overdraft had reached £663, and Mrs Clarke still required £1,012 for expenses to the end of August. Mr Sebright allowed that the Sinking Fund, now worth £800, might be used as security. Nothing fruitful had emerged since the last meeting. Fearing that publicity of the predicament would do more harm than good, the Committee decided against any form of appeal.

In this bleak moment Mrs Clarke changed the entire outlook by a suggestion which was the direct outcome of the Government decision to set up 'National Kitchens' to feed the public. When Mrs Homan had earlier mooted the idea of co-operation in this policy, Mrs Clarke had assured her that should the training of cooks and supervisors for this purpose become urgent, she already had a scheme drawn up in readiness. Possibly with the memory of the successful dinners served at the South Kensington Exhibitions, which had founded the fortunes of the School, she now made the practical proposition which saved the day. She suggested that one kitchen should be set aside to cook food for staff, students and the general public, with two teachers in charge, and the declared aim of making as much profit as possible 'as is the way in all restaurants.' In unanimous relief this lifeline was grasped, and the scheme was put into immediate effect.

The venture proved an unqualified success. By December 1917 Mrs Clarke reported 100 per cent gross profit. Indeed it deserved to succeed. The food was 'of good quality and very carefully prepared.' Meals cost 9*d*, 1*s* or 1*s* 2*d*; but soups, meat and puddings sold in individual portions for 2*d*, 3*d* or 4*d* according to the cost of ingredients. Poor rations and fuel shortage made it a hard task for the average small family to serve many good meals, and the provision of food such as the School produced was a godsend. It was a godsend too for the School, for it literally enabled it to survive.

The overdraft had progressively diminished during 1917 from £5,647 in August to £1,318 in October; by December it was down to £1,157. Mr Sebright after an absence now returned to say that in his opinion 'No action need be taken; he hoped someone he knew would come to the rescue, and that for the present the School would continue to float.' Nothing more was ever revealed of this anonymous would-be benefactor. In fact, the Public Kitchen had come to the rescue. By February 1918 returns were so much increased that the Committee decided to publicise the enterprise and extend the provision.

Gratitude to Mrs Clarke was genuinely felt and officially expressed, and there was sincere rejoicing when her work was recognised in the New Year Honours by the award of Member of the newly founded Order of the British Empire. The same February Committee, acutely aware of how the National's life had hung by a thread, passed a special vote of confidence in Mrs Clarke and her daughter.

It was one thing, however, to advocate extension of the Public Kitchen and Restaurant service, and another to achieve it. As always, it was a question of money, but at the beginning of 1918 the need for trained supervisors of the 'National Kitchens' now being established throughout the country did indeed become urgent and Mrs Clarke recognised that here lay an opportunity. The School approached the Ministry of Food offering to train some of these supervisors and it was agreed to accept groups of twelve students, all enticed by the prospect of a future salary of £150 a year, to train in the School's Public Kitchen and Restaurant. The Ministry paid the National the official grant of £1 a week for each student, which in addition to the student's weekly contribution of 12s for her midday meal, was all grist to the mill.

In March 1918 a larger kitchen was pressed into service and further restaurant space was secured by taking over the office by the front door. At the end of the month the profit had risen to £123. The demand for meals had increased. Mrs Clarke reported 324 luncheons served in two hours with a staff of eleven: Supervisor, Cook Supervisor, Cook, two vegetable maids, two kitchen maids, two waitresses and two washers-up. In May 1918 the total takings were £399, giving a net profit of £166.

The following month there was a radical change in the Committee. Sir Guy Sebright had succeeded to the baronetcy, and with other demands on his time he resigned from the Honorary Treasurership in June 1918. Mr Charles Buckmaster took over this post, to hold it for the next thirty years.

The enforced economies of the War years had taken toll. In particular, equipment was worn out. With the end of the War in sight, there was no longer the same spirit of suffering in a good cause, and although the faithful staff and students belonging to the School soldiered on without complaint, the embryo Supervisors understandably could not feel the same loyalty; in June

1918 they voiced their feelings about 'inefficient equipment and lack of appliances.' Their demands proved the spur which was needed. The following month the Ministry of Food accorded full recognition as a 'National Kitchen', which entitled them to grants for all necessary purchases.

Even so, the profits could not meet all the other expenses, and as War tensions eased, a host of problems clamoured for attention.

A Hostel still had pressing claim, both 'on account of accommodating students from different parts of the country, and the competition of other Training Schools,' and also to provide a practice house for Home Management. Mrs Ward, who had joined the Committee in 1911, ran several hostels in London, and she offered one of these, at 10 Pembridge Square, W.2, to the National. Prolonged negotiations ended satisfactorily and amid considerable publicity the Hostel was opened in September 1918. The Guild Reunion was held there in October, thronged with members, friends and officials, 'who were all charmed with the place.' But their joy was short-lived. Only two months later, on 10 December, the Committee learnt from Mrs Ward that she required the house by July 1919. After countless propositions proved useless, and with time running out, Mrs Ward responded to a Committee suggestion that as the School could not afford to buy, she herself might do so. She bought 6 Linden Gardens, W.2, repaired, equipped and let it furnished to the National at a rent of £220 a year, including rates and taxes. The house held twenty-two students and was also suitable for Home Management practice. After the vicissitudes of six years, at last, in the autumn of 1919, the Hostel problem seemed to be solved.

Under the Board of Education's ruling of August 1918, in addition to the £20 *per capita* grant to the Training Schools, a maintenance grant of £15 per annum was allocated for each day student and £28 for each resident. The Principal had agreed to use £15 for remission of fees to all students, and to give to the hostels the balance of £13 a head for each resident, which was felt to be a fair decision.

Some of the earlier Board regulations were neither so welcome nor so explicit. Commending a newly appointed office helper, Mrs Clarke said she was 'very intelligent; at present the forms

of the Board of Education were the only things which she did
not seem to have mastered.' Miss Caddow expressed 'the School's
gratitude' to H.M.I. Miss Sillitoe for her help in 'interpreting to
us the new rules of the Board of Education.'

A recurring illustration of official complexity lay in the diploma examinations. The system veered from strict control by
the Board's own officials to recognition of examiners chosen by
the School. The varying permutations led to a series of running
battles which Mrs Clarke did not always win. A defeat which
she felt bitterly resulted from the Board's decision in 1916 to
change the examination marking from numerical to alphabeti-
cal; to omit the separate Science theory paper and instead to set
all Science questions with the various pertinent subject papers;
and furthermore, to introduce the 'sample' method by examining
selected students to represent the different grade marks allocated by the School staff.

Feelings ran high and there was considerable opposition; it
was argued that finer shades of marking were impossible; that
the loss of the Science paper not only belittled its importance
but also curtailed the scope of the other subject papers, and
finally that the 'sample' of students bedevilled their chances,
placing too heavy a burden on some who might not shine in
examinations while depriving others of the opportunity to
redeem or even to distinguish themselves.

In spite of strong representations, the Board's decision was
adhered to and the first group took the new form of examination
in July 1917. The practical tests were also set and marked by the
Board's Inspectors. It was not as bad as expected; the students
'rose to the occasion'; the standard was reported as uniformly
good with no failures but several distinctions. The new pattern
seemed to have worked; even the dissenters were slightly molli-
fied. But the corollary was recorded sadly by Miss Caddow: 'The
Board of Education Diploma which is now awarded instead of
our own beautiful parchment is plain and uninteresting, and
bears no "Class." The detail as to attainments, excepting in
the rare cases where distinction is achieved and inscribed on
the Diploma, is to be found on the stamped "Record of Training"
issued by the School authorities. Our Diploma, with its beautiful
design, will be reserved for the two-year students who come on
for a third year course.'

It was a foretaste of the impersonal world to come. It was not Mrs Clarke's world. She was an individualist and she did not relish it.

When the Armistice was signed on the raw winter day of 11 November 1918, there were many casualties among the old established institutions. The National was exhausted and drained and at the end of its tether, but it was alive, and at that moment jubilant. Staff and students alike rushed with the crowds which converged on Buckingham Palace, to cheer to the echo the King and Queen on the balcony and to acclaim the victory.

Mrs Clarke too was acclaimed. She had led the National through the War; she was a Member of the Order of the British Empire. No one deserved it more.

REVIVAL

CHAPTER XXVII

THE WAR TO END ALL WARS was over. It was to be a 'brave new world' in a 'land fit for heroes to live in.' The great depression, the General Strike of 1926, the mounting unemployment, the hunger marches from Jarrow – all the problems of the next decade – were not even glimpsed as shadows.

The first priority for the National was to put its own house in order. As with everything, Mrs Clarke faced the position realistically. In 1917 she had yielded to advice not to pursue the question of retirement, but in 1919 she was in her seventy-fifth year, and no longer felt able to do justice to the School in meeting public demands and increasing professional pressures. She made her decision resolutely, and on 18 February 1919 she placed her resignation before the Executive Committee, to take effect on 31 July.

It was the end of forty-five years of dedication. In all, she gave over half a century to a branch of learning which in many ways was alien to her upbringing and natural inclinations. To the task of improving health and hygiene, she brought her gifts of intellect, administrative ability and vision in a rich personality which inspired both devotion and respect. It was the contradictions of her inheritance that endeared her. Music and the arts were the fibre of her being. Both grandfathers were men of distinction in public office, and Thomas Love Peacock was a master of burlesque as well as a serious minded man of affairs. Mrs Clarke shared many of his traits as she shared much of his life, and with dispassionate assessment of situations and people went an ironic enjoyment of follies and foibles and the gift of

swift repartee, which an unswerving sense of duty often compelled her to control. Personal reminiscences nevertheless
reveal the heart as well as the head, for Mrs Clarke's rejoinders
might be tart, but never petty; spoken perhaps with asperity,
but never unkindness.

The reins were handed over to her daughter, Miss Gladys
Clarke. 'In her capable hands the work has gone forward smooth-
ly and efficiently,' recorded Miss Caddow in the Autumn of 1919.
But it had not been plain sailing.

On 20 May 1919, with Mrs Homan in the Chair and three other
members present, the Executive Committee had 'unanimously
resolved that Miss Gladys Clarke be appointed Principal, at a
salary of not less than £500 a year, the appropriate amount to
be decided at the next meeting.' When this took place, within
a month on 17 June, Mrs Homan reported that Sir Cyril Cobb,
Chairman of the London County Council Education Committee,
had protested officially that the Council should have been consulted and the post advertised. As certain negotiations with
the Council were in progress, this view was supported by some
influential members of the Executive Committee, who also felt
it to have been too important a decision for such a small committee.

Mrs Homan then revealed that their action had been prompted
by a letter from H.M.I. Miss Sillitoe, urging that 'steps be taken
without delay to secure Miss Clarke's services on her mother's
retirement at the end of July,' and further recalling the Minute
of 18 February 1913, 'appointing Miss Gladys Clarke as Vice-
Principal . . . and to be trained to succeed Mrs Clarke on her
retirement.'

There was no going back on that decision; indeed it did not
seem that anyone wished to do so, but Mrs Clarke's retirement
lay only a few weeks ahead and there had been no official appointment of her daughter. The Board of Education, doubtless concerned over the invidious position, had drawn the attention of
the Committee to this lack of ratification. There was also query
about 'the appropriate salary; £350 a year, rising by £25 to £600
was now proposed.

By 1 July the situation was cleared in letters received from
both the Board of Education and Sir Cyril Cobb, on behalf of the

Education Committee of the London County Council. Miss Edith Gladys Clarke was appointed Principal of the National as from 1 August 1919.

The transition of power had been slightly clouded. The dominating personality of Mrs Clarke inevitably overshadowed that of her daughter, whose gifts were not fully evident until she blossomed later in life when her academic and artistic abilities were given scope. But she had also inherited the streak of steely resilience which now enabled her to ignore the little passage of arms over her appointment, and to turn her mind to the work at hand.

Premises called for urgent attention. Enemy raids during the War had been 'too near to be pleasant,' again recorded Miss Caddow, 'but mercifully there were no casualties except for a few small hits by our own shell splinters.' She continued by stressing the need for enlarged premises, 'to accommodate all the aspirants to the various trainings. As it is "the coat has to be cut according to the cloth," an annoying state of things, when so many are anxious to be put in possession of the knowledge without which no one can be said to possess the rudiments of home making.'

The building was run down and shabby, and space at a premium, though there was more room for manoeuvre after the Public Kitchen and Restaurant moved in May 1919 to 4 Eccleston Street, there to continue its success, crowded out every day with appreciative customers, the number of lunches served averaging 1,400 – 1,600 a week. These premises, adapted and equipped at 'a moderate cost of £260,' were rented for three years at £150 a year.

A certain nostalgia followed the transfer; the Kitchen had been quickly absorbed into the School and especially welcome in the charge of Miss Gordon, as 'efficiency, peace and contentment abide under her rule.' Profits, too, were considerable. The Restaurant came to the rescue many times in the following years, and it was estimated that it contributed well over £5,000 to general funds before it closed in 1927.

A previous children's kitchen was now used as the School catering kitchen; the arrangement for serving midday meals for the kitchen staff at 12 noon, the students at 12.30 and the staff at 1.15 proved so satisfactory that it continued to hold good for the next twenty years.

The vacated Public Kitchen once more became a normal practice kitchen, and made ready to receive the contingent of Australian Nursing Sisters under the tuition of Miss Rotheram, soon to transfer to the Training side, as Head of the Cookery Department.

The former Demonstration Room was pressed into service as a classroom for training students following 'the very large entry in September of thirty-five.' But there was nothing like enough room, and scores of applicants for Technical classes had to be turned away. The School continued to be thus besieged and in the following years squeezed in relief classes as best they could, particularly in the ever-popular Cookery and Needlework.

Miss Clarke in 1920 redeployed her staff as members returned from war-time activities, and later as new appointments were made in the next decade.

Miss Underhill, fresh as ever in spite of arduous work for food campaigns and service with the W.R.N.S., now began her reign in charge of the Public Demonstration and Practice classes. Totally different from the 'Flashing Iceberg,' as Miss Rotheram had been known, Miss Underhill's twinkling blue eyes and gift for establishing relaxed, friendly relations with the public as she demonstrated skilfully with her small plump hands, inspired unquestioning confidence in her devoted audiences.

In addition to the Naval Paymasters, from the rank of Commander downwards, who continued to attend, Miss Janie Clark trained generations of excellent craftswomen. Miss Broderick was renowned for her brilliance in flower making. In this art she admitted no standard short of perfection. There were others of like mind, and Miss Marsh in the Laundry ran her close. The work in this department was always meticulous, and the same pertinacity and insistence on skill marked the twenty-one year rule of Miss Lancaster when in 1928 she succeeded Miss Marsh, who had come in 1903, as Head of the Laundrywork Department.

The Needlework and Dressmaking Department was led ably and unobtrusively by Miss Emily Wallbank, whose small team was headed by Miss Quick. They were both members of the staff before the First War, and their era covered nearly thirty years.

With rare understanding and wisdom Miss Wallbank used her
very deafness to ignore the unimportant and encourage everything of value. Widely read and of catholic taste, innate com-
passion combined with shrewd insight into human nature
resulted in strong Socialist beliefs, serious efforts to help the
under-dog and a refreshing capacity for amusing and surprisingly worldly advice. She was the repository of many secrets,
and once averred that she led 'a very exciting life by proxy.'

Miss Gladys Quick's integrity shone through every action;
never lowering her own superlatively high standards, she possessed humorous tolerance and great kindliness.

Miss Eckford was another stalwart who came in 1900 to remain
thirty years. Taking charge in any subject as required, solid and
reliable as her own upholstery, she could always be counted on
to entertain everyone by remarks such as her famous 'First
find your middle, then stick in a pin,' as she initiated a delighted
class into the art of chair making.

A wide range of work was covered in the Home Management
Department where Miss Marsden even included the re-soling
of shoes as a relaxation, among the myriad activities connected
with running a home. She had held sway for many years when
she was followed in 1929 by Miss Grace Eland, an outstanding
Old Student who came direct from the Headship of the Housewifery Department at Gloucester Training College to hold the
reins briefly in 'this most responsible and to a certain extent
lonely' post, as Miss Caddow expressed it, since most of the practical work was now carried on at the Hostel. Miss Eland's able
regime lasted a brief five terms before she joined the Board of
Education as one of His Majesty's Inspectors in 1931, but she
returned in 1937 to make her sustained contribution to the
National during her twenty years as Principal until 1957.

Recognition of broader issues became apparent in the Education and Science Departments, now established since 1918 under
Miss Weldhen. Her colleagues, Miss Charlotte Morgan (who
in 1922 became Mrs Hutchinson) and Miss Kathleen Lough, the
latter in charge of the Children's Kitchen, had both joined the
staff in 1919. Thereafter, for nearly twenty years, these two
highly different personalities complemented one another. Miss
Lough's skill and competence were constantly in demand both

on the Training and the Technical Departments, in all subjects including High Class Cookery. Forthright, firm in convictions, she guided generations towards her own high standards, and with undeviating purpose through the Second War and beyond.

When Miss Weldhen left in 1925, the Departments were re-organised, and Miss Hilda Shaw, B.Sc, already for the previous three years a vigorous and enthusiastic member of staff, took over the Science Department, which she conducted with fore-sight and zeal until her retirement over thirty years later.

Mainstays on the Technical side were Irish Miss FitzGerald, elegant and witty, who gave thirty years of service from near the beginning of the century, and the versatile and urbane Miss Walker-Jones. Miss Louisa Thorpe gave unstinted measure for well over forty years. Her outstanding contributions as one-time Head of the High Class Cookery Kitchen and as Examiner nevertheless almost paled beside her superb skill in sweet-making, epitomised in her little book *Bon-Bons,* published for 2s 6d in 1921. She always brought out the best in everyone, for her gifts were matched by her unfailing courtesy and kindness.

These were the chief members of staff, many of whom had worked together before the First War, who were to carry the School during the next decade and many much further. They were independent-minded women of character, firm in their conviction of the unassailable status of the National. Inevitably it tended to isolationism. Barely perceptible at first, the vice of the virtue was evident at times in some of the Cookery, where the impeccable standards stood in danger of hardening into rigidity. The original inspiration of a dish was lost in obscurity, but the hallowed practice remained. Insistence on the use of certain containers and identical garnish had become of equal importance to the high standard of the actual cookery. No alternative could be even considered, as witnessed by the oc-casion when perfect chocolate puddings, cooked in china basins instead of the accepted tin moulds, were without question regarded as 'a catastrophe.'

Occupied with maintenance of standards and pride in achieve-ment, any thought of control passing beyond that of the School authorities and the Board of Education was a matter of concern only for those closely connected with the negotiations. The full

implications of the agreement with the London County Council
which cut at the National's precarious independence thus went
at first unregarded.

This agreement had been precipitated by the problems of
salaries, which became pressing towards the end of the War.
Wages of the domestic staff were raised to give an increase for
kitchenmaids from 12s to 15s a week, which within a year, by
1919, became 17s and £1. Grace (Mrs Wright), who had been
with the School since its inception, received 21s, and when she
retired in 1924, the Committee expressed appreciation of her
fifty years' devotion by a gratuity of £100. In 1928 Jane North,
one of the oldest members of the domestic staff, retired. She had
worked for Miss Fitzgerald after being in Mrs Clarke's private
service, and her very real loss was followed in 1929 when Emily
Piper died. The latter had been House Cook for over thirty years,
and connected with Mrs Clarke's family since the age of sixteen.
Sheldrake's weekly wages after the War were raised from £2
to £2 5s, and his thirty-two years of dedication were rewarded
in 1928 by the gift of a gold watch and £50 'in recognition of his
faithful and devoted service.' As Supervisor of the Public
Kitchen, Miss Gordon's hard earned £168 salary was increased
to £210, and the Storekeeper's from £100 to £115.

A vote of thanks was given to the Teaching Staff for their
'help and loyalty during the War,' and a Sub-Committee set up
to review the question of salaries.

During 1918 the Board of Education had been approached by
Mrs Clarke with Miss Calder of Liverpool, supported by a letter
signed by the staff teachers, to ask for increases in salaries.
The Board had made history that same year by their offer of £15
to each Domestic Subjects student in training, as well as an
improved Capitation grant, in return for an anticipated five
years of teaching service. The official Circular stated that the
Board of Education 'rely on the Training College authorities to
have due regard to the predominant importance of providing
adequate remuneration for the Teaching staff.' This proper
obligation inevitably offset any benefit from the increased
grants. The Committee agreed to £1 a month bonus, 'to merge
with any future scale the Board approve.'

Ideas put forward by the Training Colleges and various bodies,
including the London County Council, were considered by a

Committee set up by the Board of Education, under Lord Burnham. The proposals negotiated over the next few years finally
crystallised in the acceptance, in 1932, of a new scale, known as
the Burnham Scale, backdated to take effect early in 1921.
Increases were substantial. The maximum for Honours Graduates was £490, for Graduates £440, and for non-Graduates £360.
The Principal's salary became £560 a year, rising by £25 to a
maximum of £720.

Welcome and necessary as the Burnham Scale proved, nevertheless the School's exchequer was bound to suffer. In an effort
to repair, enlarge and modernise premises and equipment, and
at one and the same time fulfil all other obligations, the over-
riding need was to restore stable finances. Only a further steady
income could save them. Yet all the time basic expenses mounted.
A deficit for each training student had risen from £6 in 1915 to
£25 in 1919, and every one of these students therefore added to
the debt. Fees from the Technical classes could not cover the
losses on the Teacher Training side; the Restaurant alone made
a handsome profit.

The Committee faced the situation squarely, and reviewed
the position *vis-a-vis* the London County Council. Due in no
small measure to the efforts of Mrs Homan and Major Salmon
following previous exchanges, the hatchet had been buried. So
when in 1918 the question of the School's entitlement to further
maintenance grant was again raised, it was decided to place the
problem before the Council, and Major Salmon, devoted as ever
to the cause of the National, agreed to act as go-between. He
reported in November that the immediate reaction of the London
County Council had been to state categorically that they could
not meet past debts unless the School were taken over. He had
assured them that such an action was not in question; the School
could clear its overdraft by other means, but did need a block
grant for three years to meet the rising cost of Teacher Training
work. The Education Committee of the Council had viewed the
position with sympathy, and placed it before their Finance
Committee. As a result, in March 1919, the London County
Council promised an official grant of £1,500 which was paid a
year later, together with a supplementary £965 to help with
staff salaries.

In a subsequent interview with a deputation from the School Executive Committee, genuine concern felt by the Council was expressed by Sir Robert Blair and Miss Fawcett, who 'fully appreciated that it was impossible for the National to meet the cost of the Teacher Training work and the Hostel rent from the present fees combined with the Board of Education grants.' They agreed that the Hostel was essential for training as well as for living, and therefore part cost could rank for grant.

This timely intervention nevertheless proved the first breach in the walls of the National's dearly held independence, which up to now had withstood all attacks. It was the first of the annual grants which the National was henceforth to receive from the London County Council, and as such, it introduced a measure of control which inevitably tightened in the following years in proportion to the School's needs.

The Committee was still faced with the problem of the bank overdraft which increased during 1919 to reach over £2,000 by July. In an effort to wipe off this deficit a series of well-tried ideas was attempted. A Bazaar and a Dance 'on a big scale' both fell through in the Spring before a professional fund raiser was asked to undertake an appeal for £10,000. Mrs Clarke herself, at the eleventh hour before her retirement, offered to write personally to Her Majesty the Queen and to the Duke of Westminster, Lord Sheffield and Mr Burdett-Coutts. Maybe her instincts were right and her approach might have been more successful than the professional campaign, for twelve months later only £180 had been raised. In December 1920 this sum was amalgamated with two other small funds to total £383, and further attempts abandoned.

Meantime a serious proposition was entertained to set up a Food Preservation Department in the charge of a former member of the Board of Agriculture, whose personal work had impressed some of the Committee. Fortunately before the necessary kitchen and laboratory were prepared, the Board of Agriculture decided to hold all such courses in Gloucestershire, and the idea was quashed. There were no profits to be gained there. A City charity which had helped during the War, made a further gift of £200, but even so, with the agreed London County Council grants not yet actually paid, the overdraft rose to well over

£2,500. It was felt that drastic action was required to get rid of the millstone round its neck, and in November 1919, the Executive Committee agreed 'to dispose of the overdraft by transferring £2,600 from the Public Kitchen and Restaurant accounts to the General Funds,' thus squaring the School's accounts.

To remain in the clear was more difficult, but by judicious dipping into the Restaurant resources for minor items, a balance of nearly £1,000 lay at the Committee's disposal at the end of 1920.

Amateur Decorators at Work, 1920

REVIVAL

CHAPTER XXVIII

THE NEGOTIATIONS with the London County Council, with their promise of a grant towards hostel expenses, and the acceptance of Mrs Ward's offer of 6 Linden Gardens, Notting Hill, were both ratified by the Autumn of 1919.

The School was still clamouring for extra space, when a house which seemed as if it might fill a variety of purposes, was brought to the attention of Mr Buckmaster. It was Gunnersbury Lodge in Gunnersbury Park, Ealing, built in 1780, a 'beautiful property' belonging to the Rothschild family. Previously a Girls' School, which his own daughter had attended, it had been standing empty for seven years and was conveniently close to Acton Town Station. The house had a good hall and lecture rooms, and would take forty residents; it was thought that some of the extensive grounds might be used for growing fruit and vegetables for the School and the Public Kitchen. The main fabric was in good condition, but after the years of neglect a considerable sum was needed to put the place in order, estimates varying between £1,000 and £5,000.

Even so, it was felt to be an opportunity not to be missed, and Major Lionel de Rothschild was approached to know if he would repair, sell or let on a twenty-one years' lease. Shortly afterwards, Mr Buckmaster reported to the Committee that the Bank had promised a special loan of £9,000 to cover the purchase, repair and furnishing of Gunnersbury Lodge should negotiations prove successful. The rejoicing, when Major de Rothschild agreed to sell for £5,000, was short lived, for on 9 December 1919 Mr Buckmaster again reported to the Committee that he had

151

proceeded in a personal interview to confirm the deal with the Agents. He considered 'they had been guilty of a gross breach of faith,' as directly after his call they had written to say that the property in fact was sold, 'though this was not known to Major de Rothschild.' They had added that a chance still remained open, as 'the Major's Secretary had attached certain conditions to the sale which might yet turn the scale' in favour of the School.

Further approaches, however, proved negative. It appears that a film company bought the property and put up hoardings, so that it was generally assumed that alterations were in progress. About a year later it was realised that nothing further had happened, for at some point in the proceedings the film company had withdrawn and the Committee had been given the slip. By that time the Committee was involved with other prospective purchases and the matchless opportunity was lost.

Somewhat sick at heart at being double crossed, the Committee again reviewed the Hostel position. It was already clear by the New Year of 1920 that 6 Linden Gardens was too small to pay its way. The estimated receipts from January to April were £440 and the expenditure was rated at £450 in addition to the Warden's salary. It was resolved to take urgent steps to secure a Hostel sufficiently large to take some of the Training Classes.

An exhaustive search followed. During the next few months over two dozen houses were seriously considered and on 11 May 1920 it was reported that although 'all members of the Committee had been worked very hard, it was very difficult to find a suitable house at a resonable price.'

It was agreed not to spend more that £4,000 pending a revised estimate of revenue and expenditure. On 1 June after reading this latest statement, the hope of purchase receded and the Committee resolved to inform the Board of Education of its problems, emphasising that because of lack of space both in School and Hostel, twenty-five students who had applied for admission in the Autumn could not be accepted. Placing faith on personal contact, Mr Buckmaster was asked to take the letter himself to the Board, but experience prompted his opinion that 'it would not be the slightest use' for him to go. The letter was posted, but at the same moment the National was faced with a new problem. Mrs Ward announced that she would 'allow the

School to remain for a further period at 6 Linden Gardens, provided the Committee will agree to increase of rent.' Considering this ultimatum on 8 June it was decided that however dire their financial problems, these 'must in no way prevent the Committee from continuing to seek a Hostel.' Mr Buckmaster further stated strongly that he would even be 'ready to agree to a loss of £500 per annum on a Hostel, inclusive of the percentage payable on any loan,' and therefore he would be quite prepared to offer on behalf of the Committee the sum of £5,000 for a freehold, if sufficient for forty students.

By 13 July only a couple of houses on repairing leases were in view. Mrs Ward now asked the Committee to buy the furniture at present in 6 Linden Gardens, which she valued at £425. Replying that in order to give time for both consideration and official valuation this matter must be left until the next meeting in September, the Committee nevertheless agreed to increase the rent from £220 to £246 a year.

Houses in Princes Gate and Warwick Square came up for discussion at the end of September. The Sub-Committee with Lady Baring as Chairman was strongly supported by Mrs Karslake, who had joined the Executive in January 1920. In October still nothing had materialised, although by now properties had been considered in Russell Square as well as Brixton, Kennington, Putney, Clapham and Wandsworth. The Committee agreed to pay rent for the furniture in Linden Gardens at a rate of 10 per cent a year on the now official value of £427, 'until the Hostel question is settled.' Mrs Karslake urged renewed effort, reminding the Committee of the June resolution. Mrs Clarke suggested appealing to the Duke of Westminster 'for one of his empty houses' but this came to naught.

At the next meeting Mrs Ward made an impassioned plea. She felt 'the quarters at 6 Linden Gardens were unworthy of the National. Money was secondary to the splendid spirit animating staff and students who had been promised larger premises. It would be breaking faith if the ideas were allowed to drop.' She pressed for a Hostel by the following January, 1921. Mrs Karslake agreed, but pointed out that 'no suitable house had so far been found.'

The search continued. Later, in November, a leasehold house in Cromwell Gardens, with twenty-five years to run, was on offer for £2,000, with a ground rent of £140. This brought to a head divergent views as to whether the house should really be bought, or indeed, as no assistance was forthcoming from either the Board of Education or the London County Council, the whole Hostel question should be temporarily 'postponed without prejudice' until the financial position had improved. The Committee scrupulously considered these alternatives and finally, though still seeming in two minds, Major Salmon proposed raising a loan of £5,000 from an Insurance Company in order to procure 25 Cromwell Gardens, which he considered 'admirable and not dear at the price.' This idea was pursued, with promising results, but on 29 November during a meeting to concert plans, all hopes were shattered by a telephone message from the Insurance Company with their decision 'to do nothing in the matter of allowing a mortgage.'

The quest had again proved fruitless. Time was passing and Miss Caddow, in the *Guild Magazine*, reflected the growing concern when she hoped that 'all the efforts would soon be crowned with success.'

The end, indeed, was in sight. On 14 December, Mrs Ward laid before the Committee 'a few ideas she was working out with regard to 35 Linden Gardens' as she considered it would make a very satisfactory Hostel. She could not yet name her required rent, beyond an approximate £500 to £600 a year, based on £2,800 for purchase of freehold, expenditure between £2,000 and £3,000 on the house, and 'a large bill' from her lawyer. When in March 1921 she finally offered the house, the Committee unanimously resolved that Mr Buckmaster should meet Mrs Ward and 'all details concerning Agreements and other matters' should be considered with caution before being finally drawn up. The same Minutes record that 'a cordial vote of thanks be sent to Mrs Walter Ward for her great kindness and efforts on behalf of the School.'

At the Committee meeting on 24 May, Mr Buckmaster reported his interview with Mrs Ward's solicitor, 'who will of course safeguard Mrs Ward's interests, but thought that agreements might be drawn up to cover both parties.' A lease of up to twenty-one years, with option to buy, was suggested. Before any settlement, but after considerable discussion, it was decided to accept provisionally Mrs Ward's offer of 35 Linden Gardens, and Miss Caddow was instructed to accept students for the coming Autumn.

Negotiations continued during the summer of 1921 concerning the lease, repairs, redecorations, hot water supply, and the London County Council's approval of fire precautions and exits. The Committee gained the right to make interior alterations and to use the Hostel 'not solely for the pupils of the School.' An Extraordinary Meeting in November resolved on a twenty-one year lease, terminable only at tenant's request at five, seven or fourteen years, at a reduced rent of £210 per annum, and no option to buy. After further parley, this agreement was signed and sealed in March 1922. By January 1922, Mrs Ward had been paid £401 for her furniture, being 'the amount expended less the 10 per cent for two years.' A total of £2,500 insurance was taken out on 35 Linden Gardens to cover rent, furniture and fittings and personal possessions of staff and students.

It was pointed out that Mrs Ward had forfeited her position on the Committee under certain articles of the Memorandum of Association whereby no member could receive profit connected with the School carrying interest of more than 5 per cent per annum. She was invited to become a Vice President and after certain legal enquiries were satisfied she eventually accepted.

Number 6 Linden Gardens had been vacated, and the students transferred in September 1921, to number 35, with Miss Prior as Warden. 'The house,' again recorded Miss Caddow, 'has been beautifully adapted for our needs. The Refectory, Common Room and Drawing Room are charming, and the bedrooms are provided with hot and cold water. The Hostel also provides class rooms for the Housewifery students.' A small new Hostel sub-Committee, elected in November 1921, now met regularly at the Hostel a few days before each Executive Meeting. The situation was reported as 'very satisfactory.'

When Mrs Clarke had retired in 1919, it was decided 'to raise some memorial of a lasting nature which shall keep her memory green.' A long letter was sent to past and present staff and students and 'all to whom the School has rendered service,' stating that 'The Committee is unanimously of the opinion that such an occasion should not be allowed to pass without some tangible expression of their affection for Mrs Clarke, and admiration of her magnificent work and ceaseless devotion, not only to the interests of the National Training School of Cookery, but to every branch of women's work where progress, efficiency and welfare are concerned.' It continued, 'It is only in keeping with her character that anything of a personal presentation should have been declined. The Memorial will probably take the form of the foundation or endowment of a Hostel, to be known as the Edith Clarke Hostel, for the students of the Training School, this form of presentation being the most acceptable to Mrs Clarke.' There followed a brief account of her work and achievements in the various fields, and the letter ended on a note of optimism: 'The Committee confidently hope that all concerned will subscribe generously to the Fund, and while there is no limit to the size of donations, all contributions, however small, will be gratefully received.'

A year later, towards the end of 1920, with Hostel affairs at a low ebb, the sanguine expectations of a splendid response to the 'Edith Clarke Fund' had been sadly dashed. In recording that subscriptions only amounted to £254, Miss Caddow added, somewhat reproachfully, 'a disappointing result, when one considers how much the profession and how many past students owe their present prosperity to her pioneer work.'

A further letter was now circulated to say that 'The Edith Clarke Fund has reached the sum of £254, there being two hundred and thirty subscribers. With their permission, the Committee propose, as the amount is quite inadequate for providing a Hostel as desired, to make a presentation to Mrs Clarke personally, this to take the form of a booklet containing a short dedication, the names of the donors and a cheque.' Another circular stated that the Committee had been informed that 'the idea of a School Hostel is not popular with many old students.' The reasons were unknown, but it was recognised that the demands of the hospitals and the needs of the ex-soldiers and sailors came first in the interest of the public. The Fund was to be held open until after Christmas, and it was proposed to make the presentation in the New Year, 1921. Eventually a cheque for £260, 'a small personal gift and a beautiful little vellum book with all the names of the donors' were presented to Mrs Clarke.

She did not use the cheque. When the new Hostel was opened in September 1921, she gave yet another instance of her selfless devotion to the National. In her Presidential letter to the Guild, dated December 1921, she wrote 'I rejoice to hear that the long needed Hostel is now in being at 35 Linden Gardens, and I have given your cheque to the Committee to spend upon it. The Committee have handed this to our Honorary Treasurer, Mr Buckmaster, and in consultation with the Principal, have decided to furnish the Drawing Room-Library, calling it "The Edith Clarke Room." I hope this arrangement will please you all.'

Loading a Mobile Kitchen, 1917

Students' Common Room, 1920

REVIVAL

CHAPTER XXIX

WHILE ATTENTION was riveted on the Hostel affairs much else was afoot.

Among a variety of issues following the Education Act of 1918, the official status of the National had been raised by the decision that all 'Training Schools' should henceforth be designated 'Training Colleges.' Gratifying as this seemed, it understandably created problems. It was not easy to accept a change of name after forty-five years, and for a considerable time it was largely ignored. For another decade, although loosely termed either School or College, it remained legally unchanged, registered under the title of 'The National Training School of Cookery and Other Branches of Domestic Economy' until 1931. Then, at an Extraordinary General Meeting on 14 December, the Committee formally agreed that 'the name of the Company be changed to "The National Training College of Domestic Subjects (founded in 1873 as The National Training School of Cookery)".' But old associations died hard, and senior members of staff and old students long continued to refer, somewhat wistfully and lovingly, to the 'dear old School.'

The scheme of training, drawn up by Miss Clarke and agreed in principle before the War, called for amendments to meet the changed times. The desire to broaden the whole approach with a wider range of studies, was strengthened by the Education Act of 1918, known in honour of Lord Fisher, then President of the Board of Education, as the Fisher Act. The Preface to the Memorandum underlined a new latitude in training in practical subjects and included the words 'The aim of the Board has been

159

to recognise and promote the unity of the teaching profession, and to remove barriers which have existed between its different branches. They believe that freedom and variety are as essential in the training of teachers as they are in other forms of education, and that Training Colleges should be encouraged to plan their schemes of training on different lines so as to provide in the best way for the requirements of the various kinds of schools included in the national system of education.' This indeed broke new ground and seemed to point the way towards the academic aspirations long cherished by the National. But the new Act admitted no advanced work in Domestic Subjects by keeping the improved teacher training grants to the two-year course. Thus any third year student was classed as Technical, to suffer accordingly. There was an immediate outcry, and the Training Colleges concerned united in protest, submitting in a petition to the Board of Education a variety of schemes incorporating a third year of training which they considered should be eligible for full grant.

A prolonged investigation followed, not only into the proper provision for advanced work in both theory and practice of teaching and connected with staff qualifications, but also into the always vexed question of accommodation and equipment. In the eventual agreement students retained their choice of two or three years training, but the course was to be integrated throughout, sharing the first four terms in common. It was a far reaching decision and paved the way to the full three-year course inaugurated ten years later.

In 1920 another advance was made when the Committee accepted the proposals put forward by the Principals of Domestic Subjects Training Colleges for a uniform entrance examination, with raised standards and to cover a range of general subjects. Retaining the right to conduct its own examinations, the National revised its entrance requirements to include papers on (i) English and History, (ii) Geography and Elementary Science, (iii) Arithmetic and Elementary Mathematics, (iv) Essay and French, (v) Reading Aloud. This last test, dating back to the autumn of 1875, shortly after Mrs Clarke's installation, was still felt to be infallible. Recognition of this variety of subjects for entrance qualifications opened the door to their inclusion in the actual course, which in consequence rapidly widened in scope. In grasping these opportunities the National was further stimulated during a Full Inspection by the Board of Education in 1925 when the Committee was urged 'to pursue a progressive policy.'

Affiliation with the University began in 1926 when the Board of Education decreed that their present system of examinations should cease in 1929. The Training Colleges, contented with the smooth running of the examinations now standardised through-out the country, at first regretted this decision. It seems that the Universities also showed a certain reluctance to shoulder the burden, and in London it was pointed out that if undertaken several conditions would follow: The University would 'have to take surveillance of Domestic Subjects, and the Central Examination Body be represented by the Board of Education and the University; there would be a quinquennial inspection and University representatives on the Training College Com-mittee.' It was hoped that the Board of Education would keep the inspection of the practical work in their own hands. The Board agreed, offering the services of His Majesty's Inspectors. They were also prepared to allow £1 10s a head towards the cost of the examinations, but as the University estimate was £4 a head, the Committee viewed the situation with some alarm and resolved that 'no expense must fall on the College.'

The Universities perforce accepted the organisation of the examinations and the advantages soon became apparent. As the responsible examining body they issued the final award, thereby bestowing increased status on the course. In addition, the close contact while the proposals were under discussion proved of lasting benefit in all future negotiations.

A minor repercussion involved the discontinuance of the January 1928 entry of students; admissions were henceforth to be restricted to September since there would be no provision for examinations in December. Plans for the new system, though complicated, ran fairly smoothly. Training Colleges were divid-ed into six groups around a University College. Domestic Sub-jects Colleges were attached to King's College, and allowed one representative on the University Delegacy. As this body had the right to criticise syllabuses and alter the scope of the examinations, it was held in great importance, and the Committee expressed pleasure when the Domestic Subjects Colleges elected Miss Clarke as their representative.

No drastic changes were ruled under the new plan, but the machinery set up for the purpose was to prove of inestimable value, for with the whole bias changing, a full three-year integrated course came under serious consideration.

The Hadow Report of 1926, carrying the Fisher Act a stage further, and stating amongst its ideals: 'The training of the tastes which will fill and dignify leisure; the awakening and guiding of the intelligence, especially on its practical side,' once more stressed the value of Domestic Subjects. It was also urged that these specialist teachers should be trained to teach efficiently one or more general subjects as well as their own.

Therein lay the problem, for it was essential to channel this development into acceptable academic depth while retaining the high standards of craft. This was emphasised by Miss Clarke who wrote 'in spite of a much wider field now and in future we are still specialists, and our technique must be above criticism.' It was realised that a proper qualification to teach any other subject beyond the recognised specialist field must be based on an agreed syllabus. The National already included English and other general subjects as part of the course, but this led to no teaching qualification. To achieve this involved a completely different outlook and plan.

The project was after Miss Clarke's own heart. Always of an intellectual bent, her grasp of affairs was of great value in the ensuing discussions with the University and her own specialist colleagues. The schemes, which she described as 'quite thrilling to work out,' finally culminated in the full three-year course under the auspices of the University, which began in London in 1931. The plan for the double qualification was submitted to the Board of Education at the end of 1930 and with the University's final approval went the award of 'certification' for the teaching of English and other school subjects, as well as the specialist qualification in Domestic Subjects. Miss Clarke recorded 'in September 1931 all those entering the Training College will take a three years' training in which English will be included.'

At this same time the Committee abolished the Two Years' Teachers' Course, but the deferred third-year courses and continuous third-year courses for two-year students from other Colleges were to remain.

At the Board's Full Inspecition in March 1925 H.M.I. Miss Sillitoe led her team for the last time before her retirement and was succeeded in her connection with the National by H.M.I. Miss McCall. The Report advocated both teaching practice in rural areas and some residential experience in Home Management. In discussion in December the Committee considered the idea of acquiring another Hostel in a rural area where both recommendations could be achieved. Miss Sillitoe, now retired, had become a member of the Executive Committee and she suggested that liaison with Gloucester Training College could be of benefit in this matter and that 'some of the picked students might be interchanged' as an initial experiment. Although neither suggestion proved immediately feasible, a week's interchange between a small group of students from the National and Gloucester was first arranged during 1927, 'a most interesting experiment' which, as it continued through the years, strengthened the link between the two Colleges.

It was realised that any informed teaching in rural areas necessitated a knowledge of rural subjects and it was decided to extend the scope of the third year by their inclusion as an optional choice. The syllabus presented great complications, but in July 1927 the Board of Education approved additional courses to be held in conjunction with Swanley Horticultural Training College in Kent. By this agreement students in their third year could spend either one, two or three terms living at the Swanley College where the subjects included Dairywork, Poultry Keeping, Rural Economy and Gardening, with the alternative terms at the National, for a choice of Cookery or Needlework. For those who went to Swanley it also provided the answer for experience in residential Home Management, for with the cooperation of the Principal, Dr Kate Barratt, the National was able to appoint a member of staff for this purpose. There was a limited but steady demand for the course, which continued with happy relationships until the connection perforce was broken by the Second World War.

The new curriculum called for a more academic element on the staff. Miss Gladys Plummer, appointed Education Lecturer in 1925, became the second Honours Graduate on the staff after Miss Hilda Shaw, Head of the Science Department. Gifted and imperturbable, she brought a widening of outlook, carrying on her broad shoulders the burdens of conflicting demands for the next six years, until she accepted the newly created post of Organiser of Women's Work in Southern Nigeria. In 1931 Dr Evelyn Lawrence was appointed Lecturer in English and Psychology. Her erudite scholarship gave distinction to her Department, where she was joined two years later by Miss Jaques, whose responsibilities also covered Art. Their combined talents opened new fields and their work was reflected particularly in the approach of teaching and a growing range of activities. English was a popular subject and the interest in drama gathered momentum. Dr Lawrence's research into Child Psychology gained greater scope when she was made Director of the Froebel Foundation in 1943, but apart from a two-year wartime secondment to an Emergency Training College at the request of the Ministry of Education, Miss Jaques, ably and loyally assisted by Miss Covington, led her students into the realms of literature until the end of the College life.

It was however Miss Clarke herself who steadily fostered increasing interests and she was the inspiration of most of the social clubs springing up in the College.

Sports had early been recognised and both Tennis and Hockey Clubs were formed in the summer and autumn of 1921. It was difficult to find the necessary ground and the former club had the use of courts for limited periods at Paddington Green, while the latter went to Clapham. There was no trouble, however, about the Swimming Club in the summer of 1922, with St George's Baths next door to the College. Netball at Ravenscourt Park followed in 1925. The popular Badminton Club opened in 1929 when, conveniently near the College, St Philip's Hall, Eccleston Place, was procured for play twice a week. Classes for Greek Dancing began in 1932 and the original twenty-four enthusiastic supporters increased so rapidly that in 1934 the classes were split into two groups, for beginners and the more advanced. After the Second War in 1948 a group joined the Salle Paul Fencing Club, which met in a nearby school.

Miss Clarke retained clearly in her mind the image of the degree course envisaged by her mother in 1908, and shared her belief that any advanced work in Domestic Subjects should have roots in the Arts as well as in Science, and she was anxious to encourage aesthetic interests wherever she glimpsed them. Her own sympathies lay in this direction and her somewhat mercurial temperament revelled in the outlet.

Music always remained for her an abiding passion and she personally started the College Choir, with forty members, in the autumn of 1924, handing it over in 1925 to Miss Adelaide Rind, who consented to become its Conductor. A born musician with a beautiful voice, one of Miss Rind's great gifts lay in her sympathetic handling of voice production, a subject which she taught for many years at the Royal Academy of Dramatic Art. She and Miss Clarke worked closely together for the following twelve years, during which time the Choir, as well as twice winning the Shield at the London Music Festival, Westminster, took an increasingly large share in the life of the College. Both by precept and example they illustrated their interest, and at parties where much of the entertainment was devoted to musical items, Miss Clarke and Miss Rind would themselves contribute many songs.

Largely due to Miss Clarke's influence the Dramatic and Literary Society was formed in 1925, and in its early years was greatly helped by both Miss Rind and Miss Elinora Clarke. These were the beginnings on which future English and Education lecturers were to build.

In 1927 it was decided to combine all the College activities into a Students' Union, to be governed by a General Council, whose members were elected as follows:

   i) President – Miss Clarke
   ii) Two members of staff (elected by staff)
   iii) Student representatives elected from each Division
   iv) Senior student, *ex officio* Chairman
   v) Hostel senior student, *ex officio* Secretary

The annual subscription became one guinea, and the following sub-committees, having a member of the General Council as Chairman on each, were formed for Winter Games, Summer Games, Drama, Entertainments and Finance.

An early Upholstery Class

REVIVAL

ALREADY IN THE EARLY NINETEEN-TWENTIES there were signs of the economic crisis and social unrest which were to plague the decade. Some of the post war enthusiasm in educational advance was dimmed by an unexpected shortage of posts accentuated by the closure of the compulsory Day Continuation Schools, which since their inception in 1919 had claimed a steady supply of teachers. After three years, during which their annual cost had risen from £180,000 to £303,000, their maintenance had been judged too costly. The action was deplored, both as a retrograde educational step and as a contributory cause of unemployment in the immediate loss of teaching posts.

As the spectre of unemployment became more apparent, the Board of Education limited the numbers of training students to be accepted in 1923 and 1924, and the National took steps to find other openings for their teachers. Enquiries cpncerning work in the Dominions, including a personal approach to their old friends, the Agents General for Australia, revealed that while there was a great demand for 'women trained in Domestic Subjects,' the posts for teachers proved to be negligible. Neither demand could really satisfy the other, although some past students were taking temporary posts in this country as cooks and parlour maids in private houses, thereby 'adding very much to their prestige and experience,' as Miss Caddow recorded in a tribute to their mettle.

Miss Clarke was now asked both to give evidence to the Committee of Enquiry into the Shortage of Domestic Servants and to say whether the School would be prepared to give practical help in this respect. On the horns of a dilemma, though still divided in opinion, the Committee finally submitted a statement to the Enquiry that 'the School is prepared to train cooks for service and that there is the necessary accommodation.' Even with the numbers limited on the Training side, this space could only be found at the expense of the Technical classes, which were far too valuable an asset to be permanently reduced.

Shortage of posts on the one hand, and of personnel on the other, was all part of the repercussions of economic stress which rocked the country as a whole, and the National could best contribute to stability by keeping its own finances steady. Fees for the Technical classes had been revised in 1921 and still proved a reliable source of income at the following rates:

TECHNICAL COURSES – REVISION OF FEES, JULY 1921

Courses	Existing Fees			Revised Fees		
	£	s	d	£	s	d
Cordon Bleu	45	0	0	60	0	0
Household Management	14	14	0	21	0	0
Housekeepers' Course	14	14	0	18	18	0
Ladies' Short Cookery Course	15	15	0	21	0	0
10 Plain Cookery Lessons	2	10	0	2	2	0
10 Superior Household Cookery Lessons	3	10	0	4	4	0
Cooks' Plain Cookery Certificate	6	6	0	8	8	0
Cooks' High Class Cookery Certificate	12	12	0	16	16	0
10 Lessons in Needlework, Dressmaking and Millinery	2	10	0	3	3	0
10 Lessons in Tailoring	3	10	0	4	4	0
Plain Needlework Certificate	7	7	0	8	8	0
Dressmaking Certificate	14	14	0	16	16	0
Millinery Certificate	6	6	0	8	8	0
Advanced Needlework	7	7	0	8	8	0
Advanced Dressmaking	22	1	0	25	0	0
10 Laundry Lessons (2 hours)	2	10	0	2	10	0
10 Laundry Lessons (3 hours)	3	10	0	3	10	0
12 Lectures Home Management *each*		15	0	1	0	0
2 Courses of Home Management		—		1	10	0
12 Superior Household Demonstrations	1	0	0	1	5	0
Single lessons		2	0		2	6
10 Odd Jobs Demonstrations	2	10	0	2	10	0
Single lessons		5	0		7	6

In 1922 Miss Caddow recorded in the *Guild Magazine* that 'a Scholarship has been generously presented to the College by the Proprietors of Borwick's Baking Powder,' to bear this name. The annual value of £75 for Out-County students or £50 for a London student meant an additional £20 a year beyond the fees. The final selection from candidates, testified by their Head Mistresses as to their suitability and possessing the necessary entrance qualifications, was to lie in the hands of a Committee at the National. The Scholarship was greatly sought; after the first few years it was awarded only biennially, and later every three years to cover the three-year course. Unfortunately it was discontinued shortly before the Second War.

Afternoon classes for 'debs' once more claimed their fashionable clientele, especially for the ever popular Needlework and Dressmaking taken by Miss Brand and Miss Howlett, the latter to follow Miss Wallbank some years later as Head of the Department. Luxury fabrics, including a nightdress for the Queen of Spain, were again used as in the early pre-War days, but now occasional economy was practised as when with a novel conception of thrift a student cut up her mother's Coronation Robes to make her own evening dress. The habitual overcrowding, which drastically limited cutting out space, in no way restricted the range of work, and the big room on the first floor, with its great windows on to Buckingham Palace Road, was an incessant hum of activity.

There was activity in other ways, too. On a hot afternoon towards the end of the summer term in 1923, the Needlework classes were almost driven to distraction by the throbbing of what seemed to be a giant drill piercing the ground at their feet. This was exactly what was happening, for the Committee had decided that electricity should at last be installed throughout the building. It was said that the work was made peculiarly difficult because Mrs Clarke's insistence on additional fire precautions had resulted in specially reinforced floors at the time when the School was built in 1889, and the sufferings of the class were due to the necessarily prolonged drilling.

It took all the summer holidays to complete the electrical work and a new laboratory on the second floor which was created 'from the front and back rooms and a slice of landing,' and described as 'well appointed, well lighted, of excellent proportion, and since ventilation can always be effected from the back, the front windows can be kept shut against the noise of the traffic.' Fifty years later, not even closed windows could shut out the roar as the one-way traffic thundered by.

All this work made a heavy drain on expenditure, to the concern of the Committee, who only after 'some considerable discussion' agreed to accept, for a trial twelve months, Messrs Drake and Gorham's estimate of £1 10*s* a year for the inspection of the electric installation throughout the College.

Costs indeed were mounting as the National strove to keep pace with demands. Hostel space was again short. In the Autumn of 1922, Miss Clarke reported that 35 Linden Gardens was 'quite full, with a total of forty-one students, six having bedrooms outside,' so when an upper maisonette at number 16, a couple of minutes away, became vacant in 1923, the Committee secured it on a seven-year lease at £200 a year, thus relieving the situation by housing another ten students and Home Management practice.

It was also a great gain for the Needlework and Dressmaking classes to secure the entire top floor at St Peter's Institute, a few doors from the back entrance in Eccleston Place, instead of having to share the Boys' Club Room and remove all traces of occupation every day as they had done since 1921. Even so, the premises were hardly ideal; at a rent of £60 a year the landing at the top of seventy-eight stone stairs provided a store cupboard and inadequate cloakroom facilities, while the large class room, with a small corner shut off for an extra demonstration and fitting room, was warmed by oil stoves and shared by some forty-odd students from a variety of classes. They included the third year Teacher Training specialists from both the National and other colleges; qualified teachers taking a deferred third year; and a number engaged in Technical courses varying in length from a term to a year; who all worked together in great amity and close juxtaposition.

Finally the Committee agreed to extensive repairs and re-decoration through the entire School, both inside and out, long overdue after the enforced neglect of the fabric during the War and its aftermath.

All was now set to present a new face to the world to celebrate the Golden Jubilee. Although the School was founded in July 1873, with the first Minutes of the Executive Committee recorded on 6 November 1873, the regular classes were established in March 1874. It was therefore decided to commemorate the fifty years during that month, and great festivities were planned for the week beginning 3 March 1924.

Mrs Homan had retired as Chairman in 1921. She was parted with reluctantly, for her devoted service since 1905, particularly in the difficult War period, had been invaluable. Sir Cyril Cobb, who for some years had been Chairman of the Education Committee of the London County Council, succeeded her. Lady Baring, who joined the Committee in 1907, became Vice-Chairman in 1920, to continue in that office for the next fourteen years and the Committee had also been strengthened by Mr Lesser, who took an active share from 1921 onwards until 1939.

In January 1920 the Executive Committee decided to consider the appointment of a Vice President. This office had been in abeyance since 1913, when Lord Sheffield had followed the Duke of Bedford as President, and each member of the Committee was asked to make two suggestions. At the next meeting on 10 February, with a rich variety of names of eminent personalities, it was difficult to make a choice; after some discussion it was decided that, as well as the official Vice President, it would be of great value to the status of the School to have additional Vice Presidents of distinction.

By 9 March a choice of names for this purpose had been agreed, and on 13 April it was reported that Lady Barrett, Lady Cooper (the Lady Mayoress), Sir Almeric FitzRoy and Sir Guy Sebright had accepted invitations to become Vice Presidents. In the following year, wishing to add to this list, consultation with the School's lawyers in July 1921 elicited that there would be 'no objection to an indefinite number of Vice Presidents as long as they were not guarantors.' This was felt to be a satisfactory position, for the services of old friends and supporters could now be enlisted.

Sir Almeric FitzRoy was elected as official Vice President in March 1922, and held this position for over ten years. In 1930 the officers were established as follows:

Patron: HIS MOST GRACIOUS MAJESTY THE KING
President: The Viscount Burnham, C.H. G.C.M.G.
Vice-President: Sir Almeric FitzRoy, K.C.B. K.C.V.O.

Hon. Vice Presidents

Lady Betty Balfour   Mrs Homan
Lady Barrett, C.B.E. M.D. M.S.   Sir Guy Sebright, Bart.
   (London University)
Lady Cooper, O.B.E.   Mrs Walter Ward
   (Ex Lady Mayoress)
Professor Winifred Cullis, O.B.E. D.SC.

Executive Committee

Chairman: Sir Cyril S. Cobb, K.B.E. M.V.O.
Vice-Chairman: Lady Baring, M.B.E.
Honorary Treasurer: Charles A. Buckmaster, Esq.

Lady Denman   Ernest Lesser, Esq.
Frederic J. Dryhurst, Esq. C.B. Sir Edwin Cooper Perry,
F. W. Goodenough, Esq. C.B.E.   M.A. M.D. F.R.C.P.
Mrs Karslake   Miss Sillitoe
                             Miss Souter

Major Isidore Salmon, C.B.E. D.L. M.P.
   (representative from the London County Council)
Professor C. K. Tinkler, D.SC. (representative from
   London University)

Principal: Miss E. Gladys Clarke
Vice-Principal: Miss Caddow

In the Autumn of 1923 a Jubilee Sub-Committee, with Lady
Baring as Chairman, was elected to organise the Commemoration. It was decided to inaugurate the celebrations with a Reception, followed by a Concert and Dance; to hold an Open
Exhibition of Work for a couple of days, and to conclude with a
Thanksgiving Service at St Peter's, Eaton Square. A fund for
a permanent Jubilee Memorial was started; the specific object
'to be decided according to the amount raised and the wish of
the majority.'

The Duchess of Atholl agreed to open the Exhibition, and a
galaxy of distinguished well-wishers promised their support.
Search for accommodation suitable for the social events of the
first evening met with a slight set-back after a personal appeal
to the Duke of Westminster failed. Miss Clarke reported that

the Duchess was willing to allow the use of rooms at Grosvenor House, but the charges would be over £50, which put it out of reach. Lady Cooper then most generously came forward with the offer of £25 to cover the hire of the Princes Galleries in Piccadilly, thereby 'making it possible to charge a very low fee for admission to these spacious Galleries, including a sit-down supper, orchestra and artistes' fees.' Fortune smiled too, when in answer to Lady Baring's approach, Her Majesty Queen Mary graciously agreed to visit the National privately on Thursday morning, 6 March, to see the Exhibition of Work, which gave a great fillip to these preparations.

A private reception for the staff and friends on the previous Saturday, 1 March, was the forerunner of a series of successful functions the following week. Monday evening at the Princes Galleries was an unqualified success, but Tuesday brought a sad blow, for Miss Clarke summoned all the School to give them a message from Her Majesty Queen Mary, who, owing to a severe chill, was unable to carry out her eagerly anticipated visit. It was a bitter disappointment, but 'we tried not to be depressed,' said Miss Clarke. Providentially the indomitable Mrs Pillow was at hand and she soon rallied any deflated spirits.

The Duchess of Atholl opened the Exhibition on Wednesday, 5 March, at 2.30 pm in a packed hall, where students and visitors stood all round the walls, filled the aisles, and even sat on the edge of the small platform erected for the speakers. In a tribute to Mrs Clarke and the School, Sir Cyril Cobb spoke of the early history, with amusing reference to the cartoon in *Punch's Almanack* for 1874, showing Mr Punch as Demonstrator to a crowded audience. Rear-Admiral Sir William Beresford White in proposing the official congratulations on the Golden Jubilee, emphasised the debt of gratitude owed by the Navy to the National, recalling the atmosphere of 'enjoyment, keenness and enthusiasm' during his own attendance at a 'short course in this house, a good many years ago.'

The Exhibition filled the building. A popular item was the miniature cottage made and furnished by the third-year Science students, fitted throughout with electricity generated in a small engine house set behind cut hedges in a little garden with rustic bridge and ornamental waters. The house with its tiny switches had electric lights, fire and a bell, as well as a minute radio set. The large Jubilee Cake also excited enthusiasm, with its design, painted in vegetable colours on white icing, of two students in the uniform of 1874 and 1924, playing tennis. Their ball was a raised impression of the College crest, and across the top stretched a scroll bearing the College motto of 'Semper Fidelis.'

Crowds flocked in ceaselessly, augmented on the last day by teachers who had come to London to attend an A.T.D.S. Conference. In all about 1,500 people visited the Exhibition, and Lady Baring and Mrs Karslake passed a special vote of thanks to Miss Clarke and Miss Caddow, including the staff at Miss Clarke's express desire, for the 'extremely satisfactory work accomplished for the Jubilee.'

There was a large congregation at St Peter's for the Thanksgiving Service on Friday evening, 7 March. 'An old friend,' who also read the lessons, had arranged for the altar to be decorated with white flowers, and the full choir attended.

The Jubilee had done much to restore morale and prestige. Her Majesty Queen Mary accepted a box of Miss Thorpe's chocolates and bon-bons with 'most appreciative' words, and in recording the pleasure felt by this message, the Committee cherished the hope that the National might yet be honoured by a visit at some future date.

The reckoning was not so profitable as hoped. Printing costs were borne by the College, and to reduce any further expense on this side it was decided to record certain speeches in the *Guild Magazine* and to keep a copy of newspaper notices and other information, rather than issue them in pamphlet form.

The Jubilee Fund amounted to £405 16s. It was insufficient for two of the purposes suggested, either to found a scholarship or to acquire a Hall for conferences and entertainments. Finally, at the request of the students, the fund was set aside for College activities and the various clubs. A mural plaque to commemorate the Jubilee was considered; meantime £374 was invested and a small committee representing staff and students elected to allocate the annual interest.

One of the first uses of this money was to aid members of the newly formed branch of the Student Christian Movement to send representatives to the Annual Summer Conference at

Swanwick in Derbyshire, by supplementing their own determined efforts to raise the required funds. The College Branch of this movement continued throughout the life of the National with a staunch but limited band of loyal supporters, greatly encouraged always by Miss Eland when she became Principal.

It was 1929 before the plaque was put up in the Hall. Made of solid bronze, with a monogram of the School in coloured enamel, it bore the following inscription:

THIS TABLET COMMEMORATES THE JUBILEE OF THIS PIONEER

TRAINING COLLEGE AND TECHNICAL SCHOOL OF DOMESTIC SCIENCE

FOUNDED AS THE NATIONAL TRAINING SCHOOL OF COOKERY

AT SOUTH KENSINGTON 1873

THE SUCCESS AND GROWTH DURING FIFTY YEARS OF THIS

IMPORTANT NATIONAL WORK IS CHIEFLY DUE TO THE VISION AND

LEADERSHIP OF MRS EDITH CLARKE WHO WAS PRINCIPAL

FROM 1875 TO 1919

Needlework and Dressmaking, 1921

REVIVAL

CHAPTER XXXI

THE NATIONAL, having set much of its house in order, prepared for the next phase. There were continuing changes on all sides, in the courses, the curriculum and the buildings. Immediately after the Jubilee, on 31 March 1924, Mr Buckmaster reported that the lower floors of 16 Linden Gardens were on the market. So anxious was he to prevent any possible complications with a new tenant, that the Committee decided to strike while the iron was hot and offer £350 a year for the whole house, only £150 more than the present rent paid for the top three floors. It was accepted so quickly that only a week later on 7 April Sir Cyril Cobb and Mr Lesser protested at the speed of such an important step without further consultation. Both were appeased, however, by the reminder of the imperative need to avoid 'the very serious consequences of the wrong kind of tenant' in the same house, and the lease, to run concurrently with the existing one, was signed and sealed in May.

It was the beginning of a far reaching change, for the Warden, Miss Prior, who 'had done excellent work,' decided to resign in order to run her own Guest House, involving also the resignation of some of her staff. A new appointment became a matter of urgency, and with the overall responsibility for two houses, the salary was reconsidered. On the present scale of £135 rising by £10 to £210 a year, Miss Prior received £165. A new scale of £160, with yearly increments of £10 to reach £250, was now agreed, with the proviso that the new Warden should receive 'whatever was appropriate to her experience.'

In June Miss Frances Hosegood, who had trained at the School just before the First War, was appointed; the sub-committee responsible was unanimous in her favour, and the sanction of the Board of Education was expressed verbally as 'a very wise choice.' Miss Hosegood agreed to go into residence towards the end of July, to accustom herself to the workings of the Hostel, and to secure her staff. Thus began her fourteen years as Warden until she resigned in 1938 to find wider scope as a private Consultant in Domestic Affairs. She was zealous in her stewardship, husbanding resources and guarding the meagre finances. Cookery was her speciality, and her skill was often deployed in sharing intricate work for special occasions with Miss Broderick. Slow to judge and slow to speak, the Hostels were fortunate in her general organisation and talents for house-planning and decoration, while her flower arrangements, often using the simplest materials, revealed the country woman born and bred with her knowledge of plants and hedgerows.

There were other changes connected with the staff, for in 1923 the Board of Education and the London County Council allowed six posts of special responsibility to qualify for an extra £40 a year. These were allocated to Miss Caddow as Vice-Principal and five Heads of Departments: Miss Rotheram for Cookery, Miss Marsh for Laundry, Miss Marsden for Home Management, Miss Wallbank for Dressmaking and Needlework and to Miss Weldhen, Science and Education. This pattern was soon to alter; there were several retirements during the next few years, but the most immediately felt was that of Miss Maud Rotheram in 1925. Vitally connected with the triumphs of the early years of the century, after she joined the staff in 1902, her place in the annals was secure; but her mantle was of many colours and no one ever quite replaced her. Since the War Miss Rotheram's work had lain in every branch, and now the members of the Cookery staff combined their skill with the tradition of her supreme art to lead their departments in new and different ways.

The Report of the Full Inspection by the Board of Education in March 1925, considered by the Committee the following November, concentrated on the extensive lack of accommodation. Another recommendation, unanimously agreed, resulted in the appointment in January 1926 of Miss Florence Graham who joined the staff as College Accountant. She became a loyal and integral part of the National life, constantly consulted by all and sundry.

The Board had drawn attention to the urgent need to provide properly for a Library, a Lecture Room, Common Rooms, Cloak-rooms and a Larder, as well as all the Needlework teaching, quite apart from the overcrowding of most of the other craft rooms and kitchens. It was a formidable task, but the Committee faced it realistically and unamimously agreed to consult an architect.

The choice fell on Mr Bennett, a practising architect in charge of his own firm of T. P. Bennett & Co, and also Head of the Building Department at the Northern Polytechnic. He attended the next meeting on 14 December 1925 to discuss proposals already circulated to the members. Setting out the pros and cons with clarity, he suggested as three alternatives:

 i) To build on to the front of the building. This would increase problems of administration, give very little extra accommodation, and be very costly.

 ii) To build on to the back. This would provide very little extra accommodation; existing walls were insufficiently strong.

iii) To build a block over the large kitchens, 70 feet by 30 feet; three storeys with an area of 2,100 square feet on each floor would provide ample accommodation for all the rooms required.

The Committee decided to pursue the last proposal and agreed Mr Bennett's fees of ten guineas for his preliminary report, and seventy-five to one hundred guineas for full plans. As yet, no estimate was available, but the Bank was willing to lend £7,000, and no difficulty in procuring a loan of £10,000 for this extension was anticipated. Full of optimism, the Committee authorised Mr Bennett to go ahead.

Mrs Charles Clarke, M.B.E. in her eightieth year
Principal 1874 – 1919

REVIVAL

REJUVENATION was in the air, but the sands were running out for Mrs Clarke. She kept her clear mind and keen faculties alert to the end, using her influence as an elder statesman in the background during the seven years of her retirement, and never attempting to impose her own views. Physically she was frail, but her spirit was as vigorous and her humour as sharp as always. Miss Clarke gave thanks that she endured no suffering or illness, and 'enjoyed her wonderful independence to the end.' Believing with unshaken faith in the virtues of high principles and hard work, in youth and in the future, she died tranquilly in her sleep on 20 August 1926. In a tribute Miss Sillitoe wrote that 'Age could not lessen her courage nor quench the gleam of eternal youth in her eyes.'

Although the new generation of students did not know her, everyone had been conscious of her tradition and influence, and among the 'Old Guard' her loss was irreparable.

The hundreds of letters of sympathy to Miss Clarke all expressed a sense of personal loss; among many tributes 'she was a great lady and of the very salt of the earth' was among the most treasured. A Memorial Service was held at St Paul's, Knightsbridge, on Saturday, 13 November, with a moving address from the Bishop of Kensington. Once more Miss Sillitoe wrote 'I felt we should please her best by not sorrowing over much, but by trying to carry on the high traditions of service which she maintained so long.'

Ideas for a permanent memorial were considered by a small sub-committee representing both the Executive Committee and

181

the staff. A favoured suggestion was to collect together mementos, medals and photographs from childhood up, 'in a good
cabinet to be fixed in the Dining Room, until such time as the
College has a Hall of Assembly worthy of it.' This delightful
idea was not pursued, and so the interesting collection was
never made.

Finally it was decided to have a silver medal struck, named
The Edith Clarke Medal, to be awarded to 'the best student of
the year,' specifying that 'character, personality, ability and
proficiency were to be taken into account in making the selection.' The medal was to bear the presentment of Mrs Clarke as
she was when the School was founded, and it did not prove easy
for Messrs Spink to catch her likeness from the early photographs. The first award was made in 1927, and from then on
became the highest honour for any student to attain.

The die cost £25, with 35s for each medal. Two guineas was
also to be given to the recipient. The choice was often so difficult
that it was decided to have a Special Merit Board, on which the
names of a few students who had made outstanding contributions were inscribed each year. The Committee decided that the
total expenditure for the medal should be met from the Restaurant profits. At the same time Miss Clarke drew attention
to the fact that for the first time since 1895 the College was out
of debt. It was a fitting close to Mrs Clarke's 'great gift of organisation and her continuing efforts for its success,' as recorded
by the Committee.

REVIVAL

IN RETROSPECT, Mr Bennett's plans never really got off the ground. The College did not remain long out of debt and there were endless queries and frustrations. Early in 1926, the cost of the proposed extension of three storeys above the large kitchens to provide a total area of 6,300 square feet, was estimated at £15,000 and the first concern was to secure this sum.

Sir Cyril Cobb reported an interview with Mr Gater, who had succeeded Sir Robert Blair at the London County Council in 1924, to the effect that there was small chance of such a building plan receiving approval, but if reduced to two storeys it might possibly be considered in 1929. Mr Gater stressed that the training of teachers should continue to be restricted to match the fall in number of children entering schools, which statistics anticipated reaching the lowest ebb in 1930. He believed that the Training side should be reduced and the Technical expanded, and this would not necessitate so large an extension.

In September Miss Fawcett, Miss Margaret Jones and Mr Smail all visited the School on behalf of the London County Council, but although unanimous in their opinion that 'new, larger and better premises' were required, they queried the spending of a large sum merely on an annexe to an inadequate building. Mr Gater was supported in his views as to numbers of teachers required; already it was stated that by 1930 sixty less Domestic Science teachers would be needed in London.

A year later, in May 1927, with Mr Bennett still working on detailed plans, the Higher Education Committee of the Council, in reply to the National's Memorandum of the previous summer,

183

reiterated their statement that fewer teachers should be trained and in these circumstances an expenditure of £15,000 could not be justified. To this was added that 'in view of the expiry of the National lease in 1978 and bearing in mind the geographical position and nature of the building,' the Council was not prepared to consider any grant in their 1927/1930 programme. Amazed at such grounds for refusal, the Committee sent an immediate reply making it clear that these arguments could not be accepted. The Council remained unmoved; no change of policy ensued and the National was as far as ever from attaining its goal.

Indeed, it was almost further away than before, for number 4 Eccleston Street, which housed the Restaurant, had just been sold to new owners, who had proposed to increase the rent from £200 to £450 a year, or alternatively to charge £300 a year with a premium of £1,000 for a seven-year lease. Miss Gordon also wished to resign after her years of successful and valiant service, and a further problem was raised by queries from the Income Tax authorities concerning certain regulations, which although now satisfactorily settled, suggested a less easy passage in the future. In view of the sum of these difficulties, the Committee felt it expedient to withdraw from the premises and to close the Restaurant.

Realising how valuable it had proved, both in large scale Cookery training and in supplementing the School's income, Miss Clarke asked for permission to find other premises and run it herself, but this the Committee could not countenance. During the five years since its opening the Restaurant had contributed £4,950 to the School's main funds, in addition to paying for the electricity installation and many other items. In respect of dilapidations £100 was accepted, and on 31 May 1927 the doors were closed and the goose that laid the golden egg disappeared.

Practice in large scale cookery was arranged at the Cowdray Club, then the largest Women's Club in London. Founded in 1922 by the Viscountess Cowdray for nurses and other professional women, by 1930 it had a membership of over four thousand and served an average of five hundred meals a day, including functions such as dances, weddings, and all kinds of receptions. All cakes, bread and rolls were home made, and in addition the

Miss E. Gladys Clarke, O.B.E.

Club bottled its fruit, and made its own jams, marmalade and chutney. The efficiency and high standards of the complicated organisation were invaluable, and the students continued for many years to benefit from this experience.

An additional grant of £1,500 from the Board of Education enabled the final bank loan of £1,000 to be repaid, but brought no nearer the £15,000 so urgently required.

Then in November 1928 a far reaching decision was made, when the old established firm of Barton and Mayhew was appointed, at a fee of 45 guineas, to be the official Auditors for the National. From this time on the finances were scrupulously guarded, and consolidated wherever possible. World events and the depression in the national economy eventually proved overwhelming odds, but sound advice was thenceforth at the disposal of the Committee. Mr H. O. H. Coulson, who first came to represent his firm as a young man, remained as one of the most loyal and able supporters to the end of the National's life. Dispassionate judgment enabled him to weigh the merits of a situation, and when convinced of the proper course of action, he was tenacious in its pursuit, shrewdly assessing all the ways and means.

In spite of all Mr Gater's prognostications, the National was not only crowded to the doors but besieged by applicants for all courses. Miss Caddow, in 1928, deplored a situation where there were 'far more rejected than accepted,' lamenting that 'it does seem a shame that all this thirst for sound sensible knowledge cannot be satisfied,' simply through lack of space.

In 1929, while the Committee was still trying to raise money and to win sympathy from both the Board of Education and the London County Council, another issue came up for decision. Miss Caddow was due to retire in March; there could be no query over her excellent health and Miss Clarke represented that to lose her second in command would be detrimental to the work and organisation of the National. The Board readily gave their sanction, but owing to a misunderstanding with the Committee, the extension was granted by the latter only for one year, thereby promoting a tiresomely recurring issue.

Another source of irritation was connected with residence. Miss Clarke, since becoming Principal, had joined Miss Caddow living in the College, and though they shared residence and even converted the Students' Common Room each evening to their own sitting room, the use of the space thus occupied was continually queried, although its release could have made virtually no contribution to the envisaged extension.

Professionally Miss Clarke's name was now well to the fore. She was asked by the Editors of the *Encyclopaedia Britannica* to write the article on Cookery for their new edition, and she made her first radio broadcasts at Savoy Hill in the Summer Term 1928, at the invitation of the National Federation of Women's Institutes, when she gave several talks on Dietetics. It was noted that as 1,900 words made up fifteen minutes talk, she had a chance of saying 'quite a good deal in a short time.' The talks were printed in pamphlet form and the enterprise aroused great interest. Widespread correspondence resulted, all of it expressing appreciation not only of the content but of the delivery, for in addition to her own clear and well trained voice, Miss Clarke had inherited her mother's gift of speaking.

She was bending her mind and energies in all directions. Working intimately on the schemes leading to affiliation with the University, she readily assessed the potential value of the new B.Sc.(Dom.Sc.) Degree Course at Bristol University, agreed in 1927 with the Gloucestershire Training College of Domestic Science. Provided 'to meet the need for women of University standing possessing specialised skill,' the course covered four years. The first three years were to be spent at the University in Bristol, with four weeks in each long vacation and the final year at the Training College in Gloucester. The overall plan was designed to meet the requirements of future practical work, and covered a wide range of subjects, viewed from a variety of angles, so that students sometimes shared certain allied studies in fields such as agriculture or medicine.

Swift to recognise the scope of such flexible approach, the Committee decided to take action. The University of London was committed to the Honours B.Sc. degree in Household Science at King's College, and it was agreed to approach Bristol with a view to association similar to that arranged with Gloucester. It was also felt that the link with the rural studies at Swanley made the National peculiarly fitted to cover this aspect in depth. With the sanction of Bristol the first active participation in the Bristol Degree course of B.Sc.(Dom.Sc.) began in September 1931, when one student entered for the recognised three years at Bristol and the fourth at the National. The course was not supported as fully as hoped, possibly because it carried no professional training for teaching, and to gain this qualification demanded a fifth year. Miss Clarke was undeterred, for as early as December 1927 she had reported to the Committee that 'the association with the University of London may eventually lead to a state of things where degrees will be awarded.'

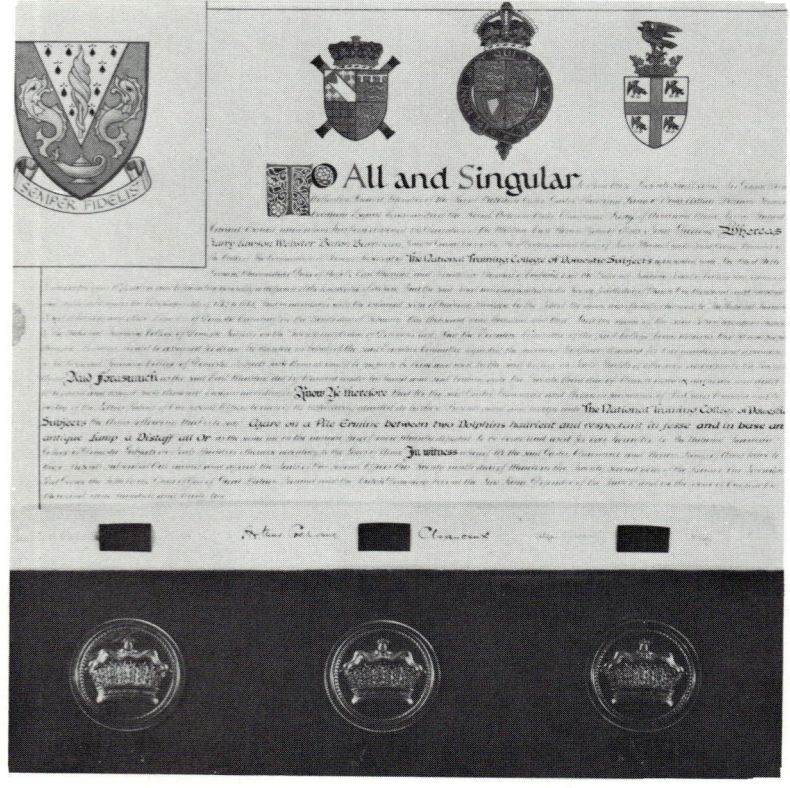

Coat of Arms of the National Training College of Domestic Subjects, 1931

REVIVAL

CHAPTER XXXIV

IT SEEMED A FITTING TRIBUTE when in June 1931 Miss Clarke became an Officer of the Order of the British Empire. 'I need hardly say how proud and delighted we all are at this honour,' wrote Miss Caddow in expressing the general pleasure at the award, 'We value it firstly for its recognition of the splendid work done by her, and secondly for its recognition of our special branch of Education.'

Three pictures appeared in the 1931–1932 issue of the *Guild Magazine*, of Miss Clarke, of Miss Caddow, and of the new Arms of the College. Miss Caddow explained: 'Miss Clarke had to appear, because she has received her O.B.E. and is a person of growing importance. It was decided that I must also appear because I am a person of diminishing importance. The third illustration, our Armorial Bearings, will I am sure delight you all. We all feel the design and colouring are delightful, and worthy of the National College of Domestic Subjects and of its long tradition.'

The question of Miss Caddow's retirement had again been raised; although the Board of Education had no query 'provided she was able to carry on her present duties,' the London County Council were unable to concur, and there were anxious moments until a friendly compromise was reached. Miss Caddow retired officially as College Secretary in August 1931, but remained as 'College Warden,' to keep a watching brief on the College, and to support Miss Clarke through the next few difficult years.

Everyone now wanted to show affection and appreciation of her long devotion. It was amply demonstrated at the Guild Reunion on 24 October 1931 when there were speeches and presentations. The response to the suggestion that Miss Caddow should be given a diamond ring from the Guild members proved so great that in addition she received an antique miniature bureau, with lists of the names of the donors in the tiny drawers, an antique washing chest, and an illuminated address. She was received with tremendous applause and, as expected, made a charming speech. 'The best part of all,' it was recorded, 'was the knowledge that Miss Caddow is only beginning another sphere of life that includes the old College in a wider embrace.'

It was decided to try a completely different plan of administration. The Vice Principalship temporarily ceased with Miss Caddow. A Secretarial Department was set up with Miss E. H. Garnham, M.A. in charge as College Secretary, and Miss Ashford, a stalwart helped since 1893, and Miss Forbes as assistants. But the scheme did not prosper, expenses proved too heavy, and in 1934 both Miss Garnham and Miss Forbes left.

There had long been a fervent wish that the National should have a Coat of Arms, and in July 1930 the students voted a sum of money for this purpose from the funds of the Students' Union. At the request of the Executive Committee, Lord Burnham, who had become President in 1925, agreed to make proper representation to the Duke of Norfolk, Earl Marshal of England, and in 1931 the Arms were granted.

There followed an immediate appeal for ideas for a design suitable 'to portray woman's work, the practical bias as well as the academic side, and our "National" character,' with an endeavour 'to get away from pots and pans.'

The following year the *Guild Magazine* proudly displayed, in colour, 'The Armorial Bearings of the National Training College of Domestic Subjects,' the new title under which the School was now registered at Somerset House. In her Foreword, Miss Clarke gave a description transcribing the heraldic terms: 'The Coat of Arms denotes royalty, dignity – the ermine; woman's work – the distaff; learning – the lamp; ethics and spirituality – the dolphins, the fish being the ancient symbol of Christ.'

The cost was recorded as £76 10s for the fee to the College of Arms and £2 10s for the designs and sketches. The old College colours were no longer appropriate, and it was reported that

Miss Alice M. Caddow, 1931

'the Azure blue of the shield with gold and red necessitated a change in our College Colours from dark to azure blue, and from silver to gold – the red remains the same,' so that 'the students have also changed the College blazer which in future is to be black with stripes of red, blue and gold, with a plain black pocket, on which the Coat of Arms shows up exceedingly well.'

The illuminated parchment, with great beauty of decoration, and bearing the Seals of Garter, Clarenceux and Norroy Kings of Arms recorded that the Earl Marshal 'did by Warrant under his hand and seal bearing date the twenty-third day of March instant authorize and direct Us to grant and assign such Armorial Ensigns Know Ye therefore that We the said Garter, Clarenceux and Norroy, in pursuance of His Grace's Warrant and by virtue of the Letters Patent of Our several Offices to each of us respectively granted do by these Presents grant and assign unto the National Training College of Domestic Subjects the Arms following, that is to say: Azure on a Pile Ermine between two Dolphins haurient and respectant in fesse and in base an antique lamp a Distaff all Or as the same are in the margin hereof more plainly depicted to be borne and used for ever hereafter by the National Training College of Domestic Subjects on Seals, Shields or otherwise according to the Laws of Arms.

'In Witness whereof We, the said Garter, Clarenceux and Norroy have to these Presents subscribed our names and affixed the Seals of Our several Offices this Twenty-ninth day of March in the Twenty-second year of the Reign of our Sovereign Lord, King George the Fifth by the Grace of God of Great Britain, Ireland and the British Dominions beyond the Seas King, Defender of the Faith, and in the year of Our Lord One thousand nine hundred and thirty-two.'

REVIVAL

CHAPTER XXXV

AN IMPETUS WAS GIVEN to the plans for building an extension
to the College when in May 1929 a team of London County
Council Inspectors visited the National for a week, to carry
out 'a most thorough and detailed inspection of work and buildings.' The work, including both content of courses and standards achieved, won high commendation. The Committee,
however, found it difficult to reconcile their advocacy of more
specialist Needlework training to support the widely shared
view that 'the neglect of Needlework in Secondary Schools must
be remedied,' with their recommendation to increase the Cookery course by two weeks and decrease the Needlework equally.

The buildings were another matter. Although showing sympathy for the problems involved, there was trenchant criticism
that since 1925, when the Board of Education had detailed the
most urgent needs of accommodation, there had been no improvement whatever.

But with no funds to meet the cost, no improvement seemed
likely. Miss Caddow, reporting the London County Council
visit, wrote 'We do *need* an extension, and if any past or present
students know a millionaire with money to burn, do please send
him along.' In the same spirit, Miss Clarke was inspired to start
the Building Fund, and in her Christmas letter of 1929 she outlined her hopes in the *Guild Magazine* as follows: 'I am very
keen that we, students of the College, should show our love for
it and for our work by doing our bit. I should like every student,
past and present, to shoulder this responsibility and each one
to form a centre for receiving funds. I suggest that each should

set out to raise £5 (one hundred friends giving one shilling or forty giving 2s 6d). I suggest £5; some might collect more and others less. Some of us could find friends and colleagues who again could be centres to collect £5 and so on. Two thousand £5 gifts would bring in £10,000. I cannot imagine anything more splendid than that we ourselves should be the means of contributing a substantial sum to the Building Fund. Will you all become enthusiasts and help?' A year later, somewhat crestfallen, she wrote that 'our Building Fund had been started at a bad time, just before this terrible trade depression, affecting rich and poor alike.' Only small sums had been received, amounting to £309, a far cry from the thousands needed. For the first and only time a note of dejection crept in when she admitted to 'many a despondent moment.'

It was a bad time to propagate any plans requiring money. Widespread unemployment, bitter disillusionment and dire economic depression had brought the country almost to its knees; within sight was the formation of the National Government one of whose first actions in dealing with the state of crisis was to make a clarion call for retrenchment. In response to this appeal to patriotism, Civil Servants and all whose emoluments were in any way the responsibility of the Government agreed to a so-called 'voluntary' cut in salaries, whose temporary nature slipped imperceptibly into the accepted norm.

Nevertheless the National, both suffering and being rebuked over the lack of space, was forced into action, bad time or no. Mr Bennett's plans had now risen to four storeys and thirty thousand pounds.

A review of the position in consultation with the London County Council was essential, but in subsequent meetings their Inspectors were adamant in support of Mr Gater's opinion that less room was needed for fewer teachers. The National in return pleaded the Hadow recommendations to raise the school-leaving age in 1931, which would necessitate at least as many teachers as at present, and reminded the Inspectors that the College had received no grant of any kind from the London County Council until 1919, although three quarters of the Council's Domestic Subjects teachers had been trained at the National. Finally Miss Sillitoe pressed that Domestic Subjects teachers should be considered for Headships of Schools. The London County Council then reverted to their previous statements. They endorsed the need for the extension of premises; indeed they wished to promote further developments of the Technical side, but on no consideration could they agree to rebuilding on a site where the lease ran for barely fifty years.

The new relationship with the London County Council created by the acceptance of grants carried an obligation to conform to the general direction of the Council, and the view now propounded seemed to offer the National, if the College were to survive and prosper, no alternative but to find another site with a considerably longer lease. In this predicament, even with no visible means of obtaining funds, the Committee decided to abandon Mr Bennett's plans for an extension, and bend all energies towards building a new College on a new site.

In June 1929 Sir Edwin Cooper Perry, who represented the University of London on the Executive Committee, proposed the transfer of the National to another site on the Grosvenor Estate, and at his instigation, Mr William Walford, of the firm of Perry and Walford, Architects and Surveyors, approached Miss Clarke to discuss ways and means. It was thought that if the existing College building in its valuable position could be exchanged for a less expensive site, a modern College might be erected 'at very little extra outlay of money.'

A Building sub-Committee was formed with Sir Cyril Cobb, Sir Cooper Perry and Mr Lesser, and in the same summer month Mr Walford was encouraged to proceed with searches, surveys and plans. It proved to be the beginning of nearly five years of discussion, thought, negotiation and frustration.

The new plans allowed for 50,000 square feet of floor space to provide ample accommodation for an Assembly Hall, Dining Hall, Library, Common Rooms and cloakrooms as well as Laboratories, Kitchens, larders, lecture and class rooms for greatly increased numbers of students, and a margin for even further expansion. The idea was attractive and tempting. It remained however to find both the site and they money.

A personal approach was advised to Mr Detmar Blow, the Grosvenor Estate Architect; it was also agreed to submit Mr Walford's plans to the Board of Education asking for assistance to implement them. Their reply stated that though unprepared

to give financial help, they might approve a 50 per cent reim-
bursement on a grant from the London County Council. The
conditions appeared complex; it was feared that the status of the
College might be altered, and the admission of students from
outside London jeopardised.

Sir Cyril Cobb reported that the London County Council
would be willing to allow a grant of £10,000 towards rebuilding,
with no supplementary grant for four years, which the Committee viewed as totally inadequate. Major Salmon proposed an
appeal to the City Parochial Charities, who had previously
helped with small gifts, to advance the required sum at low
interest rates, but this lay beyond their scope. The Restaurant
profits were gone; all that was left was the Building Fund.

Plans dropped into abeyance. There seemed no point in pursu-
ing designs and estimates and entering into negotiations for a
site, with no means of footing the bill.

Renewed pressure however came after the Visitation by the
Training Colleges Delegacy of the University of London in
March 1931. Favourably impressed by the tone and work of the
College, their Report also included some pertinent comments
concerning the organisation. Praising the freedom of the
students to control their own affairs and finances in the Students
Union, they drew attention to the position of the teaching staff
in having no share in the government of the College, recom-
mending that some means should be found to associate them
with this, and also that the Principal should have a seat, *ex
officio*, on the Executive Committee. Both these suggestions
were queried by the Committee and not pursued. Mrs Clarke
had been invited to join the Committee personally in 1912. She
had continued to attend the meetings for a couple of years after
her retirement, but the privilege had not been extended to her
daughter. The lack of close contact between the staff and the
Committee was always a matter for regret, and to some extent
prevented the co-operation which could have eased later
troubles.

But the immediate nub of the Report lay in the stark reminder
that new ideas and experimental work were heavily penalised in
the almost ludicrous inadequacy of the premises. Faced with
this statement and the continuously increasing pressure on
space, another review of the situation was held in December 1931.

The sub-Committee dismissed any idea of an extension as 'totally inadequate provision' and maintained that an alternative site on the Grosvenor Estate for a new College still seemed the only solution. Mr Welford, lately returned invigorated from a sea voyage, insisted that 'financial help would be attracted far more strongly to a definite plan for a new, up-to-date building, rather than for a makeshift conversion.'

Earlier, in 1930, Mr Detmar Blow had visited the National and admitted its needs, so it was felt that the ground was prepared. In a spirit of renewed confidence, the Committee decided to re-open talks with the Grosvenor Estate officials. A satisfactory interview immediately before Christmas 1931, even with the hint that negotiations 'would need to be most delicately handled' and that 'no financial concessions would be contemplated,' produced the belief that, on proper application, the Estate would be willing to arrange the exchange of the present building and site for another in a less valuable position. 'Thereby,' it was recorded, 'enabling the National to secure a new building, still within reasonable distance of Victoria Station, and with a minimum of disruption of teaching practice.'

By April 1932, with the necessary designs and drawings prepared, Mr Walford was authorised by the Committee to reopen negotiations with the Estate. Valuation of the lease of the National at £15,000 was regarded as a fair assessment, but events moved slowly. With the end of the year in sight, the Grosvenor Estate officials advised a different plan – to recondition the present building and erect a new block on a vacant site in Eccleston Street East, at the back of the College.

Once more all was in the melting pot. In spite of the continual setbacks, Miss Clarke wrote in the *Guild Magazine* at Christmas 1932, 'The actual date of the foundation of the National was on 17 July 1873' and she continued, 'I hope I am not too optimistic, but my thoughts often fix upon the laying of the Foundation Stone of a new College on 17 July 1933. Negotiations are going forward, and this makes me more hopeful than I have been for many years. Our own Building Fund now stands at £607 9s 6d.'

In March 1933, Miss Clarke's incurable optimism seemed no nearer fulfilment when Mr Walford produced a comprehensive report. He stated that if a new building on the existing site were carried up to the height needed to provide the required accommodation the National would be involved in serious difficulties regarding 'Ancient Lights' and that the College would have to close during the entire rebuilding, as to continue any form of practical work would be impossible.

He pointed out that the present total site was only 9,150 square feet with a floor space of 12,000 square feet, and that for some years the National had been forced to procure temporary accommodation outside the building on short tenancy agreements, always a costly arrangement. Detailed investigation had determined that a superficial floor space of about 39,000 square feet would be requisite, and it was estimated that for this purpose a site area of 15,000 square feet was desirable.

Shortly after this, Mr Walford reported that the Grosvenor Estate had indicated that a site of 8,755 square feet with a frontage of ninety feet to the southern side of Eccleston Street East, immediately behind the College, might be available. The ground rent was £750 per annum for a lease of ninety-nine years. It was at present let, but possession was possible within twelve months.

Further extension of this site was possible at an additional ground rent of £800 a year, if four houses with their gardens, numbers 49, 51, 53 and 55 in Ebury Street also became available, since the properties fronting on to Eccleston Street East and Ebury Street lay back to back, and could be connected

There were therefore two recommended propositions. Firstly to acquire the site in Eccleston Street East, build thereon and connect with the present College by a bridge crossing that street; for this the cost would be approximately £45,000. Secondly, both sites might be acquired, to give a total area of 16,000 square feet at a suggested ground rent of £1,600 per annum, and at an additional cost of £35,000 to £40,000, depending on the 'elaboration of the Frontage Design.'

By the second means, the National would acquire a new College of six storeys, with 'requisite light and air to all parties and owners concerned, and with facilities to add other storeys in the event of future development of the College.'

It seemed an exciting prospect fraught with interesting possibilities, but the total sum required was approximately £80,000. This would be substantially reduced by the exchange of sites and certain sales, but even with possible grants from the Board of Education and the London County Council, there was still a long way to go.

But now, for the remainder of the year 1933, the Grosvenor Estate officers brought all attempts at negotiation to a standstill. Personal approaches from Miss Clarke were acknowledged, but definite replies postponed; even letters sent by Special Messenger required to await an answer received the same fate.

Early in 1934, Major Salmon, now Sir Isidore, wrote to Sir Cyril Cobb that he felt it was useless to press for an interview with the Grosvenor representatives 'unless the way is clear on financing costs' and that 'the School must put up proposals to secure income to meet outgoings.' In March, Mr Walford said he had understood that the new accommodation would be adequate to produce the extra revenue to meet the rebuilding costs, but it now seemed that either a generous donor or substantial annual surplus income was essential. The first part of the scheme would cost £45,000 entailing a Sinking Fund of £2,500 a year.

Miss Clarke was appalled. She thought a 'possible extra income from students would be £950 a year.' Even with the release of the rented outside premises, such a charge as the one suggested could only be met, if no generous donor appeared, by 'increasing the Technical side far beyond the capacity for the new building.'

In December 1934 it was reported that the London County Council could not consider a capital grant large enough for a new building, and once more the Committee discussed the situation at length.

There seemed no means of raising sufficient money to meet the cost of a new College, and no means either of guaranteeing the annual heavy toll of mortgages and maintenance.

There was no generous 'millionaire with money to burn' for whom Miss Caddow had vainly sighed. The plans were still-born.

There was one more attempt to transfer the site of the National when in the following April 1935 Miss Clarke herself produced her own ideas for a new building outside London. She had gone into the possibilities very thoroughly, but by this time she was ill, and in a generally dispirited atmosphere over the premises, her suggestions were never considered.

Public Practice Kitchen, 1921

REVIVAL

CHAPTER XXXVI

AS THE NINETEEN-TWENTIES drew to a close, the very difficulties produced an upsurge of resilience, as if the staff and students were on their mettle to maintain high standards. Troubles over the premises were taken in their stride, and established traditions held good. The old feudal regime still existed, and was so firmly entrenched that it persisted until the Second World War. There was strict order of seniority, accepted as of right by both older and younger generations. A junior member of staff recalled without any rancour that she rarely had any tea, for it was unquestioningly assumed that she should make the toast for each senior member who came into the staff room.

Miss Clarke herself brooked no further question once her mind was made up, and for all her aesthetic susceptibilities, she could be a dictator if she wished. When a member of staff protested that she knew little about a subject which it had been decided to entrust to her, Miss Clarke merely drew herself up and replied 'You have enough intelligence to learn,' and there was nothing more to be said. Intuitive in her judgment, she backed her trust with loyalty but without favour; 'ever a believer in the loose rein,' as Miss Caddow wrote later, she never relinquished control, although insisting on individual responsibility.

Her attitude was reflected throughout the College and no slackness was tolerated. But the transformation of the course with its widening outlook encouraged a freedom in which staff and students alike revelled, creating an atmosphere of confidence and enjoyment. No longer was it a 'catastrophe' if the wrong dish were used; rigorous standards were still the order

201

of the day, though in paying tribute to the insistence on perfection a student added in delighted remembrance 'But I have never laughed so much.' Another recalled 'Everything had to be perfect, but it was always fun and never dreary.'

It was as if the National's ardour burnt with a particular radiance until the flame was temporarily snuffed out in the difficult years of the mid-thirties.

However acceptable the new approach was in general, the Committee did not find other ideas of change equally welcome. When in March 1929 Miss Clarke reported a proposal from the London Housecraft teachers that the name of the profession should be changed from Domestic Subjects to Home Economics, the members of the Executive felt this was going too far. They registered disapproval, decided not to take action, but 'to wait and see.' Perhaps they felt justified in this decision when over thirty years later they had still not been called upon for any further views.

More pleasing were the results of the new University of London examinations. Both in 1930 and 1931 the students acquitted themselves with credit, and the first group of Third Years in 1931 were awarded Distinctions in Cookery, Needlework and Dressmaking, and Teaching.

The more academic bias determined the Executive Committee, in May 1930, to form a Standing Education Committee, 'of not more than five persons, to consider and make recommendations on all educational purposes.' The University representative, Sir Cooper Perry, concerned for the interests of the staff, was informed that the latter were not represented on any sub-Committee. In pursuance of the question, the Committee finally agreed 'to consider the matter at some future date in the event of forming another sub-Committee,' and thus the issue was indefinitely postponed.

The first Education Committee consisted of the Chairman, Vice-Chairman, and Hon. Treasurer, *ex officio,* and four other members: Mr Dryhurst, shortly replaced by Miss Souter, Mr Lesser, Sir Cooper Perry and Miss Sillitoe, the latter losing no time in using her pertinacity and persuasion in negotiations with the University, particularly over the practical examinations.

There were bound to be teething troubles. The sample method of examination, which had aroused so much strong feeling at the National when first introduced in 1917, was now regarded with such favour that there was great concern when the University opposed the practice. The London Principals were not united in this view and in June 1931 Miss Clarke sent a Minority Resolution to the Examinations Council to ask for individual freedom for each College, but the plea was rejected. Still unconvinced, the Committee was strengthened in its views by the unanimous decision of the Principals outside London that the sample method should continue, and in February Miss Clarke wrote to the Senate to point out that as the Two-Year Course ended in July 1932, there would be no students in their final year until 1934, 'by which time the method of examination could be further discussed.'

In reply, the Vice-Chancellor invited the Chairman, Sir Cyril Cobb, to a meeting on 9 March 1932 'at which the Principal of the National Training College and the Principal of the University should both be present.' They were sympathetically received and the University conceded that the present sample method 'should continue for this year, subject to Delegacy approval.' The National got no further. On 14 March a letter from the Delegacy gave the desired permission for July 1932, 'provided the College definitely accepted the new policy in principle.'

Miss Clarke replied, at the direction of the Committee, that 'the Members cannot abandon the attitude they have adopted with regard to the principle of the method of examinations, as that would be to stultify all they have said on the respective merits of the two systems, based on experience and full consideration. On the other hand, they cannot expect the University to reverse their decision; therefore they will feel bound to accept the new policy in practice.' The letter concluded with a graceful expression of gratitude to the University 'for having so generously met us over the postponement of the new system for this year 1932.' The matter was closed. From 1934, every student took every practical test.

There were other problems to be resolved. The relationship and degree of responsibility as between the External and Internal Examiners called for diplomatic handling. The University appointed the former to work each year in turn with the individual member of the Training College staff nominated for the particular subject. Together they visited all the Colleges concerned, and their joint assessment of the students was submitted to an Independent Moderator, also chosen by the University, who judged a representative sample of theory papers. The final mark was agreed after any necessary discussion. At every point there was room for manoeuvre, and the eventual harmony and smooth running achieved was due largely to the readiness of everyone concerned to co-operate.

It was far less easy to deal with the position when at the final meeting of the Examiners the Principals were excluded. They at first resented being debarred from a share in the grading of their own students, but came to appreciate the University practice of limiting attendance at Examiners' Meetings to those members of staff academically responsible for the various subjects. This policy continued until after the Second World War when the organisation was changed by the establishment in 1948 of the London University Institute of Education.

Meantime there had been no reprieve over the Hostels. In 1925 Mrs Ward, anxious to realise capital, had asked the Committee to buy 35 Linden Gardens; but with the two Hostels separated at numbers 16 and 35, it was felt unwise to consider the purchase of either. Anxiety lest they should be forced to leave number 35 was eventually allayed when Mrs Ward agreed to continue the existing arrangement.

When, however, Lady Greenwood's house at number 33 came up for sale in 1929, the Committee felt that the chance of acquiring this adjoining property must be grasped, and Mr Lesser urged the purchase of number 35 at the same time. Lack of means prevented this, but a mortgage and a loan from the Bank enabled number 33 to be secured for £3,800 with a further £500 for conversion. Fortuitously the lease of number 16 Linden Gardens expired the following year in June 1930, so the Home Management Department was transferred to the new Hostel, with the London County Council promising £600 towards the equipment. Doors were cut in the party walls between the two houses and all the students were at last under one roof.

Mrs Ward died in the summer of 1931. The Committee decided

to reopen negotiations for the purchase of number 35 Linden Gardens, and in November the price of £4,686 was agreed. The property comprising the two connected houses, bought for a total of £8,486, was felt by the National to be a substantial asset, although the sum expended had made another hole in the exchequer.

But they were still short of accommodation, and thus at the same time were forced to negotiate for the lease of a maisonette in number 61 Linden Gardens, which was taken over in October 1931 at a rent of £175 per annum. This was regarded as particularly satisfactory, for the yearly expenditure was estimated at £428 and the income at £708, to give a balance of £280.

The demand was not yet satisfied, and in May 1933 the acquisition of another Hostel at Camden Hill, for an extra thirty-five students, was being considered. It proved unsuitable, but in November 1933, the suggestion of a house in Hampstead, number 19 Fitzjohn's Avenue, N.W.3, was felt to be worth pursuit. Further investigation revealed that the present tenant wished to leave and the owner was willing to assign the lease to the National. The furniture and fittings were bought for £1,600. In spite of its distance from Linden Gardens, the choice was approved, and Miss Caddow described the new Hostel as a charming house with a garden large enough for a tennis court. It was opened officially on 1 March by the Parliamentary Secretary to the Board of Education, who declared that 'the work of Domestic Subjects teachers could do more to improve the conditions of the country than any other form of education, a great deal of the social unrest and discomfort being due to mismanagement in the home.'

The flat at 61 Linden Gardens was given up during this Spring Term. Miss Hosegood, Senior Warden, became responsible for 19 Fitzjohn's Avenue, and after a brief interlude, Miss Haydon was appointed in July 1934 as Warden for the Linden Gardens Hostel.

The pressure on space in the main building in Buckingham Palace Road brought home the imperative need for extra outside accommodation. In particular the Needlework and Dressmaking classes were at full stretch and in the New Year of 1932 this Department for all the Training and Technical students was transferred to a first floor flat in Lower Belgrave Street. At a rent of £275 a year for five rooms and excellent lighting, they felt in clover, especially as the three years lease gave the right to the leads at the back, 'a boon during the summer months.'

This freed the Needlework Room in the College for a Lecture Room and Library, but could not satisfy the increasing demand for Technical classes. To provide for these, including an extra group of Housekeepers, other premises were acquired on a seven-year lease on the third floor above the Coastal Coach Station at the corner of Buckingham Palace Road and Elizabeth Street; in January 1933 a large up-to-date kitchen and a room equipped for Needlework and Upholstery were ready to receive Housekeepers, Cordon Bleu and Short Course Cookery students, about fifty in all. The cost of the adaptation was £700.

Satisfactory as these additions were, organisation inevitably became more difficult, and Miss Clarke, in querying whether 'the spirit of co-operation may suffer with so many students away from the main building' was underlining the ever increasing claims of a new College. As these hopes dimmed, the need for further reorganisation became apparent. Lower Belgrave Street no longer filled the bill, and early in 1934 the Committee discussed in detail the question of moving the Needlework Department to additional premises at the Coastal Chambers. Finally it was decided, in spite of the continued disadvantages of separated premises, to lease the second floor, comprising 2,300 square feet, at Allington House in nearby Allington Street, which seemed to offer good facilities for Needlework. The London County Council agreed a special capital grant of £1,750 to cover £1,000 for equipment and £750 towards the first year's rent of £1,000 per annum, exclusive of rates and heating. The lease of twenty-one years was terminable at five, seven or fourteen years.

Miss Clarke, still hoping that it was 'only a temporary arrange- . ment,' wrote that the new Department was 'a delight with its light and spacious rooms and up-to-date equipment and furniture,' while Miss Caddow stressed that it provided comfortable accommodation for all the classes, and paid tribute to Miss Howlett, who had succeeded Miss Wallbank in 1933 as Head of the Department, for her share in this work, as everything was 'extremely well planned and the decoration and lighting perfect.'

'A handsome gift' of cordless electric irons was given by the General Electric Company and the estimated cost of £728 for adaptation was exceeded by a few pounds only. The National took possession on 25 June 1935. Provision both for Hostels and classes was indeed spread, but it seemed the best that could be done.

The Secretarial side was temporarily steady and the cramped quarters improved. In 1932 Miss Caddow recorded that 'a new office has been constructed on the roof of the Staffroom, and is very light and well ventilated. Miss Garnham and Miss Graham are housed there, and we find the extra accommodation very useful.' After Miss Garnham and Miss Forbes both left in 1934, Miss Rennards was appointed as College Secretary, with Miss Russell and the Principal's private secretary, Miss Louie Ashford, to help. But the latter's retirement was due, and on 31 March 1936 a party was given for kindly plump Miss Ashford, with her flaxen head, who knew 'just about everything about everybody.' Her knowledge of the College ran even Miss Caddow's pretty close, for she had come as a young junior clerk in 1893, and the Executive Committee now showed the appreciation of her forty-three years of 'ungrudging service' with a cheque for £250. Other personal gifts from the Principal and the staff included another cheque and typewriter, an eiderdown and deck chair. But in spite of these lures Miss Ashford never lost one of her abiding interests, the performance of *Hiawatha* at the Royal Albert Hall where every year she sang in the choir, 'made up all brown,' as she used to declare, and 'wearing a string of beads.'

Punch Almanack

REVIVAL

CHAPTER XXXVII

THE YEAR 1934 was heralded on Monday, 1 January, by a Refresher Course attended by forty-six students, 'of all ages and at all stages,' who packed into the days, and also many evenings, practical work, lectures, demonstrations and entertainments until Tuesday, 9 January. It was the year chosen to commemorate the Diamond Jubilee, and to signalise the occasion, the Executive Committee decided to award two full three-year scholarships, one to a student beginning her Teacher Training Course in September 1934, and another, particularly to honour the Silver Jubilee of the National's Patron, His Majesty King George V, to a student beginning her course in September 1935. Both were to be designated Diamond Jubilee Scholarships.

Celebrations were not confined to any particular dates, as with the Golden Jubilee. In April 1934 the staff of the College raised and invested a small sum of money to provide an annual prize for craftsmanship, a Book Token valued at one guinea, to be given alternately to a Training and a Technical student. The staff also presented the Principal at a teaparty on 17 April with a platinum and diamond brooch, bearing the College Arms in enamel, and the dates 1874–1934 in diamonds, together with an engraved panel of their names.

A few days later, on 20 April, the College students organised a Ball at Chiltern Hall, Baker Street, where two hundred and seventy guests were received by the Chairman of the Executive Committee, Mrs Karslake, with Mr Buckmaster, Mr Lesser, Sir Isidore Salmon and the Principal. Dancing was from 9 pm to 2 am, and it was recorded that 'at supper there were three high

209

tables. At the centre table were the Governors, the Principal, H.M.I. Miss McCall, Lady Salmon and two senior members of staff; at the other tables were the staff and senior students with their parties.'

About this time the Executive Committee was sometimes referred to as the 'Governing Body,' and the members of the Committee loosely termed the 'Governors.' Gradually, as time passed and the practice continued, the different name became generally accepted, although to the end of the National's life, the 'Governing Body' remained legally registered under the title of 'Executive Committee.'

Jubilee celebrations continued into the following year, culminating on 10 and 11 April 1935 in an Exhibition which was visited by over two thousand people, among them many of eminence in the educational world. The keynote of the Exhibition was the progress of Domestic Subjects through the past sixty years, illustrating the changing methods and equipment, as well as the materials and fashions, including the students' original uniform.

It was evidence of a gallant effort on the part of Miss Clarke and her staff. In the Autumn of 1934 she had had a serious operation, and although she returned to duty in January 1935 a series of misadventures prevented her from fulfilling all her duties. During her absence Miss Underhill, who had succeeded Miss Eckford as Head of the Cookery Department in 1930, was in charge, but in the summer the Committee decided to appoint a Vice-Principal, and Mrs Hutchinson was invited to fill this post from 1 July 1935. It was a popular appointment, for Mrs Hutchinson possessed humanity and understanding in a rare degree, qualities needed in the increasingly difficult situation. It restored confidence, too, for Miss Clarke's health continued to cause concern, which inevitably diminished much of the general zest.

At the Guild Reunion on 18 October Miss Clarke returned briefly to greet a large gathering. 'We were very glad,' Miss Challen wrote, 'that Miss Clarke was able to receive us and give her customary address on the College activities of the year.' Work continued under the cloud of her illness and in May 1936 Mrs Hutchinson was appointed Acting Principal. Although

both the Committee and the London County Council were united
in their offer to grant a further six months leave of absence, Miss
Clarke offered her resignation as from 30 September. The Committee accepted it on 22 June 'with the very deepest regret,' and
continued: 'The Executive wish to place on record their great
admiration for the years of service Miss Clarke has given to the
College. This being an inherited tradition from her Mother,
they realise how difficult it will be to replace her in any way.'
A month later, on 22 July 1936, she died at home in the charming
thatched cottage which she shared with Miss Caddow and Miss
Rind at Finchampstead, Berkshire.

   The year 1936 was a sad one for the country as a whole, and for
the National in particular. Beginning with the death of His
Majesty King George V in January, the College not only shared
the nation's sorrow, but also lost its 'beloved King and Patron.'
In Miss Clarke's death in July it lost its visionary Principal.
When Miss Helen Sillitoe died on 17 September, an irreplace-
able friend and supporter had gone. Finally on 23 September
Edwin Sheldrake died, the unforgettable loyal commissionaire.
   There were many tributes to Miss Clarke. She was acclaimed
in the educational world as a practical idealist with a keen mind.
Never so robust as Mrs Clarke, her distinguished mother, she
was emotional yet unexpectedly tough. Many acts of personal
kindness have been recorded by individual students, and where
much was at stake, her sympathetic interviewing was remarked
on. The student who was awarded the Diamond Jubilee Scholarship for 1935 remembers:
   'I found her resting on a couch, looking tired and old, but she
smiled at me, held out her hand, and made me feel at ease while
she questioned me.
   'I have thought many times since of the effort that must have
been required from someone mortally ill, to appear so genuinely
interested in what a young student had to say, and it was a
measure of her kindness that must have prompted her to ensure
that the letter containing the unexpected and pleasant news of
the conferring of the scholarship, was posted to arrive at home
on Christmas morning, thus making the day a doubly happy
one for us.'

Another tribute from a student training in 1921 gives a revealing picture of the contrasting sides of her character. The student was 'worried and exhausted' shortly before her Finals, and recalls: 'One day Miss Clarke sent for me during one of Miss Rotheram's demonstrations. I went in fear and trembling, wondering what I had done, but after a very kindly greeting she said, to my astonishment, 'We think perhaps a fortnight at Herne Bay with an old Cordon Bleu who has a boarding house on the seafront would do you good,' and then 'Of course you would go at our expense.' As I was still dumbfounded with surprise, she added encouragingly, 'You could have the same room that I have when I stay there.' All was arranged, and the student was told to call at the office for a sealed envelope – 'When I opened it, it contained notes covering all my expenses for the fortnight, including pocket money. It was an astonishingly generous gift.' The holiday was 'a supreme joy,' and had the desired effect in that she duly achieved her Diploma. Later she tasted Miss Clarke's astringency. 'She could be very forthright when occasion required; feeling greatly discouraged in my first post, I wrote to Miss Clarke expecting sympathy, and instead received the reply "Don't be so chicken hearted. You should be glad you have been given a job straight away. Some students are still looking for one." It was just the tonic I needed, and did me good.'

Perhaps the last word should rest with Miss Caddow, faithful recorder and intimate friend for nearly forty years. In the *Guild Magazine* Miss Caddow wrote, 'Miss Clarke was singularly gifted: she had an original intuitive brain; great powers of organisation from broad outline to minute detail; she was practical, yet artistic; simple, yet deeply wise; acutely sensitive but courageous; and she had inspiration which quickly fired those with whom she worked. She had a marvellous gift for friendship, a deep love of music, of children, of birds and flowers. Her speaking and singing voice had a particularly beautiful quality, the remembrance of which will always remain to those of us who knew her best.

'Above all, she possessed a deep and true religion. The message she sent to us all last year "Be strong and of a good courage" is her message still.'

It was indeed the end of an era. The family régime was over, and at first it could hardly be realised. Miss Caddow left the National shortly after, and the small private apartments which she had shared with Miss Clarke were altered and redecorated. One became the Principal's sitting room and the Vice-Principal's office, and the other was fitted up as a Science Lecture room to relieve the overcrowding of the Laboratory next to it.

The College had been Miss Caddow's home since the beginning of the century, and to her now fell the onerous task of clearing the accumulated possessions and papers and letters dating back to the early days. It was essentially a personal affair, and the sorting and reading of this mass of material, involving much of purely private concern, as well as taking the ultimate decision on its disposal, must often have been painful and certainly difficult, to achieve single handed. Over long periods she returned to toil daily, and her mammoth task was barely ended in 1938 when the threat of another World War and the approach of the Munich crisis claimed all attention.

In the ensuing preparations for possible evacuation, and the final urgent plans to meet the climax on 3 September 1939 when the Second World War was declared, it was not easy to keep records of the storage of multifarious possessions. By the end of War, it was even more difficult to trace them. Enemy action everywhere took its toll; in some cases records were overlaid; in others, memories were faulty or those who knew the answers were no longer alive. For many of the National's affairs Miss Caddow held the key, and it was only long after her death in 1953 that it was realised how much information had died with her. At the close of the College, when records proved untraceable and meagre, there was no Miss Caddow to fill the gaps with her prodigious memory.

Although no longer an integral part of the College life, she kept in close contact, always remaining Vice President of the Guild. She took an active share in the consideration as to the best use of the legacies from Miss Clarke and Miss Sillitoe, although ultimate decisions were perforce indefinitely postponed by the intervention of the War. The latter bequeathed to the National the sum of £200 in addition to one fifth of the residue of her estate, which proved eventually to total over £1,100.

Miss Clarke left to the College her copyrights, the proceeds to be used for social activities of the staff and students. She desired that the senior staff should keep her books up to date. One hundred and eighty-two books belonging to Miss Clarke and Miss Caddow were presented to the College Library. Miss Caddow resigned the Editorship of the *Guild Magazine*, and from henceforth her vivid and witty comments no longer illuminated the pages of 'College and Staff News.'

At the close of the sorrowful year of 1936, the retirement in December of H.M.I. Miss McCall left another void. The College had found her a tower of strength, and in the eleven years since she had followed Miss Sillitoe she had earned affection, respect and total trust. Impressive in person and knowledge, her domination could strike awe and even terror into the hearts of many who met her professionally. Her standards were almost unattainably high and she tolerated nothing slipshod or indolent; but where encouragement, support and practical help were genuinely needed, she spared no pains, and her strong character could lift an individual or a situation through a period of crisis. It was her truthful, clear headed judgment allied to positive action which made 'the great Miss McCall' so universally admired, but it was her loyalty, shrewd understanding and generous sympathy, not readily revealed, that made her loved. Recognition of these traits prompted Miss Eland's statement that 'personal experience at the Board of Education had shown her that Miss McCall's wisdom and humanity made her the first to be sought in times of trouble.' Under her authoritarian air, an innate humbleness manifested itself in the declaration of her cardinal belief that 'it is not the holder of an office, but the office itself' which commands respect.

Fortunately for the National, she agreed to join the Executive Committee and gave ungrudgingly of her thought and time to the problems which beset the College throughout the Second War.

REVIVAL

THE NATIONAL had now, in 1936, to set out on a new road to suit the changing times. There had been recent changes in the staff on whom heavy demands had been made following the University regulations which involved Heads of Departments for all subjects acting as Internal or External Examiners.

Miss Underhill retired in 1935. In 1930 she had handed over her domain of the Public Demonstrations to Miss Challen, a skilled craftswoman who had lately trained at the National and was already a member of staff. Miss Underhill then temporarily succeeded Miss Eckford, now retired, as Head of the Training Kitchen. Miss Eckford and Miss Underhill had been sltawart members of the staff since 1900 and 1902 respectively, and through the years had carried many posts of responsibility. Miss Challen shortly left for a year's exchange in South Africa, and on her return in 1933, at Miss Underhill's own wish, Miss Challen became Head of the Cookery Training side, thus enabling Miss Underhill, who gloried in her relations with the public, once again to enjoy the Public Demonstrations until her retirement.

Miss Challen was ably assisted by Miss Florence Watson, lately in charge of Cookery at Edinburgh, and by Miss Georgina Knight, a recent student who gave her gay and versatile services to the College at intervals during marriage for many years. When Miss Underhill, in 1935, relinquished the Public Demonstrations with her adoring audiences, Miss J. N. Edward succeeded in this field. She had taken her High Class Cookery Diploma at the National in 1929, joined the staff in 1932; deputised for Miss Challen during the latter's absence abroad, and now with marked success, took the responsibility for the Public Demonstrations.

Miss Edward's appointment to the staff was to prove one of the most far reaching in the history of the College. A Scot of impeccable standards and principles, she was both astute and farseeing, and to the end of the National's life she remained one of its finest exponents, unstinted in devotion and generosity.

Another Scot, Miss Mary Swanston, came to help Miss Underhill in 1930. Even tempered and philosophical, with a fund of knowledge and common sense, Miss Swanston had a lasting influence on staff and students alike; always ready to listen, and with her pawky humour, to give stimulating yet acceptable advice.

In 1929 Miss Walker Jones had succeeded Miss FitzGerald on her retirement, and Miss Woodham arrived to assist on the Technical side with the Housekeepers' and Brides' Courses, remaining in charge when Miss Walker Jones left in 1933. There was ever increasing demand for these courses, and in 1935 Miss H. M. McIntyre joined the Cookery team at the Coastal Chambers where the classes were full to capacity.

Needlework and Dressmaking were thriving under the leadership of Miss D. M. Howlett, whose skill and liberal outlook brought a new challenge. It had been sad to part with Miss Wallbank, 'one of the outstanding people whom it is impossible to replace,' when she retired in 1933, after twenty years of 'wonderful service.'

There was reorganisation in the Home Management Department which since 1934 had been in the charge of Miss Dumas and Miss Cottrell. Miss Patience Dumas, B.Sc., who first came to assist in the Science Department in 1928, was inescapably claimed by reason of her ability and clear mind to answer a variety of calls. When Miss Eland, as Head of the Home Management Department, joined the Board of Education in 1931, she was succeeded by Miss D. K. McCracken, who reluctantly left the sphere of Dressmaking as Miss Wallbank's assistant. An inspired decision resulted in Miss Dumas coming to help. With many tastes in common, including enjoyment of the quirks and vagaries of life, it proved an appreciative and happy partnership. Miss Dumas became the right hand undertaking in particular the essential scientific side of the training. Miss McCracken resigned shortly after her marriage to Mr B. G. Stone towards the end of 1933, and it was on Miss Dumas that responsibility for the Department fell in the summer of 1934. Miss Gertrude Cottrell joined her and they worked together until Miss Cottrell was appointed Head of the Home Management in April 1935. When Miss Kennett came to assist Miss Cottrell, Miss Dumas was realeased to devote her talents to the Science Department. But the names of Miss Dumas and Miss Cottrell are inseparably linked in the records of Home Management, for they were soon to join forces and make history during the years of evacuation at Torquay.

Miss Lancaster ruled in the Laundry, and Dr Lawrence held sway in the Department of English and Psychology. Responsibility for the complicated organisation and myriad problems connected with the teaching of 'Method,' involving children's classes and teaching practice in all subjects, was shared by Mrs Hutchinson and Miss Lough. But with the recent claims on Mrs Hutchinson consequent on Miss Clarke's illness and death, the enormous spread of the work had devolved on Miss Lough, who shouldered the burden, as she did many others, with a complete grasp of the situation, imparting a feeling of confidence and stability – no mean feat in those days of insecurity.

The Governing Body had suffered some changes. The President, Lord Burnham, had died in 1933, and this office fell temporarily into abeyance. The Vice Presidents also were depleted by the loss of Sir Almeric FitzRoy, Sir Guy Sebright and Mrs Walter Ward, who had died, and of Lady Cooper who now had too much else to do. On the Executive side there was no longer either Lady Baring or Lady Denham. Some of the gaps were filled by Mr Abady, J.P., Miss Boulton, H.M.I. (retired) and Miss Margaret Jones, O.B.E., L.C.C. Inspector (retired) and an old student of the National.

The Chairman, Sir Cyril Cobb, resigned in 1937, shortly before his death the following year, and Sir Isidore Salmon thenceforth carried the Chairmanship up to the early years of the War. There was personal sadness when Lady Baring, Vice Chairman for the past eleven years, died in June 1934. She had served on the Committee since 1907, and to exceptional administrative ability she allied 'never failing help and sympathy' with charm of personality. Her place was taken by Mrs Karslake, who had already been a Committee member since 1919.

In 1936, both Lady Max-Muller and Miss Reynard, Warden of King's College of Household Science, were welcomed as new members of the Committee. The former had long been sought, and she now began a span of twenty-two years of energetic interest.

But there had been one outstanding joyous event among the shifting sands, when on 29 May 1934 the National had the pleasure of entertaining at tea Mr and Mrs Charles Buckmaster, and their eldest daughter Ursula, a former student, to celebrate Mr Buckmaster's eightieth birthday. With a personal gift went a framed and illuminated address in recognition of his staunch friendship and constant care for the College for nearly twenty years, which he was to continue, with apparently undiminished vigour, to give in all, thirty-three years of devoted work as Honorary Treasurer.

When the members of the Executive Committee in June 1936 accepted Miss Clarke's resignation, they knew full well, as they recorded in the Official Minutes, how extremely difficult it would be to replace her. They therefore gave particularly heartfelt thanks when, on 19 October 1936, Miss Grace M. Eland accepted the post of Principal. In her many contacts with the National, including her time as Senior Student and later as Head of the Home Management Department, she had always been held in high repute. A devout churchwoman, a most able teacher and administrator, it was felt that her abilities and integrity marked her out for this high position, and with her deep voice and rather grave manner she was a commanding figure. There was double rejoicing when the Ministry of Education agreed to release her from her post as His Majesty's Inspector of Schools, to enable her to take up her duties at the College in January 1937. Her salary scale, as Principal, was agreed by the Board of Education at £640, rising by £25 to £750 a year.

Among the early events of Miss Eland's Principalship the most auspicious was the agreement of Her Majesty Queen Elizabeth to continue the Royal Patronage of the College by becoming its Patron in 1937, after His Majesty King George VI had succeeded to the throne. This honour was to prove one of the

Miss Grace M. Eland, O.B.E., 1946
Principal 1937 – 1957

happiest of the National's connections. Her Majesty's interest and sympathetic understanding were an unfailing support for the next twenty-five years, and extended beyond the life of the College to encourage the Educational Trust which was later formed to perpetuate the spirit of the pioneer founders.

The happiness occasioned by this Patronage comforted the National and heartened everyone to deal with the wrack left by the ebb of Miss Clarke's life. On all sides there was much to do, but the loyalty and steadiness of the staff did much to mitigate the labours. A critical review of the work was essential. At the first Executive Committee Meeting which Miss Eland attended on 18 January 1937, the Report of the London University Visitation of 1936, referring to some 'excellent work,' was received with considerable satisfaction. But Lady Max-Muller, who had joined the Committee the previous November, had some strictures to make over certain cakes displayed at the Annual Cake Show on 17 December 1936. She felt 'there was room for improvement,' and pressed for the engagement of a first class chef 'to give lectures, demonstrate and criticise,' concentrating on the Advanced and Cordon Bleu courses.

The matter was taken up seriously, and on 24 May 1937 the Committee authorised the expenditure of from three to five guineas for a chef to come once or twice a term, leaving the matter in the hands of the Principal. Lady Max-Muller was indefatigable in pursuit of her aim, and through her intervention, Miss Eland reported in June that Mr Edward Hulton had very kindly given £200 to be spent at the Principal's discretion, in consultation with Lady Max-Muller, 'to raise the standard of Cookery at the College.' In grateful acceptance of this unexpected gift, it was agreed to name it the 'Edward Hulton Grant.' In spite of all the enticements, the quest for the master chef proved vain. History did not repeat itself, and this time there was no Herman Senn to come to the rescue and bully or cajole.

Two years later, in February 1939, Miss Eland at last announced the 'engagement of a chef to demonstrate to the staff and some of the students,' but events were catching up with them and before any results were possible, the National was plunged, with all the country, into the Second World War.

Towards the end of May 1937, Mrs Hutchinson formally

resigned as Vice-Principal and a farewell party was given for her on 15 December. Among the gifts presented by staff and students were a set of silver soup bowls, a silver coffee pot, jug and sugar basin, and a Sheffield plate coffee tray. These were some of the tangible tokens of affection and esteem, for her retirement was felt as a personal loss. In a delightful 'Appreciation' in the *Guild Magazine*, a vivid pen picture is drawn. Emphasising her consideration of individual needs and points of view, it stresses her essentially personal approach. Small, neat and precise, she was also 'the enemy of dull routine,' a 'lover of gay, pretty and growing things,' and 'would relieve a sober discussion by adjusting perhaps a misplaced flower in a bowl, or a crooked rug.' This same personal interest allowed her to discern capabilities and cherish a good idea; with quick reactions 'of varied mood,' she was courteous and tactful. Gratitude for her services to the National, during eighteen years as Mistress of Method, Vice-Principal and Acting Principal, 'was placed on record in the books of the Association, with their deep appreciation by the members of the Executive Committee.'

At the Committee in July 1937, the question of the post of Vice-Principal was seriously canvassed. Miss Eland pointed out that the administrative work was necessarily at a stage of transition, and that as the Principal no longer resided on the premises the domestic side also needed adjustment. She suggested that before making any appointment time should be given to consider general reorganisation. The wisdom of this course was immediately apparent, and the Committee agreed to postpone the matter until later in the year.

A month earlier, in June 1937, a new regime had begun in the secretarial department when Miss Rennards left with two juniors, and in her place Miss J. E. Taylor was appointed as College Secretary. It was the beginning of a long, unbroken tenure of this office, for Miss Taylor, impervious to the pressures of life, remained at the National for the next twenty-five years, creating an atmosphere of charm and leisure.

Reorganisation was certainly called for, since as well as the loss of Miss Caddow and Mrs Hutchinson, there were other moves pending, and the year 1938 saw several changes on the staff. Miss Challen left to take charge of the Women's Department at Wolverhampton Technical College. Miss Watson followed her at the National as Head of the Training side, with Miss Edward as first assistant. Her place in the Public Demonstrations was taken by Miss King; Miss Crawford, famed for her delicacy of touch in craftsmanship, joined the Cookery staff. Miss Duckworth, who became Mrs Walsh, brought her flair for the work to enhance the Needlework and Dressmaking Department, and Miss F. N. Clarke, as 'Lady Housekeeper,' came to relieve Miss Ker of some of the responsibilities of the domestic side. Miss Joan Ker, a skilled Cordon Bleu, came after the First War to carry singlehanded for many years the responsible and arduous post of Storekeeper. Her well-stocked, orderly storeroom tucked away in the basement could always fulfil any demand, no matter how sudden or extraordinary. This however was but a part of her wide duties. She was responsible not only for the proper ordering and distribution of stores for all the Cookery classes, but also for catering for the endless meals and snacks served daily to the students, the teaching staff and the array of domestic helpers, allocating every scrap of food cooked in every kitchen. Any superfluous dishes were sold each afternoon to an avid public. Miss Ker, zealous in these multifarious charges, certainly stood in need of regular assistance.

There were Hostel changes too, for Miss Hosegood resigned in the Spring of 1938. After her long and devoted Wardenship of the Hostels, both at Linden Gardens and Fitzjohn's Avenue, many good wishes went with her in her venture as 'Domestic Consultant.' She was followed at Hampstead by Miss Mercier, while Miss Haydon, loyally supported by Miss O'Keeffe, continued at Linden Gardens.

The new Vice-Principal, Miss I. H. Bewick, came in the summer of 1938. A Cambridge graduate and former Vice-Principal of the recently closed Peterborough Training College, she had both wide experience and farseeing interest in students, who sat at her feet during her talented and entertaining lectures. Later, in Torquay, she opened vistas of other worlds with her wit, vivacity and jewellery during the years of austerity in the Second World War. Administration was not really her sphere; she and the Principal were poles apart, and in 1945 she bade farewell and returned eventually to her much loved Cambridge, shedding her brilliance meantime on another adoring set of pupils.

As well as the new disposition of staff, there were alterations in the premises, particularly in the main building. In addition to the changes in Miss Clarke's and Miss Caddow's quarters, a former maid's bedroom on the top floor was converted into an office for Miss Graham, thus releasing her old office above the Staff Room for assistant secretaries. The dismantling of the old Children's Flat provided lecture rooms for Education, English and Elocution; much needed alternatives to the Library. Many improvements were made in the Laundry, including, as the *Guild Magazine* recorded in 1938, 'well planned cupboards, and new and ingenious equipment,' describing some of the latter as 'wringers that close down into tables, extra sinks fitted with hot and cold water, and a new kind of iron that gives out steam from the point, thus damping the clothes before they are ironed.'

Such improvements seemed a superficial scratching of the surface compared with the basic problem, and in spite of all efforts, the question of the premises remained.

In February 1938, the Education Officer and other officials of the London County Council had visited and been 'very impressed with the way the Departments were run; they realised more than before the need for a new building,' but there came also a letter regretting that 'no capital grant for re-building can be recommended during 1938–1941.'

A Full Inspection by the Board of Education followed in October 1938. In their Report they paid tribute to every department, stating that the students were fortunate in the keen and cultured group of lecturers who 'encouraged independent thought.' But they emphasised that in such restricted and inadequate premises good work could only be achieved under considerable strain. They urged the necessity for peace and quiet for reading and private study, and warned that to maintain the National's high reputation and continue to attract the best material, its amenities must be worthy of the content of the training.

The College was commended for the range of courses undertaken at the request of Government Departments, among them the Army, the Navy and the Hospitals, including a valuable course in Sick-room Cookery, followed by examinations, which had started at Guy's Hospital in 1931. Praise was meted out to the 'overburdened, self-sacrificing' members of both Training and Technical staff, who achieved high standards while often carrying the additional burden of separation from the main College.

The expense of these far-flung departments was a matter of concern. The total of these rents in 1937–1938 amounted to £1,973; 'two thousand pounds as near as makes no matter, annually down the drain,' was one pungent comment.

It all added up to the same tale, the crying need for a new College, with all departments under the same roof. Every official report for the past twenty years had emphasised the urgency, but this was not the moment in time when plans for any building could even be contemplated.

The College had returned as usual to begin the Autumn Term in September 1938, only 'to be scattered to the four winds' as Miss Eland wrote in her Guild letter of November, under the threat of War. Already by June 1938 preparations for possible evacuation had been well in hand, but even in August it was devoutly hoped that these plans, involving endless consultations and journeys, need never materialise.

For those in charge of Colleges and young students, however, the Munich crisis allowed no risks to be taken, and the National was temporarily closed. Returning with many others in similar plight after the immediate danger was averted in October, there was a general desire to clutch at the 'peace in our time' promised in the 'scrap of paper' signed by Hitler and Neville Chamberlain. The latter's 'Out of this nettle, danger, we pluck this flower, safety,' was on everyone's lips, and a vast majority grasped at the proferred reprieve.

The nervous tension of this national crisis took its toll, and settling into routine and hard work was not helped by finding the road outside the College in process of being dug up. It was something of an anticlimax to discover that these excavations were totally unconnected with the Air Raid Precautions immediately surmised and merely part of ordinary road repairs. But no matter what the cause, the noise and dirt were the same, and it seemed hard that the first Full Inspection of the Board of Education for thirteen years should coincide with such an upheaval. Miss Eland wrote that H.M. Inspectors 'were most sympathetic and understanding, but we were a little sorry that lectures in the Library and both Science rooms had to be delivered to the full accompaniment of electric drills.' Nevertheless, as already stated, the ensuing Report was both appreciative and encouraging.

Definite plans had now to be worked out in detail, to be put into immediate effect in case of war. In March 1939 Miss Eland and Mrs Karslake represented the National at a Conference sought by the Training College Principals who, concerned to safeguard the interests of the training courses in particular, decided to discuss the problems involved. The Board of Education had their own lists of possible reception areas, where Local Authorities and institutions were approached with a view of requisition or sharing of premises and resources in the event of emergency. The magnitude of the task taxed some of the most able and resolute in the country, but eventually a scheme so detailed and comprehensive was evolved that order, systematic though flexible, emerged from what might have been chaos.

Each Training College was given a certain individual responsibility over the investigation of premises, and Miss Eland, sometimes accompanied by a member of the Committee or the Board of Education, went far and wide to view possible homes for the National classes and Hostels. It was irksome and time consuming, but Miss Eland's deep sense of duty would not permit her to impose extra burdens on others, though the help, during these trips, of an experienced Hostel Warden could have both lightened her labours and shortened her journeys.

The final decision lay with the Board of Education, and on 19 June 1939 the Executive Committee learnt that 'arrangements had been made whereby it was hoped that the National Training College would be accommodated at the South Devon Technical College, Torquay, for classes during a national emergency.'

Details of 'billet fees,' the contribution expected from parents if they agreed to their daughters going to Torquay, and any guide as to the general cost involved, had still all to be worked out.

Time was short, even shorter than they knew. In July a letter was sent out to all parents, asking for their decision should the College move to Torquay; assurance was given that 'residential grants would be paid by the Board of Education to recognised day students who become residents,' but no information was available as to the cost of billets, 'though in due course no doubt the figure will be fixed by the Government.' It was in October 1939, when all the students were already installed, that it was announced that 'the billeting fees of students have been provisionally fixed at 30s a week plus the usual College charge for lunches.'

Early in the year 1939 both Mr Lesser and Sir Cooper Perry had died, and their loss was keenly felt. Mr Guy Thorold now joined the Committee, and gave his able services for another twenty years.

Miss Janie Clark, skilled member of the staff since 1908, hot tempered, obstinate and staunch as ever, left also in 1939, to enjoy well earned retirement; Miss Quick endeared by both her personal and professional qualities agreed to stay on for another year, and at the same time Miss Margaret Breukelman, another excellent craftswoman, joined the staff to add her gifts to the Needlework team.

Only a few who had known the College in the nineteen twenties now remained, to work under strange conditions with a different staff, but still zealous to maintain standards in a changing world. The buildings were inadequate; there were no funds in the Exchequer to meet the inevitable and increasing demands and to carry the burden of accumulating debt.

As the holocaust of the Second War threatened to engulf the world, the National had reached a watershed.

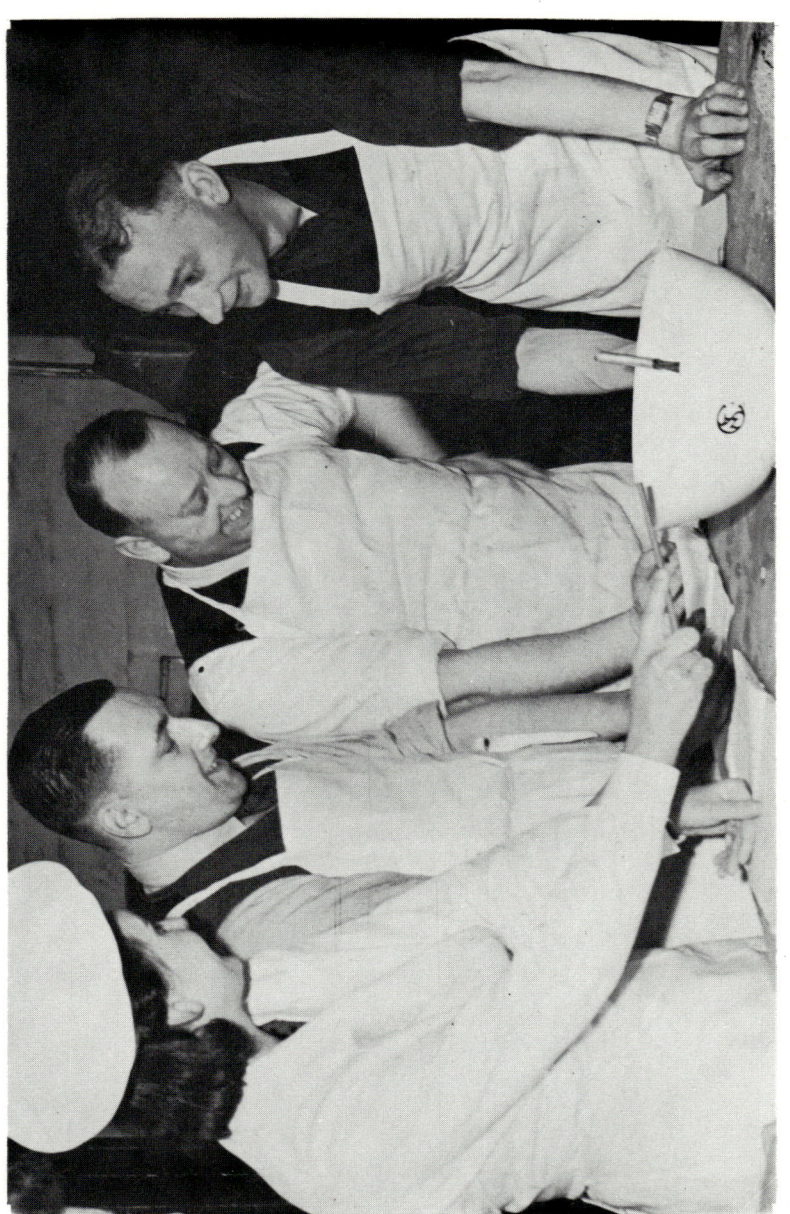

The Afternoon Session was fairly lively!

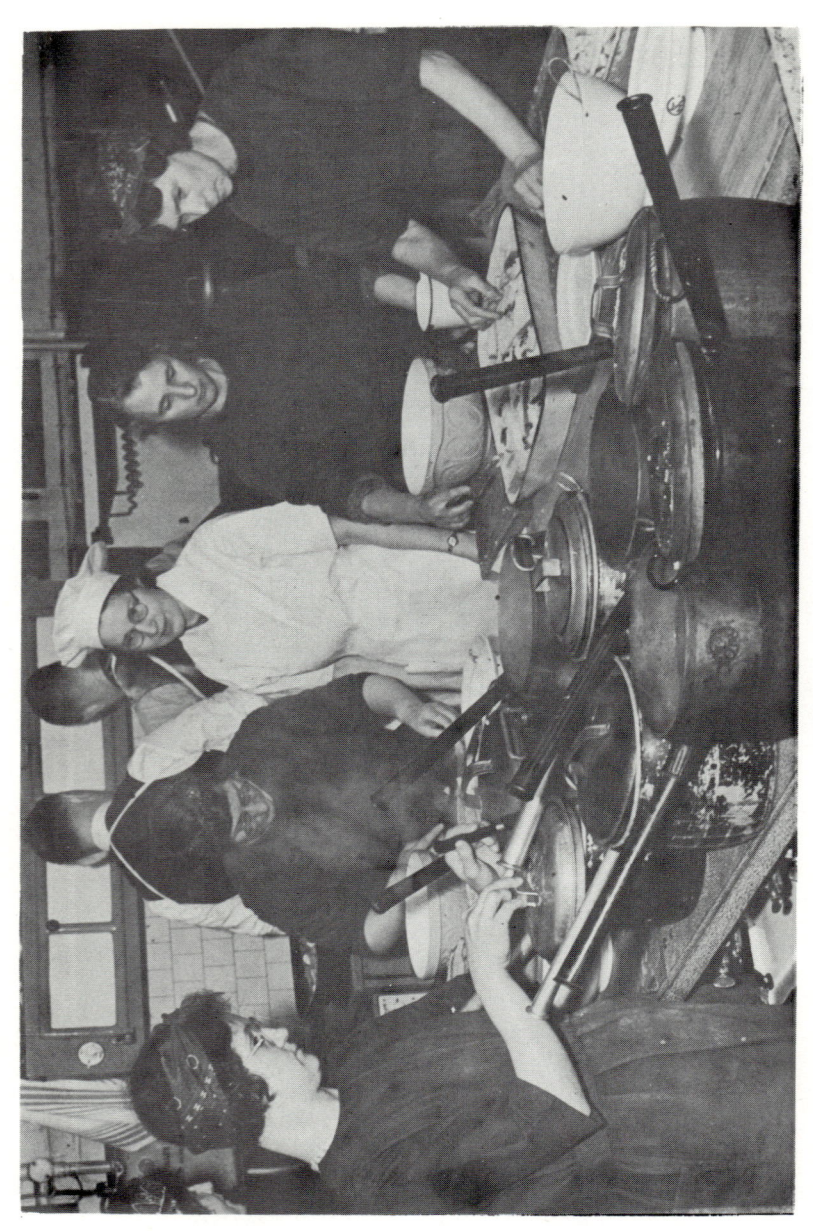

Canteen Cooks, 1943

WAR

CHAPTER XXXIX

WHEN THE ANNOUNCEMENT OF WAR was made at 11 o'clock on Sunday, 3 September 1939, the National had moved to Torquay. So much forethought had gone into this tremendous undertaking that Miss Eland was able to write 'When War was imminent, some of the staff joined me at Torquay, and together we found billets for staff and students, and worked out a new time table.' Students began to arrive on that bright sunny September Sunday, within hours of the Declaration. 'Perhaps not many educational establishments in exile began the Autumn term on the opening day appointed long before,' it was recorded, 'but the National was among the few that did,' and on 13 September, there were 191 students, soon rising to 200. Of these, 141 were on the Training side, including the Bristol Degree and Continuous Third Year students; the remainder were Technical students preparaing for the Cordon Bleu, Short Course Cookery, Needlework Diploma and Housekeeper's Certificate examinations. Only a handful were day students, nearly everyone living either in Hostels or in billets supervised by the College.

It had always been expected that the main building in London would be snapped up quickly for Government purposes, but 'events,' wrote Miss Eland in her first *Wartime Letter* of March 1940, 'have proved to be quite different from our anticipations. Miss Taylor, the College Secretary, has been on duty at 72–78 Buckingham Palace Road, and is still there, but all through the autumn of 1939 the building stood empty and desolate except when processions of furniture removers passed in and out loading lorries with gas cookers, laundrywork and cookery equipment, books, office files, stationery, etc. to be transported to

229

Torquay, or alternatively unloading equipment brought from Coastal Chambers and Allington House to be stored in College, both these outside premises having been vacated "for the duration".'

This had resulted from the decision of the Executive Committee at their first meeting of the War, held at the Trocadero Hotel, London, on 18 October 1939. With Sir Isidore Salmon in the Chair, there were ten other members; apologies being received from Lady Max-Muller, Miss Reynard and Professor Mottram. It later proved impossible for the two latter members to attend at all during the War, but they were not replaced until September 1945, when Miss Proctor, M.B., Ch.B. and Miss Dent joined in their stead.

Sir Isidore was deeply concerned about the financial position of the National on evacuation to Torquay. He had personally consulted both the President of the Board of Education and the Education Officer of the London County Council, who were unable to give any extra help. As long ago as 1931, Miss Sillitoe, during discussions with the London County Council, had drawn attention to the anomalous position of the College, stating that 'This is the only College without money behind it. All Domestic Science Colleges in other towns have been taken over by the Local Authorities.' It was certainly a difficult position now, and the vast main building threatened to become a white elephant.

Sir Isidore carried the Committee with him in unanimous agreement that there 'must be no thought at present of the National returning to Buckingham Palace Road,' but in view of the serious implications, the Auditors were asked to prepare a statement showing the financial position 'as if the College were to close.' It was also agreed to give notice in respect of the premises at Coastal Chambers, Allington House and Fitzjohn's Avenue with possible reduction of rent. Later, a reasonable agreement concerning rebate of rates was reached, and all the premises were vacated.

There was genuine appreciation of the way in which all the work had been transferred to Torquay, and also gratitude to all the staff for their public spirited acceptance of the position, for it had been feared that some might prove redundant and they had been notified accordingly. Happily this was not the case,

and all the Teaching staff remained, apart from those left voluntarily to undertake other War duties, mainly at this moment
service in the Red Cross and NAAFI. There was, however, no
place for some members of the clerical and domestic staff, and
it was with regret that Miss Emery, who for many years had been
in charge of the telephone, left with a gratuity of £25 in appreciation of her long service, and Mrs Jackman, who had given solid
help in one of the big kitchens, received £15. Benning, who had
been handyman since 1908, was given £10 on this compulsory
retirement.

By the next Committee Meeting in December 1939, with Sir
Isidore in the Chair and seven other members present, things
looked brighter. Enquiries for Cookery classes were pouring in,
and the Committee decided to exploit these demands and make
use of the building now lying idle in Buckingham Palace Road.
Two members of the Cookery staff were released from Torquay,
to be aided by Mrs MacGregor, together with Mrs Barnes and
Benning from the domestic staff, the latter now recalled at a
higher wage, to remain faithful for another four years. With this
minimal staff, classes in Cookery opened for the public in
January 1940, and were held throughout the week, all of them
thronged with people eager to acquire even the simplest knowledge.

By this time it had become apparent that training in large
scale Cookery was essential if workers everywhere were to be
adequately fed. A Ministry of Labour *Bulletin* of this period,
referring to the wide extension of communal feeding, including
the great increase in the number of industrial Canteens, continued 'It is not, however, enough that there should be simply a
factory Canteen; it must provide good food, well cooked and
served, despite restrictions on supplies. The need is both to
supply additional Canteen staff, and to equip existing Canteen
staffs with the necessary knowledge.'

The College was approached by the Board of Education, who
had learnt through the WVS that the Ministry of Labour was
in urgent need of courses in Canteen cookery. The Committee
was swift to recognise its particular contribution in this field.
With further reorganisation of staff at Torquay the National,

Her Majesty Queen Elizabeth with Naval Paymasters, 1943

in July 1940, under the leadership of Miss J. N. Edward, opened a Canteen with the double purpose of training Canteen workers and feeding the public.

To meet this twofold need, the Ministry of Labour and National Service in conjunction with the Board of Education instituted a variety of courses to train Canteen Cooks, Manageresses and Supervisors, as well as short courses in Canteen Management and Administration. As Industrial Canteens, War Workers' Hostels, Schools Meals' Centres, British Restaurants and other communal feeding were everywhere established, the need for Supervisors and Manageresses rose swiftly in proportion.

The National was admirably suited to these purposes, both geographically and professionally. Courses varied in length from two weeks to three months. The first to be trained were men from the Friends' Ambulance Unit and the National Fire Service. The latter had two travelling kitchens outside the back door of the College, where a group of four cooked for a hundred people in each van. These vans were 'beautifully equipped,' and valiant work was done during the Blitz, serving soup and snacks to firemen who were often on duty without respite for interminable hours.

There was also some wonderment at the patience of the neighbours 'who forebore to complain of the smuts puffing out from the self contained Blitz cookers.' The men from the Friends' Ambulance Unit later went out to Libya and North Africa, using vans supplied by the Canadian Red Cross.

Cooking in College was done in two of the main kitchens. Staff and students ate at 12 noon, and opened the doors to the public at 12.30; Wednesdays and Fridays were meatless days, but always the two-course luncheon for 1s proved so popular that the College was almost besieged.

In November 1941 Miss Edward led a course for a limited number of staff teachers from Colleges in all parts of the country to determine on methods for teaching Canteen cooks quickly. The Ministry of Labour initiated this six weeks' course, and the first recruits arrived in January 1942. It was like a snowball; as other organisations applied for training, more and more courses were added until there were trainees from the RN, WRNS, RAF,

WRAF, ATS and NAAFI, and eventually every branch of the Services was included, as well as Refresher Courses for all types of students. The first five-week course for the WAAF, at the request of the Air Ministry, began in July 1942, and set the pattern for many others in that the courses followed consecutively without a break.

The first day the Canteen opened to the public, 26 lunches were served; by the end of the week they had risen to 89. When on 25 June 1942 the numbers had reached over 700 a day, the Committee felt that there was too great pressure on the staff, and decided that the lunches should be reduced to 500 for the public and 50 for the staff. It proved impossible to conform to this ruling and a year later it was recognised that the numbers could not be curtailed if the individual trainees were to have the proper experience in large scale cooking. The same Committee in June sanctioned a 'Responsibility Allowance' of £48 a year to Miss Edward 'in respect of Canteen and Training Courses in London.'

As courses and students increased, more members joined the Buckingham Palace Road Staff. Miss Loader, who had taught Technical classes since 1913, returned after a year in Torquay. Always kindly, renowned for her skill with yeast mixtures, in 1941 she resigned to be married and the College felt the loss of this pleasant member of staff who had unobtrusively helped many people with scant previous knowledge, really to enjoy Cookery.

In addition to the full-time lecturers, there were part-time helpers; Miss Graham, the Accountant, with one assistant dealt with the finances for both London and Torquay. Miss Taylor, the College Secretary, actually occupied the top flat throughout the War, and remained in charge of the office, 'a post,' it was said, 'which has involved her in many unwonted tasks at all hours of the day and night.' There were extra assistants, some voluntary, as well as the domestic helpers, led by faithful Mrs MacGregor.

Among other activities, the staff, in groups of three, took their turn of duty practically every week in the rota of Fire Watching at the vast Baths next door.

By now the 'phoney war' which had taxed nerves until the Spring of 1940 had long since passed, and civilians were in the

front line, calmer and steadier than in the early months of uncertainty. The first false air raid warning which resounded over
London and parts of England within half an hour of the declaration of War on 3 September 1939 left an indelible impression, and
for months afterwards many people on their journeys would
scurry like rabbits from one air raid shelter to the next, lingering
at the entrance to the imagined haven, like a group in a game of
grim musical chairs.

In Buckingham Palace Road, the brunt was borne by Miss
Taylor and Miss Edward with her staunch team including
Miss Atkinson, Miss Bennett, Miss Fulleylove, Miss Main,
Miss Pearman, Miss Wagstaff and Miss Watts, who did yeoman
service and to whom tribute should be paid. They were never
fainthearted.

For the ordinary person, even at the blackest moments of the
War, the possibility of defeat simply did not exist. Everything
was accepted as it came, no matter how daunting, and the in-
corrigible sense of humour which had inspired Bruce Bairns-
father's famous cartoon of the First World War 'If you know of
a better 'ole, go to it,' was never far from the surface.

Miss Edward wrote 'Fortunately memories of the bombing of
London endured in the War years are short, but everyone remembers cooking on oil and solid fuel stoves and makeshifts because
the supply of electricity and gas was cut. Makeshifts indeed
were many; as someone later remarked 'Miss Edward at times
was cooking almost on a candle.' There was exhilaration in
'starting out for College at the height of the Blitz at 6.30 am,
before buses were either available or re-routed because of glass
strewn streets, and being given a daily lift to Victoria by a farmer
with a lorry load of empty bins, on his way round the hotels to
collect pig waste.' The outward journey was more agreeable
than the return, with the bins full. Another recollection of Miss
Edwards was 'The day when a bomb dropped near College during
the lunch hour on 21 December 1940, the Canteen was full to
capacity. The inside windows burst open and the customers all
rose to their feet simultaneously, just as if they were standing
for the opening chord of God Save the King. This was followed
by a dead silence, and when they found they were unharmed,
all sat down quietly and continued with their meal as if nothing
had happened.'

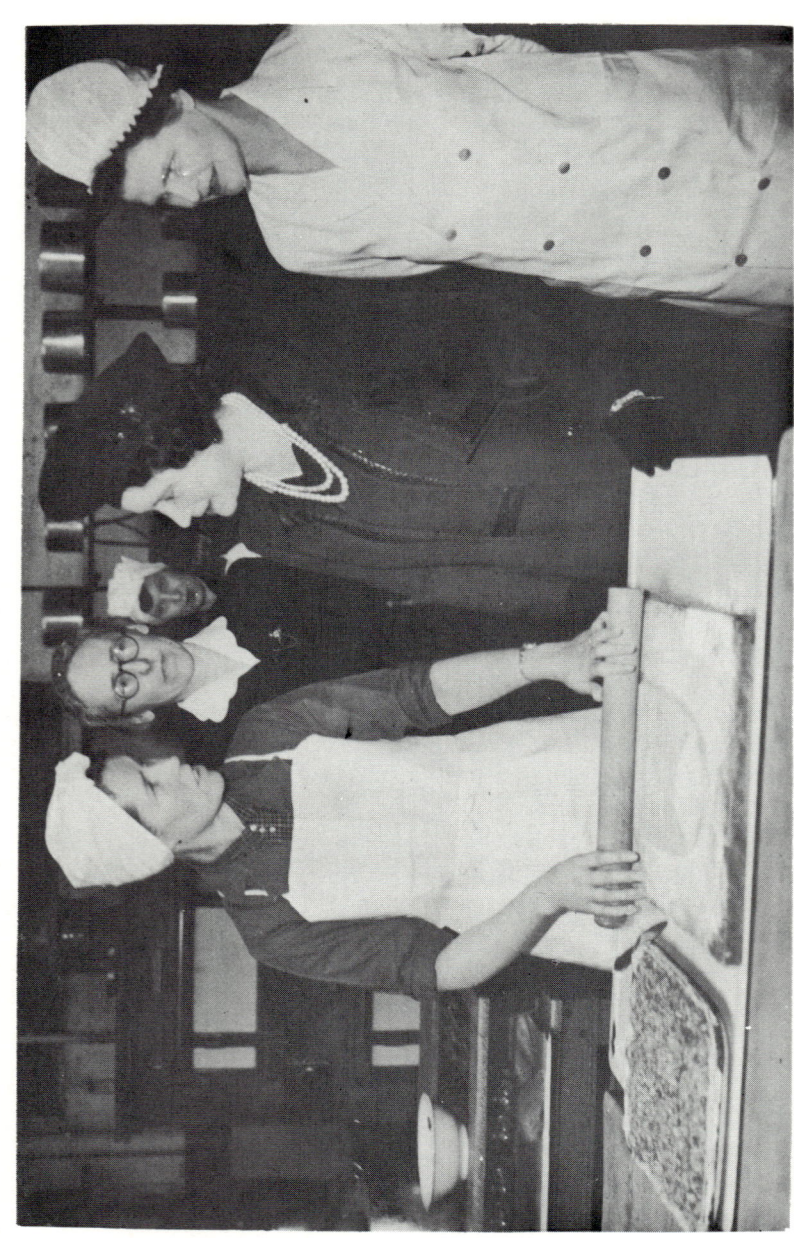

Her Majesty Queen Elizabeth talking to Canteen Cook (with Miss Eland and Miss Edward, 1943

To repair the material damage of that day cost £125, happily the only War Damage Claim which the National suffered from enemy action. But there were many near misses.

In common with the Windmill Theatre, the National at Buckingham Palace Road could claim 'We never closed.' Miss Edward wrote 'We all took our holidays in turn, and I remember telephoning from Scotland at 4 pm one day during the buzz bomb raids, to make sure everyone was safe. Miss Taylor answered the 'phone, assured me everything was all right, and then said "Hold on a minute." This was followed by sounds of commotion and peals of laughter. When she spoke on the 'phone again, I was informed that all the staff had dived under the table, when a buzz bomb "cut out," but they were all safe, and no damage to College.'

The pressure of training increased. Miss Main recalled that sometimes she had a group for a bare fortnight; at another time 'it was decided in consultation with RAF personnel that we should take Catering Officers for four weeks in College. I had a new intake every two weeks. They cooked all their meals during this time, as we had their rations, taking back food for the week-end to their quarters near the Albert Hall.'

Among some of the officers was 'Mr Bentley of *Bentley's Oyster Bar*, who had never cooked before.' With another set a sergeant, who was sent to help with the class, later became a Professor at the University of Strathclyde. The Navy sent three men at regular intervals from each port of Portsmouth, Plymouth and Chatham for a three weeks' Instructors' Course; some of whom had virtuously taken high class cookery lessons in preparation.

Certainly the trainees, drawn from all walks of life and all parts of the country, seemed highly appreciative and often liked to celebrate the end of their training by taking their instructors to a theatre, to everyone's pleasure. One group evidently enjoyed a daily fillip, for they 'used to go to Grosvenor House for a drink after luncheon, so that the afternoon session was fairly lively!'

But everyone helped. Miss Edward recalled that 'an out-standing recollection of the War years was the friendly and cooperative spirit encountered everywhere, not only among the staff in College, but in all the groups being trained, as well as in buses, in trains and everywhere.'

Nevertheless it was unremitting labour throughout the War.

Rare alleviation was a godsend. It was therefore the most tremendous uplift to everyone's spirits, and far beyond their wildest
dreams, to learn that Her Majesty Queen Elizabeth proposed
to visit them in the midst of their work.

The glow of this visit remained like the warmth of radiant
heat long after it was over. Her Majesty arrived on 24 March
1943 in time to see both the cooking and serving of the meals, to
the surprised delight of the general public; but first she was
shown round the kitchens by Miss Eland and Miss Edward. As
always, the Queen showed great interest in all that she saw,
speaking to the men and women in the different courses about
the work which they would be doing on completion of their
training. Her kind comment on the happy atmosphere in the
College was an added comfort, and the National was left inspirit-
ed and revived as she passed to her car through a guard of honour
formed by students drawn from the Services in training.

Her Majesty had most kindly given £10 to the College in both
1942 and 1943, and the Committee decided 'that a Silver Rose
Bowl be bought with the £20 so graciously donated by Her
Majesty Queen Elizabeth.' It was agreed to engrave on it annually the name of the outstanding student of the year, and this
honour continued through the length of the National's days.

By the end of the War a thousand meals a day were being
served, with the College Library converted into an extra dining
room. Nearly three thousand students of all kinds had been
trained at Buckingham Palace Road since the Canteen opened
in July 1940.

Miss Edward's contribution to the achievement of the
National during the War can never be overestimated. One of
her team wrote: 'Looking back over those War years, we all
realised we owed everything to Miss Edward, whose drive,
enthusiasm and skill carried us along.' Always 'on the spot,' she
was also 'always immaculate,' and her team strove 'to emulate
her in every way.'

WAR

THE NATIONAL was split into two parts, and few could be cognisant of what went on in both. In neither London nor Torquay were there facilities or time for constant inter-communication, and it was left to Miss Eland to journey to and fro, act as liaison and report to the Committee. There were changes among the members of the Executive, and the death of Sir Isidore Salmon in September 1941 deprived the National of an able Chairman who had represented the London County Council on the Committee since 1910. Mrs Karslake was unanimously elected Chairman in his place, and Mr Abady, K.C., became Vice Chairman. In her 1942 *Guild Letter* Miss Eland wrote of Sir Isidore 'Amid all the activities of an intensely active public life in his capacity as a Member of Parliament, Managing Director of J. Lyons and Company, and Honorary Catering Adviser to the Army, he was always ready to spare time for College affairs and to do anything in his power to further our interests. His knowledge of finance and great business gifts were brought to the service of the College as its Chairman, and those of us who knew him in Committee will remember not only these qualities, but also his characteristic insistence on fair dealings to all, and his kindness of heart, especially to any subordinate members of College who might be in difficulties.'

A new Finance Committee was formed in December 1931 to include Mrs Karslake, Mr Abady, Mr Buckmaster, Mrs Lowe (who was the new London County Council representative), Mr McFarlane and Mr Thorold; at the same time an Education and Appointments Committee was elected of Mrs Karslake, Miss

Boulton, Mr Buckmaster, Miss Margaret Jones, Lady Max-
Müller, Miss McCall and Miss Souter. Inevitably it was difficult
for the members of the Executive Committee to meet as regularly
as they wished, but three or four meetings a year were managed,
totalling twenty Committees during the War; the average
attendance was eight including Mrs Karslake who took the
Chair unfailingly. Miss Eland acted as go-between; some members visited Torquay, among them both Mrs Karslake and Miss
Souter.

Miss Eland made her headquarters at Torquay, and from there
she wrote her *Wartime Letters* to the Guild members. It was
obviously impossible to hold the Annual Reunion as usual in
October 1939, but the Old Students Guild Committee held an
Emergency Meeting in November. It was realised that the
enforced economy in the use of paper would prevent the issue
of the *Guild Magazine*, and it was decided to send out a *News
Letter* instead. The bulk of this was written by the Principal;
there were also brief factual items concerning students. In her
three *Wartime Letters* of 1940, 1941 and 1942, Miss Eland ranged
over wide ground, sketching a picture of the College life, with
its daily doings and its hopes and its plans. After this, there was
a gap of four years before the *Guild Magazine* was resumed
in 1946.

The move to Torquay, although the circumstances were
hardly propitious, was not without a certain sense of elation.
The weather was glorious, and far removed from the grime and
smuts of London, especially Victoria Station, the buoyant air
and open skies tended to make the sinister purpose a little more
remote. Anxiety there was, but unlike the First World War,
there was no false sentimental patriotism. Youthful students
obviously had no personal experience of War, but it was only
twenty years since the 1918 Armistice, and almost everyone had
some connection with those who had gone through it. The older
generation, though fortunately with no possible fore-knowledge
of what now lay in store, knew too many bitter facts which simply
resulted in a stiffening of purpose to counteract the sinking of
heart. When the blows did fall, young and old alike closed ranks,
and as the years brought disasters to one and all, even when
depleted, they were tighter knit than ever.

The golden Autumn of 1939, when even in October people breakfasted out of doors, blossomed again in the lovely Spring and Summer of 1940. The 'phoney War' had persisted, but in the late sunshine of a long summer's day, following the enemy occupation of Belgium and Holland, the guns of France could be heard across the Channel on the still evening air, to reach towns and villages in the South and up to the fringe of London. Families went nightly to bed with little cases packed with emergency food and clothes, ready at hand to snatch in the event of an Invasion in the small hours, and each morning the sunshine seemed doubly glorious, with another night passed.

But after the Miracle of Dunkirk, with the Battle of Britain in full spate, everyone knew that total War had started. Even after the threat of imminent invasion was over, there was a chill foreboding for the future. With Norway and France fallen, to ring England by the enemy, and the War news deteriorating, so the weather worsened. The gales which had shattered the projected Invasion now swept the country with rain to give a wet, bitter winter.

To settle in Torquay and find Hostels was no easy task. The first to be acquired, for twelve guineas a week, accommodated fifty-six students, who with Miss Haydon as Warden, lived at Ferny Bank, Babbacombe Downs, with the magnificent view across the bay. By January 1940, Miss Cottrell and Miss Dumas were installed at the Villa Rosa, Trumlands Road, rented unfurnished for three guineas a week. This charming house belonged to Mrs Dashwood, the authoress E. M. Delafield, and the aura of *The Provincial Lady*, together with certain mementoes, enhanced the sense of a real home, so long desired. It seemed ironic that it had taken two Wars to bring this about, for not since Mrs Clarke had lent her house at Porlock in 1915 had there been any residential practice in Home Management.

The house remained the base for this Department until Easter 1946. Second year students, numbering seventeen at a time, spent a month twice a year in the Spring and Autumn terms in rotation; First and Third year students were fitted into the Summer term, when an ex-technical student came in as residential cook. Furniture and equipment were brought from Fitzjohn's Avenue, and since realistic running of a home called for

Villa Rosa Hostel in Torquay, 1940

far fewer than seventeen students, the opportunity was taken to cover other ground, some of the most immediately useful being extensive renewals and repairs to furniture and furnishings. So it proved 'an ill wind' in many respects; the results of the refurnishing were so evident that when at one stage, with the possibility of the place being sold over their heads, a prospective buyer was so impressed by the immaculate condition that he enquired 'the number of maids kept.' Miss Cottrell, concealing her secret delight, replied simply 'Seventeen.' Happily, the Villa was not sold.

In addition to Home Management, Miss Broderick and later Miss Crawford taught Technical classes, by this means also providing the midday lunch. 'There were occasional crises,' Miss Dumas recalled, 'when it was found that these students had used our egg ration for some elaborate, but alas, not filling dish.'

The actual Cordon Bleu course was soon forced to disappear temporarily, as war conditions made it impossible to continue the high class cookery of the final term. Instead the National offered a third term of Institutional Catering, or alternatively the option of postponing the third term until conditions after the War should make the proper ingredients available.

Students at the Stall in Torquay Market, *c* 1942

South Devon Technical College, 1939

Staff and Students of the National, July 1945

Life in the Villa Rosa seems to have been an enjoyable experience, many of the students declaring how valuable the training had been. Labour expenses were kept to a minimum, limited to the cook's salary in the summer terms, and wages for kitchen cleaning in the evenings. Full use was made of the house; even in the holidays the Villa was occupied, either by members of staff or for Refresher courses.

They were blessed to escape War damage; when a plane crashed at the bottom of the hill on the tragic afternoon when St Mary's Church was hit during Sunday School, 'as soon as possible the students went out to give any help they could.' Villa Rosa itself was left with 'nothing worse than the loss of some ceilings and several windows.'

Through the courtesy and co-operation of the South Devon Technical College, the complete reorganisation of the work of both Colleges was made possible. Accustomed to the entire disposition of their individual resources, the National and the South Devon College now had to share premises and facilities, and without the willing effort of the hosts, the jigsaw could never have been fitted. It was recorded that the 'Principal of the Devon Technical College has been most generous in the space he has placed at our disposal,' and there was warm appreciation

Group photographed at the South Devon Technical College

of 'our most hospitable reception.' An official letter to express the gratitude of the Executive Committee was sent to thank the Principal personally for his kindness 'to our Principal, staff and students' for the co-operation of the Devon staff.

The Technical College had only one kitchen and one laundry, and the National had therefore to seek the use of Housecraft kitchens in neighbouring schools, who in turn adjusted their own work in order to provide National students with extra training space. Miss Jaques wrote, 'Some classes are held in the afternoon, and some demonstrations in the evening; but the main working hours, in the Technical College, are from 8.45 to noon; round about 8.30 am the approaches to College are full of the whirr of students' bicycles free-wheeling down hill – or the labouring of those mounting up.'

Later, these hours were often extended; work sometimes began at 8 am and continued until the South Devon Technical students came in for their sessions beginning at 1.30 pm. The National again had the use of the premises for more classes from 5.30 to 8.30 pm.

It was a test of temper as well as organisation; nevertheless even with the prolonged strain of war conditions taxing daily endurance, it was the exception for anyone in authority to vent their feelings on others with equally frayed nerves.

Needlework and Dressmaking were also taken mainly in the

Principal, Chairman of Governors (Miss F. M. Pugh) and some of the
Staff of the South Devon Technical College, 1951

Technical College, with Miss Howlett and Miss Breukelman
coping with the inevitable limitations. Miss Quick had retired
at the end of 1939, to throw herself for another twenty years
into wartime needs and social work in her home town of
Hastings, where she was acclaimed, as at the National, for her
undeviating standards and her kindness.

Miss Shaw tackled the Science with her usual vigour. She
recalled a meeting on a hot afternoon in the Mayor's Parlour
to discuss 'how people could be kept well fed and happy on the
food available.' The members present included representatives
of the Electricity and Gas Boards, the WVS, various local
Guilds and some of the National staff. A plan of campaign was
drawn up, everybody undertaking certain individual responsibilities on behalf of their own organisations.

Within the National, the Science Department undertook all
the Dietetics, to be illustrated practically by meals and dishes
prepared in the kitchens. The nub was how to get this over to the
public, and as in the First World War when a shop had been
taken temporarily in the Old Kent Road in 1917 for the purpose
of 'demonstrating wholesome cookery,' so now the first step in
the campaign was the loan of a tobacconist's shop in Castle
Circus. Miss Shaw wrote, 'This was an excellent spot, as it had
a small kiosk where a student could stand and demonstrate to

the passers-by; the window showed dishes illustrating the subject for the day, such as 'Sugar substitutes, to supply both energy and flavour; the Herring, to supply good body building material, heat and energy.' It was a great attraction, the audience offering their own views and oral contributions, while the fishmonger opposite found the display brought a good source of income. 'All the while,' continued Miss Shaw, 'we kept in mind the use of home supplies, thus saving shipping. Other days were devoted to vitamins, their sources and functions; to meat and fat substitutes; a well-balanced diet for all ages; encouraging fresh vegetables wherever possible, even growing mustard and cress and parsley at home.'

The Third year students, entering with alacrity into this unusual plan, decided that unconventional advertisement was equally essential, and Torquay witnessed them, in the College uniform, acting as 'sandwich men,' with board back and front proclaiming the week's programme, marching down Fore Street to the Pavilion, incidentally disturbing many of the townsfolk who thought this to be a demonstration of the hotel chefs about to go on strike.

Later, a stall was taken in the Market, where a junior member of staff was deputed to rally the public through a megaphone. 'It was like calling people to a Punch and Judy show at a Fair,' said one, or a new version of Gilbert and Sullivan's 'Come, walk up and purchase with avidity; overcome your diffidence and natural timidity.' As the War continued, new concoctions were added to the accepted dishes, among the more strange being a single sprat wrapped in potato pastry, and baked with head and tail projecting at each end, euphemistically dubbed 'Star gazing pasty.'

Simple talks on dietetics were given to various Guilds and Schools, and detailed help on 'food for the family' stressing body building and energy giving foods, were offered locally when the Electricity and Gas Companies lent their showrooms for this purpose.

It was a comprehensive undertaking, and the smooth running was made possible by the very able organisation and secretarial work given voluntarily by Miss F. M. Pugh, M.A., later Alderman and Governor of the South Devon Technical College, with whom the Committee worked in amity.

Miss May Pugh's friendship, begun in days of trouble and
uncertainty, was forged during the years of struggle, remaining
unswerving throughout the life of the National, to give her
allegiance finally to the Trust.

Miss McIntyre was in charge of the Cookery Training Department helped by Miss Crawford. Both shared the same high
standards and superb technique. Miss Crawford was often
claimed for Technical classes and in January 1940, Miss Barbara
Visick, an Old Student recently trained, joined Miss McIntyre.
Gifted with professional expertise and blessed with warmth of
temperament, Miss Visick was a pourer of oil on troubled waters,
with a great sense of fun. She carried out complicated and often
contradictory orders responsibly, but even in the most trying
situations she could find lively amusement, and made it equally
so for others.

Her story of the near-loss of stewing steak bought for the
entire class, brings up a vivid picture of waiting in a bus queue,
with these rations, almost as precious as gold, wrapped inadequately in the flimsiest bit of paper, when 'all the dogs in Torquay
came from miles around, rushing and leaping, foaming at the
mouth,' while Miss Visick held her arm higher and higher in an
effort to keep them at bay until she reached the safety of the bus.
Another experience was also due to the difficulty of transporting
damp and perishable food; for this time, as she stepped from the
bus with a whole consignment of herrings, the paper broke. All
the herrings fell out; only some in the road, but the passengers
rushed to the rescue, 'throwing out herrings, left, right and
centre, as the bus moved on!'

In Torquay the winter cold was accentuated on those wind-
swept hills, when people skidded on the snow and ice of the steep
slopes. In several layers of coats and jerseys, Miss Lancaster
made her way down Teignmouth Road carrying an enormous
bag of College possessions, chiefly huge heavy bunches of keys,
and a large flour dredger filled with cinders which she sprinkled
on the ground before her as she walked, going in to any known
port of call to refill her dredger. Rain was an added trial – 'I never
imagined it could rain so much,' and 'there always seemed to
be a deluge' were typical recollections; Miss Visick 'wore out

Restaurant Queue, 1940

five mackintoshes' during those War years, and eventually equipped herself with fisherman's oilskins: trousers, sou'wester and all. The tight schedule of work allowed her, at one time, only a quarter of an hour between two classes a couple of miles apart. When she reached her second class 'sodden from the lashing rain,' she found she had left her skirt at the first, and so was obliged to teach in her dripping trousers, somewhat to her own discomfort, the slight dismay of the Principal, but the great enjoyment of her class.

If the elements outside were unkind, conditions inside were often not much better, for the enforced economy in the use of fuel meant that there was little or no heat. Not only mackintoshes, but jerseys were worn out too, as one after another was put on, in order to keep warm. As food became scarcer, it was imperative to try to eat the most warming and filling. Another of Miss Visick's memories is of sharing the small practice house belonging to the South Devon College, where, as they had a constant stream of visitors, they 'invariably gave them a supper of lentil soup and baked stuffed potatoes' – the stuffing being 'the most minute bit of cheese.'

WAR

TORQUAY was full to overflowing with evacuees, both young and old, and Hostels were at a premium. By June 1941, thirty students were billeted in the beautiful Forest Hotel at a cost of £150 for forty weeks of the year. They were able to remain until December 1944, and then transferred to Frognal Hall, temporarily taken over furnished in January 1945 at a rent of £20 a week. At the Forest Hotel, in spite of 'rather peculiar sculleries,' Technical classes were held in the kitchens, including Cookery for the Housekeepers Course.

Two more Hostels were acquired on 1 January 1942: Ferny Combe, the house adjoining the original Hostel at Ferny Bank, was rented for six guineas a week, and Beechcroft where students had already been billeted, was taken furnished for £4 a week. It greatly eased the situation, and in October that year, Miss Eland was able to write 'We now have a mere handful of students in billets, in contrast to the number in private houses when we were first evacuated.'

Cookery provision called for attention, and in 1941, the Committee agreed to spend £150 on new large-scale equipment for use in Torquay, on condition that the South Devon Technical College accepted that it must be brought back to London after the War. After 'some slight discussion,' it was decided to accede to the request of the Devon Education Committee for an extra £50 a year rent for the use of the Technical College.

There was a spate of minor financial claims for attention. Somewhat belatedly, a subsistence allowance of 5s a week to the staff compulsorily evacuated to Torquay, as from September

1939, plus single train fare was sanctioned. The wages of certain domestic workers at Buckingham Palace Road were raised, among them Mrs MacGregor, who with an increase of 5s a week, now received £1 7s 6d.

The Auditors also raised their fees, and an agreement was reached of seventy-five guineas a year to cover College and Hostel accounts both in London and Torquay. Their statement for 1940 – 1941 showed the prospect of a substantial profit at Torquay, as well as cautious hopes for the Canteen in London; hopes which were to be more than fully realised.

Miss Woodham retired in 1942, and the subsequent staff changes released Miss Visick from the beck and call of the Cookery Department, to share responsibility for the House-keepers Course. By helping with some of the students' cookery teaching in the schools, Miss Visick was also able to add her weight towards supporting Miss Lough in the mammoth task of planning and supervising all the teaching practice for the College. Miss Lough had returned to London for a brief three months in 1940, to launch the new Canteen with Miss Edward, and then went back to Devon.

The second year of War had brought two other Training Colleges to Torquay: St Katharine's, Tottenham, and Stockwell; with increasing pressure everywhere, the available areas for teaching practice became more far flung. The 'Normal' Training Colleges did not infringe on the Housecraft preserves; it was only Dr Lawrence in her field of Education who faced problems over any claims for practice in general subjects. Arrangements called not only for the highest degree of organisation, but also of acumen. 'First catch your school, then know it,' was a reversal of thought provoked by the exigencies of War, but it involved a never ending check on students and conditions. Schools every-where were co-operative, but they also were beset by loss of staff and the material difficulties of packing more and more children into often inadequately heated and lighted buildings. 'For the first time,' wrote Miss Eland, 'some of the schools are experiencing an inrush of students for teaching practice.'

Miss Lough had her work cut out. As Warden of the small Hostel 'Beechcroft,' she was impelled to return to Torquay every night, often to face notes of lessons to be checked and possibly discussed. Her area spread in all directions, from Barnstaple in the North to Plymouth in the South, and as far afield as Taunton in Somerset. No town nor village, however remote, escaped her net. Setting forth between 7 and 7.30 am, covering the countryside, not in a dog cart as in the last century, but in a country bus meandering through the highways and byways, Miss Lough was a worthy successor to the early undaunted pioneers. In places such as Bampton and Buckfastleigh, Totnes and Teignmouth, Kingsweir and Newton Abbot, lovely Honiton, Dawlish and Dartmouth – the latter incredibly difficult to reach by the little ferry in rough weather – in all weathers, at all times and in every school, 'the one thing we always got,' said Miss Lough, 'was a welcome.'

The students themselves often perforce lived during the week in the place where they were teaching while on 'intensive' practice. In spite of all the handicaps, even maybe partly because what they had lacked in ordered, conventional training had been compensated by the flexible approach which demanded that everyone should be resilient, both the students who took their Finals in 1941, bearing the brunt of the move from London, and those who took all their training at Torquay, did exceptionally well in their Final examinations. The first set gained Distinctions in Education, Advanced Cookery, Advanced Needlework and Dressmaking, with many Credits. Those who finished in 1942 amassed two Distinctions in Education, five in Advanced Cookery, five in Advanced Needlework and Dressmaking, as well as Credits in Cookery, English and Science and seven in Home Management. Perhaps the Villa Rosa had had its effect.

Although Torquay, with rare and terrible exceptions, did not suffer like some of the 'Baedeker Towns,' there were constant raids, aimed in great part at the shipping in the Bay, or when bombs were dropped en route to and from Exeter and Plymouth. Maybe also the stimulus to be constantly 'at the ready' was strengthened by the continued presence of the Services, particularly the young men of the RAF, who delighted in the proximity of so many attractive girls, and contributed to many memorable occasions, some less romantic than others. Food regularly had to be transported from kitchens to Hostels, and Miss Jaques wrote 'Hence the need for *Sammy,* the tricycle, who in peace-time threaded his way along Buckingham Palace Road, laden with food from Coastal Chambers, and now does his bit in less traffic, but on more exacting contours – as the students who act as combined convoy, brake and charioteers well know.' The Air Force boys knew it too, and many would line the route, hailing the students with ribald remarks. Attractions, at times to the detriment of work, were strong. 'I think,' Miss Eland once wryly said as she addressed her students, 'you must remember that down here the Sea and Air tend to go to your heads,' a remark received with rapturous delight by her appreciative audience.

As early in the War as December 1941, the Education sub-Committee decided to make plans for post War needs. Their immediate concern was for accommodation both for courses and Hostels, but specific search was obviously dependent on any contemplated change in the actual training. Miss Eland re-presented the Principals of Domestic Science Colleges on the Joint Standing Committee for the Training of Teachers, and in June 1942, she was appointed to serve on a sub-Committee of the Training Colleges Delegacy of the University of London 'to consider the post War training of teachers.' These deliberations prepared minds for the change of thought which followed the McNair Report of 1944; this Report emphasised many of the principles embodied in the Butler Act, of that same year, and eventually, among other recommended reforms, crystallised in setting up the Institutes of Education whose policy was later to produce complicated problems and precipitate many battles.

In the dispensation of the Act, the Board of Education became a Ministry, with Mr R. A. Butler as its first memorable Minister.

Meantime the Executive Committee of the National decided to concentrate on the basic problems whose solution, whatever the duration of the War, called for advance planning. Miss Eland's position as a member of the Training Colleges Delegacy of the University was undoubtedly a great advantage in judging the way the wind was blowing in regard to the policy for future teacher training. Taking time by the forelock, the Committee asked Miss Eland, in March 1943, to prepare a memorandum 'giving some idea of the amount of accommodation necessary

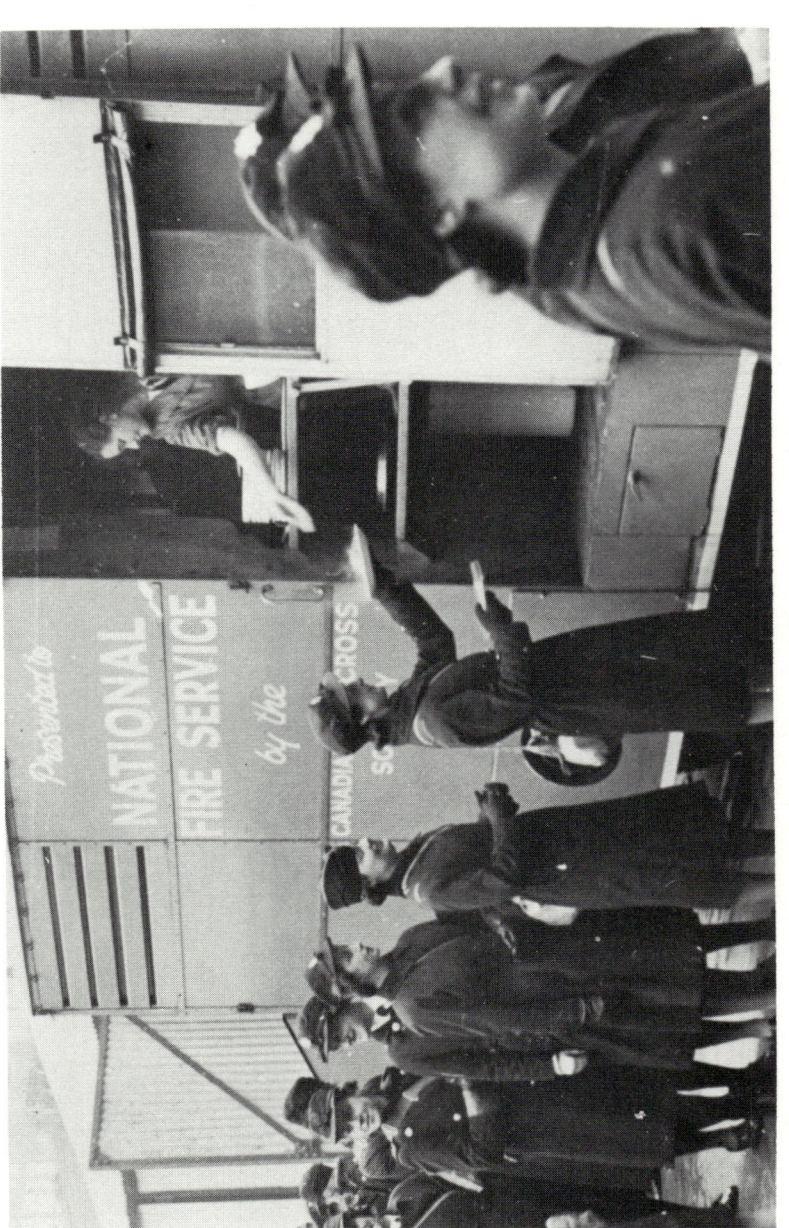

Travelling Kitchen presented by Canadian Red Cross, 1943

for students after the War, taking into account the money available for rents in comparison with pre-War figures.' As, at this
stage, any comparison of rents would be purely hypothetical, it
could not be an exercise with any degree of accuracy, but at
least the Committee, having more than a shrewd idea of its own
financial limitations, could look for premises within its means.
It was also agreed to discuss, as soon as possible, post-War plans
both with the Board of Education and the London County
Council Education Officer.

By the following June 1943, unanimous agreement had been
reached that the building in Buckingham Palace Road should
be retained, with the suggestion that the College should become
residential. This would involve a far greater range of Hostels
than formerly, and the Committee decided that suitable houses
should be sought 'as near to the main building as possible, for
the purpose of residence, Home Management practice, lecture
rooms, student and staff common rooms and Assembly Hall,'
authorising the Chairman and Principal 'to investigate all
possibilities.' In a reply to a questionnaire from the Board of
Education concerning future plans, the National stressed the
'urgency to acquire Hostels without delay, as the rented accommodation at Torquay must be given up immediately on cessation
of hostilities.' In the event, this anxiety fortunately proved
groundless.

There now began an intensive search for Hostels. London
was racked by the devastating hail of buzz bombs; property
slumped so heavily in value that much of it could be had for a
song, but while there were shrewd buyers, able and willing to
take a risk, there were owners equally astute, and the National
could not hope to have it all its own way.

In October 1944, the Committee was considering Eccleston
Square, whose proximity lent favour to the possibility of acquiring a range of adjoining houses. Numbers 53 and 54 were the
first on the market, and aware of the continuing risk of destruc-
tion by enemy action, the Committee offered to rent them for
£1,800 a year. Equally aware of their potential value, the owners
cavilled at anything less than £2,500 per annum, and eventually
in December 1944 struck a bargain at this price for a thirty-one
year lease.

Deciding to concentrate on Eccleston Square, numbers 33 and 35 Linden Gardens were sold early in 1945. They had been bought for a total sum of £8,486 in 1931, but in Notting Hill at this time, it was not a seller's market, and the price fetched was £7,700; a loss, after nearly fifteen years, apart from considerable sums spent on conversions and improvements, of £786.

Even so, there was something to add to the exchequer, and the Committee invested £2,000 as 'Reserve for contingencies,' and £300 for non-teaching staff gratuities, in 3 per cent War Bonds. There was constant call on the latter fund; Benning, retiring finally after thirty-six years' service, received a gratuity of £100 in December 1944.

In September 1945, the leases of numbers 55, 56 and 57 Eccleston Square were offered for sale, and purchased for £2,250 each, on a forty-three year lease to terminate in 1988, at an annual ground rent of £154. The Grosvenor Estate gave permission for all the houses now acquired by the National to be used jointly as Hostels and 'extensions of the main building, as necessary,' and both the Ministry of Education and the London County Council sanctioned the enterprise.

The houses were still subject to War-time requisition; they also required extensive alteration. Realising the size of this problem, the Committee were thankful to be able to rent number 72 Eccleston Square offered by the Grosvenor Estate for £275 per annum. It proved immensely useful both for classes and as a temporary Library until the Estate called in the lease at the end of September 1949.

Even though the National never became a residential College, and the Hostels only catered for those who needed to live within reach, the additional space in the new premises was absorbed by the claims of both Training and Technical courses. To replan, alter and adapt, equip and furnish the houses for their dual purpose of residence and specialist teaching, with facilities for private study, proved a major undertaking.

The main building in Buckingham Palace Road had deteriorated badly during the War, and although £100 had been spent in 1942 to clean the gutters and repaint the back of the building, this at best had been patchwork. The whole place needed complete replanning. Short of gutting and re-building, any alterations were bound to be makeshift.

Application was made to the Ministry of Education for capital grant towards the increased accommodation in Eccleston Square and also for work in Buckingham Palace Road designed to provide new cloakrooms and lavatories, alterations to kitchens on the ground floor, and the addition of two storeys at the back of the building. The estimated cost for the main building alone was £11,275, and the present resources available, consisting of £5,474 from the Contingencies Reserve, £1,732 from the Bequests Reserve, and a cash balance of £4,000, totalled £11,206.

The allocation of resources called for careful thought, and there were personal affairs also to be dealt with. 'Special Services' during the War were recognised by a bonus of £50 to Miss Edward, £35 to Miss Taylor anv £20 to Miss Graham, though some of their services could never be assessed in terms of money.

The previous years had taken their toll, apart from enemy action. Two real friends of the National who were grievously missed were Miss Wallbank, always incomparable, who had died in 1938, and Miss McCall, after a life-time of gallant and efficient service, on 12 October 1945.

The time at Torquay was coming to an end. Strong as was the desire to pick up the threads and return to their rightful place in the centre of events in London, a certain degree of sadness was inevitable. In spite of the myriad difficulties, the inconsolable personal losses and tribulations of War, the years in the main had been basically happy ones, and it is the remembrance of the amusing episodes and the humour of situations, including the constantly bandied excuse of 'you know there's a War on,' that come uppermost in all the recollections.

In June 1945, Miss Pugh, who was now Chairman of the Domestic Science sub-Committee of Devon County Education Committee, gave positive proof of her friendship for the National by offering an Annual Prize as a token of remembrance of the Torquay days. She suggested that it should be a companion prize to the award made alternately each year to a Training and a Technical student, which the staff had given in 1934 to commemorate the Diamond Jubilee. This happy idea effectively dispelled any sense of grievance should a gifted student fail to gain recognition simply because it was the turn of the other course

'Interval in the Day's Work'
Pre-War Catering Kitchen

to receive the award. The Executive Committee of the National sent its official thanks, but it was everyone who shared in the pleasure of Miss Pugh's generosity.

At a final celebration, when the National wished to show its appreciation of the co-operation and friendly help of all the staff of the South Devon Technical College, a gold watch was presented to the Principal, Mr S. W. Smith, B.A., as a tangible memento of lasting gratitude. In turn, the National also received many warm tributes, including one from the Torquay Food Campaign, 'to thank the College and staff for valuable help.'

Catering Kitchen, 1958

Field Kitchen, First World War

SURVIVAL

CHAPTER XLII

VICTORY IN EUROPE, announced on 8 May 1945, to be known henceforth as VE Day, found people everywhere drained and exhausted. In this respect, conditions were comparable with the end of the First World War, but here the similarity ended. There was nothing like the same wild exultation of 1918. The Second World War had been too widespread; there had been too many known horrors to stomach; it was not yet even finished in the Far East. Swift on the heels of victory, thankfulness that the carnage was nearly over was tempered for the ordinary man and woman by a vague misgiving over erstwhile partners and mistrust of the future. Under the relief lay disillusion; never a propitious basis for warmth of understanding or generosity of purpose.

The National's London premises were nothing like in order when VE Day came in May, and although sixty students returned in January 1946, it was a long haul before the College was once again united in London in January 1947. In the meantime, some members of the staff remained with groups of students in Torquay, returning to London as and when accommodation became ready; a state of uncertainty almost more unsettling than the War years. Problems of Final Examinations were solved when the Ministry of Education agreed that they should be held in both London and Torquay.

One of the most significant decisions taken by the Committee early in 1945 was the invitation to Miss Lough in March to become Acting Vice Principal, following Miss Bewick's resignation, and the full appointment, with an allowance of £50, was ratified in September. It was particularly fortunate at that moment, for in the general exodus from Wartime quarters, when Miss Eland stayed behind to wind up affairs in Torquay, Miss Lough returned to London to join Miss Edward, where together they coped with a host of pressing problems.

The material deficiencies of premises and equipment demanded immediate attention. Apart from the sheer commonsense of having the College figuratively under one roof, it was essential to end the Torquay costs, which were sapping the funds so badly needed for the work of major reconstruction in London. But now, with the War over, it was not just a question of money, important as that was.

There was so great a call on builders that permits were issued both in regard to official consent to proposed plans and also for priority for the work. Institutions which had either been demolished or badly damaged through bombing, obviously had first call. The National did not come into this category, and so its claims lay low on the lists. Uncertainty over satisfactory provision threatened the recruitment of students; it was not easy to dispel this doubt and the repercussions continued to be felt years later.

The Butler Act of 1944, following the McNair Report, was a milestone in the history of Education, both stimulating and offering an answer to the youth of the nation, about to be demobilised. As the War ended, there was clamour for greater provision for further education and a strong assumption of the right to better conditions. Students applying to Training Colleges naturally were attracted by modern buildings, with individual study bedrooms. 'Utility' was the official term applied to the basic standard of all modern materials, and no matter how much austerity inevitably attached to the new 'Utility' buildings, they were welcomed as a symbol of the contemporary scene. The great Universities were in a class apart, but otherwise, with few exceptions, solid worth and long established traditions housed in shabby, out-of-date premises understandably stood no chance of initial selection by the young now making their choice. A small fortune was needed if the National were virtually to rebuild the College in Buckingham Palace

Road, and at the same time provide it and the newly acquired Hostels with modern, labour-saving equipment.

The College did not possess a small fortune. The Public Restaurant, as in the First World War, had been a triumphant success. Wise husbandry had also been practised; following the combined advice of the Auditor and the Committee, the National at the end of the Second World War, had not only survived, but was solvent.

They also had one tremendous asset in the clear mind and capable hands of Miss J. N. Edward. As the War had progressed Miss Edward's responsibility had grown in proportion to the ever-widening gap between London and Torquay, epitomised in the Wartime slogan 'Is your journey really necessary?' as limitations on travel were continually imposed.

The planning of post-War policy and training made increasing inroads on Miss Eland's time, so it was indeed a relief to have Miss Edward, conversant with every aspect of the needs in London and willing to give every spare moment of her time to solve them. She it was who discussed overall and detailed plans with the architects, even to working out on squared paper, the exact position of equipment and furniture. She it was who also not only supervised these alterations in both the main building and the newly acquired houses in Eccleston Square, but when the need arose, shared the physical work involved. She recalled, with dry humour, how in the last minute preparations of a Hostel, she herself had 'finished scrubbing down the basement staircase as the first student arrived at the front door.'

It says much for the calibre of both Miss Edward, who 'had reigned supreme,' and of Miss Lough who now arrived as Vice Principal to represent Miss Eland, that their mutual appreciation of each other enabled them to work together in harmony and lasting friendship. Miss Lough's staunch loyalty, wide experience and strong common sense, firm amidst the welter and swirl of events, provided the bulwark the College needed.

Early in 1946, a building licence was granted for the expenditure of £13,500 for alterations at Buckingham Palace Road, and finally the Eccleston Square houses were derequisitioned. Reconstruction of all these premises was laboured, for the vast programme envisaged depended on continued licences, available builders and ready money. All these were uncertain quantities. It was therefore imperative to decide on an order of priority, and the Committee unanimously agreed that basic preparation of the Hostels should have first claim, to be followed by alterations in the main building. It was found expedient, however, in order to make the best use of permits and money, and so hasten the return of the students, for much of the work to run concurrently.

Only part of the premises in Buckingham Palace Road had been needed during the War. The entire ground floor had been devoted to large scale cookery, and some of the front rooms on the floors above also used for various purposes. The laboratories and all the back of the building had remained empty, and it was now decided to make temporary use of some of these rooms, pending the proper reconstruction.

Such was Miss Margaret Begg's introduction to the National in London. She had joined the staff in Devon in September 1945, as Head of the Teacher Training Cookery Department, after Miss McIntyre had taken another appointment, and was immediately plunged into organising the transfer of her students from Torquay to London in readiness to begin work there in the New Year of 1946. After a packed Autumn term of full course work, time had still to be snatched to prepare all the equipment for transport, with the students 'cleaning and polishing with the utmost vigour.' This was only the first stage. During the Christmas holidays of 1945 the previous Children's and Technical Home Management Kitchens on the first floor at the rear of Buckingham Palace Road were put into order, so that in January 1946, the third year Training students 'quickly settled into their new environment, well established and ready to take, very successfully, their Final examinations in March.'

The comparative peace of the new quarters was soon to be shattered. Two floors were to be added above the Laundry at the rear of the building, to provide three kitchens and a lecture room, two rooms on each floor. Miss Begg remembered that 'workmen moved in; the roof was removed and scaffolding erected inside and outside,' which meant that huge steel stanchions were driven through her kitchens, and the glass taken out of the windows. 'The kitchen ceilings,' she continued, 'through which the scaffolding passed, were naturally not weatherproof, but at least one could not see the sky through them. Rain, however, came through with no difficulty, and progress round the kitchen was impeded by numerous buckets and other containers more or less catching the rain' – thus graphically reviving memories of the early days in South Kensington; though when the rain pelted down, the tarpaulins now stretched overhead were less noisy than the old corrugated iron roof.

The remaining reconstruction was gradually accomplished. The Demonstration Room was gutted and refitted as the main store room, and thus ended the great days of the Public Demonstrations which had brought such glory to the College. There were very few people who remembered 'those times of excitement and purpose,' as someone expressed it, when in 1956 the old Laundrywork room was converted into a Science laboratory, and thus the transformation of the rear of the building was complete.

At an early stage the Library was restored to its true purpose, releasing the space at 72 Eccleston Square. Considerable ingenuity in the organisation of classes was called for during the reconstruction of the ground floor. The Catering Kitchen and Kitchen 2 were thrown together to make the new kitchen for large scale work; the big Technical Kitchen became a Dining Room and Assembly Hall to seat two hundred and fifty people, with a 'small but adequately equipped stage.' Behind this a new staff cloakroom was fitted in. The provision of the vast electrical installation to service the needs of the College now filled the two old basement cloakrooms which had witnessed the daily change and chatter for nearly sixty years, and for which staff and students alike felt a strange nostalgia.

The last piece of reconstruction was a corridor on the first floor, built on top of the one below, and flanked by groups of cloakrooms and lavatories. This corridor linked the front and rear of the building, and thus at last saved the time and energy long wasted in going up and down two separate staircases at opposite ends of the College. Its completion was acclaimed as 'the greatest boon of all.'

By January 1946, Miss O'Keeffe was back from Torquay,

grappling with the preparation and daily demands of the Hostels, while the provision of permits, proper fire precautions and essential amenities produced endless delays. Any member of the staff with a moment to spare helped with general clearing up, washing paint and arranging rooms.

The first students arrived at numbers 55 and 72 Eccleston Square, to begin the Spring Term 1946 in London. They were followed by other groups as the Hostels at numbers 56 and 57 were opened, with the three adjoining houses linked by communicating doors. By the Autumn a hundred students were in residence and the Torquay Hostels were ceasing to take their toll in rent. Miss Haydon had returned earlier in the year, and after twelve years as Warden at both Linden Gardens and Torquay, she was greatly missed when she retired in December. The Hostels at numbers 53 and 54, run jointly as one unit, under the comfortable rule of Miss Winifred and Miss Rosamund Attrill were ready for the final group of students in January 1947. Miss S. R. J. Fraser had arrived to succeed Miss Haydon, but Miss Attrill and her sister left in the following Spring of 1948. There were constant changes, but through them all, Miss O'Keeffe kept the flag flying.

The six Eccleston Square Hostels shared their premises with various Departments, and 'every inch of space was filled.' Needlework, Home Management, English and Education were all taught there, while the Library was temporarily housed at number 72.

Conflicting claims on available kitchens and classrooms during the early post-War years inevitably resulted in changes and eventual loss of many of the established Technical courses. The Cordon Bleu and the 'Brides' Course were not revived, and this deprivation was felt keenly. The Naval Paymasters attended for a further brief period, but were then precluded by the acute pressure on space during the extensive alterations to the building. The Admiralty also felt by now that they had a sufficient number of experienced staff to train their own men.

It was thus the final chapter in the long series of courses at Buckingham Palace Road for the Royal Navy. But in their own quarters some of the traditions of the National were preserved, as Miss Lough discovered. After her retirement as Vice Principal, she was invited to Chatham, 'to be treated royally at the

Officers Mess,' and then found, to her great pleasure, that the Head of the Naval Catering Training Establishment had actually in use in his kitchens the High Class Cookery Book first published in the preceding century.

The old cookery books continued to hold their own. In 1952, the British North Greenland Expedition wrote for a copy, 'to use during the next two years,' of Mrs Clarke's *Plain Class Cookery Book*.

The existing large scale courses for the Services changed in purpose. Towards the end of the War, in preparation for a return to civilian life, short courses in Homecraft, in place of Canteen Cookery, were arranged for members of the ATS and the WAAF. The Ministry of Labour courses were coming to an end but there were still courses of varying lengths for Canteen Caterers and Cooks. The one-year Housekeepers' Course developed into the Institutional Management Course which started at the National in September 1947. The syllabus was wide ranging and comprehensive, preparing students for the recognised Certificate of its Association, obtainable after a year of paid supervised work in an Institution, following two years of full-time College training.

In 1951, a shorter course, to respond to certain needs of Industry, was planned with a first year of general Housecraft and a second with emphasis on Cookery and practice in demonstrating. This led to the Demonstrator's Certificate, awarded by the College until 1955, when the National Council for Domestic Studies undertook responsibility for the examination.

The disappearance of the Housekeepers' Course was regretted, and the Principal in 1950 proposed its reinstatement, but there were many problems stemming from policy and premises, and even the one-year Cooks' Certificate Course, in the charge of Miss Crawford after her return from Torquay, faded out in 1955 when she left for another post. This Cooks' Course had comprised two terms aimed at achieving a high standard of cookery, followed by a final term of large scale work in the Canteen Kitchen, helping the IMA students to prepare meals for the Public Restaurant.

Canteen service was by now established as part of the National life, and gone were the days when special meals were served at different times. There was no longer any pandering to whims and fancies in the new, well organised, labour saving system.

The IMA students ate the canteen meals; others had the dishes from the Training Kitchens, supplemented as necessary by the Canteen, which supplied approximately one thousand meals daily to a faithful public. Nor was their loyalty surprising when a two-course luncheon could be relied on to be well chosen, cooked and served for the price of a shilling. Neither did it escalate with the passage of years. Tea and coffee, raised from 1½d, remained at 2d a cup until it became 3d in 1955; the luncheon was increased to 1s 2d in August 1946, and thereafter rose slowly to reach 1s 9d in 1951, and finally to 2s in 1958.

But there was affection for the College, and regret for more than material values, when the Public Restaurant closed in the sad days of 1962.

The IMA Course made its presence felt in other ways besides the valuable Canteen. In preparation for subsequent posts in a wide variety of Institutions the training entailed residential experience in Home Management, which involved the use of three Hostels.

The Grosvenor Estate now required number 72 Eccleston Square, the house which they had temporarily lent to the National, and it behoved the Committee to find a replacement. Bearing in mind the additional needs of the IMA Course, it was decided to seek a larger property. The main problem, as always, was the cost, and the Bank was approached for an overdraft to cover the outlay. In October 1949 St George's House in Vincent Square was approved, and the price of £28,000 agreed. The Committee's initial rejoicing was somewhat harshly dispelled when the owners then accepted an offer of £35,000 and withdrew.

Two adjoining houses, numbers 101 and 103 Eaton Place shortly became available and were secured in June 1950 for £4,000 each. The Ministry of Education approved estimates for repairs and decorations at both houses at a cost of £2,890, with consideration of a further £2,140 for the conversion of basements into a dining room and kitchens. Even though the price paid was considerably lower than that contemplated for the Vincent Square property, the Bank was asked to increase the overdraft to £20,000. By June 1951, it was raised to £30,000.

SURVIVAL

CHAPTER XLIII

THE NATIONAL, in the month of January 1947, with Miss Eland returned and affairs at Torquay wound up, was once more set on its path in London, for better, for worse; for richer, for poorer. What the ultimate state would be, only time could tell, but at least the immediate situation could be gauged by taking stock.

The College was richer in experience and achievement; its horizons were wider and more academic; its reaction to changing times more flexible and tolerant. It had gifted and valuable members of staff. The Public Restaurant was flourishing and prosperous. There was considerable reconstruction, refurbishing and new equipment.

It was poorer in the loss of some skilled and loyal staff of long standing and in the practice of certain craft techniques. In spite of rebuilding, the basic design and material condition of the premises and much of the equipment stood to endanger both the College's status and its future. It had no endowment fund, and no proper capital.

To retrieve the position and exploit the assets, prospects depended on a firm financial basis, and although in this respect there were certain promising features, to establish the necessary security was by no means straightforward.

The issue was forced in connection with Ministry of Education regulations concerning apportionment of income and contributions towards rent. It was complicated by the official designation of the National as a 'Voluntary' institution, and by the two sides of its work, the Teacher Training and the Technical, now separated physically and with differing aims and incomes.

The closest scrutiny of the position with all its implications was called for, and in a masterly survey, the Auditor, Mr H. O. H. Coulson, elucidated 'the effect of the Ministry of Education proposals upon the revenue and expenses of the College,' and laid his findings before the Finance Committee on 15 May 1947.

Referring to the reorganisation and additional building, for which 'a total expenditure of some £27,000 is envisaged,' he explained that on 31 March 1946, after the sale of properties, the College had in hand a total sum of £21,000, and 'under the provision of schemes made by the Ministry of Education' claimed to be 'entitled to a grant of 50 per cent of its capital expenditure, after taking into account the proceeds of any capital realisation.' A problem, however, lay in the assignment of the various claims, covering Training and Technical Departments, as well as Hostel accommodation. After sorting out these issues, the conclusion was reached that 'the College, therefore, claims from the Ministry some £9,500, so that after discharging the whole of its programmed capital expenditure, it should have approximately £3,000 of liquid capital available for the normal conduct of its affairs.'

This indeed would have been quite a comfortable position, but there were far more strings tied to it. In a tight packed argument, the Auditor continued:

'Under the conditions attaching to the Schemes of the Ministry of Education, it is understood that, in future, the fees to be charged by the College will be fixed by the Ministry which will also make certain stipulations as the amenities to be offered to students and the additional charges, if any, which may be made to them. These stipulations relate primarily to the "Training" side of the College, although there will also be restrictions upon the acceptance of private or Technical students and upon the fees to be charged to them. In determining the fees which the College may charge to "Training" students, the Ministry will have regard to the reasonable costs of operation but, where the whole or major part of the premises occupied are rented, will require a College of this type (described as a "voluntary" college) to find from "voluntary" sources one half of the total rent payable, allowing one half only as part of the reasonable costs upon which Training students' fees are based.

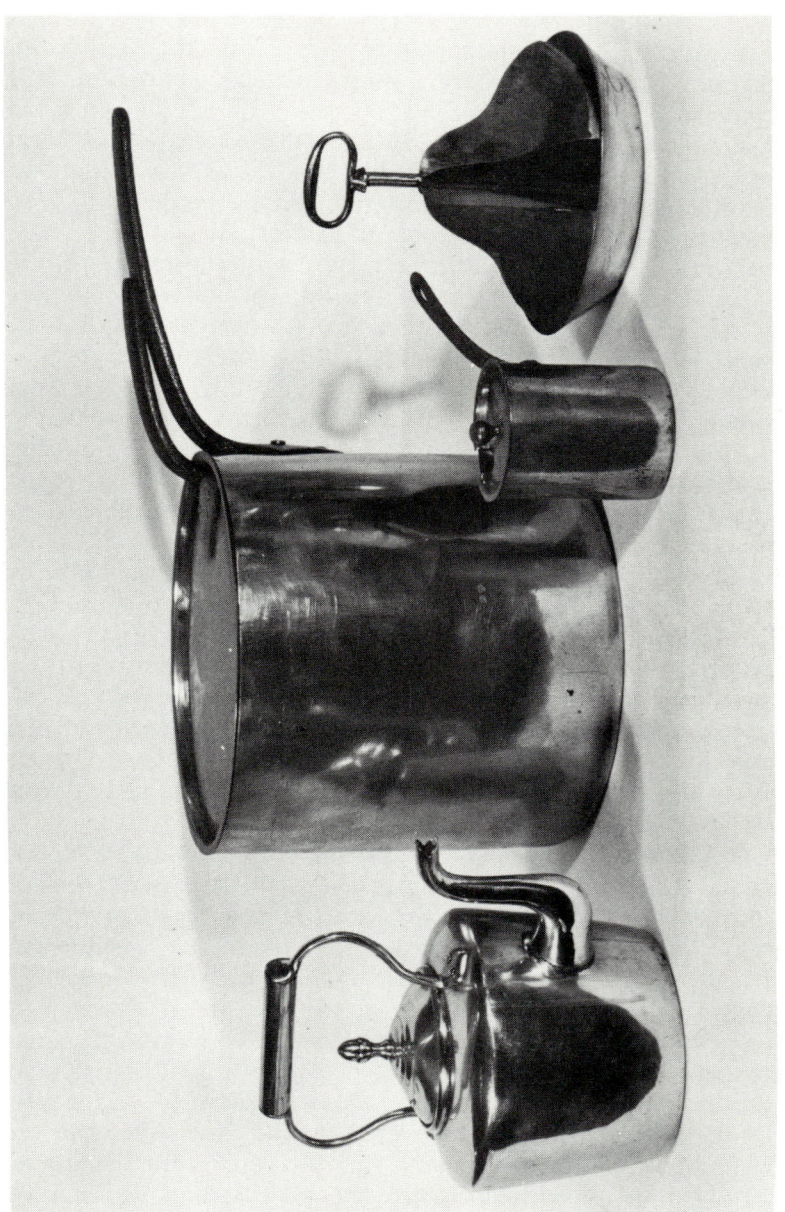

Selection of the National Copper (now in Brighton Pavilion)

'The College holds some four leaseholds expiring in 1978, at comparatively low rents, but pays for two other buildings, 53 and 54 Eccleston Square, a rental of £2,500 per annum. It is understood that the Ministry proposes in the calculation of the fees to be charged to "Training" students, to disallow one half of these rents, or approximately £1,500. The Ministry enquires from what "voluntary" sources the College would propose to meet the disallowed portion of the rents.

'The College is described as a "Voluntary" college on the ground, apparently, that it has in the past derived some part of its income from sources other than fees and grants. In fact, the College has obtained only a trifling income from sources which might strictly be designated as "voluntary," but has from time to time obtained substantial profits, which have been taken, in effect, to an Endowment Fund, from the operation of canteens and national kitchens. As matters now stand, it is proposed that the present canteen operations should be continued as an essential outlet for the food cooked by students taking courses in big-scale cookery. Inasmuch as these sales of food are, in effect, the disposal of a by-product of the operations of the College, it may be argued that virtually the whole proceeds may be regarded as "voluntary" income as defined by relation to the sources of the revenue of the College in former years. It is impracticable to draw up accurate separate accounts of canteen operations, as the preparation of food is an essential part of the teaching activities of the College wholly on the non-Training or "Technical" side.

'It is submitted that the College should contend that its so-called voluntary income has, in the past, been derived from sources similar to the present canteen operations and from relatively small surpluses derived from the fees of "Technical" students whether residential or day. In so far as the College is permitted to charge adequate fees to "Technical" students to cover the cost of their teaching and to retain as voluntary income receipts from the sale of by-products of the teaching operations, it may anticipate receiving an income in the future adequate to meet any charges not covered by the fees receivable on account of "Training" students. Provided, therefore, the Ministry of Education does not so use its powers as to make it impossible for the College to continue to cover its costs of the "Technical" as well as of the "Training" side, the College is in a position to continue its operations unless and until there is some substantial change in existing conditions.

'If, however, the Ministry indicates that it will so use its powers it would seem that the College is in a position, for a comparatively limited period of time, to use its accumulated funds to meet annual deficits resulting from the fixation of its fees at less than the actual cost of teaching. If and when its resources had been substantially absorbed, the College would have no alternative but to close down and the Company would be liquidated.'

In this succinct Note, the tocsin had sounded.

There were, however, many moments of pleasure after the War ended, and an event which gave widespread gratification was the recognition of the National in the honour bestowed on Miss Grace Eland, when in the New Year of 1946, she became an Officer of the Most Excellent Order of the British Empire. The award was a stimulant at this time when everyone recognised the long hard road which lay ahead.

Miss Eland herself was now immersed in the reorganisation of the Teacher Training Courses which followed the recommendations of the McNair Report. At the Committee Meeting on 26 October 1944, this Report was discussed in connection with a Memorandum of 23 September from the University of London, proposing to set up a School of Education at the University, where approved Teacher Training Institutions within the area would be included.

Cautious over committing the College to a new idea whose significance was difficult to assess, it was eventually agreed to reply that 'The Committee accepted the proposed Scheme in principle, but wished to place on record its opinion that the members of staff of Domestic Subjects Colleges with high specialist qualifications should be accepted as members of the School of Education on equal terms with colleagues of comparable academic distinction.'

The new idea, in fact, had come to stay, and the memorandum of the University was the prelude to sustained and concentrated effort to grasp a new concept, translate it into workable shape and hammer out every detail. Miss Eland's intellectual approach now came into its own, and stood the National in good stead during the prolonged ensuing discussions.

There were thirty-four Training Colleges in the ambit of the University of London, and the McNair Committee on the Training of Teachers, to which a great number of witnesses were summoned, studied their diverse aims and needs in considerable depth. These Training Colleges were now to be linked to the University's own established Department of Education, which dealt with advanced and graduate courses and research, to form in a new amalgam the London Institute of Education, soon to become a power house under the forceful and dominating Directorship of Professor Jeffreys.

The recognised teaching qualification for all teachers, whether of General or Specialist subjects, was to be the Certificate issued by the Institute, and no time was lost in setting up a working party to agree basic requirements and seek common ground between the Colleges, without loss of individuality. None the less, the first draft produced considerable anxiety in the Training Colleges for some of the ideas mooted seemed to cut at the roots of established beliefs.

Emphasis was placed on 'educating' as opposed to 'training.' To this end, it was suggested that a compulsory main subject, or 'Field of Study' as it was originally termed, 'not to be considered as part of the curriculum studies,' was to be chosen by each individual student for the development of his, or her, own education.'

The implication caused heart searching, and at times hurt, particularly to the craft teachers, among whom the wise and intelligent had always striven to 'educate' in the wider sense, as well as 'train' in the narrower vocational field. As each student must stand or fall by this test, it became the keystone of the course, demanding much scheduled and private time and study; to the detriment, it was often strongly felt, of the recognised training originally undertaken by the student.

The demand for additional time for private study directly connected with specialist training competed further with the claims of craft technique. A fair allocation of hours at first seemed an insuperable problem, not only within each individual college, but even more so when comparison between Two and Three-Year Courses had to be made.

Repercussions were felt in every subject and at every level. The course in Principles of Education had hitherto been planned between the three London Domestic Subjects Colleges, setting a common paper with special reference to their own needs, and marked to an agreed standard, but now they would have to meet the requirements of the full Education Board of Studies of the Institute. Although certain aspects of the revolutionary change might be welcomed, it was obvious from the start that feelings ran too high to allow of easy co-operation. Battles were fought every inch of the way before understanding, tact and compromise eventually achieved overall agreement.

An Area Training Scheme was set up, whereby, for the purpose of joint consultation and conduct of final examinations, colleges were divided into groups of five or six, chosen to give amongst themselves variety and interchange of ideas. The National initially belonged to a group including a highly academic Roman Catholic College, a Physical Education College, and one with a bias towards Nursery and Infant work.

Discussions at meetings with a Professor or Senior Tutor of the Department of Education in the Chair, were always stimulating; the arguments usually hot. Miss Royston recalled 'one felt that one was always fighting' and continued, 'The fiercest battles were in the full meetings of the Education Board of Studies, where over two hundred Education Tutors and University representatives gathered in the Beveridge Hall to fight for the freedom of individual colleges, which many felt was threatened by the new regime.' She summarised some of the duties which now fell to the share of college lecturers: 'Every subject had its own Board of Studies, and the three Domestic Subjects Colleges were joined by the newly established Seaford College in Sussex, to determine the academic content and examination procedure for all subjects under their aegis. In this they were helped by the Education Tutors from these four colleges who formed a separate Committee to deal with aspects of curriculum and practical teaching.'

The choice of a Field of Study nearly brought the walls of the National about its ears. Convinced of the potential academic value of the practical subjects, it proposed that students should 'choose an aesthetic, scientific or social studies approach, and from this angle make an integrated study of some aspect of Needlework, Cookery or Home Management.' It was an unheard of idea. 'According to the Institute,' Miss Royston recalled, 'the only choice open to the National, as a specialist Domestic Subjects College, was English,' and it was 'made quite clear that full agreement was a compulsory condition of acceptance as a Constituent College of the Institute, and therefore the National's interpretation of Fields of Study had to be approved at the highest level.' She continued, 'At a meeting with the Director, there was considerable opposition, Professor Jeffreys expressing the fear that 'vocational training was coming in by the back door,' and that the real aims of the Fields of Study would be defeated.' Alarm bells rang on all sides, for the path now lay along a knife edge where a false step could have spelt disaster.

Wits, patience and determination were all fully deployed before the claims of the National were recognised. Finally it was agreed 'that the College should be allowed to experiment.' In heartfelt relief it grasped this opportunity to prove its case. Not only did it succeed, but at the same time remained true to tradition, for again in its history it had been a pioneer.

The developments following the establishment of the London Institute of Education were swiftly discernible in the improvement of all Library facilities, and the craft subjects were enriched by the generous allocation of funds for a wide range of books. Appreciation of this was reflected in Miss Eland's words that 'they might have to live with the limitations of the building, but to a great degree books could compensate.'

There was no short cut through the maze of prolonged negotiations, fierce arguments and patient discussions which finally led to agreement. It was December 1948, the year of the College's seventy-fifth anniversary, when the Senate of the University invited the National to become a Constituent College of the London Institute of Education, and Miss Eland was elected to serve on the Council of the Institute.

The changed standing of the College immediately became apparent in a new relationship. The status and title of 'Lecturer in the Institute' was conferred by the Senate on all members of

the staff concerned with the training of teachers, whether dealing with academic or craft subjects. The pooling of ideas and
resources made for much closer association, not only between
the lecturers of all the thirty-four training Colleges, but with
the central purpose of the Institute, including the prospect of
periodical service on the Council or Academic Board. The
Association of London Education Students spread the net still
wider, for it was so designed that all men and women students
of the Constituent Colleges could share University activities.

A repercussion of the new set-up was the break with Bristol.
In 1949 the National's connection with that University in the
practical training of their Home Economics students finished.
No longer was the little group to be found at Buckingham Palace
Road or at the Hostels, for henceforth this side of their work was
shared between Bath and Gloucester.

A year later, in December 1949, the Chancellor of the University of London, the Earl of Athlone, formally inaugurated the
Institute of Education. The National was represented at the
ceremony by the Principal, the Vice Principal, three senior
members of staff, and six student representatives, including the
President of the Students' Guild. Miss Eland had already written
'The wide implications of the scheme can be achieved only by
the efforts of all members of the Colleges as well as of those of us
elected to serve on the Council or the Academic Board.'

There was genuine desire and unremitting work for the
success of the new concept. Yet some twenty years later Miss
Royston again commented that although 'academic standards
had certainly risen,' she wondered whether 'the specialist
Colleges had found a really satisfactory adjustment and balance
between craftsmanship and the other demands of the course. It
seems,' she concluded, 'to be an unending search.'

Every searcher finds his own answer. However wide the gaps
between the points of view, the final consensus of opinion seems
to reflect the philosophy of 'losses on the Roundabouts means
profits on the Swings!'

Her Majesty Queen Elizabeth and Canteen Cooks, 1949

SURVIVAL

CHAPTER XLIV

THE INAUGURATION of the London Institute of Education in December 1949 had been preceded by a red letter day in October. The seventy-fifth anniversary of the National, originally planned for celebration in 1948, was postponed for twelve months, to conform to the pattern of the previous commemorations, and the importance attached to the occasion was highlighted when Her Majesty Queen Elizabeth agreed to honour the College with a visit. Excitement ran high. It was six years since she had heartened everyone by coming during the hard days of the War, so it was a double delight to welcome her now at a time of real rejoicing.

A great part of the College was changed almost beyond recognition, for the main building programme was complete. The new Assembly Hall was filled to overflowing with staff and students, and the little platform transformed with flowers, ready to greet the Royal Patron when she arrived, with her Lady in Waiting, the Lady Katherine Seymour, at eleven o'clock on the morning of Wednesday, 18 May. There were spring flowers everywhere, arranged in the big polished copper pans and the long *bain-marie* from the old kitchens, as well as in the 'Queen's silver Rosebowl' on the platform.

It was a sunshiny morning, and Her Majesty's loveliness in powder blue and grey was complemented by the delicate tints of the lilies of the valley, delphiniums and roses in her bouquet. After this had been presented in the Hall, and she had been officially welcomed by the Chairman and the Principal, Miss Eland conducted Queen Elizabeth around the College. Even those who had been previously privileged to meet Her Majesty were struck afresh at her interest and kindness. Miss Lough recalled how she amazed everyone with her practical knowledge, appreciating the value of macaroni cheese as 'a stand-by,' and when a student ventured to warn her that an iron was 'hot,' Her Majesty revealed her own knowledge of the degree of heat required 'for such fine material.'

It was this friendly understanding allied to her charm which enslaved the College anew. She was untiring in seeing work in all subjects of both Training and Technical students; in gracious conversation over coffee with the Committee members; in recognition of any helper, and of the students who lined the corridors and formed a guard of honour to her waiting car after a memorable visit.

The final episode was unplanned and unusual, for the glorious morning sunshine unexpectedly dissolved in rain, and Her Majesty the Queen left the National under a borrowed multi-coloured golf umbrella whose brightness could not outshine the glow of her personality.

Now once more life was earnest. The new Teacher Training Course was being implemented, and all students entering the College in September 1950 were to follow the different plan. There were staff changes, too. The half century marked the close of many associations, but it was the beginning of others. Miss Chart, who had come as Education lecturer in 1943, resigned in 1948, but continued to give Miss Royston, the Head of Department, some part-time help until 1950. Mrs Baranyay then arrived, and with her clear mind and sympathetic approach helped students to an awareness of social problems. Both she and Miss Henwood, an Old Student who returned in 1948, loyally supported the College to the end.

At the end of the summer 1949, six members of staff left, chief among them Miss Lancaster and Miss Howlett. Miss Lancaster's gift as a miniaturist, showing at the Royal Academy, was matched by her scrupulous technique and knowledge of very different materials in the sphere of laundrywork. Both she and Miss Howlett shared an artistic appreciation of fabrics, and in the Needlework and Dressmaking Department, Miss Howlett

Her Majesty Queen Elizabeth with Lady Katharine Seymour
and Miss Lough

encouraged lively experimental work. She was succeeded by Miss Breukelman who carried on the tradition of high standards and deft handling which had always marked these subjects.

Miss Main, Miss Tait and Mrs Brown, the latter since her pre-War days as Miss Winthrop known for her Cookery expertise, all left at the same time. They had all been National students, steeped in its ways, and as with many others of this ilk, they continued to uphold the College even when other posts took them elsewhere.

It was also at the close of this summer term in 1949 that Miss Swanston's 'characteristic practical generosity' was demonstrated in the first award of her prize. She had died two years earlier, and left 'one hundred pounds sterling . . . to be invested and the interest thereon to be used to provide prizes for students taking the Housekeepers' Course only,' and to be given to the student who did outstanding work in Cookery. The prize was to be 'preferably a Text Book or some apparatus of special use in the subject.' As the Housekeepers' Course had already become part of the Institutional Management Course, the prize was awarded to a student then finishing her two-year College course.

The Committee, in June 1948, had raised the wages of the domestic staff to 2s an hour and granted two weeks annual holidays. They now resolved to exercise justice towards the members of the non-teaching staff who were still out in the cold in regard to pensions. This timely action was clinched in 'a fair scheme' contracted with the Alliance Assurance Company in 1949, but it nevertheless drew Ministry of Education censure, expressed in a note to the Committee in October 1950, at the 'lack of previous consultation' over these commitments. The rebuke met with no comment, but a certain acrimony in the relationship was evinced when in January 1951, the Ministry of Education classed the National as a 'Profit-making Limited Liability Company,' to which the Auditor took strong exception, and a reply was sent to the effect that the College was an 'Association not trading for profit.'

It was a hard time for the Committee. Everyone was fully aware of the shaky state of the finances, and equally of the heavy drain imposed by the latest Burnham and Pelham salary scales for lecturers. Later in the year, the Ministry were persuaded to raise the fees to £210 for Tuition and to £141 for Board for 1951–1952, and to pay an extra £9 per student towards meeting past deficits since July 1946.

On a more profitable note, a new Course for Commonwealth students was initiated. From the end of the Second War, the College had accepted individual students sponsored by the Colonial Office, who in 1951 proposed that the National should 'inaugurate a course of Teacher Training planned to meet the needs of students from Overseas territories.' The idea was a welcome one, and the Principal was authorised to proceed. A three-year scheme to begin in 1952, and relating specifically to the needs and problems of the developing countries of the Commonwealth, was prepared and accepted at the Colonial Office by the Students' Department, which in consultation with the Overseas Governments, took overall responsibility for training and welfare.

It was particularly fortunate that the first ten students from eight different Colonies were able in June 1953, both to enjoy the College decorations and gay window boxes, and also to share the students' celebration of the Coronation. The wet cold night of Tuesday, 1 June, even though protected from the hard ground by mackintoshes, blankets and hot water bottles, and fortified by sandwiches and drinks, may not have been an entirely enjoyable experience, but at least they were all splendidly positioned 'to give loyal support to Her Majesty Queen Elizabeth II on her way to and from the Abbey.'

Among these first Overseas students were three from Ghana who had received their initial training in that country from Miss Asari, herself a former National student, so they quickly made themselves at home. So completely did the new arrivals become part of the College life that it caused no surprise when in 1954, the charming Miss Evelyn Tan from Singapore made history as the first Overseas student to be elected President of the Students' Union; culminating in the award of the Queen's Prize for service to the College.

There had been a renewed and pleasurable link with South Devon Technical College when approximately two hundred and fifty of their students stayed at the Eccleston Square Hostels

(at a charge of 12*s* 6*d* for bed and breakfast), during the summer
vacation of 1951 while they visited the Festival of Britain. Miss
Cottrell, whose name was forever connected with the Villa Rosa
at Torquay, had just retired, and the Home Management Department had bidden her a reluctant goodbye. Miss Kennett, her
assistant for many years, succeeded her.

During this time in a period of under five years the older members of the staff and the Committee were saddened by a series of
deaths, following the loss of the vital bond with the National of
Mr Charles Buckmaster when he retired in 1948. He had joined
the Executive Committee in 1915, and for the thirty years since
1918 had been the Honorary Treasurer. He resigned in June, and
died the following 24 May 1949, a week after his ninety-fifth
birthday. He had much in common with his famous predecessors:
his own father, Mr J. C. Buckmaster, who had lectured at the
Great Exhibition of 1873, and Sir Henry Cole who had initiated
the whole National enterprise. Miss Caddow recorded that
Mr Charles Buckmaster was 'most truly a guide, philosopher
and friend, an ardent Anglican, a Liberal, a man of high attainments, fond of travel, with a fund of humour and great capacity
for happiness reflected in his happy home life.'
In 1951, Miss Broderick died in January and Mrs Hutchinson
in November; then Louisa, aged ninety-two, at the end of December 1952. There were still fewer to mourn the old *régime* by the
end of 1953. Miss Caddow, the mainstay, died on 27 August 1953
in her ninetieth year. Miss Louisa Thorpe had died in January,
and Mrs Stanley Jones in July; as Miss Lydia Loader the latter
had worked closely for many years with Miss Walker Jones,
whose own death followed in November.
Mrs MacGregor had known and worked with them all. When
she retired in October 1953, the Committee marked the unanimous appreciation of her thirty-four years of service with a
gratuity of £100 – but it could in no way lessen her desolation
at the end of this sorrowful year.
Each one was forever a part of the fabric of the National, and
each had brought her own gifts in tribute and in affection to the
'dear old School.'
Miss Caddow represented the flower of the early days, and
had become a legend in her own time. In recalling her vivid

interest in everyone and everything, which remained undimmed to the last, Miss Eland quoted, in illustration, 'I warmed both hands before the fire of life. It sinks, and I am ready to depart.'

In her ninety years, Miss Caddow witnessed many events, and always revelled in the exhilaration of Celebrations and Jubilees. It seemed fitting that the last one she enjoyed held the promise of youth and happiness in the colourful Coronation of the young Queen, Her Majesty Queen Elizabeth II, the daughter of her most cherished member of the Royal Family.

Miss Alice Caddow bequeathed to the Guild one hundred pounds, which provided a handsome clock from Camerer Cuss and other improvements for the Library. A Memorial Fund was set up to benefit the Hostel, and used for the Quiet Room in Eccleston Square, including the purchase of an electric heater and a new blue carpet.

Miss Eland wrote in May 1953, of 'two big changes of personnel.' The first concerned the Executive Committee, with the resignation from the Chairmanship of Mrs Karslake, who had become a member in 1920, Vice Chairman in 1934 and Chairman in 1941, and to whom, 'always sagacious and kind,' the College already owed so much during these thirty-three years. She agreed to remain on the Committee; Mrs Dally, who had joined as Mrs Page Roberts in 1947, now accepted the Chairmanship.

The second change resulted from Miss Lough's decision to retire after the Summer Term of 1953. She had given unswerving help to the College for nearly thirty-five years; undaunted and with shrewd understanding, she had rescued many a student from an attack of nerves before a lesson by her firm and simple dictum 'Take a deep breath, and speak up.' Miss Eland regarded her as 'one of the most helpful colleagues any Principal could wish to have,' and continued 'My sense of loss in her departure is mitigated by the knowledge that I am to have Miss Edward as Vice Principal in her place.'

At the end of this same term, Miss Fraser resigned from the Hostel. She was succeeded by Miss Kelleher who came to join Miss O'Keeffe in this exacting task.

Another break followed in the December of 1953, when Miss Royston returned to her native county of Yorkshire, to become Vice Principal of the College of Housecraft at Ilkley.

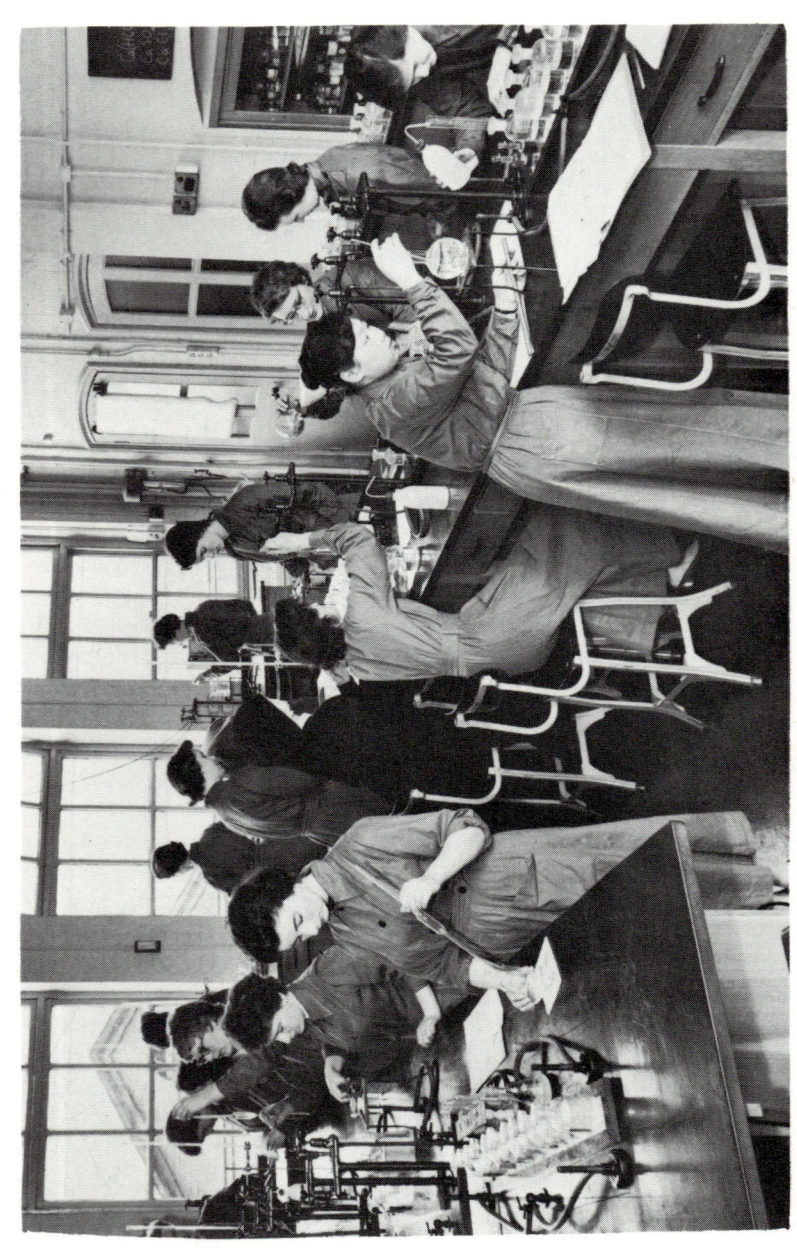

Science Laboratory, 1958

SURVIVAL

CHAPTER XLV

THE UNIVERSITY VISITATION of 17 May 1951 had shown appreciation of the conduct of the National in dealing with the changed conditions and new courses since becoming a Constituent College of the University. The content of the curriculum was felt to be in good hands, but in spite of all the recent extensive material improvements, the Visitors deplored the still existing deficiencies, which they regarded as limiting the range of work. In especial, they noted the lack of an Assembly Hall, and they advocated the conversion of the top floor into a laboratory. They asked specifically for the views of the staff, particularly in regard to the Library. The answer to each point raised was a matter of importance.

The Committee had recently been reconsidering possible means whereby the teaching staff could officially express their views. In the previous March, 'feasible arrangements to enable the academic staff to formulate and express a corporate policy on academic matters, and to take part in the management of the College' had been discussed at length. It was finally resolved however that 'representations from the College Academic Board, on academic matters,' would be received by the Committee members, as brought to their notice from time to time by the Principal, and further 'that the Minutes of the Meetings of the College Board be laid on the table at Meetings of the Executive Committee for their information.' Miss Eland had just been elected an *ex officio* member of the Executive Committee, and thus through her, a channel of communication was opened; but the staff had no direct official access to the Committee, and

289

there was no thought of implementing the suggestion that they should 'take part in the management of the College.'

The ideas of the University Visitors for improving the premises were costly. The Committee considered them in detail at the Meeting on 13 December 1951, during a prolonged discussion of the present financial position. This followed a Finance Committee Meeting the previous week on 6 December, when the Auditor, in presenting his Report and Balance Sheet for the year ending 31 August 1951, had drawn attention to the 'very grave financial position of the College, owing to the non-payment of capital grant by the Ministry of Education on the houses in Eaton Place, and the decline of fees for Training students,' whose recruitment suffered from the out-of-date premises. It was also reported that during that year the assets of the College had been decreased by £8,000, and that 'if this amount were withdrawn annually in future, the College would have to close down within a very short period.'

The Honorary Treasurer summed up the situation, pointing out that 'the crisis could only be postponed for a time' unless the Ministry of Education agreed to a higher fee for the Training students, and to an annual grant towards the cost of the Technical training.'

It was a bitter reflection that lack of space and restrictions imposed on fees exaggerated the general problems, and so prevented expansion of the once profitable Technical courses. Only the Institutional Management Course, supplying the Public Restaurant, well and truly earned its keep.

It was unanimously agreed that it was imperative to make a further appeal to the Ministry of Education, stressing that the very life of the National was dependent on adequate fees and grants. In response, the Minister, early in 1952, announced that 'a full review of the College's financial position should be undertaken,' and requested a statement of accounts.

The Auditor was again asked for a memorandum, and in April 1952 'with a view to getting some kind of realism into the grant procedure,' Mr Coulson prepared a Report designed for discussion. In it he reverted to his earlier suggestion of 1947 that the surplus profit of some £5,000 a year from the Public Restaurant should be transferred to an Endowment Fund, which

Cookery, 1958

could be used 'to cover expenses disallowed by the Ministry, and at the same time use any balance to build up a fund out of which the College could discharge its own share of capital expenditure.' The ensuing discussion was of great value. The idea was accepted by the Ministry, and by this master stroke the College was enabled, over the next few years, in considerable measure to rebuild its capital position. In addition, the Ministry also approved a back-dated grant of £4,000 for 1950–1951, to be regarded as a basis for the following three years.

The Committee felt justified in judging these moves to indicate that the College was regarded as worthy of long-term support. Mr Max-Muller, who had joined the Committee two years previously, suggested that this belief might be substantiated by an exchange at high level with the Ministry to discuss means of putting the College finances on a permanently firm footing, and it was again urged that on this security rested the whole future of the National. A 'most satisfactory personal talk' resulted; it brought a degree of reassurance, and the Committee in December 1952 recorded its official thanks both to Mr Coulson and to Mr Max-Muller, for all their help, including the discussion with Sir John Maud at the Ministry. Finances were temporarily steadier, and for a short space of time, there was a lull in the anxiety.

After the University Visitation of May 1951, a 'suitable reply' from the National had been despatched, implying that the Committee would pursue the recommendations of the Visitors' Report for improving the premises. In answer, the following June 1952, the Director of the Institute of Education 'noted with satisfaction the steps taken to meet the points raised.' The parlous state of the National's finances, however, had prevented any steps being taken.

The College was therefore in somewhat of a quandary when it was learnt that another Visitation was forthcoming on 14 November 1955. Estimates for the proposed conversions were hastily sought, but fulfilment seemed as far off as ever, with an Assembly Hall over the Catering Kitchen rated at £12,000, and tutorial rooms and laboratory at £15,000. It was agreed that the Principal should explain that 'only in the last two years had it

Laundry, 1958

been possible to put money aside for this purpose; that the Assembly Hall was deemed impracticable,' but it was 'hoped to acquire the other important accommodation.' Against all probability, the last statement proved to be quite correct.

The subsequent University Report was both complimentary and stimulating. The Visitors accepted the difficulties connected with a new Assembly Hall, but the Committee was galvanised into compliance with their other suggestions. By the following June 1956, plans for a new laboratory and modernisation of an old laundry were agreed with the Ministry of Education, the Committee confirming its decision that 'the College's part of the expense should not exceed £6,000.' The figure was realistic, for with a revised estimate of £4,112, there was still good margin for additional heating and equipment. The plans were at once put into effect, and completed with surprising speed.

The new laboratory was a tribute to Miss Hilda Shaw who had raised Science to a position of recognised eminence far beyond any resemblance to the subject or its status when she had joined the staff in 1922. It was ironic that the larger, quieter laboratory should materialise so soon after her retirement in the summer of 1956. She had so often related how she was constantly compelled to shut the windows against the distractions of the traffic and the Guards' Band, with subsequent lack of oxygen and onset of sleep, which seemed singularly inappropriate during lectures on Hygiene. Now, in the new laboratory at the back of the building, the comparative quiet allowed open windows to let in air, even if polluted and smutty; air conditioning still belonged to the future.

Miss Eland echoed the feelings of many when she wrote of Miss Shaw: 'Always she has been ready to strive to the uttermost to enable even the most unscientifically minded to gain some understanding of scientific principles,' and that 'no one could have been more zealous to help every student.'

Miss Dumas now became Head of the Science Department, and with two laboratories in use it was planned to have an additional full-time Lecturer as well as two part-time.

There had been changes on the Executive Committee. In 1952 Mrs Dally took over the Chair from Mrs Karslake, with Mr

MacFarlane continuing, since 1945, as Vice Chairman. Mrs Karslake agreed to remain as a member of the Committee, and her son Mr E. K. Karslake had followed the honoured Mr Buckmaster in June 1948 as Honorary Treasurer. He resigned in 1953, when Mr (later Sir Guy) Thorold ably guided the finances towards a more stable basis until his appointment to the Embassy at Washington in 1956.

Mrs Cash became a member of the Committee in 1953, and her husband Mr (afterwards Sir William) Cash accepted the invitation in 1956, to take over as Honorary Treasurer from Mr Thorold. It proved an onerous period with the fortunes of the National at stake.

The Committee members included Miss H. Dent, who, coming in 1946 as a University Representative, had served as an Independent Member since 1947. Miss Souter, who had joined in 1916, Lady Max-Muller in 1936, Mrs Lowe in 1941 and Lady Monckton in 1942, all continued their support.

Mrs Lowe died in 1956 at the age of eighty-six. She had been the first woman Chairman of the London County Council, and an active member of the Executive, Finance and Education Committees at the National who keenly felt the loss of her experienced judgment.

Mr John Max-Muller came in 1950 to give able and pertinent advice; Mrs Osman and Mr D. C. Dally joined three years later in 1953. Lady Heath and Miss M. J. Sargeaunt, Principal of King's College of Household Science (which became Queen Elizabeth College in 1953) had represented the University of London since 1947, and Miss S. Griffiths the London County Council from 1956.

Both Mrs Karslake and Mr MacFarlane, faithful friends of long standing, died in 1958. Lady Max-Muller resigned in the same year.

Miss Dent then became Vice Chairman, Miss Karslake took her Mother's place on the Committee, but her brother Mr Karslake resigned in 1959. When Sir Guy Thorold rejoined them in the midsummer of 1959, the Executive Committee numbered fifteen.

These were the representatives of the National whose fate it was to take official responsibility and pilot the College through

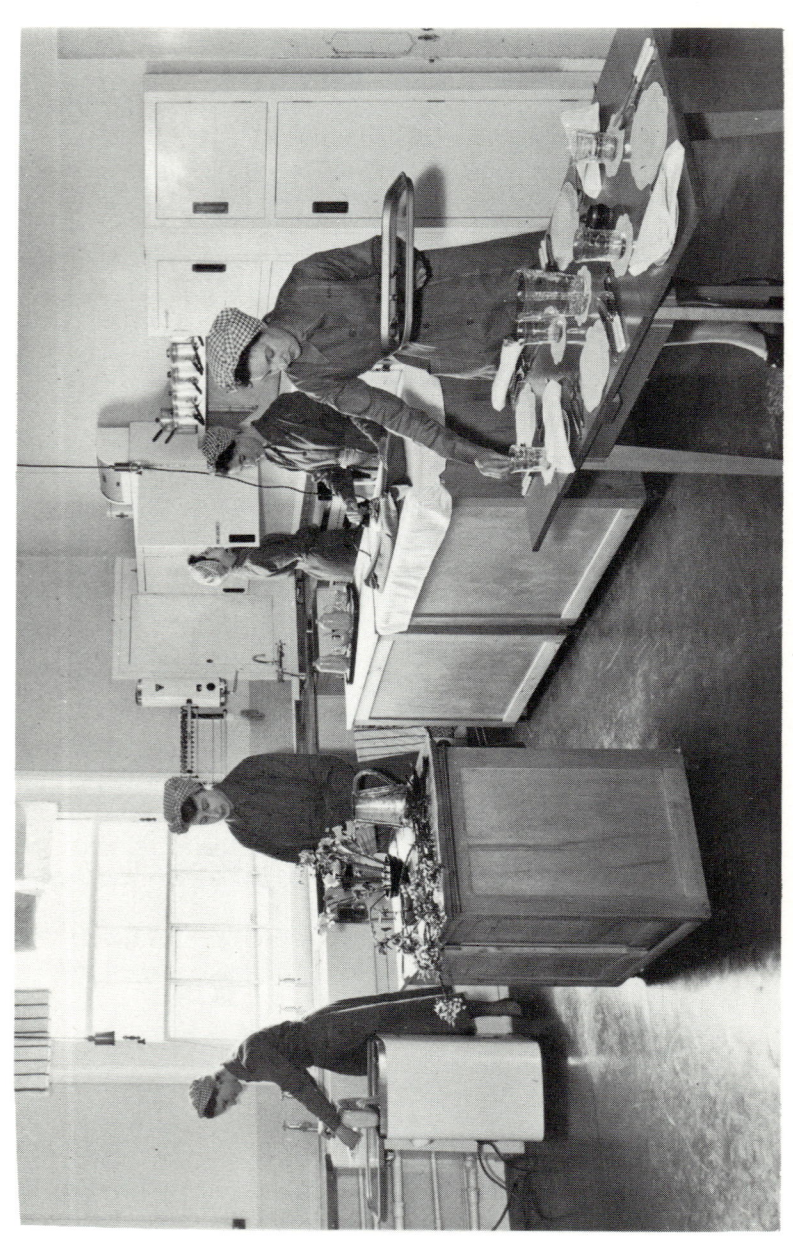

Home Management, 1958

the treacherous currents of the remaining years.

In December 1953, Mr Coulson reported that although great care in expenditure was still needed, the net assets had improved by £7,500, and a year later, still repeating his warning over expenses, he was yet able to report that the College was 'getting back to a state of solvency.'

During September to December 1955, the number of Canteen meals increased by four thousand as against the same period in 1954, and it was noted with satisfaction that 'if this were maintained for a full year, it would add £970 to the takings.'

In 1956 the Ministry reopened the accounts for the years 1954–1955, in order to make their grants up to £6,000 a year, promising to raise them again in the following year and pay three instalments of £3,000 a term, to total £9,000 a year.

It really seemed as if the National might be turning the corner, but there was still a nagging uncertainty. Maintenance and repairs were a constant drain, and the recruitment of students continued to be erratic. It became increasingly evident that nothing short of up-to-date premises could stem this drift away from the College, but the cost of a new building was estimated at over £400,000. It seemed that the premises could not usefully be replaced on the present restricted site, and problems of accommodation for the College during rebuilding almost insuperable, even if the Grosvenor Estate had been prepared at that moment to enter into a firm agreement over the extension and terms of the lease, which was by no means the case. Until the future should be reasonably assured there could be no confidence in planning. The National as the only Domestic Science Training College in the country not taken over by its Local Education Authority had no further way of increasing its income, and therefore was dependent on the Ministry of Education and the London County Council to keep it afloat.

The only means of obtaining funds towards rebuilding was by the sale of its properties and leases. At this time, the later inflationary spiral in prices had not made itself evident, and the assessment of the College's assets of necessity had to be cautious. It was also realised that much of the appeal of the National throughout its life had lain in its geographical position, and that any transfer beyond the present district would rob it of half its magnetism. No longer would it be associated in everyone's mind with Buckingham Palace Road, Victoria Station, the Band of the Guards, St James's Park and the Palace.

Faced with this predicament, the Committee sought further discussion with the Ministry. At the same time, appreciating the sound grasp and keen intellect of their Auditor, he was invited to become a member of the Executive, a proposal which Mr Coulson was obliged to refuse as long as he continued his services as Auditor, though he never wavered in placing his advice at their disposal.

At the end of the year, Miss Eland tendered her resignation, to take effect on the following 31 August 1956, but she finally yielded to requests to stay until August 1957. It was not an easy passage. Miss Eland's unquestioning sense of duty drew great strength from her religious beliefs, and she was an ardent churchwoman. Unfailing attendance at Service was the prelude to each day, so that the administrative and secretarial affairs were timed to begin at ten o'clock, though official hours for classes were unaltered. The same stern self discipline which would not allow her to share or delegate many of the burdens of her office, resulted in an ever increasing load which the help of others might have lightened. So anxious was she never to impose on anyone, that wherever possible, she bore the responsibility with her Committee, of unwelcome if unavoidable decisions, shielding everyone within the College from their impact. The staff in consequence were ignorant of the implications of the financial problems which were inexorably dragging down the National.

It was an increasingly unhappy situation, though a brave face was shown to the world. The students, with no suspicion of the approaching rapids, continued to enjoy their courses and succeed in their examinations. Both Training and Technical sides brought credit to the College.

Miss Eland's retirement was marked by a tribute from Miss Souter, on behalf of the Executive Committee, in June 1957, when she spoke of 'the value of our gain in your loyal co-operation in all the exigencies of our policy' and 'wished to say how genuine is our appreciation, in full measure, commensurate with the work you have done.' In July, a small party in her honour was attended by all the members of the Committee, and the College and Hostel staff, when she was asked to accept a small gift and their good wishes, gratitude and affection.' The previous 18 May 1957, had seen about 150 members of the Guild, trained between the years of 1901 and 1956, gathered at the Trocadero Restaurant for a Luncheon and tea to bid her farewell and to present her with an illuminated leather book with signatures of the subscribers to a £200 cheque. Miss Eland later wrote of her enjoyment 'in turning over the pages and picturing you in my mind's eye'; she felt that there was not much doubt that she would use some of the cheque for a holiday abroad.

Ferny Bank Hostel, Torquay, 1940

Miss Barbara S. Briggs
Principal 1957 – 1962

LAST DAYS

CHAPTER XLVI

THE APPOINTMENT of a new Principal to succeed Miss Eland was made in February 1957, when the Committee was unanimous in offering the post to Miss Barbara Briggs. She had been trained at Gloucestershire Training College of Domestic Science, where she had been one of Miss Eland's students, and during that time had come on a brief exchange visit to the National. She taught in the Midlands and at Roedean, and during the War went with a group from this School to another in Nova Scotia, where later she became Head Mistress. Returning from Canada in 1954, she was appointed as Her Majesty's Inspector of Schools, and assigned to the South West of England. Unaware of the abyss ahead, Miss Briggs accepted in good faith the invitation to become the fourth Principal of the National and took up her duties on 1 September 1957.

She was not left long in ignorance. Soon after her arrival she was taken into Mr William Cash's confidence over the state of the College. She learnt that 'Finances were at a very low ebb, staff salaries and domestic wages were rising, and the whole place run on a knife edge. The tiny balance was quite inadequate to replace or provide for new equipment or furnishings. Each year, the requirements estimated by Heads of Department were cut drastically.' That the premises were outdated and could not compare with those of other institutions was of course quite evident; the Library was too small and the College lacked proper provision for tutorials, private study and an Art Department. Hostel accommodation was poor, with shared bedrooms and inadequate washing facilities.

Now there seemed to be virtually no hope of changing these conditions, for the funds of a Voluntary College were very different from one owned by a Local Education Authority, and could by no means meet the cost involved. The present conditions deterred prospective students, and as the dedicated, long serving members of staff left, it had become increasingly difficult to appoint their successors. Miss Briggs was in a cleft stick. In the circumstances long term planning became impossible, and as all Committee matters were confidential, open discussion equally banned.

Mr William Cash, the Honorary Treasurer, had reported in the previous December 1956, that during a talk with Mr Nenk, the Accountant General at the Ministry of Education, it had been agreed that the situation should be reviewed the following year, after the 1956–1957 accounts became available. By June 1957 the Bank overdraft had been reduced to £10,000, but other issues now loomed ahead and when at a meeting in October, the Ministry suggested a visit to the College from Mr Warlow, a member of their Cost Investigation Unit, the National agreed with alacrity.

It was hoped that the subsequent findings might clarify the position and illumine the future, which had again become obscure since the Ministry had made known its policy over Specialist Training Colleges. This lay in overall acceptance of General Purpose Training Colleges, with various 'wings' wherein students could specialise in certain branches, while sharing subjects common to all. This design, it was felt, would be more economical in premises, staffing, general facilities and amenities, including grounds and sports, while at the same time enriching the students' experience with daily interchange of ideas in work and social life. In some cases, co-education was advocated, as approximating more to University life. There was no encouragement to build single sex, specialist colleges, even if the site and the money were available.

The National was still in the dark a year later on 16 October 1958, when Miss Briggs went with the now Sir William Cash for a talk at the Ministry with Mr B. L. Savage, the Territorial Officer for the College, which resulted in speeding up matters. The Ministry made it clear that nothing definite could be stated until they had studied the report of the Cost Investigation Unit, but Mr Savage indicated that a deputation from the National would be welcome early in the year 1959.

Mr Warlow eventually visited the College for two weeks on 28 October 1958. No report had been received when Sir William Cash, after a further personal exchange of views, told the Committee in February 1959 that he 'now understood that the Ministry wished the College to continue for another twenty years, and would welcome plans for the future.' At the request of Mr Savage and of H.M.I. Mrs House, Staff Inspector of Housecraft, who was responsible for the National, a list of new equipment and furnishings estimated at £5,710 was forwarded for consideration to the Ministry. Plans for further adaptation of the main Eccleston Square Hostel were costed at £7,600; tentative suggestions for extending the building at Buckingham Palace Road, or finding alternative premises were again brought forward. It was reported at the Finance Committee that the former proposition would entail at least £28,500, judged to be not worth while in view of the limited length of the lease. Mr Max-Muller had investigated prices and been advised that with approximately twenty years to run, the lease of Buckingham Palace Road might be worth £60,000 or £70,000, but with anything less than fifteen years, it would probably not realise more than enough to pay for dilapidations. The market was uncertain and a slump in property was feared. It was, however, learnt that in the London County Council Development Plan, the building was zoned for offices, which would be advantageous for value. The present Hostel leases could also be useful assets.

The Report from Mr Warlow was still awaited as the Spring of 1959 passed into early Summer. Conscious of the Ministry attitude over Specialist Colleges, it was like living on the edge of a volcano, and the Committee decided that while awaiting Ministry action it would be wise to initiate exploratory talks; it was agreed that the Chief Education Officers of both the London County Council and Middlesex should be approached unofficially.

Urgent consideration of the immediate position followed. It was reported that Middlesex would be interested in further discussion if a substantial sum of money were forthcoming. The

Committee had sought to approach various Trusts and Foundations in this connection, but no move could be entertained without Ministry approval. Miss Briggs underlined the problems of the staff and students and the planning of time tables; Home Management teaching suffered from lack of residential accommodation. Finally it was emphasised that in any negotiations claims must first be met in regard to 'dilapidations, staff and pensions.' It was agreed that Mr Max-Muller should obtain a realistic valuation of all the properties, and that as soon as Mr Warlow's Report came, the Ministry should be asked to receive a deputation.

The Report from the Cost Investigation Unit finally arrived and was fully considered in mid-June. Mr Warlow gave a brief *resume* of the original aims and Constitution of the National, and a factual account of the present position with regard to premises, courses, staffing, students and finance. He confirmed the assets and liabilities already known and recognised by the Committee. Although grant-aid from the Ministry for 1958–1959 was agreed at £472 per student, 'the estimate submitted by the College for that year showed a net excess of expenditure over income, excluding any grant from the Ministry, of £13,615.'

Mr Warlow felt that economies could be practised in reduction of secretarial and domestic staff, and also in purchase of stores, by pooling certain resources. The completely separate administration of the main College and the Hostels involved duplication at all levels, extending to Bank accounts. Admitting the problem 'in buildings of such a rambling nature,' he underlined the disadvantages of basement kitchens and dining rooms, shared bedrooms, and the gas fires for which individual students bore the cost of two thirds of the coins which they fed into the slot meters. He emphasised the effect of these conditions on the recruitment of students, so that those who came had not often put the College high on their list of priority.

The financial liabilities and assets were set out in detail. Fixed assets were judged at £44,000, and the addition of Reserve and Endowment Funds brought the estimated total to some £72,000. Against this, liabilities, including Bank overdraft, the Leasehold Redemption Fund and the accumulated deficit on income and expenditure account amounted to nearly £56,000.

Library, 1958

The National was by no means bankrupt, but the steady annual deficit of approximately £8,000, due to the gap between expenditure and the fees and grants sanctioned by the Ministry for both Training and Technical courses, would obviously within a few years drain away any surplus.

The climax of the Report lay in the brief Summary which stated succinctly that 'In view of the general financial position of the College, its whole future should be considered as a policy matter.' The issue was forced.

Mr Coulson confirmed that the figures given in broad principle were correct, and undertook to send written comments to the Chairman, to be forwarded to the Ministry. Mr Coulson stated in his letter that 'no distinction could be drawn between the finances of Teacher Training and Technical Departments, as their actions are closely intermingled so that the one tends to stand or fall by the other.' He continued 'The College could carry on, and in so doing, run down its assets, but only for a relatively short time. The position is, indeed, likely to worsen more rapidly than at the pace dictated by recurring deficits. The properties of the College are wholly leasehold, and with the passage of time, leaseholds, as wasting assets, lose their value and the loss of income is very much more rapid in the latter years of the lease.'

He gave as his opinion that 'The Executive Committee should direct its attention to considering more immediate steps so to arrange its affairs that the capital resources of the Company should be deployed to enable the work of the College to be carried on elsewhere with greater effect,' and continued that 'steps taken now to reorganise the basis of the operations of the College, and possibly to seek some other support in so doing, would be likely to maximise the amount of capital which could be found from the assets, and make it more likely that the work of the College could be continued upon a basis falling more nearly within the intentions of its Founders.' Finally he stressed the importance of Ministry approval for any new scheme, otherwise 'even the capital funds available to the College might be gravely depleted by claims for the repayment of past grants.'

The last statement held vital implications. Mr Coulson later emphasised that legally the College was compelled 'to appropriate to any new capital expenditure the whole of its realisations from other capital assets. If, for example, it realised investments or property and invested the proceeds in new premises, the capital grant claim was limited to the cost of the new premises, reduced by the amounts realised from other premises and assets, and then one half was paid by the Ministry and the other half expected to be met out of the voluntary funds or endowments of the College.'

It was essential to consult the Ministry, and the Executive Committee sought an early date for discussion with Mr Nenk. The mounting problems gave rise to considerable apprehension on their part, for Mr Nenk in whose hands the final decision seemed to lie, was known for his stern, incisive mind and implacable judgment, which would not permit the claims of tradition and humanity to weigh against calculated material factors. The Committee's fears, indeed, were well founded. A date was agreed for 3 July 1959. It was to prove the death knell.

The National was represented by Mrs Dally, Chairman of the Executive Committee; Miss H. Dent, Vice Chairman; Sir William Cash, Honorary Treasurer; Sir Guy Thorold; Miss B. S. Briggs, Principal; and Mr H. O. H. Coulson, Auditor. They were received by Mr Nenk, Miss Bell, Mrs House H.M.I. (Staff Inspector for Housecraft), Mr Warlow and Mr Savage.

Sir William Cash stated the case for the College. He explained how the finances were bound up with the leasehold property. It was clear, he continued, that the College could not be run for ever in its extremely inadequate premises; nor could it be rebuilt on its present site. The Governors could not afford to transfer it to new premises elsewhere, but they were anxious for the sake of students and staff not to close it down forthwith; they wondered whether it would be possible to amalgamate with another College, while retaining the National's traditions; in that case the Committee would be prepared to dispose of the present premises and put whatever money accrued to them into the new organisation. He referred to his informal approach to Middlesex. If none of these things were possible, then 'the College would have to face the disagreeable process of a gradual winding up, during which it would be likely to lose essential staff; while running costs per student, as the College emptied, would be very high.' The Committee thought this would be generally bad for morale, and ought to be avoided if possible.

The rejoinder was cold. Mr Nenk stated that 'the matter had been given full consideration and it had become clear to the Ministry that as a long term proposition the College was not viable. The question was simply, therefore, how soon it could be closed.'

Whatever were the previously expressed private views of his colleagues, no voice at this moment was raised in the National's defence.

Mr Nenk pointed out that subject to repayment of capital grant received from the Ministry, and to any contractual liability to existing students, the Executive Committee was technically free to close whenever it wished. He hoped, however, that the members would be prepared to consider the Ministry's position in the light of the present need for teachers. Without any break for comments, he asked if it would be possible to accept students until 1961 and close in 1964 when these students had completed their course? The Ministry would be sympathetic to the proposal that the College's tradition should be perpetuated elsewhere, but that was a matter which would require a good deal of consideration.

There was no room for manoeuvre. The decision to close the National had been made, and the fiat issued.

The remainder of the gloomy morning was concerned with the pros and cons of alternative dates for closure and the ultimate future. Finally the Ministry agreed that there should be further discussion 'to secure a decision by the end of the year.' The following depressing weeks were filled with restless activities and confidential discussions.

Sir William Cash had an unofficial talk with Miss Bell, to discuss dates for closure. The Ministry were not prepared to countenance overtures either to the Middlesex or London County Councils, but she revealed that a 'certain, unnamed College' could receive some forty students in 1962 in a new Wing which could preserve the name and traditions of the National. If 1962 were acceptable, the Ministry would proceed with negotiations. Meantime they suggested 'disposal of some Hostels and discontinuance of the Institutional Management Course,' adding the warning that 'at the end, capital grants would have to be repaid to the Ministry, which could absorb the whole of any final surplus.'

Needlework, 1958

Discussing this position on 2 September 1959, Mr Coulson strongly advised keeping open the Canteen and therefore retaining the Institutional Management Course up to the last possible minute, to safeguard the income. Mr Max-Muller had recently acquired new leases for some of the Eccleston Square Hostels as an investment, and preferred 1962 for closure in order to give time for negotiation in selling. Neither Miss Briggs nor Miss Edward, however, wished to remain after 1961.

It was agreed that when the news should be broken to the staff, the Committee must be in a position to be explicit as to the date of closure and plans for the future. They must be informed of the College to which any remaining students would be transferred, and also definite prospects about posts.

It was unanimously resolved that the College should not continue after July 1961, and that a Meeting of the full staff should be called for 22 September, to inform them of the decision taken.

Before any of this could be implemented, another Meeting was called at the Ministry on 15 September when Miss Bell, Mrs House H.M.I. and Mr Savage met Mrs Dally, Sir William Cash and Miss Briggs. 'The unnamed College,' announced Miss Bell, was the Gloucestershire Training College of Domestic Science; extensions could be built to take extra students, but could not be ready until 1962. Again the alternatives of 1961 and 1962 were debated, the Ministry favouring 1962 for closure, and stating that 'the National owed an obligation to the 1959 entry of students to finish their three-year course in London.'

The Executive Committee met on 21 September to reconsider the case yet again. Finally it passed the Resolution 'It is agreed that provided satisfactory arrangements can be made with the Ministry of Education regarding finance, the National Training College shall continue the intake of Teacher Training students until 1961 and shall remain operating until the end of the financial year 1962, after which date the College shall cease to function as a Training College, and the Teacher Training activities shall be transferred to the Gloucestershire Education Authority.' It was carried unanimously.

It was agreed that entries should be accepted for the two-year Technical courses up to 1960, and for the one-year courses until

1961. Anxiety was expressed that the staff should have every help towards new posts; a small sub-Committee would deal with personal problems. It was learnt that the Principal would return as Her Majesty's Inspector to the Ministry of Education.

The Resolution to close the College was sent to the Ministry, and the Committee agreed to inform the staff of this decision.

Students from Ghana

LAST DAYS

THE CHAIR was taken by Mrs Dally on Wednesday, 30 September 1959, at a Meeting attended by seven members of the Executive Committee, Mr B. L. Savage of the Ministry of Education, the Principal of the National with the Vice Principal, all the College Lecturers, Hostel Wardens and the Heads of Department of the non-teaching staff. The Chairman opened the proceedings by saying that 'the Ministry of Education had put forward a plan to transfer the College to Gloucester in 1962' and that the Executive Committee 'had approved this plan in principle.' She asked that this information should be regarded as confidential 'until settled; full information will be given immediately the position is clarified.' She felt it was 'only fair to tell the staff of the proposal at the earliest possible moment.' She then left the field to Sir William Cash for an explanation of the financial issues.

Sir William said that the Committee had been forced into this position for the two main reasons of the depreciating value of the leaseholds and 'the drawbacks of this old building which the staff would know only too well.' As a result, the Committee had finally come to the conclusion that 'a planned withdrawal was the only solution.' The position was further explored by Mr Savage, who stressed the necessity of continuity in the training of students.

The members of the Committee supported Mrs Dally in expressions of appreciation of staff loyalty, concern for future prospects, and 'very deep regret.' After a reminder that the matter was not yet public, the Meeting closed.

'It was like a blow between the eyes,' said one member of staff later, and another 'We were dumbfounded; it felt as if the ground had opened under our feet.' At first few could see beyond the yawning pit in front. Any previous suspicion of what was in the wind seems to have been confined to the idea that the College might be forced to continue elsewhere under different conditions, but never to contemplate final closure. The injunctions as to the highly confidential nature of the proceedings remained, but open discussion was inevitable once the position was disclosed to the Guild.

The news was broken at the Reunion on Saturday, 17 October 1959, at the close of the Speeches and Reports on the year's work. In shocked silence a packed hall listened to Miss Briggs' plain statements of fact; comments were invited, but no one spoke. It was left to Miss Eland to say 'I think everyone is too stunned,' and suggest a move to tea.

There the storm broke. In virtual ignorance of the long years of unceasing struggle against insolvency and the mounting problems which had precipitated the present crisis, reactions were swift and unrestrained. Bitter, overwhelming anger that the beloved National should be 'written off in this way' before anyone had even known of its plight, was voiced with force. It was too soon for coherent thought, but the idea of immediate protest to the Committee by individual members ran through the gathering like flame through a cornfield crackling and generating heat as it took hold. With no conception of what might be done, members were united in a blind determination 'somehow to save the College.'

The fire unexpectedly kindled that afternoon was never quenched. It flared and flickered before it was fanned to life to burn clearly and steadily. The sudden upsurge of feeling revealed loyalty and affection which were eventually channelled into a strong force of activity.

Much later, with the hindsight of achievement, Miss Shaw said of the first flare up 'It was the squib which lit the rocket which hit the moon.'

The initiative lay with the Guild members. A small group immediately organised itself, determined to ascertain the facts behind the apparently arbitrary ruling of the Executive Committee, and if possible avert the demise of the College. Among them, Mrs Margaret Plumstead staunchly rallied others;

hundreds of individual letters of protest had been sent, and the
Committee in acknowledging these, declared itself willing to
meet a deputation of Old Students.

But no meeting could bear fruit unless the Guild knew the
true position, and continual contradictory rumours only served
to confuse the issue. The prime movers were resolved on no
account to be deflected from their purpose, but in this small
group they were all fully occupied in professional posts which
in some cases debarred the holders from taking any official
part. The reverse of this medal lay in access to higher authority
for consultation, and the ensuing confidential discussions were
of inestimable value. The insight thus gained into actual facts,
as well as other points of view, cleared a great deal of misunderstanding. It also made plain that for those who had public
commitments, any open campaign could only be led, as by the
Duke of Plaza-Toro, from behind.

The need for a Guild member able and willing to share the
avowed activities and speak openly on their behalf, led to an
approach, in December 1959, to Miss Violet Brand, who was as
yet ignorant of the situation. After a varied career, she was no
longer tied by any public duties; the call on her personal interest
in a cause which held infinite possibilities made an immediate,
irresistible appeal, and her long association with the National
clinched her championship. The small 'ginger' group went into
action. In independent isolation it lacked any official authority,
and it was felt essential to gauge the extent of Guild support.
After consultation with the Committee of the Old Students, an
Extraordinary General Meeting of Guild members was called,
to learn their views, and if possible to achieve unity both in any
approach to the Executive Committee of the National, and also
in any plan which might enable the College to continue in being.

The response was tremendous. On the cold, snowy afternoon
of Saturday, 9 January 1960, from all over England from Cumber-
land to Cornwall, two hundred Old Students gathered in the Hall
of Westminster Technical College in Vincent Square, S.W.1.
Another hundred sent apologies and wished to be identified with
the cause. Miss Brand was elected to the Chair, and Miss Eland
supported her on the platform. An able exposition put into perspective both Ministry of Education policy with regard to
Teacher Training Colleges, and also the problems of the Govern-

ing Body of the National connected with fees, grants, and the condition of the buildings. Discussion of possible ideas for the future produced a wide range of suggestions, practicable and otherwise. It was appreciated that any activity undertaken by the Guild would be dependent on funds, and the members declared themselves ready to help in this way.

Finally, the Meeting passed a Resolution deploring the decision to close the College and transfer its name and students to another Domestic Subjects College: 'While appreciating their difficulties, this Meeting most earnestly desires the Governing Body to reconsider their decision, and to consider sympathetically suggestions to be put forward which would enable the College to retain its identity and to remain nearer London. This Meeting further pledges itself to do all in its power to support the Governing Body to achieve this end.'

Sir William Cash had received Miss Brand on 7 January, and had sent a message 'welcoming the help of the Old Students,' and expressing his own pleasure 'if the life of the National could be saved.' He had repeated 'the readiness of the Governors to receive a delegation.'

This Meeting sowed the seeds which matured eighteen months later when the Guild on 22 July 1961 brought into being the Educational Trust to be known as 'The National Training College of Domestic Subjects Trust.'

An unofficial overture had been made on behalf of the Old Students to the Surrey Education Authority towards the end of the year 1959, when the Director of Education had shown considerable interest. This possibility was therefore discussed in a high level confidential talk with an Under Secretary at the Ministry of Education, during which it was claimed that great efforts had been made by the Ministry to save the National, and that the Governors' decision to close had been accepted with reluctance. Several alternatives previously canvassed were enumerated and although by now all these earlier suggestions had been ruled out, it was said finally that should a direct approach to the Ministry be made by the Surrey Authority, it would be 'considered on its merit, provided the Governors of the National agreed.' The first step was to discover whether the Surrey Education Authority were really serious and prepared to act. A further interview with the Director confirmed their interest and readiness to go ahead.

On 24 February 1960, the Executive Committee of the National, now generally referred to as the Governing Body, received four Guild representatives. Mrs Dally in the Chair was supported by Lady Cash, Miss Dent, Miss Griffiths, Miss Souter, Sir William Cash, Sir Guy Thorold, with Mr Coulson and Mr Savage in attendance. The Principal Miss Briggs, and the Vice Principal Miss Edward were present, and the delegates from the Guild to plead their cause, were Miss Eland, Miss Brand, Miss Tait and Miss Visick. Miss Eland, deploring the emphasis on financial and material problems, thought that more stress should be laid on the intangible assets such as the skill of the staff and the high standard of work. Miss Brand now brought forward the subject of Surrey. Sir William Cash had himself seen their Director of Education and felt that the project seemed worth consideration. It was agreed that the Surrey Education Authority should be informed of the present situation, and asked to write officially both to the Ministry of Education and to the Governing Body.

Mr Coulson gave particulars of the financial position, which was confirmed by Mr Savage, who added the statement that 'had the Governors been able to offer £100,000 last year towards the cost of rebuilding the College elsewhere, the Ministry would have sanctioned 75 per cent grant towards the ultimate cost of £400,000 to £500,000' – information which seemed news to everyone. Whether, in the event, this would have worked out so comfortably cannot be known, for Mr Savage was definite that such a moment had passed; indeed he was convinced that no change in the present plan would be sanctioned.

There was considerable surprise when Mrs Dally read a letter from the Governors at Gloucester, who 'liked the idea of a badge to be designed for the Gloucestershire Training College, which would incorporate the National's Coat of Arms, and also felt that the name National should be included in the title of their College.'

The Guild representatives left feeling depressed. It was therefore with surprise that they learnt that the Governors had considered their pleas with sympathy and had written to the Ministry stating their willingness 'to fall in with the Old

Students' wishes if such a change of plan could be favoured.'

Hopes still centred on Surrey. Both the Ministry of Education and the Governors of the National expressed themselves as prepared to receive an approach from the Surrey Education Authority, whose Director maintained their intentions. All seemed set fair. Everyone was ready at the very least, for serious discussion, and a date in March 1960 was agreed when Surrey would send their official letter. It never came. In spite of last minute confirmation by the Director, some internal issue produced disagreement on their Education Committee, and he simply withdrew.

The small fighting group of Guild members had made all the running. After this somewhat mortifying experience, they were back where they started.

In June 1960 the Guild forwarded a Resolution of their Committee 'most earnestly desiring the Governors to investigate all possible ways and means of keeping the College alive after 1962, perhaps in association with some other Body or Trust; and also to preserve the assets from the sale of the existing properties, after satisfying all necessary obligations, for this purpose.' They also felt most strongly that the Records, the original 'Grant of Arms' and portraits should not be dissipated or handed over to any other College or Authority without full agreement of the Guild. Finally they would welcome an early opportunity of discussion, and sought assurance that no positive actions contrary to their proposals would be taken meanwhile.

The Governors replied that with every sympathy for the desires of the Old Students, it must be realised that the College was a Company, and therefore bound by law as to future procedure, whatever their personal wishes might be. They pointed out that all grants towards Teacher and Technical training, rebuilding and refurnishing, must be repaid to the Ministry, and continued: 'If, on the winding up of the Association, there remains any balance over and above the amount required by the Ministry – which seems unlikely – then legal advice will be sought to deal with such matters as are entirely beyond the control of the Governing Body.'

With regard to the Grant of Arms and the College Records, the Governors stated that they would be happy to discuss these

matters at a later date with representatives of the Old Students'
Guild, but there was little they could say at that moment.

Meantime, the College carried on. The surface was calm;
students continued to enjoy their training and to achieve excellent examination results.

Miss Graham, after thirty-three years service, retired at the
end of 1958. A luncheon and a dinner party were given in her
honour, when both the Governors and the staff presented her
with cheques to mark their appreciation and good wishes. A few
months later Miss Louie Ashford died at the age of eighty-six –
the last survivor who had served the College in the nineteenth
century.

The next year, in 1960, there was sadness with the deaths of
Miss Cottrell on 25 February and of Miss Quick on 20 September.
The former, endearingly known as 'The Cot', was always remembered for her vitality, integrity and sense of humour. Miss Quick,
indeed 'a trusty colleague,' embarked on a full twenty years of
tremendous work in the Women's Voluntary Service and Civil
Defence in her home town of Hastings after she retired. She
dealt with everything that came her way, in addition to the
duties of Clothing Officer and the organisation of relief work
for stricken areas. Her true epitaph lay in an appreciation
which read 'No truly voluntary worker will be more missed by
the hundreds of old people, the poor and the lonely in Hastings,
than our beloved Miss Quick.'

The Senate of the University expressed official regret at the
formal intimation of the closure of the National in 1962, offering
to assist any members of the Teaching Staff who might be uncertain of their future. A dispersal of staff was inevitable, and
the Governors, although grateful that some were able to remain
until the end, expected and encouraged those who found other
openings to take up their new work as soon as the opportunity
presented itself. Miss Dumas's retirement in July 1960 broke
the long continuity of the Science Department, and the College
regretfully accepted her loss.

Long-term planning was at an end, though policy had to be
agreed with Gloucester in regard to the National students who
were to finish their training there.

During 1960, plans for closure in 1962 were constantly under review. The Governors confirmed the recommendations of the Finance Committee for an improved pensions scheme for the non-teaching staff. They also learnt from the Ministry that while 'not concerned with any disposal of assets,' the repayment of capital grants was estimated at approximately £24,000.

In spite of the earlier Ministry ruling that negotiations with the London County Council could not be countenanced, certain moves were now found to be taking place. The Executive Committee, on 26 October 1960, 'agreed in principle' to the L.C.C's request to take a small group of Housecraft students from the Sidney Webb Day Training College for part-time training, to begin in September 1961. It was then revealed that they 'planned to use the Buckingham Palace Road premises for these students until alternative accommodation should be available.'

It was the thin end of the wedge, and it shortly became apparent that an offer for the leasehold was expected from the London County Council. In these circumstances Mr Max-Muller advised that it would be 'unwise to enter into any other negotiations until the position was clear.'

By the time the Governors met on 15 February 1961, a date in September had been settled for the reception of the small group of Sidney Webb students. There had also been a visit from the Chief Housecraft Inspector of the London County Council and the Principal of the Women's Department at Regent Street Polytechnic. During their tour of inspection of all the premises, including the Hostels, they had intimated that students from the Polytechnic would be in training at the National in September 1962. They had also asked specifically for an Institutional Management Course to be started, on behalf of the London County Council, a few months hence in September 1961.

Dismissing the latter proposition as obviously not feasible, the apparent assumption of a take-over was disturbing. No firm offer had been received. Driven by circumstances, the Governors decided to write at once to the Director of Education to enquire if he were yet able to clarify the position with regard to the purchase of the leases of the National properties. Over two months later, towards the end of April, the Director's reply merely confirmed the London County Council's interest in the main building, but found it was 'not economic to consider the Hostels.' It was a wearisome affair.

The Governors also felt under attack through rumours which had circulated impugning their motives, especially what they regarded as an untrue allegation in a professional journal implying deliberate intention on their part to close the National, come what might. On reflection they decided to ignore it, but it rankled, and in June 1961 the College Academic Board proposed that a factual account of the closure should be circulated. The Governors decided that they had nothing further to add to their official Press statement of November 1959, but they agreed that at the forthcoming Reunion of the Old Students Guild in October 1961, as many Governors as possible should attend, and Mrs Dally, as Chairman, should address the assembly and explain the position.

Although the closure of the National now seemed fixed beyond recall, a last appeal had been made by the Principal in April 1961. Pointing out that if the premises were purchased by the London County Council, they would be used for exactly the same purpose as at present, even though now condemned as inadequate by the Ministry of Education, she pressed for a direct approach to the Minister. It was urged that the National might even yet be linked to a General Subjects Training College and Sir Guy Thorold undertook immediately to seek an interview with Sir David Eccles.

The attempt proved abortive. No interview materialised, and on 27 July 1961, the Minister wrote to reiterate the impossibility of continuance as a Voluntary College; that no Local Education Authority near London was in a position to take it over, and that arrangements were already completed to transfer the third-year students to Gloucester in 1962. With regard to the London County Council using the premises for a similar purpose as at present, this was brushed aside when the Minister stated that although their inadequacy had been recognised, the sale of the lease was purely a matter for discussion between the Governors and the London County Council.

Nothing was achieved; matters had moved too far.

Inextricably bound with the fate of the National, now in the melting pot, was that of the Old Students Guild. Its future, as a matter of immediate concern, was discussed at the Guild Committee Meeting preceding the Reunion on 15 October 1960. It was agreed that all members of the Guild should share in any decision, and a sub-Committee including the President, Hon. Secretary and Hon. Treasurer was elected to draft a circular letter, and deal with the replies. Four hundred, more than half of those approached, sent answers, all favouring some form of continuance. Proposals, thus stimulated, now poured in on all sides, and included projects connected with research; social, cultural and community purposes; scholarships and exchange visits; cake shops, libraries and refresher courses.

Among this surfeit of ideas, some were chosen and published in the *Guild Magazine* of May 1961. All were directed at perpetuating the name, aims and ideals of the National. Among the suggestions was one for 'The formation of a permanent organisation in the form of a Trust; the administration to be in the hands of a Committee composed of Old Students, Friends of the College, and such eminent educationists to be co-opted as occasion may arise,' and continuing with proposals covering possible projects and means of financing.

These ideas were brought forward to the Governors at their Executive Committee on 14 June 1961, but they decided to defer consideration until their next meeting in November, 'as so few (four hundred) replies had been received.'

On 18 July 1961, a small independent Meeting was convened, with Miss Pugh in the Chair, and attended by Miss Briggs, Miss Brand, Miss Edward, Miss Jaques, Miss Shaw and Mr B. G. Stone. The latter had long and close connections with the College, professionally through the Colonial Office, personally through his wife, and as a friend of the National in his support of their present efforts to save it.

The upshot of the Meeting was a Recommendation submitted to the Guild Committee, endorsing the idea in the May Magazine, 'that a Charitable Trust be set up, to be known as The National Training College of Domestic Subjects (Founded 1873) Trust,' and setting out specific terms.

The Guild felt that four hundred replies from their members provided sufficient backing to justify investigation of all or any of the myriad schemes which they had by now received. They came to the conclusion, after considerable debate, that the immediate move should be acceptance of the idea to form an Educational Trust dedicated to certain definite purposes. Accordingly, on 22 July 1961, the Committee of the Old Students Guild resolved unanimously 'to set up The National Training College of Domestic Subjects (Founded 1873) Trust,' and specified the terms already put forward, as follows:

AIMS
1) To perpetuate the name and work at home and overseas of the National Training College of Domestic Subjects, and the aims and ideals of the Founders.
2) To make a contribution to the future work in the same and allied fields by:
   a) Awarding studentships for research in Domestic Subjects.
   b) Travelling Scholarships.
3) The permanent Trust to be established with not less than three Trustees.
   The administration of the Trust to be in the hands of a Committee composed of Old Students, Friends of the College, and other interested persons to be co-opted as occasion may arise.
4) The Trust to be financed by:
   a) Personal donations.
   b) Covenanted yearly subscriptions.
   c) Possible assets after the winding up of the College.
   d) Possible contributions from Industry.
   e) Grants from Responsible Bodies.

A sub-Committee of Miss Briggs, Miss Eland, the Hon. Secretary and the Hon. Treasurer met to consider details before Miss Briggs, as President, consulted a solicitor over the legal proceedings, and Counsel's opinion was taken. A Draft Deed was drawn up by Messrs Radcliffes and Company of Little College Street, S.W.1, for submission to the Ministry of Education and the Charity Commissioners; private legal advice was also sought.

Since the Guild had sponsored the Trust, it followed that every Guild member would automatically be associated. The whole Trust, therefore, comprised the Old Students Guild and any interested individual or Association, the latter to be entitled Friends of the Trust. It was agreed that the Trust Committee, in addition to a Chairman, should consist of the President and Hon. Secretary of the Guild, *ex officio*; five representatives of the Old Students, and five Friends.

The Guild Committee now nominated the Officers of the Trust, whom they invited to serve as Trustees or as members of the Committee. Acceptance was received from two Trustees, the Honourable Mrs Donald Kershaw, an Old Student of the College, and Mr B. G. Stone; and nine Committee members, the five representing the Old Students being Miss V. Brand, Miss G. M. Eland, Miss B. M. Fisher, Mrs F. S. Standley and Miss M. J. Voyce. The four Friends of the Trust were Miss I. S. Gibson, Mrs E. R. House, Miss M. S. Jaques and Miss F. M. Pugh.

The Inaugural Meeting of 11 October 1961 was attended by the two Trustees, seven members of the Committee, the President, the Hon. Secretary and the Hon. Treasurer of the Guild and the Vice Principal of the College. Mr B. G. Stone was elected to the Chair which he occupied at every subsequent meeting of their Executive Committees.

The Trust was in being, and from now on it took active responsibility.

At this first meeting, the aims and administration of the Trust were given close consideration and it was obvious that finances were a matter of some urgency. Miss Eland's proposal that the purpose and position of the Trust should be explained at the coming Reunion on 21 October was unanimously carried, and Miss Brand agreed to speak. Thus, at the final Reunion to be held at Buckingham Palace Road on Saturday, 21 October 1961, both the Governors and the Trust were represented. Mrs Dally was supported by Miss Dent, Lady Cash and Lady Monckton. She gave a *résumé* of the events leading up to the decision to close, stressing the financial troubles which made it impossible either to rebuild, or bring the College up to date. She referred to the meeting when the Finance Committee 'saw it was obvious that the Ministry of Education was not prepared to continue financing the College, and were also officially informed of the Ministry policy of enlargement of General Colleges with a Domestic Science wing.' Finally came the Ministry's refusal to accept any approach either to Middlesex or the London County Council, culminating in the decision that the National Teacher

Training students should be gradually absorbed into the Gloucester Training College by 1962, in accordance with Ministry
policy.

Mrs Dally spoke of the efforts with Sir David Eccles which
had ended with an official reassurance that no decision had been
taken as to the future use of the building. She said that the London County Council had been considering whether it might be
suitable for teaching accommodation as an annexe to an existing Technical College. If acquired for this purpose it was proposed that 'a small part of the premises should be used for a very
limited period for students from the Sidney Webb Training
College, and would cease after one or two years,' which was 'a
very different matter from retaining the premises for permanent
use for Teacher Training by any other Authority.' In the event,
this forecast hardly proved to be accurate. Mrs Dally paid
tribute to the Principal and staff for their loyalty and help,
before leaving with her three fellow Governors.

The audience, although not entirely prepared to be convinced,
listened with close attention and turned over the proferred
explanations in their minds, with mixed feelings.

Miss Violet Brand then spoke to the Resolution proposing
the formation of a Charitable Educational Trust, outlining
various projects and possibilities. She believed there was 'still
much unfulfilled' and made a plea 'to back a scheme devised to
keep the name and ideals of the place alive, because we all owed
it a debt.' Miss M. S. Jaques seconded the proposal, asking and
answering some pertinent questions, and ended with the rallying cry of 'Do it now!'

It was two years since the initial blow had fallen at the
Reunion on 17 October 1959. Within this time, the burning
feelings then aroused had forged an instrument designed to
shape the pattern of the future. This was the Trust, complete in
form, but not yet fully geared for action.

Miss Briggs informed the Governors on 1 November 1961 of
the official formation of the Trust, explaining the Constitution
and Aims, with some ideas as to the type of work which might
fulfil these. She emphasised the suggested means of finance,
drawing attention to the 'possible assets after winding up the
College affairs.'

Discussion followed before the Governors agreed 'to inform the Trust Committee that after winding up the College they would be willing to transfer some assets to them, provided the Constitution of the Trust came within the Articles of Association;' they added that they would like this Constitution to be circularised before their next Meeting in February 1962.

Attention was then bent on finances and Hostel affairs. Eaton Place had been closed in August 1961; it was agreed to aim at selling the Eccleston Square leases during the summer of 1962, and to arrange for an auctioneer to take the furniture, apart from certain soft furnishings sold to the domestic staff. A Hostel which had been let during the vacation added £254 to the Endowment Fund.

The Committee resolved that Mr Coulson, who had made helpful suggestions concerning the repayment of the grant claimed by the Ministry, should 'be appointed Liquidator.' In view of his advice that as many matters as possible should be settled in advance, other affairs were discussed. It was left to the Principal to arrange with Berridge House over the sale of certain cookery equipment in which they were interested; it was agreed that after proper assessment, the disposal of the Library contents should be decided, and any surplus sold to the Sidney Webb College.

The idea of amalgamation and pooling of resources with Gloucester Training College had inexplicably lapsed, apparently with mutual agreement and Ministry acquiescence. The Committee now wished to record their appreciation of the close and cordial relations by presenting them with a piece of silver and, if possible, 'any rare Library books.'

By the next Meeting, on 14 February 1962, tension was eased all round. It appeared that the London County Council had now become *persona grata* and had made a firm offer for the lease of 72–78 Buckingham Palace Road, agreeing 'to pay all expenses of the transfer.' The offer was accepted with apparent satisfaction, and legal arrangements as to cost, completion date and other details were left in the hands of Mr Max-Muller.

It was now necessary for the Executive Committee to make a statutory declaration of its intention to wind it up, and Mr Max-Muller also undertook this formality.

The weight of suspense was lifted, and the burden consequently lightened. In spite of many unavoidable and sorrowful tasks which still lay ahead, there was more heart to tackle them. In fact, one of the first actions on this February day was of rejoicing, for Her Majesty Queen Elizabeth the Queen Mother had agreed to pay a farewell visit to the National before it closed, and the Committee accepted with delight the proposal of 5 June 1962.

At this same Committee, as requested by the Governors, the Trust submitted their Draft Deed, seeking comments. The Trustees, 'greatly encouraged by the Governors' interest,' reiterated their aims, with the desire to sponsor serious investigation, or some form of advanced work or research, both in this country and overseas. They drew attention to their need for funds, stating that covenants and donations at present amounted to £323 10s. Finally the Trustees reported two Meetings held since November 1961 and their fourth planned for 9 March 1962.

The Governors did not wish to comment on the Trust Deed. In reply to a request from the Principal that a sum of money might be given to the Trust now, they stated that they were in no position as yet to offer substantial financial support, and would not in fact be in such a position until after the liquidation of the Company in 1963. The rebuff was softened by the intimation that they might consider a small contribution in response to an appeal, but added the warning that they 'could not give any undertaking regarding the application of their funds for the use of the Trust.'

The last Annual General Meeting of the National's Executive Committee took place on this same 14 February 1962 when there was a final re-election of the Committee members. It was also reported that as the staff, both Teaching and non-Teaching, were gradually finding other posts, it 'looked as if there was not too much difficulty in everyone finding a new sphere of interest,' a reflection which gave rise to great satisfaction at this surprising turn of Fortune's wheel.

The question of a third Trustee had been exercising the minds of all concerned with the Trust, for it was strongly felt that the invitation should go to an educationist of repute who would give wise counsel. The conviction that the holder should be no mere figurehead led finally to the unanimous choice of the Right Honourable Dr Robert Stopford, Lord Bishop of London.

Dr Stopford, after being Senior History Master and House-master at Oundle School, had been Principal of Trinity College, Kandy, Ceylon, and of Achimota College in the Gold Coast (now Ghana). On his return to England at the end of the War, he served as Moderator of the Church of England Training Colleges and General Secretary of the National Society before becoming successively Bishop of Fulham (with diocese overseas), Peter-borough and London. This unique experience combined to give him exceptional knowledge of conditions and problems both at home and overseas, and his sound judgment over a course of action invariably proved the accuracy of his swift appraisal of the situation.

An approach elicited that he would be interested to hear about the Trust and its aims and objects, and it was a matter of heart-felt rejoicing that, after further investigation and a talk with the Chairman, Mr B. G. Stone, the Bishop agreed on 18 June 1962, to become a Trustee. From then on his wisdom and judg-ment were freely at the disposal of the Trust, in advice over all professional matters, where his foresight particularly in the fields of education and finance was invaluable.

The Deed of Trust after close scrutiny was agreed and signed by the Trustees for registration as an Educational Charity with the Ministry of Education in September 1962.

By now the Trust had found some headquarters. In March 1962, a most agreeable small eyrie was acquired at 251 Brompton Road, S.W.3. With wide outlook across the intervening junction of broad roads to Brompton Oratory and the Victoria and Albert Museum, it was easily accessible by public transport. The annual rent of £150 was settled anonymously for the first year.

The tiny office was soon filled to overflowing; there was just space to squeeze past the tables, bookcases and filing cabinets, while treasured photographs, portraits and the magnificent Grant of Arms covered the walls – all valued gifts received from the Governors when the College closed. The unfailing help and sympathy of the British Dietetic Association who sublet this

little room, and their landlords, the National Advisory Council
for Careers (formerly the Women's Employment Federation),
the two friendly neighbours who shared this same top floor,
made for a most happy relationship throughout the Trust's
tenure, which continued until March 1971. Not the least of the
kindnesses was shown personally by Miss B. J. Jamieson and
Miss I. F. Hilton, the respective Secretaries of these Associations, who at considerable inconvenience regularly handed
over their own rooms to give the Trust Committees space to meet.

Elizabeth R

March 24ᵗʰ 1943

Elizabeth R

May 18ᵗʰ 1949

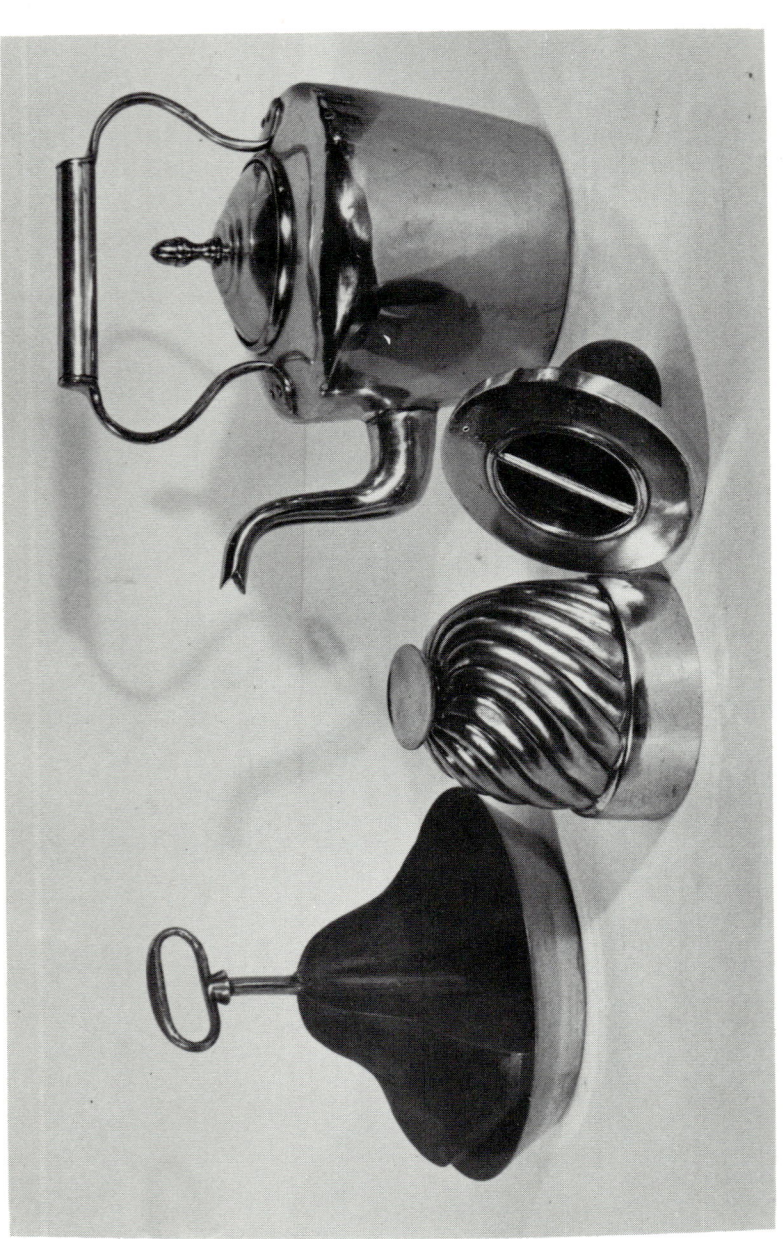

LAST DAYS

THE GOVERNORS met on 2 May 1962, to arrange the final programme for the Royal visit of 5 June, and for a brief spell all
hearts were lifted as thoughts turned from the galling and
dismal future. The preparation to receive Her Majesty was in
itself a stimulus, and something of the old exhilaration swept
through the place. When eventually on the bright morning of
Tuesday, 5 June 1962, Her Majesty Queen Elizabeth, now the
Queen Mother, attended by Lady Jean Rankin, arrived at the
National, any lingering trace of sadness was immediately dispelled by her joyous warmth and radiance.

Invitations were deliberately limited to College personnel;
so that in the Hall, seated to capacity, the Governors and the
staff, teaching, administrative and domestic, could all see and
hear Her Majesty, on this her farewell visit as Patron of the
National. As always, the grace of her appearance with a bouquet
of roses, orchids, carnations and lilies of the valley against the
soft lilac of her dress, epitomised the delicate bloom of the lovely
flowers.

Mrs Dally, in thanking Her Majesty for the honour of her
visit, spoke of the changed times which had forced them to close
their doors; she referred to the Educational Trust lately set up
'to perpetuate the name and work of the College, together with
the ideals of its Founders, so though as a College we may die, as
a name we live.'

Her Majesty the Queen Mother, in her sympathetic answer,
recalled that she had followed the College's activities with
interest and admiration for a quarter of a century, and knew

Her Majesty Queen Elizabeth the Queen Mother with the Principal and Students, 1962

that with no endowment, it had waged a continuous struggle for existence; and she paid tribute to those who had 'guided it so wisely throughout its eighty-nine years.' As the oldest Domestic Subjects College in the country, the pioneer work of its early days had led to the founding of similar Training Colleges, and Her Majesty was confident that the principles for which it had stood, and the high standards it had upheld, 'would continue to influence and inspire future generations,' and that those who had trained at the National 'will be ready to play an important part in the life of the community.'

She continued, that sad as indeed it was, that present-day requirements made it necessary to close the College, 'the establishment of an Educational Trust to perpetuate its name and aims will be welcomed by all who are connected with it, and who have its interest at heart.' This was balm indeed, and it strengthened and inspired as well as solaced.

After gracious acceptance of a crystal vase, a brief tour of the College followed to see the work of various courses. Tea was served in the Library, where a small group of students were especially honoured when Her Majesty sat with them. At the close of her visit, students formed a Guard of Honour down the steps, but as Her Majesty Queen Elizabeth, the beloved Queen Mother, passed down these to cross the pavement to her waiting car, she stopped to speak yet again to all who tried to cluster round. There were full hearts welling up in tears of happiness and devotion as she drove away. For a few short glorious hours, the nightmare ahead had been kept at bay.

Elizabeth R

_June 5th
1962_

The state of euphoria surrounding Her Majesty's visit stimulated an atmosphere of generosity. Maybe it was this influence which inspired the Governors, when the Principal reported that Gloucestershire Training College would prefer a monetary gift 'to perpetuate the name of the National,' to respond by voting the sum of two hundred and fifty guineas to be given for the purchase of a piece of plate, only stipulating that they should choose the inscription.

The Finance Committee of 30 May 1962 discussed pensions and gratuities. The auction of the leases for the Eccleston Square Hostels had been arranged for 14 June, and of the contents for 19 July. A letter from the London County Council stated that they hoped to complete the sale by 1 September 1962, the date fixed for vacant possession. Equipment at Buckingham Palace Road not required by the London County Council was to be sold by public auction on 27 August. The official closing of the College accounts was fixed for 31 July 1962, with the audit to commence on 20 August, to give time for the Declaration of Solvency to be made on completion of the accounts. It was agreed to hold a General Meeting towards the end of September at Alderman's House, E.C.2, which after 1 September would be the Registered Office of the Company, and where Mr Coulson kindly offered accommodation for the Accountant and the account books.

At the Executive Committee on 13 June 1962, a Rose Bowl for Gloucester was now on view, with neither plinth nor inscription. It was decided to add both, the wording of the latter to read 'Presented to the Gloucestershire Training College by the Governing Body of the National Training College of Domestic Subjects, 1873–1962.'

A request from the Old Students that a plaque should be placed on the outside of the building to commemorate the National was referred to the Architects' Department of the London County Council, who confirmed on 11 July that this should be put up and paid for by the Governors with the approval of the Council.

A letter from the Trust provoked considerable discussion. The Governors had earlier offered a small contribution to their funds, and desirous of retaining all possible donations and covenanted subscriptions towards their future activities, the Trustees had nonetheless to meet administrative expenses. So the Governors' eventual decision to give £100 for this purpose during the next year was a welcome addition to their meagre funds.

Letters of thanks were read from the Principal of Berridge House and the Chairman of the Ranfurly Library for gifts of books. On behalf of the Committee, Mrs Dally thanked Mrs Osman for her long service as Chairman of the Hostel sub-Committee.

The Governors had now to face the inevitable and melancholy task of disposing of any College property not already allocated. The list was formidable. Some decisions, dependent on further enquiries and consideration, inevitably had to be postponed, but a number of items were recorded as follows:

1) *a)* The College Seal, Minute Books and College Records to be sent to the Liquidator in compliance with the law.

   b) Students' Records to be microfilmed and kept by the Principal.

2) To be given to the Trust:

   a) Signed photograph of Her Majesty the Queen Mother.

   b) Silver Rose Bowl, purchased by donation from Her Majesty the Queen Mother.

   c) Grant of Arms.

   d) Old College photographs and some assorted books.

3) Brass Cross and candlesticks. Enquiries to be made as to where they might be useful and welcome.

4) Copper. The Minutes record: 'After the Governors have selected pieces (to be inscribed "National Training College of Domestic Subjects, 1873–1962") the lecturers and staff, in order of seniority, to be allowed to choose pieces.'

It was also agreed 'to consult the Curator of the Victoria and Albert Museum as to the remaining copper utensils. Failing acceptance of this gift by any Museum, the collection, numbering approximately four hundred pieces, should be sold by auction.'

The Committee then decided that the sum of £1,365 9s originally in the Building Fund should be presented to the Old Students
Guild; it was reported in the following September 1962 that this
had been handed over.

Certain pensions and gratuities not already arranged with
the Alliance Assurance Company were considered, but following the practice of the later Finance Committees, discussions
of financial reports were held *in camera* and few records survived. The end of the National was appallingly near; the affairs
of the Committee were confidential and nothing was bruited
abroad.

The Governors met again in force on Wednesday, 11 July, to
deal with a number of items still outstanding. The Trust meantime had recorded their appreciation of the £100 donation, and
the Society for the Propagation of the Gospel was grateful for
the gift of the cross and candlesticks, which were sent abroad.

Sir William Cash gave a *résumé* of the sale of the properties
to date. Sadly, there was no Miss Souter to listen with the others,
for she had died in July 1961. She had been still alive to know of
the final appeal to Sir David Eccles, but not of the failed hopes.
She had been a devoted member of the Committee since 1916,
and during these forty-five years was always known for the
invaluable help which she gave so willingly.

Items agreed and recorded at the Finance Committee immediately preceding this Executive Meeting of the Governors
were now reported as follows:

1) The lease of the Eaton Place Hostel had been sold in October
1961 for £32,000, and the Eccleston Square Hostels in June
1962 for £45,000, totalling £77,000.
2) The London County Council had agreed to purchase the lease
of 72–78 Buckingham Palace Road for £95,000.
3) The above sum of £95,000, when received (completion date
3 September 1962), to be invested with a local Corporation for
six months.
4) The present investment of £20,000 to remain with the Royal
Borough of New Windsor for a further period of six months.
5) Monetary gifts to lecturers to be paid after 1 September when
their service with the National ceased.
6) The records of recent students to be microfilmed, and the

Ministry of Education, instead of the Principal, asked to keep
them in safe custody.

Finally the Governors placed on record their thanks to Mr
Coulson for his 'help and extra unpaid work,' and hoped that he
would take an adequate fee for the onerous task as Liquidator.

A Finance Committee was fixed for 18 September, the Annual
General Meeting for 10 October, and an Executive Committee
for 6 November 1962. By this time the National would be closed.
Apart from those in the confidence of the Committee, no one had
any inkling of the intentions of the Governors with regard to
these ample funds now at their disposal.

Since its inception in 1961, the Trust had given unremitting
thought to its future enterprises, but all plans were perforce
governed by their purse strings which at this time were deci-
dedly restricted. Their ideas, however, were by no means narrow
or circumscribed, and although as yet only in embryo, it was
clear that they would need money.

As the only representatives of the long line of National members, and brought into being by the Old Students Guild, the
Trust were regarded as the 'moral heirs' of the National, and
thus entitled to any surplus funds after all proper commitments
had been satisfied. They therefore approached the Governors
to lay their case before them.

Although the National properties were sold during the
summer of 1962, the Trust was ignorant of the extent of the
sum realised until in October 1962, in reply to their letter, Mr
Max-Muller wrote on behalf of the Governors to say that
Ministry approval was required for any disposal of the 'substantial monies,' gained from the sale of the leases.

It was felt imperative to make personal contact with the
Governors in order to gain assurance that they also regarded
the Trust as the rightful beneficiaries. At the same time the
Trust recognised that the value of their objectives must be
clearly understood. They were particularly anxious not to rush
into any hasty or untoward decision with regard to their plans,
but wished to prove both the validity of their schemes and the
integrity of their purpose in the use of the money.

Accordingly the Trust immediately sought an interview with
the Governors to discuss the position and establish common

ground over future action, a proposal which unhappily was not found acceptable.

The Governors were understandably chary of handing over substantial funds to a Body, or for projects, of which they were largely ignorant, but it lay within their hands to obtain all this information by meeting representatives of the Trust. Knowing that the reality of any planning depended on the extent and security of funds, and convinced that co-operation could be of mutual benefit, the Trust again approached the Governors for consultation. Unfortunately the Governors felt equally unable to accede to this request; repeated attempts made by the Trust Committee, in which they were supported by their Trustee, the Lord Bishop of London, all proved unavailing.

It was tragic that the two Bodies most intimately concerned over the affairs of the National, with the newly formed Trust dedicated to perpetuating the work of the College, should never have met. They were thus denied the mutual exchange of ideas and the benefit of intellectual stimulus.

The Governors evidently believed that contact was inadvisable, and the months of 1963 went by with all approaches by the Trust ignored or evaded. The implication that the Old Students were unworthy of consideration led to renewed resentment and misgiving; in this unhappy state of affairs any straw in the wind added fuel to the smouldering fire.

One issue assumed such undue proportions as to amount almost to a conflagration. Among the sad dispersal of possessions, many cherished purely for the sake of association, was the magnificent collection of copper whose destiny was still unrevealed. Undoubtedly the copper was of some intrinsic value, but it was not for this reason that it roused such passionate interest and pride. Nor was it merely its beauty, shapely and strong, lovely in its simplicity of line and glory of colour, and the great variety of its sizes and designs and purposes, which made it so cherished. From the enormous fish kettles and *bains-maries* to the tiniest delicate jelly moulds, each piece was perfect in its own right. All who had shared in the life of the College seemed to regard it as peculiarly their own. It mattered not if they had worked in other departments and never even handled these glowing treasures. It belonged to the National; it was indis-

solubly linked with it and everyone felt a personal proprietary
interest. Its fate became a matter of burning importance. 'What
is happening to the *copper*?' was the constant, anguished cry –
almost as foster parents suffering bitterly over unknown plans
for the future of beloved children.

Actually, the fate of the copper had been decided in June
1962, when the Executive Committee had agreed that first the
Governors, and then the present lecturers and staff should
select pieces; the remainder should be offered to a museum or
sold by auction. Happily this last indignity was spared, and
the remaining members of this choice group travelled together
to a new and beautiful home. Early in August 1962 they were
welcomed at the Royal Pavilion in Brighton, whose Curator
wrote most appreciatively of the 'very fine series of copper
utensils totalling 177 pieces.' Although they already possessed
several hundred items, this was a specially welcome addition
as it included several articles not formerly represented. In
the changing displays at the Royal Pavilion, the prized copper
from the National now shares the honours in the Great Kitchen
with the famous collections from the Duke of Wellington's
household and from that of the Duke of Northumberland at
Syon House.

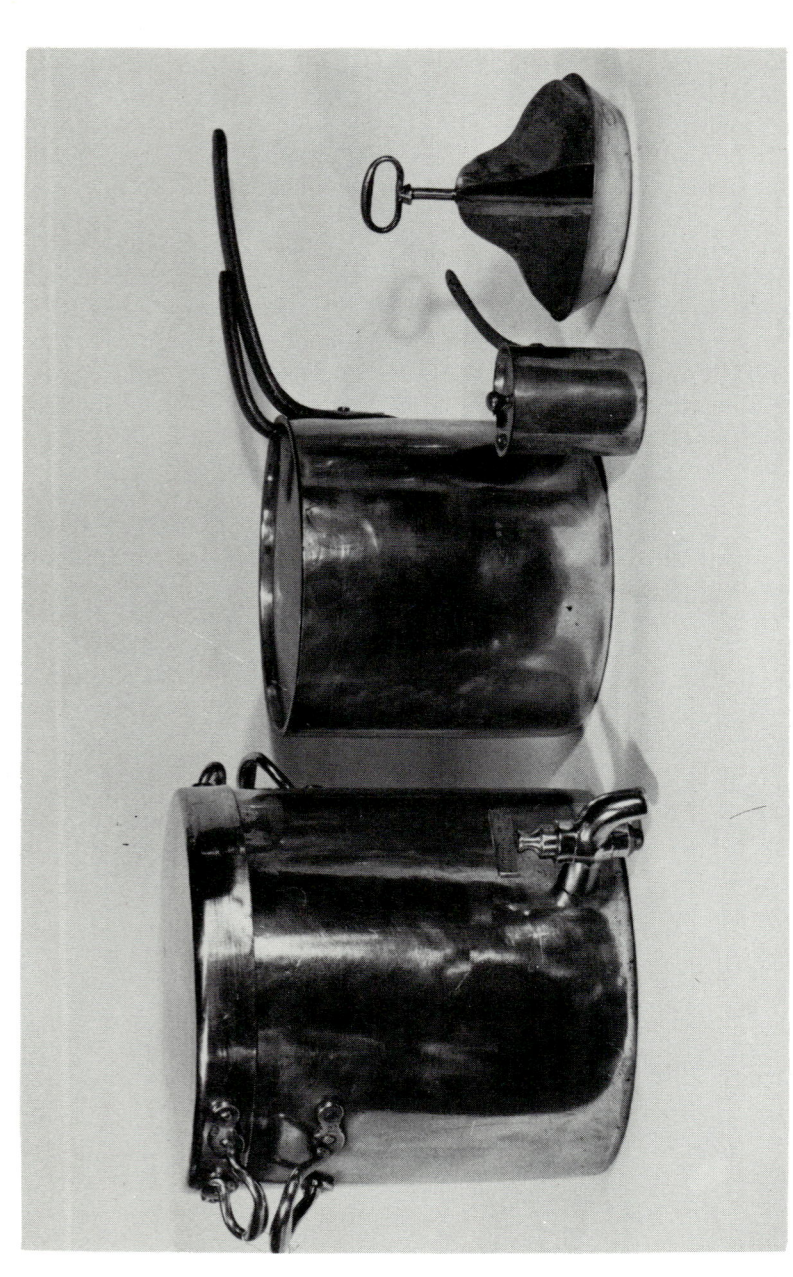

In the sea of cross currents, misunderstandings were inevitable. The three main protagonists were the Governors, the Guild and the Ministry of Education. Each represented a cross section of human society, and as such were all fallible. Often ignorant of the reasons which lay behind actions, even the best intentioned, in an atmosphere of suspicion and intolerance, could be falsely accused of ulterior motives. All were drawn into the whirlpool.

The Governors had been beset, but without cognisance of their traumatic experience neither the Guild nor the Trust could share or lighten their burdens. Had they felt able to take into their confidence the senior members of both the College staff and the Guild, they could have enlisted considerable support. But the Governors had always eschewed this contact, and in spite of repeated recommendations and requests, over a long period of years, from Inspectors, University Visitors and representatives within the College, the staff had no right of direct access to the Executive Committee, and no voice in the policy or management of the College. Candour could have opened the door to mutual confidence, but whereas the **Governors felt no obligation to reveal their intentions or their** motives, the old students felt powerless against an iron curtain.

As with the copper, the Guild was possessive over the National. After all, it was argued, the College was founded and had existed for the students, who with its staff had supported it through thick and thin. They were sore and hurt at being shut out. From its first days the School seems to have inspired an intense, almost hypnotic, but abiding loyalty, even though at times this extended for some to a 'love-hate' relationship. Yet even its sternest critics, or most apathetic members, could be roused to defend it in peril, to fight like tigers.

It was this rallying cry of danger which bound together the Guild and the Trust. At first there was but a nucleus of staunch fighters backed by a large number ready to support; there was also a small group merely wishing to follow the line of least resistance. Yet even these, watching events with some trepidation, were pricked by the realisation of need, and eventually were found to be swimming, often strongly, with everyone else; not always perhaps quite aware of the long haul of others before them.

Had a proper interchange of views been possible between representatives of the Guild, the Trust and the Governors, satisfactory personal relationships could have been established. Their joint efforts to save the life of the National might indeed have proved vain, but at least everyone could have fought on the same side.

The Ministry of Education was equally cavilled at, and there were many voices within its precincts. There were those who genuinely supported the College, and worked for its continuance, not on the same site nor in its identical form, but who nevertheless went to great lengths to save it. Others saw no future for it, and were unmoved by its fate; some veered both in views and voices.

Even the few idealists had to be realists, for they were guardians of the public purse. Materially everything militated against the College. It lacked up-to-date premises, equipment and money. It had neither land nor capital. It was the only Domestic Subjects College in England, as Miss Sillitoe had pointed out as early as 1931, which had not been taken over by its Local Education Authority.

Inevitably there was no longer a band of dedicated staff nor a shrewd indomitable leader to assess and meet the needs of the changing world. Even had there been, it would have proved a tough struggle, of doubtful success, for in the contemporary educational climate, initiative and originality were less welcome than conformity to the regulation mould. The National did not fit into this pattern; independence of mind had characterised its policy and its courses. A unique contribution might have been possible with development of the Technical side and the Public Restaurant, with the income therefrom left to discretionary powers to combat the rising cost of inflation and safeguard the Teacher Training Course. Flair, discernment and faith were all needed. Neither they, nor a genuine desire to help were entirely lacking, but in the end the intransigence of the hard headed won the day.

DEEPLY CONCERNED as they were, the Trust lost neither faith nor determination, and in May 1963 began serious work on the major enterprise which was to dominate all endeavours for the best part of a decade. A plan of this project was sent in confidence to the Governors, whom the Trust believed would find it worthy of support. Not a word had been vouchsafed as to any proposals on the part of the Governors, and the Trust felt that with their own latest scheme, original in approach and designed to fill a very real need, their claim was strong. But by this time, the plans for the allocation of the funds were all cut and dried.

On 1 May 1963, the Executive Committee had met at Alderman's House. Miss Dent was in the Chair, and presented Miss Briggs, on behalf of the Governors, with a silver salver. A gratuity and an annuity were also formally agreed in respect of her premature retirement as Principal, following the closure of the College.

The disposal of their total funds was then discussed and finally determined. An Extraordinary General Meeting to confirm these resolutions was convened for Wednesday, 5 June 1963.

On the morning of Wednesday, 10 July 1963, *The Times* inserted a paragraph, headed in distinctive type '£100,000 Gift to Queen Elizabeth College.' It informed the public that this sum had been given by the National Training College of Domestic Subjects towards the cost of building and equipping an extension to the Department of Nutrition. It enlarged further on the topic, ending with the hope that the new building would be completed in 1965.

To learn this news through the stark medium of the Press proved distressing to the Guild and Friends of the Trust, especially to senior members and those who had, for the past two years, worked unremittingly to establish contact and good relations. Even now there was no personal word from the Chairman, but at the request of the Executive Committee, Mr Coulson wrote officially in his capacity as Liquidator, to convey the views formed at their final May Meeting. He reported that 'the Committee felt unanimously that a permanent memorial to the National in this country was essential, and chose Queen Elizabeth College because it was in London, the National's original home. In addition, Queen Elizabeth College lacked research space for nutrition, was already known for training nutritionists for work in all parts of the world, and could not undertake any further projects without more space.'

The new extension would be identified with the National by a plaque bearing the words:

'Be it remembered that in the year 1963, the National Training College of Domestic Subjects (founded in 1873) provided the sum of £100,000 to the Principal and Governors of Queen Elizabeth College, University of London, to be applied by them in meeting the cost of building this extension to the Nutrition Department.'

Another Press announcement was enclosed, with further details of the decisions of the Executive Committee, who had 'resolved that the proceeds of realisation of its assets after settlement of its liabilities shall be given as £100,000 to Queen Elizabeth College, University of London; as to £5,000 to The British Society for International Health Education; and as to the remaining funds, estimated at not less than £20,000, to the National Training College of Domestic Subjects (founded 1873) Trust, for the purposes of that Trust.'

Mr Coulson continued in his letter that the relatively small donation to the British Society for International Health Education was felt to be justified by the interest which that Society took in problems of overseas nutrition. 'Even with these gifts,' he continued, 'there will remain a substantial sum of between £20,000 and £30,000 which will be made available to the National Training College of Domestic Subjects Trust and will, it is hoped, enable the Trust to fulfil its objects.' He was asked further 'to convey the view of the Executive Committee that Old Students will be very pleased indeed by the decisions which have been made by the Governors,' which on the face of it seemed a somewhat curious assumption.

One further phrase in this letter was to prove of the greatest import when it declared that 'Certain assets remain to be realised, and negotiations upon claims made by the Minister of Education require to be concluded.' Mr Coulson, with his knowledge of affairs and keen mind, tackled the intricacies of the legal aspects of the Ministry's claims for the repayment of grants with consummate skill and marked success, to the enduring benefit and lasting gratitude of the Trust.

The handsome donation of £100,000 to Queen Elizabeth College was especially valued by Miss Sargeaunt, the Principal; Miss Dent, whose long connections included two years as Acting Principal; Lady Heath, who represented the University of London; and Mrs Osman, who was a member of the Queen Elizabeth College House Committee. All these Governors of the National fully understood the scope of the University aspirations, and appreciated the value of the benefit now conferred.

Sir William Cash had earlier expressed his gratitude to the Executive Committee for their commendation of the proposed gift of £5,000 to the British Society for International Health Education, in whose affairs, as their Hon. Treasurer, he had a particular interest.

The Chairman of the Trust, on behalf of his Committee, wrote to Mr Coulson to thank him for his helpful letter, and to record the appreciation of the Trust for the sum of money which was to come to them. He also congratulated Queen Elizabeth College on their good fortune.

It was 1966 before the final Balance Sheet was issued. During this time, legal tangles were straightened and many people were involved with the rights and the wrongs and the questions of mercy and justice. The chief credit for the final settlement lay with Mr Coulson, who with tenacity succeeded in reducing by £10,000 the Ministry's original claims for repayment of grants, and who with understanding reconciled many differing viewpoints.

On 14 January 1966 the final Balance Sheet was as follows:

	£	s	d	£	s	d
Total receipts from realisation of Assets				£175,431	11	2
Total Payments	£	s	d	£	s	d
Refund of grants to Department of Education and Science	16,621	15	9			
Teachers Superannuation Scheme	3,998	9	1			
Purchase of annuity and endowment policy	3,756	11	8			
Liquidation expenses, legal charges and sundries	4,399	7	10			
				28,776	4	4
Donations to						
Queen Elizabeth College	100,000	0	0			
British Society for Health Education	5,000	0	0			
National Training College of Domestic Subjects Trust	41,655	6	10			
				146,655	6	10
TOTAL PAYMENTS				£175,431	11	2

It seemed ironic that the premises in Buckingham Palace Road were to be used for their original purpose, though no longer for their original students. The National, the pioneer College of the British Isles, was leaving, and the London County Council, with whom it had waged so many battles, were moving in.

Disposal of the posessions had been minutely planned, and now in the few weeks before 12 July 1962 everythimg had to be finally cleared for the new tenants. Officials from the London County Council streamed in and out at all hours, assessing and measuring, planning to discard or replace, often with no compunction for the feelings of those who listened to the scathing comments over the type or condition of the equipment and furnishings. The old familiar items became unexpectedly loved, and the very presence of even a considerate intruder turned the knife in the wound.

The final packing and transportation felt like an army on manoeuvres. Papers, and still more papers, were sorted to fill crates and boxes. Some were destined to be kept and others to be destroyed. In despair and fatigue, as the days passed,inevitably orderly method suffered, and some of the crammed packing cases bore witness to confusion of minds and hands. Equipment, utensils, books and pictures had all to be disposed of somewhere for the College was now to be altered, refurbished and redecorated.

Among the milling crowds, staggering under the weight of furniture and equipment, no one could keep track of all that went on. Certain books and illustrations referred to in early records were lost, and the big framed photograph of Mr J. C. Buckmaster in the Entrance Hall, meeting the gaze of all who came downstairs, was never seen again. It was a long time before such disappearances were even realised.

The staff were numb with weariness. There were few of the old seniors left, and during the last uncertain years, many new members had been birds of passage. The underlying unrest had its repercussions on the students, for there had been no settled College to absorb them into its tradition. They felt affection, and now there was undoubted sadness, but understandably those who were about to finish their training at Gloucester felt, with the resilience of youth, a sense of excited expectancy.

The last day of the College on 12 July 1962 was one of grief, especially for the few remaining seniors, who suffered stoically. There was still one more painful episode, when the final auction was held on Monday, 27 August 1962. Many of the discarded items were indeed useless for the majority of people, but there were a few bargains for those who had heart or leisure to secure these remnants of better days. Some who really cared for the place went in and out, to join the shifting audience, and listen to the dismal recital of interminable 'lots.' The sum realised was £1,035. There was neither interest nor enthusiasm; in an atmosphere of apathetic dreariness, it was a bleak affair.

THE NATIONAL had closed – the great pioneer College, visionary, idealistic and severely practical; trustworthy and courageous; eccentric and high handed; inspiring fanatical personal devotion, dedication to duty, pride in perfection of work and appreciation of the artist in whatever sphere. Always one step ahead, recognising and applying modern thought and developments; fearless, forthright, ruthless, tough and feudal, it was at the same time capable of great humanity, understanding, generosity and practical help. With humility and wisdom, the College worked with all and was beholden to none.

Perhaps its mission was accomplished. The spirit of sturdy independence, characteristic of its strengths and its weaknesses, could never have adapted itself to a conventional pattern. With the end of the family régime, the Second World War and the uniformity inevitable with the change of educational policy, the individual flavour and vivid spark of adventure were dimmed.

But it had blazed the trail. As the pioneer, it had been instrumental in leading the way to all the other Domestic Subjects Colleges which had swiftly started in every part of the country. It achieved exactly what Sir Henry Cole had in mind when he founded it, which was 'to ensure that the art and science of cookery should be made available throughout the whole country.' From his vision of 'art and science' flowed the whole concept of home-making in its fullest sense, linking, in vital interest, the aesthetic and the scientific, with a philosophy of life rooted in the understanding and care of human beings.

At the heart of Britain, in the centre of the capital, it justified its status as a 'National' College. Throughout its ninety years, everyone who worked for it brought an individual contribution, helping to shape and strengthen and colour part of the pattern. The unique design belongs to them all. When it closed on Thursday, 12 July 1962, the tapestry of the National was woven.

1873   1873

THE NATIONAL
TRAINING COLLEGE OF
DOMESTIC SUBJECTS

FOUNDED AS
THE NATIONAL
TRAINING SCHOOL
OF COOKERY

Cake presented to H.R.H. Princess Mary
on her engagement to Viscount Lascelles, November 1921

FLASH BACK

SOME OF THE MOST VIVID SPLASHES of colour in the National tapestry were the resplendent patterns of the early Reunions and the beautiful recurring gleam of the exquisite legendary cakes.

The Annual Reunions came into their own at the end of the First World War and dominated the Guild events. Always held at a mid-October weekend, the prelude was a Church Service on the Friday evening, usually at St Peter's, Eaton Square. On the Saturday evening at the National there was a Reception, with Speech, Supper, and often music and entertainment.

It was a full-dress affair and the organisation was meticulous to the last detail. The most delectable dishes were made ready in the preceding days, and executed with a degree of skill which even in those times when the mark of training was mastery of technique, was recognised as little short of perfection.

Though food was undoubtedly the main concern, all other preparations were equally scrupulous. Clean kitchens were re-cleaned; every knife, spoon and fork, dish, plate, cup and saucer, and glass was washed and polished. Tables scrubbed white with silver sand were covered with even whiter cloths; the copper burnished till it dazzled and the big fish kettles filled with Autumn leaves and flowers were displayed at vantage points throughout the building.

The whole undertaking was conducted by the staff, assisted by a small band of hand-picked students, who all arrived at the College early on the Saturday morning. Division of labour was feudal and ordained by the law of the Medes and Persians. The

Cookery staff were in the ascendant, and their lightest whim obeyed; flower arrangers also ranked high and both these groups of élite were allowed to be temperamental as the hours passed and a certain tension mounted. Juniors from lesser departments were employed in running errands and counting spoons; at times they carried tea to out of the way corners whose occupants, engrossed in mysterious ploys, were too busy to emerge.

When all was ready elsewhere, the final rite was performed. Although the College employed handymen supposedly to deal with all heavy tasks, it was always left to Miss Quick, deft but frail, sometimes aided by an acolyte, to sew together the tough red felt which she then personally rolled out along the passages.

After a brief dispersal, the staff returned in sparkling form, coiffured and gloved, the seniors in particular, magnificent in superb evening gowns, now ready to greet the Old Students thronging through the open double doors as the hour struck seven o'clock, to be wedged in the Entrance Hall. It was a transformation scene from the daily scurry of students and attaché cases; now there were chiffon dresses and satin shoes, and gloved fingers extricating small coloured tickets of admission from velvet wraps and little silver chain bags.

All who could crowded near the staircase, where in a sudden hush of expectancy, the Principal and her guests now made their entry, slowly descending under a battery of eyes, meeting first the penetrating gaze in the large photograph immediately facing them over the Dining Room door, of Mr J. C. Buckmaster who seemed to watch the little procession with a proprietary air.

The Principal and Miss Caddow received and mingled with the guests before Miss Clarke addressed them in the big Dining Room. There was always the customary blend of pride in the National's achievements of the preceding year, coupled with a slightly astringent reminder of the duties and standards expected, lest any should be tempted to rest on their laurels. With the evening thus launched, the time for the real business of food and conversation began, and before the formal interludes for music or drama, the vociferous delight of greetings and chatter mounted till it became deafening.

At eleven o'clock hot *consommé* was served, and waves of warmth from satisfied minds and heated bodies billowed into the cold night air of Buckingham Palace Road as the assembly dispersed. The great Reception was over for another year.

These stupendous functions continued until the nineteen-thirties. Even though the savour went out of them with Miss Clarke's illness and death, the pattern remained the same until all Meetings were brought to a halt by the Second World War. The first Reunion after this War had ended in 1946, in a changed world, was a very different affair. The Church Service was held as before on the Friday evening at St Peter's, Eaton Square, but the Reunion took place next day on Saturday, 19 October, in the afternoon, immediately following the General Meeting of the Guild. Relief that the National had survived the War gave to this Reunion a special spirit of thanksgiving, resulting in renewed contacts and interests and enrolment of members.

The following year saw a repetition of these times for both Service and Reunion, and this became the accepted plan, until in 1954, it was decided to hold both celebrations on the same day, with the Church Service in the morning and the Reception in the afternoon. For a few years longer Miss Caddow was there with Miss Eland to receive the Old Students as they entered at one door and went out by another of the old Dining Room. Later in the proceedings, the Principal highlighted the year's events by presenting both the College awards and her own Report; not apostrophising her audience as Miss Clarke had done, but giving an erudite review of the National's work.

There were still beautiful cakes and savouries; there were still greetings and reminiscences and talk; there were still pleasurable contacts and exchange of news. But the sense of occasion was gone. The days of dignity and splendour were over.

The last Reunion in Buckingham Palace Road was on 21 October 1961, an afternoon of sadness bordering on despair only mitigated by undaunted determination to preserve the name and aims and ideals of the National. The following year, homeless and bereft, the Old Students were heartened by the warm invitation of Miss K. M. Perry, the Principal of the National Society's Training College in Hampstead, to hold both the Church Service and the Reception at Berridge House. The Service was in their Chapel, with its striking contemporary fur-

W

nishings, glowing colours and beautiful modern silver; guests were regaled by a buffet luncheon in the big Hall which was then placed at the disposal of both Guild and Trust for their afternoon meetings, and there was welcome tea before the journey home. This generous hospitality and happy arrangement continued for two years, when sadly Berridge House was no longer available. Later their own College moved to join The College of All Saints, St. Katharine's, Tottenham.

It was then decided to approach Queen Elizabeth College, who agreed to let the Guild have, at a reasonable fee, rooms for the Service, luncheon and afternoon meetings, and for them to deal with the related arrangements planned by the Guild Committee. In spite of the helpful attention of Queen Elizabeth College's pleasant staff, and the privilege of viewing the big plaque recording the gift of £100,000 from the Governors of the National, there could never be the same family feeling of the past Reunions. It was inevitable that with every effort, the Old Students felt strangers in a strange land.

The last gathering was held here on 30 September 1972, for in 1973 the Guild closed, exactly sixty one years after its birth in 1912. It continued to live through the Trust which it had brought into being in 1961, for every Guild Member automatically belonged to both organisations. No date had yet been fixed for the Trust to wind up its affairs, as there was still some further work to be done.

Cake representing a Rockery

THE CAKES were jewels strung along an endless thread, in an infinite variety of settings; some magnificent and brilliant, some warm and glowing, some bright and gay and amusing, some modest and simple, but all beautiful in their own right. The gem itself had to be worthy of its setting, and beneath the decoration, the quality of the basic cake was the first essential. The lily could be gilded, but there could be no whited sepulchre; there was no danger of sawdust-dry or sodden centres hidden under the final image.

Although no tribute ever surpassed that of the chef at Buckingham Palace when the great sugar hawthorn bough was so life-like that he judged it to be newly picked from a tree, yet other cakes merited comparable praise. Hundreds had their hour of passing glory, remembered only by those who toiled to achieve their perfection; and occasionally also by those who ate them, sometimes in real appreciation though more often in casual enjoyment. Ignorant of the choice ingredients, the blending of flavours, the skill of the mixing and baking, and the finished artistry, the heedless were sublimely unaware that they carelessly demolished a perishable work of art.

Throughout the years, these delectable cakes appeared in assorted shapes and sizes. In the first *Guild Magazine* of 1912, Miss Gladys Clarke described some of the Christmas Exhibition work; there were a hundred and ten cakes 'hardly two alike in colouring or design', and she continued 'Among the children's cakes, one specially deserves mention; the cake was in the form of a table laid for a meal, the pie had just been cut, and the four-and-twenty blackbirds were seen emerging. The majority of the cakes were piped and decorated with roses in many sizes and colours; daisies, lavender, violets, scarlet pimpernel, water lilies, holly, mistletoe and Christmas roses. Some of the trellis work was exceptionally good. A cake decorated with large pink roses and pale blue forget-me-nots was graciously accepted by H.R.H. Princess Mary from the staff.'

Nine years later, in November 1921, in celebration of her engagement to Viscount Lascelles, H.R.H. Princess Mary accepted another cake from the National, this time decorated, not only with flowers, but with the cornucopias of plenty.

The art of flower making, not always understood, became one of the acclaimed and unrivalled skills of the National. In 1913 it was recorded that 'among the newest flowers were mimosa, daffodils, sweet peas, primroses and speedwell'. They were always adding to their repertoire. The creative urge impels the born decorator of cakes to rush to the kitchen as a painter to his palette, and as with any serious artist, both hard study and assiduous practice are needed to perfect the technique. There is no short cut, if ideas are to be translated with meaning and accuracy. Few possess the inspiration, and perhaps fewer the staying-power, but both are essential to reach the goal.

At the National, Miss Broderick's gifts in this field were unexcelled. Her thin shapely hands brought the sugar flowers to life, exact in form and colour. The perfection of these replicas was due to constant practice. She once said that although already an expert, it had taken her a year before she was satisfied with her modelling of a narcissus, where the petals were semi-transparent and grained like a true 'paper-white.' Her skill had full play when in 1935 she made a cake in the form of a rock garden full of tiny flowers, which to the great delight of all, was accepted by His Majesty King George V who had then been Patron of the National for over twenty-five years.

Miss Rotheram's genius literally flowered again in Miss Broderick, and in turn Miss Crawford carried on the tradition. The achievements of this gifted trio inspired many who came to their demonstrations and classes, both students and members of the public; some of the latter who later went from strength to strength possibly never even realised the extent of their privilege in that they had participated in virtuoso performances. There were worthy disciples within the College, but none were ever known really to compare with these three supreme exponents of their art, and when Miss Crawford left in 1955, there was no one to follow her.

At Miss Ashford's farewell party in 1936, the glory of the tea table lay in 'a cake that might have flowered for a wedding.' For christenings and weddings, Miss Broderick's cakes were especially coveted for their lightness of touch and delicacy of colour.

Miss Clarke once amazed a young man for whose marriage she was presenting the wedding cake, when on meeting him for the first time, she enquired, apparently inconsequently, as to his favourite colour. Somewhat bewildered by the query, he answered 'Blue, I think.' 'Then,' said Miss Clarke, 'you shall have blue on your wedding cake.' He was horrified. Shyness and manners kept him from any demur, but he later said to his future wife '*Blue* on a wedding cake! I thought they were always white.' When the cake arrived, it was breathtaking in its aesthetic beauty. The lovely white cake was garlanded with posies of exquisite miniature flowers, of tiny roses, lilies of the valley, mimosa and the blue of speedwell and forget-me-nots.

Cakes jostle across the canvas of the years. There were the great classical celebration cakes, handsome and magnificent; the commemoration of events such as the Golden Jubilee Cake of 1924 showing the students of the eras of 1874 and 1924 playing tennis in the clothes of their day; the occasional sophisticated experiments in bizarre colours, and novelties of every sort. These included houses, rock gardens, snowballs, chalets, cushions, hampers, bowls of flowers, a Japanese rickshaw and a sedan chair, sacks of potatoes, oranges and lemons, Humpty Dumpty, Polar bears. Nowadays there would surely have been Dougal and the Magic Roundabout.

There were large cakes, small cakes, pillared and piped, decorated with chaplets, tassels, knots, stars, rosettes, bows and feathers, all in sugar. But above all there were flowers; always flowers, blooming in and out of season in profusion and in glory. Probably the keenest nostalgia was felt for the lovely flowering cakes with their subtlety and blend of exquisite colours, reaching the height of perfection in craft.

All were ephemeral, and few living memories remain. But the cake with the immense branch of hawthorn which blossomed in May 1912 was surely the National cake of the century – and unforgettable.

University of Surrey, showing Home Economics Centre

PHOENIX RISING

CHAPTER L

Nor shall this peace sleep with her; but as when
The bird of wonder dies, the maiden phoenix,
Her ashes new – create another heir
As great in admiration as herself.

William Shakespeare
King Henry VIII, Act 3

MISS ALICE CADDOW once quoted 'The darkest night that ever fell on earth, never put out the stars.' Black night had fallen on the National, and the stars seemed very far away. After its double doors were shut and barred, and before the band of builders and decorators moved in to renovate the place from top to toe, the College was left with empty echoing rooms, dusty and deserted. It seemed as if the building withdrew behind its blank windows to brood over jealously guarded secrets; secrets locked in the hearts of those now gone, and preserved to the last within the old walls.

The tapestry, worked inch by inch for eighty-nine years, with its kaleidoscope of colours, illumined the joys, sorrows, exaltation, near despair, long strong threads of purpose, bold designs, patches muddled and mishandled, side by side with brilliance of inspiration and achievement. Imprinted on the mind, it remains indestructible. Nevertheless, when the last stitches were completed, and the National physically ceased on 12 July 1962, many felt that it was indeed the end. But as in the eternal cycle of death and life, as one story ended, so another began. Through the ashes of the old rose the new; the new life belonged to the future and the responsibility for giving it a good start lay with the Trust.

As already recorded, the National Training College of Domestic Subjects (founded 1873) Trust had been brought into being by a resolution of the Old Students Guild in July 1961, as an Educational and Charitable Trust, and by October, those who had agreed to serve were as follows:

TRUSTEES

The Honourable Mrs Donald Kershaw
B. G. Stone, O.B.E., M.A.(Cantab.)

COMMITTEE

Representing Old Students
Miss V. Brand, A.R.R.C.
Miss G. M. Eland, O.B.E., *Former Principal N.T.C.D.S.*
Miss B. M. Fisher
Mrs F. S. Standley
Miss M. J. Voyce, *Head of Women's Department,
Croydon Technical College*
Miss B. S. Briggs, *Principal N.T.C.D.S. President, Old
Students Guild, ex officio*
Miss M. Knox-Johnston, *Hon. Secretary, Old Students
Guild, ex officio*

Friends of the National
Miss I. S. Gibson, O.B.E., B.Sc., *Principal Glasgow and
West of Scotland College of Domestic Subjects*
Mrs E. R. House, H.M.I. (retired)
Miss M. S. Jaques, B.A.
Miss F. M. Pugh, J.P., M.A.

At the Inaugural Meeting on 11 October 1961, Mr B. G. Stone was elected to the Chair, and Miss Brand agreed to serve temporarily as Hon. Secretary. Apologies for absence were received from Miss Gibson and Miss Pugh; otherwise there was full attendance and the Committee set itself to study the conditions and aims of the newly constituted Trust. Under matters of finance, it was agreed that the Trustees should be the guardians of the funds, to advise, administer and allocate, but that they should not be required to act in any capacity for fund raising. The draft Deed was in the hands of Messrs Radcliffes and Co. A number of people had already promised donations and seven-year deeds of covenant.

The Committee now examined in detail the first specific aim of the Constitution: 'To perpetuate the name and work at home and

overseas of the National Training College of Domestic Subjects, and the aims and ideals of its Founders.' It was essential to
clarify this statement, both in order to define the purpose of the
Trust, and also to direct their own minds towards the proper
means of fulfilment. Any project which embraced the aims and
ideals would automatically perpetuate the work, though not
necessarily the name, of the National. It appeared also that two
separate schemes would be needed to do justice to enterprises
both at home and overseas.

The first requirement, obviously, was to discover exactly what
were these aims and ideals of the Founders. The tenets of the
National had formed the very warp and weft of the College life,
and their strength had been such as to withstand all attempts to
tear it apart. They were incorporated in a conception of home-
making which demanded recognition of certain principles and
abilities, with which the founders demonstrated their identifi-
cation by their actions. They showed foresight in assessment of
future needs and quick response; independence of mind and
courage to embark on new ventures; appreciation of a wide and
balanced outlook with integrity of purpose, faith, determination, common sense and a capacity for hard work. They believed
in the pursuit and dissemination of knowledge and the acquisition of skill; the recognition of modern thought involving a
sense of personal responsibility in the ultimate use of its development; and the exploitation of the National's assets in any field.
The founders were establishing a College, but the end of the
charge was the home as the hub, the basis of civilised life, responsible for moral, cultural and material priorities.

Few attained such heights consistently, but the students were
imbued with these standards in which they were trained by
precept and example. The principles which had given strength
and significance to the National's achievements still held good
nearly a century later, and it was on these that the Trust wished
to build. Convinced that each generation should make its own
assessment and contribution in its own way, the Trust were
concerned to provide conditions for creative work in media
suited to the time. They maintained one condition: any project
which they sponsored must be based on the aims and ideals of
the National's founders.

It was agreed that any enterprise should be interpreted liberally; to encourage mature students, and 'to give financial aid for any need deemed in the opinion of the Committee to further the aims of the Founders'; also to promote a variety of research in education and technology. Finally it was decided that 'members of the Committee were to be eligible to receive grants; age and sex to be no bar.'

At the second Committee Meeting on 7 December 1961, considerable time was perforce devoted to agreeing, clause by clause, the draft Deed of the Trust. The problem of money followed; paucity of funds led to the advisability of securing outside interest and assistance, for the choice of any project would inevitably be governed by finances. Donations and the first instalments of the covenanted subscriptions now amounted to £317 19s, with the promise of £212 income per annum, and although many friends rallied to help with incidental expenses, obviously no major undertaking could be contemplated. Any thought that the Trust were following in the National's footsteps, with enterprises curtailed through lack of money, was not admitted. Happily, in this respect a better fate awaited the Trust, though for a long time their only reliable assets were faith and determination.

Consideration of possible projects provoked a variety of unpredictable views. Inevitably there were conflicting opinions among the members of the Committee. The link which joined them was a shared determination to translate the original aims of the National into a worthy enterprise, but great patience and tolerance were called for while schemes were debated, for it was another year before a project whose value was unequivocally acclaimed bound them into a team, and harnessed energies.

Meantime it was decided that an interim plan within their means might be put into action. Work on the home front was considered first, but as many of the less costly suggestions were already assisted by established associations, it was deemed wiser not to dissipate small sums on minor projects. Attention was therefore turned to their other commitment of 'work overseas,' where it was felt that there might be some real need of a pioneer nature which the Trust could meet without draining the exchequer.

Eventually, in January 1962, following hard argument, it was agreed to pursue a pilot scheme overseas. This idea was reinforced by Miss Gibson who stressed the two-way benefit involved, as whoever was selected would both answer the need abroad, and contribute a valuable piece of educational training on overseas problems on her return.

The Committee was of one mind in deciding that acknowledged authorities in the overseas sphere should be consulted, particularly Miss D. S. Hollingsworth of the Ministry of Agriculture, Fisheries and Food, and Miss F. H. Gwilliam, the Woman Education Adviser of the Department of Technical Cooperation. Both these experts gave warm encouragement, and Dr Elizabeth Keister, of the Food and Agriculture Organisation, promised all possible help.

Before coming to any decision, however, everyone wished for the opportunity of a proper discussion with an experienced specialist in overseas work, and it was unanimously decided to invite Miss Freda Gwilliam to join the next Committee on 31 May 1962.

She developed the idea of sending a student on attachment to the educational staff of a selected country for work on some local project of community development, with the support of international organisations, and also of later offering bursaries to suitable women from that same country to come to Britain for courses in family living, study of clothing, and budgeting. Bursaries could also be offered to help Old Students to take an academic diploma course of advanced study, sponsored by a University in the United Kingdom or the U.S.A.

The scheme held great appeal and the fact that it might well prove to be a unique combination of work at home and abroad was a point high in its favour, and partly satisfied those who still craved the home front as priority.

Her talk indeed proved the turning point in the overseas project and immediate agreement was reached on approaches to friends or Old Students abroad, with professional knowledge, to seek their views on any possible local investigations which could be of value. Miss Gwilliam felt that the whole field of exchange was open to the Trust, and she emphasised the help to be confidently expected from international conferences, seminars and the F.A.O. A small *ad hoc* sub-Committee was set up to examine suggestions and recommend proposals, to the general uplift of spirit.

At this same May Committee, two schemes for work at home were also propounded. King Edward's Hospital Fund for London had set up a Working Party to consider the need for Domestic Superintendents and Supervisors for hospitals, with recommendations for training. The Committee agreed to investigate further both this position as well as the second suggestion concerning education of the handicapped. In the event, neither of these two ideas were pursued. The latter called for highly specialised skills which the Trust was in no position to provide. The former was a parochial matter which by now had been taken well in hand.

Several items of importance marked the sixth meeting on 18 July 1962. The first was a sad reminder of the reason for their own existence. The National had closed in the previous week, and the Chairman read out the telegram sent from the Trust 'Our thoughts are with all staff and students today. *Semper fidelis* remains for us all. Wishing you good fortune as you set forth.'

The next item was a happy augury, for the Right Honourable the Lord Bishop of London had consented in June to support the work of the Trust by becoming a Trustee. This gratifying news was followed by the introduction and welcome of Mr Thorold Hadrill, Manager of the National Provincial Bank, 161 Brompton Road, S.W.3, who had agreed to serve as Hon. Treasurer of the Trust, thus relieving Miss Briggs of this responsibility. It was now resolved that 'the funds at present held in the names of Miss B. S. Briggs and Miss H. M. Lancaster, the respective President and Hon. Treasurer of the Guild, be vested forthwith in the Trustees, and transferred to a separate account with the National Provincial Bank, in the name of the National Training College of Domestic Subjects (founded 1873) Trust.

From the moment when Mr Thorold Hadrill joined the Trust Committee as the Hon. Treasurer, the finances were in safe and gifted hands. Not only did he watch and guard, but he guided and advised with unerring judgment.

Replies arrived from correspondents overseas. Imagination was seized by a suggestion from Bombay, for the adoption of an Indian village, to give practical help with equipment and personnel, and informal advice was sought from a former Minister of Health, the Rajkumari Amrit Kaur. It was agreed to write personally to an Old Student in Kenya; and for the Chairman, through his professional association with overseas governments, to approach officials in Kenya, Nyasaland and Uganda for their views on a practical project of co-operation.

By October 1962 there were definite developments. The Indian scheme unfortunately fell through, as the Rajkumari was ill and unable to deal with it. Kenya and Nyasaland were appreciative, but the provision of teaching staff was their prior need. Uganda, however, responded with interest that the authorities 'expected to be able to accept and co-operate in such a scheme as the Trust had in mind.' It seemed propitious that Miss J. M. Neilson, an old National student and Domestic Subjects Organiser in Uganda, was at this moment on leave in England, so that contact could be made. Miss Neilson declared that the Trust's proposals fitted closely with her own ideas for linking the education of African women to homemaking and she undertook to follow up officially the proposals of the Trust on her return.

Enquiries had meantime confirmed that for any returning Bursar, overseas experience could be a valuable preparation towards further academic qualifications, expecially in the comparative education section of the Academic Diploma in Education of the London University Institute of Education.

The way seemed to be clearing; but funds were still low.

The Annual General Meeting was held, by kind permission of the Principal, Miss K. M. Perry, at Berridge House on 20 October 1962. The Chairman summarised the varied events of the past year, detailing the legal position of the Trust; the finances, reinforced by the kind gift of £50 from the Guild, and £100 from the Governors of the National, towards administrative expenses; and also the present relationship with the Governors. He further explained details of the proposed Bursary for work overseas and he warmly welcomed the expert in this field, Miss Freda Gwilliam, experienced in pastures old and new, who took up the story.

In her travels, she said, she had widely recognised the immense opportunities for women, through training them to play a complementary part as homemakers in the work of social education which 'leads to stability in a developing country.' She rallied the entire audience by recalling the pioneer work which the National had started in London, and was still continued by its students all over the world. She referred to many parts of Africa, North Borneo and Gibraltar, where help was planned; she was conscious that the scope was limitless, and that the imaginative scheme outlined by the Trust was just what was wanted. She ended with a clarion call: 'with such inspiration, the right motto for the Trust should be "Phoenix Rising".'

Enormous enthusiasm greeted this vivid and inspiriting talk. There was unanimous assent to the Resolution 'to pursue projects at home and abroad.' This was sent by the Committee to the Governors in a Memorandum urging the recognition of the Trust as the 'rightful heirs' of the National.

By the end of the year, progress had been made on all sides, but on 12 December 1962, the Chairman reported two personal losses which clouded the meeting. Lady Cash had died; she had been a staunch and able member of the Executive Committee of the College for nearly ten years. Mrs House felt unable to continue on the Trust Committee, and her wide experience at home and abroad was greatly missed.

Relationships with Uganda brought general satisfaction. The Chairman had been in frequent correspondence with their Department of Education; the Trust proposals had received unofficial approval, and Uganda were now prepared, at the appropriate moment, to issue the official invitation to visit as the guest of their Government; for without this no selected Bursar could undertake any assignment.

The time had now come for a realistic assessment of the sum needed for this enterprise. When Mr Hadrill had become the Hon. Treasurer of the Trust in July 1962, funds had been steady but low, and although they had increased by December of that year to reach a bank balance of £727 14s 6d, the annual income was still a bare few hundred pounds, which could in no way meet the case. Nevertheless the Trust were not the 'moral heirs' of the National for nothing; they took the decision to 'be prepared,' and during the next six months resolutely went ahead with their plans. By the summer of 1963, exchange of views both in correspondence and personal talks between representatives of the Trust and overseas advisers, particularly with Mr E. K. K. Sempebwa of the Ugandan High Commission Office in London, had led to a realistic scheme, accepted by all concerned and ready to put into action.

It remained to find the money, and although it was accepted that the Governors could not delay indefinitely the allocation of their surplus funds, no reliance could be placed either on the time or the content of their announcement. The Trust could only possess their souls in faith and patience.

They also had plenty to occupy them. The Committee Meeting in December 1962 had been important in that it was the first time that mention was made of what was eventually to become the major enterprise of the Trust. There had been much serious thought before it was decided to discuss the proposition that 'the outstanding need for Domestic Scientists in the United Kingdom was the opportunity to take a degree, and that the Trust should work towards this.' This idea crystallised an enterprise worthy of the aims of the Founders – a pioneer project which would fill a want. The challenge lay at hand.

Consultation with the Lord Bishop of London, to seek his views, was the next step. The suggestion of a degree course in Domestic Subjects, by now generally known by the title of Home Economics, interested Dr Stopford. He was in favour of it in principle, and recommended an approach to a new University where the planning gained in flexibility what it lacked in tradition. He pointed out the advantage which some financial subsidy could give, but, although fully appreciating this advice, the Trust as yet had neither money nor even a syllabus – only their convictions. Their determination, however, was greatly strengthened by the Bishop's encouragement.

There was nothing original in the idea of a degree course in this field. Leaders of the profession for over fifty years had been aware of this need, and Mrs Clarke had been a pioneer in her efforts to introduce such a course as early as 1909, in an endeavour to bring the academic content of the training into line with accepted University disciplines. Miss Clarke had again pursued this view in stating her hopes to the Executive Committee in 1927.

For many years, individuals and groups had discussed the problem as it applied to Britain. Some of the older pioneers had given it considerable study, and if Miss Gwynneth Haigh, B.Sc., Principal of Leicester Training College of Housecraft, had not tragically died while still in office, she might well have led a successful campaign. As it was, in a close friendship, she had discussed in detail many of her ideas with Mr and Mrs B. G. Stone, who were able to contribute them to the discussions which led to the shaping of the Degree Course finally devised by a small sub-Committee of the Trust.

The members of this sub-Committee, set up in May 1963, were Dr E. P. Baranyay, Ph.D.; Miss B. S. Briggs, H.M.I. and former Principal of the National; Miss M. M. N. McLauchlan, B.A., Head Mistress of North London Collegiate School; Mrs D. K. Stone, H.M.I.; B. G. Stone, M.A., Chairman of the Trust. They were authorised to consult or co-opt others for special subjects under discussion, with the following brief: 'To explore the ground and test the validity of the assumption that there is a need for a further degree course in Home Economics, to make recommendations as to the general scope and content of such a course, and to report back to the Executive Committee in the Autumn.'

The first meeting was held on Monday, 1 July 1963, at the Westminster flat of Mr and Mrs Stone, and from then on, at the end of their day's work, the members regularly met there. There followed an exciting six months.

The terms of reference were examined in detail and not until the members had satisfied themselves as to the need for a degree course, were the general lines considered. At the outset, it was agreed to work towards certain aims; these proved to be synonymous with the ideals of the Founders of the National, and it was decided to devise a course in which they could be embodied, while at the same time keeping the pattern as flexible as possible, opening the door to potential Arts and Science candidates, of both sexes. The course was to be based on the Humanities, and while recognising the inherent truth of Science, it was yet not to be restricted to a narrow specialisation.

Assessing the needs of youth in relation to the future, it was felt that there was an increasing search for a new dispensation, a turning away from the established forms of religion, scholarship and politics, from the domination of Science and Technology, towards the Humanities, with vision beyond the accepted commercial concepts of the day.

Evidence showed that there were many Sixth-formers of

University calibre who did not wish to confine their studies to
subjects such as History, or Classics, or Science, however wide
the compass, and sought instead a course dealing with people,
which could lead to many avenues. The sub-Committee became
convinced that this year of 1963 was the right time to devise a
course to meet these needs within the coming decade.

Appreciating both the University belief in the trained mind
untramelled by future demands, and also the generally existing
concern with some form of assured career, the sub-Committee
felt it incumbent on them to ensure a proper basis, so that leaving
graduates would be fitted to enter a wide range of spheres and
be capable of learning the specific needs of any particular post
or organisation, on the actual job. It was planned, as are all
University courses, to train leaders of thought with informed
minds and a sense of personal responsibility. Home Economics
seemed peculiarly fitted for this conception of a degree course;
it also complemented some of the National's ideals in the time-
less qualities of vision, courage and endurance.

It was these beliefs that the sub-Committee attempted to
translate into a specific course which would merit academic
recognition.

In the eleven meetings, with a break of two months between
July and September, hard thought wrestled with constant
heart-searchings. Once the main topics were agreed, experts in
various fields joined the sub-Committee at times to offer specialist knowledge. Each subject was considered individually and
in relation to the others, and here the cut and thrust of the little
Committee evoked both ideas and response. The members all
made very different contributions; from the National Miss
Briggs brought her experience and dispassionate approach, and
Mrs Baranyay her wide and intuitive sympathy. Miss McLauchlan was immediately in tune, for to humour and humanity she
allied a keen incisive mind and clarity of judgment. All the
Committee members shared in common a desire to give honest
assessment, to search for solutions, and to recognise the wise
suggestion without any personal axes to grind.

Schemes of work were planned in outline, then drawn up in
great detail. They were pruned heavily, but insufficiently, and
at the first official appraisal by an academic, the entire course
was shot down in flames and summarily dismissed. Fortunately
x

the sub-Committee was undaunted, and also blessed by the support of Professor Richard D'Aeth, Professor of Education at Exeter University, who now came to the rescue. Widely travelled and experienced, with sensitive perception, he had early understood and encouraged the idea of the degree course, and joined one or two Committee sessions. He now demonstrated his faith practically, by advising, not on any change of content, but on a change of presentation to a form which would be acceptable to a University.

Complete re-writing, to reduce the original detailed and already heavily pruned schemes to a minimum, produced a skeleton syllabus which could be adapted to suit the conditions and bias of any University, but not losing by jot or tittle the principles and ideals on which it was based.

On 14 December 1963, the new Degree Course, original in its approach, and devised by the Trust, was ready for submission.

Meantime the Governors had published the allocations of their funds, and the Trust had learnt that their own share would amount to between £20,000 and £30,000. The first step was to decide on its proper investment and use.

A meeting of the Trustees, Dr R. W. Stopford, Lord Bishop of London, the Honourable Mrs Donald Kershaw and Mr B. G. Stone, with Mr T. D. Hadrill, Hon. Treasurer in attendance, had been held on Thursday, 5 December 1963, at Church House, Westminster, S.W.1, to discuss the investment policy of the Trust. After Mr Hadrill had outlined the various methods open under the terms of the Trust Deed, the Trustees decided to invest the sum of £20,000 recently received from the Liquidator of the National Training College of Domestic Subjects in a balanced portfolio of Equities and Investment Trusts, in roughly equal proportions, with not more than 5 per cent in the shares of any one company, so as to safeguard both the capital and income of the Trust to the best advantage against the probable effects of future inflation. Mr Hadrill was instructed to seek the advice of a stockbroker with not less than fifteen years experience on the Stock Exchange and with specialised knowledge of Investment Trusts, and to authorise him to prepare detailed proposals accordingly for the approval of the Trustees.

The Trustees recommended that about 20 per cent of the

annual income derived from investments should be retained each year for further investment so as to build up the capital resources of the Trust, and that the balance together with the other income from donations and covenanted subscriptions should be available for implementing the schemes of the Trust as agreed from time to time by the Executive Committee. It was further decided that any additional grant which might be forthcoming from the Liquidator of the College should be similarly invested, subject to the proviso that a part might if necessary be retained for immediate expenditure on the furtherance of the Uganda Scheme towards the cost of a second bursary. Realistic discussion had produced the figure of approximately £1,500 as required to cover the expenses of one Bursar. The Chairman promised to bring these decisions and recommendations to the attention of the Committee.

Such was the importance which the Trust attached to the selection of the right candidate for Uganda, that in September 1963 it was decided to frame an advertisement designed to attract applicants of outstanding quality, and to give it the widest possible publicity in professional educational journals and the main daily newspapers. Interviews could then be arranged for the New Year, thus allowing time for the Bursar to set forth in the late summer. It was decided that at the forthcoming Annual General Meeting on 19 October 1963, Uganda interests should be given weight. Miss Voyce who had actively helped both in advice and planning, agreed to speak, and the Committee was unanimous in its wish to invite Mr E. K. K. Sempebwa, who had given continuous and friendly help, also to address the meeting.

Miss Voyce went straight to the core of the matter, appealing both to heart and mind, as she explained the potential scope and stressed how ultimate success depended on finding someone who could meet the challenge of this venture. Mr Sempebwa delighted his audience by his interesting talk on the life and conditions in his country, recalling the original link between Uganda and Britain which dated from a treaty in the days of Queen Victoria. He described their educational system, and emphasised the need for development at all levels, leading up to the degrees now to be awarded at Makerere College, in relationship with the University of London. As yet, there had been insufficient opportunities for girls and women, and it was strongly felt that on this side the Bursar would be able to play an important part. With a few telling illustrations he brought home this essential need to all who listened.

Changes were taking place in the Trust Committee. Mrs Strange had taken over the Hon. Secretaryship of the Guild from Miss Johnston in July 1963, and so became an *ex officio* member of the Trust Committee. Miss Gibson had resigned, and the regret that she showed in her letter was equally felt by all the Committee. In February 1964, Miss Brand relinquished her responsibility as Hon. Secretary which she had handled vigorously since the formation of the Trust. She was followed by Miss Katharine Worsley, who with sympathetic devotion carried out the ever increasing duties as the work of the Trust expanded, and through many vicissitudes never failed to respond loyally to demands on her time. Miss Brand remained as a member of the Committee and in June 1964, Miss Irene Hilton, with her quick grasp of essentials, added to everyone's pleasure when she accepted an invitation to join. At the same time there was general regret at the resignation, due to pressure of work, of Miss B. S. Briggs, both as President of the Guild and a member of the Trust Executive and Degree sub-Committees. The Committee was also sorry to say goodbye to Mrs Standley in 1965 and Miss Fisher in 1966.

There was great regret when Mr Hadrill resigned as Hon. Treasurer in March 1966, tempered by gratification that he consented to remain as a member of the Committee, who were thus able to avail themselves of his perception and knowledge which he continued to place readily at their disposal. Mr J. G. Page accepted the vacated office, and gave the able and devoted service on which the Trust had come to rely.

At the same date, an invitation was sent to Mr Coulson to become a member of the Committee, and it was also proposed that Mrs D. K. Stone, now freed from her Trappist vows by retirement from the Ministry of Education, should join. Both expressed pleasure in their replies; Mr Coulson was welcomed at the next meeting at the end of June, and Mrs Stone attended soon afterwards. It was also announced on 29 June 1966, that Miss Eland had been compelled by ill health to resign from the

Presidency of the Guild, and she was succeeded by Miss Barbara Visick.

Plans went ahead for the Uganda Bursarship. Five candidates were shortlisted from twenty applications, for interview on 20 March 1964. The Selection Board comprising Miss V. Brand, Miss M. J. Sargeaunt, Mr E. K. K. Sempebwa, Miss B. M. Visick, Miss M. J. Voyce, with Mr B. G. Stone in the Chair, and Miss K. Worsley as Hon. Secretary, had agreed that as funds were now available, it would be preferable to appoint two Bursars for a period of eight months rather than one Bursar for a year.

The two Bursaries were awarded, to take effect from the late summer of 1964 until Easter 1965, to Miss I. C. Begrie, a member of the staff of Queen Elizabeth College and to Miss M. S. Wood, an old National student, on the staff of Seaford Training College.

On 25 June 1964 the Chairman reported these appointments to the Trust Committee, adding the unfortunate news that Miss Wood had almost immediately withdrawn as her Education Authority was not prepared to grant the required leave. Miss Begrie would therefore go alone and was due in Kampala on 31 July 1964. All possible preparations had been made to receive her as an emissary with specific terms of reference, and to give her every opportunity to meet people and to study conditions.

The Chairman spoke again about this Bursary at the Annual General Meeting on 3 October 1964, placing on record the deep debt owed to Miss Irene Hilton, who as President of the International Federation of University Women, had conducted a Seminar for UNESCO during May 1964 at Makerere. She had been untiring in arranging introductions both professionally and socially. Miss Gwilliam had also given personal help through her wide range of contacts, so that Miss Begrie's way had been paved in advance in many circles.

Through the initiative of the Chairman, the Ugandan Government had agreed that Miss Begrie should be attached to the Inspectorate Division of the Ministry of Education, occupying the post of a Central Government Inspector of Schools, and given office accommodation, subsidised housing, mileage allowance and travelling expenses, on the same scale as in equivalent Government service. At the same time she was left free to make any arrangements she wished, to fulfil the conditions of her assignment with the Trust. She travelled extensively, and wrote 'It seems to me that I had the best of all possible worlds.' But a variety of circumstances combined to prevent fruition of the project. Changing politics allied with the general climate of opinion inhibited the outcome of constructive ideas or independent thought.

Satisfaction was expressed that the Bursar herself had been able to enjoy and benefit from her eight months' experience. Her final Report was of considerable interest, but the expectancy of receiving handpicked students to follow specially planned courses of programmes in Britain, thus to form a nucleus of leaders on return to their own country, all collapsed. With the approach of Independence, no later follow-up was practicable.

The Bursary cost the Trust £1,250, but this was as nothing compared with the loss of their unfulfilled hopes. The first venture of the Trust, nevertheless, gave evidence of Britain's concern and goodwill towards her African Colonies, which even though subsequent unhappy events in Uganda did not implement, may have shown that active help was sincerely intended.

Two years later, in May 1967, quite a different enterprise was undertaken. The Degree Course was by now being pursued with ardour, but simultaneously the Trust embarked on another project at home. It was brought to the notice of the Committee by Mr Hadrill who suggested that there was scope for a Home Economist to help the Mulberry Housing Trust. This had been formed in 1965 to acquire suitable houses in a somewhat derelict area of North Paddington, occupied mainly by Irish and Jamaican families, in order to adapt, renovate and let them in separate flats. It was felt that advice and help, given with understanding and tact, on matters of family living, especially the care and maintenance of the property, and the problems of food, clothing and budgeting, could lead to the better welfare and greater contentment of the families concerned, and thus speed up the process of resettlement. It would be an unusual form of social

work, for which a Home Economist would be peculiarly fitted
by training, but the right temperament would also be essential.

There was full agreement between the Committee and Miss
Josie Jackson, the Mulberry Housing Trust Manager, as to the
value of this contribution, and discussions between them led
to the decision that the Trust should pay the salary of such an
assistant, for two years on an experimental basis, without prejudice. The eventual agreement also ensured pension rights for
trained teachers of Home Economics.

Miss Sheila Charnley, whose previous experience had included both free lance and public relations work, was appointed, and
joined the Mulberry staff on 1 November 1967, at a salary of
£1,250 a year. This was raised to £1,500 in 1969 and the Trust
continued this responsibility for four years. Miss Charnley was
undoubtedly attracted by the challenge, and under the vigorous
direction of Miss Josie Jackson, the work flourished and grew
apace.

It was a happy and interesting relationship for the Trust, and
was another small but useful piece of pioneer work, for never
before had a Home Economist worked as an integral member of
the staff of a Housing Association. Miss Josie Jackson and Miss
Charnley both spoke at the Annual General Meetings in 1967
and 1968, and aroused great interest. In 1970 Mulberry bought
its 200th house for conversion, and a second Home Economist
was appointed. In September 1971 Miss Charnley left to take
further training in social work; her place was filled, so that two
Home Economists still continued on the Mulberry staff.

The Trust were forced to reconsider their financial commitments, for now they were deeply involved in the demands connected with the degree course. Though no whit less appreciative
of Mulberry's noteworthy achievements, the Trust did not feel
justified in continuing financial support at that moment. The
whole enterprise had been a testimony to co-operation in a
pioneer venture, and an unbroken link remained.

On a smaller scale, the Trust decided in 1966 to offer Study
Travel grants to former staff or students of the National. It was
suggested that such a grant might enable them to extend a
holiday abroad to include some educational work connected
with Home Economics; alternatively, if granted official leave
of absence by their employers, they might undertake a specific

piece of research overseas during term time. The sum generally accepted by the Committee was in the region of £100, though no actual limit was placed either on the amount or number of these grants. A big response was anticipated when the offer was widely publicised, particularly in *Guild News Letters* and at Reunions.

In the event, only one application was received. Miss Bridget Macartney, a senior dietitian, was already in receipt of a grant from the British Dietetic Association, to visit hospitals in Canada and the U.S.A., in April and May 1967. The supplement of £100 from the Trust enabled her both to extend her programme and to travel locally by air, to the advantage of her visit.

In 1972, in conjunction with the Guild, a grant of £160 was made available for four Old Students towards travel and maintenance expenses when attending the International Home Economics Federation Meeting in Helsinki.

Confidence in the Degree Course remained unshaken, though there was a long passage ahead. 'Even the weariest river winds somewhere safe to sea' wrote Swinburne, but in January 1964 no one even knew quite where the sea lay.

There had been encouragement over the final draft of the Degree Course from several academics, including the Lord Bishop of London and Professor Richard D'Aeth, to whom so much was already due. It was now decided to put the scheme to the test and submit it to a University. The Committee authorised the Chairman to undertake this responsibility on their behalf, and thus began a series of stimulating and interesting contacts which nevertheless often ended in frustrated hopes.

The first approach was to Birmingham where personal and professional relationships were already established through the Chairman's official work. The Vice Chancellor, Sir Robert Aitken, in an immediate response welcomed the proposal, and put it before his Senate where it aroused sympathetic interest. But the response of the Deans was not encouraging. The truth was that in the uncertain financial climate, there was anxiety lest even the existing, well established courses could be fully maintained, let alone embarking on the idea of a new department which could not bring with it adequate financial help.

Even so, the matter was pursued in a spirit of warm friendliness in a series of letters and meetings in Birmingham and in London, between the Vice Chancellor, the Registrar (Sir George Cartland) and the Trust Chairman. A small sub-Committee to investigate possibilities was set up at Birmingham in May 1964, and hopes rose. But the financial problems pressed heavily. By now the Trust were in a position to offer some £20,000 or £30,000, but as a sum nearer £70,000 would be required, the Trust's contribution would be a bagatelle in comparison to the need.

Genuine desire on both sides to reach a happy conclusion ended sadly in November 1965 after two years of continuous good-will, when Birmingham came 'reluctantly to the conclusion that there was no hope of exploring any new field of activity during the next quinquennium.' Sir Robert Aitken, in 1965, appealing for more 'detailed basic planning, looking ten years ahead,' described in his annual report 'the year that began confidently, with an invitation to a great endeavour, and ended in uncertainty.' 'Confidence began to ebb,' he continued, 'as it became apparent that financial support might not extend . . . to meet the needs of the students and of the country.' He pleaded for fuller discussion with the Government concerning the Universities' part in the national development.

It was an unfortunate time for all Universities, who found great difficulty in implementing their present commitments. There was no chance of the Trust endowing a Chair, and at this point they had no further capital to guarantee continuance of the course should University sources find themselves unable to meet rising costs.

The Chairman, through his professional work and personal introductions, knew many of the Universities, and he was welcomed always with kindness and also with great interest for the original scheme which he offered and discussed. In several Universities the idea was given serious consideration by the Senate; it was noticeable that everywhere the senior members were interested and quick to respond to the potential scope; it was only the immature in age or outlook who sometimes failed to grasp the possibilities.

Canterbury in particular pursued the idea realistically, but before any decision was reached, the long river wound to its last bend, and the sea was in sight.

On 28 February 1966, Mr Coulson sent the final statement on the winding up of the National. Due to his untiring efforts, another £10,000 had been released from Ministry of Education repayment, which with the residue bequeathed by the Governors increased the final sum to £41,655 5*s* 10*d*. Donations, covenanted subscriptions and anonymous gifts, including the wonderfully generous £1,000 from Miss Edward, who never let her name be known, had enabled the Trust to start. Without these gifts, it could never have survived the two years from its inception in July 1961 until the contribution from the Governors, announced two years later, was paid on 24 October 1963.

The Trust had thus been able to undertake several projects, and now in 1966 were in possession of some £43,000. How this sum, through brilliant investment, nearly doubled itself in another five years, is a financial saga which although detailed with lucid clarity, still remains a source of admiration, tinged with a certain mystery, to the average uninitiated and less gifted.

In a masterly survey, at the Annual General Meeting on 28 September 1968, Mr Hadrill wittily described, likening the whole procedure to the dressing of a boar's head, from the first essentials of sound basic knowledge to the impressive richness of the superb finished article, the rapid rise of these funds. The magnificent achievement assuredly deserved more than the 'cordial nod of recognition towards the Guardians of the funds' for which he modestly suggested 'there was room if so inclined.'

The initial credit lay with Mr Hadrill for his shrewd and courageous advice, taken in consultation with the Lord Bishop of London. The continuation of their agreed policy maintained the value of the funds, so that the Trust was finally able to give a substantial sum towards the launching of the Degree Course.

At the end of 1966, the Committee had reached its final membership. The one exception was the regretted retirement of Mr J. G. Page as Hon. Treasurer in 1972, when he was followed by Mr J. D. Collins. The tradition of ability and genuine help had remained unbroken, and while welcoming Mr Collins, who proved equally interested, there was very real gratitude expressed for all that Mr Page had done with unvarying kindness.

The Officers of the Trust were now in 1966 as follows:

TRUSTEES
The Honourable Mrs Donald Kershaw
The Right Honourable the Lord Bishop of London,
    Dr R. W. Stopford, C.B.E., P.C., D.D., D.C.L.
B. G. Stone, O.B.E., M.A.(Cantab.)

EXECUTIVE COMMITTEE
B. G. Stone, *Chairman*
Miss V. Brand, A.R.R.C.
H. O. H. Coulson
Miss G. M. Eland, O.B.E. Former Principal N.T.C.D.S.
Miss B. M. Fisher
T. D. Hadrill
Miss I. F. Hilton, M.A., Secretary N.A.C.C.
Miss M. S. Jacques, B.A.
J. G. Page, *Hon. Treasurer*
Mrs M. Plumstead
Miss F. M. Pugh, J.P., M.A.
Mrs D. K. Stone, H.M.I. (Retired)
Mrs J. Strange, Hon. Secretary Old Students Guild
Miss B. M. E. Visick, President Old Students Guild
Miss M. J. Voyce, Head of Women's Department,
    Croydon Technical College
Miss K. Worsley, *Hon. Secretary*

At the Annual General Meeting on 30 September 1967, the Chairman reported that the Trust had agreed to help the Women's Employment Federation with their Home Economics Careers pamphlet, and to cover the cost of printing. Two years later, after completion, the final sum amounted to £223.

At the end of 1968, a suggestion was made for compiling a history of the National as another means of perpetuating its memory; but any decision was to be deferred until opinions had been sought from members of both the Guild and the Trust.

It had taken two years from 1964 for the river to carry its cargo of the degree course to within a glimpse of the sea. Far from being wearisome, it had proved a most stimulating and interesting journey full of unexpected twists and turns, and only marred occasionally by the uncertainty of its length. It was another two years before the course reached its haven, but by the beginning of 1966 the way was clearing, though it was by no means straightforward.

In December 1965, the Lord Bishop of London suggested to the Chairman that the University of Surrey might be the right home for the degree course. He also suggested the new University of the City, but it proved that their programme was already full, and Dr J. S. Tait, the Vice Chancellor elect, in turn proposed an approach to Dr D. M. A. Leggett, Principal of the Battersea College of Technology, now to become Vice Chancellor of the new University of Surrey, which was rising on its site outside Guildford.

Almost at the same time, the other Trustee, the Honourable Mrs Donald Kershaw, met Mr Marchant, Chairman of the Academic Policy Committee, and enlisted his active interest. All roads were converging on Guildford. Mrs Kershaw and Mr Stone were invited to an exploratory talk at Battersea College on 11 February 1966, and by that time both Dr Leggett and Mr Marchant had given serious thought to the Trust's proposals for the degree course, as given below:

SYLLABUS OF PROPOSED DEGREE COURSE IN
HOME ECONOMICS

I *Domestic Architecture and Services*
  a) An historical introduction to domestic architecture and furnishings.
  b) Contemporary design and construction of domestic dwellings.
  c) A comparative study of the functional design and suitability of domestic furniture, equipment and services.

   d) Town planning; use of natural resources; public services.
II *The Psychology and Sociology of the Family*
   a) Personal relations, both individual and within the family; attitudes and opinions; group patterns of behaviour.
   b) Environmental forces; social mobility; expansion of automation; extension of leisure; increased longevity.
III *The Science of Food*
   a) The basic needs of the human body and nutritive content of foods.
   b) Food production in the light of scientific developments, with special reference to the work of the United Nations Agencies and Technical Assistance programmes.
   c) The economics of world markets.

It was made clear that no course could be mounted until the University moved to its new site, but it was agreed that this comparatively short delay was immaterial if firm acceptance in principle could be secured at an early date. Many of the suggested topics could be covered by present members of the staff, but there would need to be a Professor or senior member of staff in charge of the course as a whole, responsible for co-ordinating the various studies.

It appeared that the course could best fit a niche in the Humanities and Social Science Department, and would therefore come under the direction of Dr A. Tropp, the newly appointed Professor of Sociology, now on a year's sabbatical leave in the United States, and he would need to be consulted. The ball, Dr Leggett felt, was now in his own court; he would discuss academic and financial implications first with his colleagues, and then with the Academic Policy Committee, with whom there would shortly be an opportunity.

A Working Party was set up to consider the Trust's proposed course, and it was June 1966 when their report was presented. There had been queries regarding the due weight of academic content, and on 22 August this was discussed between two University representatives of the Working Party and three members of the Trust Committee, all five women. Considerable differences of outlook almost brought matters to an impasse; the University representatives firmly opining that the course was unnecessary, and lacked both preparation for any specific career and academic weight.

It took some months and was largely due to the efforts of the Vice Chancellor and the Trust Chairman, before the misapprehensions were eventually cleared.

Faith in the degree course was demonstrated by Miss Mc Lauchlan when she stated at the Annual General Meeting of the Trust on the following 1 October 1966, that she knew that students of high calibre would be attracted by its 'artistic and architectural interest as well as by its recognition of scientific development, and by the opportunity it would provide for study in depth of human relations in the place that matters most – the home.'

Although the Trust were primarily concerned with the University conception of the trained mind, untrammelled by future commitments, they decided to satisfy certain criticisms, by gaining first-hand insight into a range of possible careers for graduates of such a course, through personal interviews in a variety of fields.

A discussion with Lord Llewellyn Davies, Professor of Architecture at University College, London, who was the first President of the International Society of Ekistics, showed that his views, particularly in relation to his degree course in Architecture, Planning and Building, seemed to share many factors akin to the Trust's way of thinking. In a sympathetic talk with the Chairman, Lord Llewellyn Davies felt that the Trust's proposed course could be very useful if it qualified the graduates to take the post graduate research courses in Environmental Studies now being planned in a number of Universities, and for which Surrey also hoped to gain approval.

Other contacts were made with representatives of the world of commerce and industry. Miss Mary George, Director of the Electrical Association for Women, had long been interested and helpful, feeling that graduates would be welcome in her own field of work. Mrs Joan Robins, Home Service Adviser of the Gas Council, was now approached for the first time and immediately responded. She was anxious to recruit students whose ability and personality would enable them to take a recognised place in industry, and she not only appreciated at first sight the use of the proposed course, but at once offered to visit the University in personal support, where she thereafter took part in many ensuing discussions.

Miss Eland's perspicacity foresaw the risk that industrial interests might radically alter the bias of the course, but it was pointed out that acceptance of the basic aims would eradicate this danger.

Nothing definite could be decided before the return of Professor Tropp, but the many facets increasingly evident in the proposed course awakened curiosity in an ever widening horizon. The Trust by now were deeply drawn to the vision and vigorous enterprise shown by Surrey. When other Universities began to show interest, and certain fears were voiced that the Trust might fall between two stools, the unavoidable delays were stern tests of their endurance and belief in Surrey.

Professor Tropp returned in the summer of 1967. To the delight of the Trust, he showed himself in favour of the course, and immediately set about the necessary adaptations to fit it into the Surrey University pattern.

The Working Party of Professors, with Professor Tropp as Chairman, met on 18 July 1967. They had consulted various Home Economists on the general needs of the profession, and their present thinking led to a four-year 'sandwich' course, with the third year to be spent in attachments within industry, or gaining educational experience. The draft of the syllabus followed the general lines laid down by the Trust, with an introduction to the various branches of the subject in the first year, leading by stages to more advanced work in the final year. There should be close liaison with Guildford School of Art on the design side, possibly leading to the joint appointment of a lecturer. The position, of course, was fluid while discussions were proceeding.

The confident hopes of those unversed in the ramifications attendant on mounting a degree course were shaken when no speedy issue was at hand. At the Annual General Meeting on 28 September 1968 the Chairman likened a modern University to 'a complex piece of machinery with interlocking controls, all of which have to be operated in the right sequence and through the right people to obtain the desired result. The constitution,' he continued, 'of an Honours Home Economics degree course in the University of Surrey occupied the time and attention of three separate Working Parties and the consideration of three or four successive meetings of the Academic Policy Committee before the formal assent of the Senate was secured, and this is really only the beginning of the process of arranging a viable course to open in 1970. The immense intricacy of the operation and the spate of letters, talks and memoranda which has occupied the last fifteen months has added, just to my own comparatively small personal share, three more large files to the stack in our cupboard, and telephone calls have been legion.'

It was not until 28 February 1968 that the Trust Committee received a letter from Dr Leggett confirming that the Senate had approved the establishment of an Honours course of four years, leading to the degree of Bachelor of Science. Dr Leggett enclosed the draft which Professor Tropp had devised, based on the original plan of the Trust, and hoped that the Trust would accept this, and feel able to give financial assistance as offered. He stated that Mr John Freyne, Director of General Studies, would be Director of the course. He and Professor Tropp would work with an Advisory Committee, for which the Trust was invited to nominate two members.

The Committee approved a draft reply, making the Trust position clear while confirming its willingness to give financial assistance to the University of Surrey. The letter sent by the Chairman on 4 March 1968 stated 'As the outline planned by Professor Tropp approximates so closely, both in aims and content, to the syllabus devised by the Trust, and submitted to the University in February 1966, my Committee feel every confidence that however details may change to meet differing needs, the course will always remain a true expression of the fundamentals of civilised life emanating from the home. In these circumstances, the Committee will feel happy in confirming their agreement to give financial assistance for the course.'

A small finance group was now set up to examine the financial aspect in detail, to report their recommendations to an early meeting of the Trust Executive Committee, and then to discuss with Dr Leggett how these could best be put into effect. It was agreed that the members of this group should be the Trustees and the Hon. Treasurer with Mr Hadrill and Mr Coulson.

Consultation with the Lord Bishop in April concerning the allocation of the Trust funds led to a meeting of the small finance group with Dr Leggett on 3 May 1968, when it was agreed that the Trust should give the University £50,000, in two instalments, for the building of the Home Economics Centre. Later, to meet rising costs, this was increased to £56,000.

The Balance Sheets are quoted here for the years 1968 & 1972:

BALANCE SHEET AS AT 30 JUNE 1968

ACCUMULATED FUND	£	s	d	CURRENT ASSETS	£	s	d
Balance at 1 July 1967	47,339	2	7	Cash on Deposit A/c	174	19	1
Excess of Income over				Cash on Current A/c	1,329	18	7
Expenditure for year				Cash in hand	6	17	5
ended 30 June 1968	1,730	5	9	Income Tax recoverable	1,118	8	3
				Sundry Debtor	43	10	0
Current Liabilities				INVESTMENTS at cost	46,457	17	2
Expenses accrued	81	8	1	(market value £72,084)			
Clarke-Swanston Fund				Clarke-Swanston Fund			
Balance at 1 July 1967	2,330	8	0	Investments at cost	2,349	13	11
				(market value £3,806)			
	£51,481	4	5		£51,481	4	5

After two payments to the University of Surrey, each of £28,000, making £56,000; £10,000 for the Edith Clarke Fund; £2,000 for the Library; with some minor grants, bringing the total up to approximately £70,000, the last balance sheet, given below, for 1972, shows Trust assets of over £17,000.

BALANCE SHEET AS AT 30 JUNE 1972

ACCUMULATED FUND	£	CURRENT ASSETS	£
Balance at 1 July 1971	16,272·20	Cash on Deposit Account	4,470·18
Profits realised and appreciation of investment	1,576·20	Cash on Current Account	446·18
		Cash in hand	4·60
Less excess of Expenditure over Income for year		Income Tax recoverable	145·60
ended 30 June 1972	186·84	Investments at market value	12,639·00
	17,661·56		
Current Liabilities			
Accrued expenses	44·00		
	£17,705·56		£17,705·56

Miss Voyce and Mr Stone were nominated to serve on the Advisory Committee of the University, which was composed of University representatives and certain advisers. At the first meeting on 29 January 1969, the latter included Miss B. S. Briggs, Miss E. Gray, Miss M. M. N. McLauchlan, Mrs J. Robins, Miss M. J. Voyce and Mr B. G. Stone, to join the University members, Dr Burstall, Mr Freyne, Miss Perkins and Professor Salmon, with Professor Tropp in the Chair.

Many matters were considered, including suggested amendments of the original scheme. These were discussed at the Trust Committee in September 1969, when Miss Hilton urged that more attention should be given to Art and Design in the home. Unfortunately, a variety of circumstances combined to prevent the fulfilment of these hopes.

The work of the Advisory Committee on plans for the Home Economics Centre was helped by the visit of Mr John Freyne to the U.S.A., for which the Trust gave a grant of over £300 in the autumn of 1968, to meet Home Economists and see their departments in various Universities. The eventual plans and equipment at Surrey are a tribute to fresh ideas and imaginative thought.

A Press Conference was held at the University on 12 June 1968, when the Vice Chancellor invited the Trust Chairman to speak. A group of Home Economists was there to learn about the new course, which the Vice Chancellor lucidly explained. Advance publicity was also given by Miss Hilton in her June *Bulletin* to the four hundred schools on the W.E.F. list, by a notice of the forthcoming Home Economics degree course.

At the Annual General Meeting on 28 September 1968, there was genuine rejoicing at the happy outcome of the years of work and negotiation, sealed by kind and gracious congratulation from Her Majesty Queen Elizabeth, the Queen Mother.

At the following Annual General Meeting on 27 September 1969, the Chairman gave a summary of the general position. He explained that the new degree course in Home Economics 'has been fitted into their Humanities and Social Science Department, and the University is looking forward to welcoming the first group of about fifteen students this time next year, in October 1970, at the University's new home at Guildford.

'I expect,' he continued, 'that most of you know the magnificent site of Guildford Cathedral just outside the town, standing high above the Portsmouth Road. The University has nearly four hundred acres there; eighty acres on the steep hillside adjoining the Cathedral precincts and running down to the playing fields far below. The architects have devised a brilliant grouping of buildings in a compact campus on this dramatic site, ingeniously linking some of them together at different levels, so that one can for example walk from the fifth floor of one to the second floor of another, and from the middle of the Engineering block on to the flat roof of the Students' Refectory. The Senate House is a separate building of seven stories on the lower part of the slope. Our Home Economics Centre will be in that area. There is also a central Lecture Theatre block and a Library. They plan for Halls of Residence eventually for over three thousand students. One thousand are actually in residence this session. Some of these buildings are finished and in use, but it will obviously take several years before the present plan is complete.'

A few months later the Committee was appreciative of the invitation given, on 12 December 1969, to their Chairman, Mr B. G. Stone, representing the N.T.C.D.S. Trust, to become a Foundation Fellow of the Court of the University. Composed of about four hundred members, the Court includes:
1) Officers of the University of Surrey
2) High Officers of the Church and State for Surrey
3) Chief Officers of the Surrey County Council
4) Members of Parliament for Surrey
5) Principals of County Training Colleges
6) Directors of Industrial, Commercial and Research Organisations
7) Further representatives of religious, educational and professional bodies
8) Individual Life Members
9) Representatives of Bodies contributing to the University Foundation Fund (known as 'Foundation Fellows').
An attractive small oak plaque bearing the arms of the University had been received to mark this membership.

Through discussions at the University and the medium of the Advisory Committee, the Trust were kept in close touch with the progress of both the syllabus and the building, but contemporary ideas with their increasing pull of commercial profit at the expense of humanity caused the Committee some concern. While in full support of technological progress, the very acceptance of the word 'consumer,' with its proper meaning of one who devours as opposed to one who produces, could in itself constitute a danger, for however lightly used in common jargon, it could never represent anyone whose aim was to give.

Accordingly, the Trust Committee invited Professor Tropp and Mr Freyne to discuss the fundamentals of the course implicit in the training, including their practical application. On 1 October 1970, at Alderman's House, through the courtesy of Mr Coulson, this meeting gave an excellent opportunity to gain mutual understanding. It had long been realised that while carrying the overall responsibility, the demands on the time of Professor Tropp and Mr Freyne were too heavy to allow the close attention required, and there was urgent need for a Lecturer to translate and co-ordinate the concept of the course. The Trust offered to help initially with this salary, as there were many claims on University funds until the Quinquennium in 1972; but in the event, the University assumed responsibility from the start.

At the close of reasoned argument, Professor Tropp assured the Committee that the course was firmly based on the aims and ideals shared by all. It was generally hoped that the new Lecturer would appreciate this fundamental conviction, and combine specific knowledge with vision of the potential scope.

On 1 May 1971, Mrs Kathleen Hastrop was appointed. She had been a consultant Home Economist to organisations concerned with domestic appliances and food, with previous University experience in research at both Birmingham and Queen Elizabeth College, London. She undertook the responsibility for placing the students in their third year, when her knowledge of industrial conditions proved valuable. There were not equal facilities on the educational and aesthetic sides, but a happy connection was made with the Mulberry Housing Trust where the University students had opportunities to study welfare work under the watchful care of Miss Josie Jackson.

During the summer of 1972, Dr R. J. Irving, M.Sc. Ph.D., a Reader in Chemistry, joined the team, to bring his interpretation of the basic aims to strengthen the development of the course.

Immediately before the payment by the Trust of the second instalment of the total sum of £56,000, for the building of the Home Economics Centre, on 25 May 1971, Dr Leggett confirmed in writing to the Chairman, 'It is with pleasure that I, on behalf of the University, give formal assurance to you and your co-Trustees that the money given to the University of Surrey by the N.T.C.D.S. Trust, will be used for the purpose for which it was given, i.e. to enable the University to run a degree course in Home Economics, having the aims as conceived and presented by the Trust.'

In 1970 the first fourteen students, including one who was more mature, drawn from a wide range of 125 applicants, illustrated how the work can be enriched by different contributions. Another fifteen joined in both 1971 and 1972, and the first students of this pioneer Home Economics Honours Degree Course will graduate in 1974.

'And thus the whirligig of time brings in his' – surprises, for it is recorded that Mr J. C. Buckmaster, one of the pioneers cf the National, who lectured on Cookery at the Exhibition of 1873, was urged to take up teaching as a career by John Bright, who secured a place for him at one of the 'first regular teacher training courses, in the newly established College at Battersea.' Over a hundred years later, this College is translated to the University of Surrey, and here another pioneer course, in Home Economics, stems from the National. The wheel has come full circle.

The National Training School of Cookery was founded in South Kensington in 1873. As the centenary drew near, it was increasingly felt that its history should be recorded. Thus it was that this book came to be written.

On 9 June 1973, the Vice Chancellor will officially open the Home Economics Centre, unveiling a plaque which reads:

This Centre for the Degree Course in Home Economics, based on an original scheme of the National Training College of Domestic Subjects Trust, was given to the University by the Trust to perpetuate the aims and ideals of the above College.
The Centre was opened by Dr D. M. A. Leggett, Vice-Chancellor of the University, on 9 June 1973.

The Chairman of the Trust will hand over to the University the following possessions long prized by the National:
The Grant of Arms   Visitors Book
Framed photograph of Mrs Edith Clarke
Silver Rose-bowl (purchased with gifts from Her Majesty
    Queen Elizabeth, the Queen Mother)
Framed illustration from *The Graphic* of 18 July 1874

There will be an opportunity to visit the splendid site and new buildings before the first Edith Clarke memorial lecture 'The History and Economy of the Home' to be given by Professor John Burnett, Ph.D. He will speak on the social conditions of the last hundred years, referring in perspective to the work of the National, as recorded in this History.

A buffet supper will follow, and the Trust are greatly indebted to the University for placing at their disposal the facilities for the celebration of this day.

When the Chairman of the Trust hands over the National's possessions to the University, he has been honoured by a request from Her Majesty Queen Elizabeth the Queen Mother, to deliver to the assembly her own personal message from Clarence House, which reads:

As Patron for many years of the National Training College of Domestic Subjects, it gives me much pleasure to know that its good work is being continued in the University of Surrey in the form of the Honours Degree Course in Home Economics.

The Home Economics Centre will worthily enshrine the mementos and the spirit of the College and, at the official opening ceremony, I take this opportunity for welcoming all the Old Students who have come here today, and of wishing the present undergraduates every success.

                               ELIZABETH R
Saturday, 9 June 1973   *Queen Mother*

Plaque, Grant of Arms and Mrs Clarke's photograph
at the University of Surrey, 1973

This Centre, for the Degree in Home Economics
based on an original scheme of the National
Training College of Domestic Subjects Trust,
was given to the University by the Trust to
perpetuate the aims and ideals of the above
College.

The Centre was opened by
the Vice-Chancellor, Dr.D.M.A. Leggett
on 9 June 1973

When Mrs Clarke's life at the National ended, Miss Caddow wrote of her that she was 'one of the great pioneers of women's work, who in many respects was ahead of her day and generation,' and that 'it is hoped to raise some memorial of a lasting nature which shall keep her memory green.'

Fifty years later, a memorial, not just in bricks and mortar, has been raised. A century after she began her task, the Home Economics Centre displays the Grant of Arms, her own photograph and other treasures from the National. But the true reward lies in the work.

The words of Her Majesty Queen Elizabeth the Queen Mother express the hopes and stimulus for the unknown, exciting future, which were epitomised by Dr D. M. A. Leggett, the Vice Chancellor of the University of Surrey, when he first studied the degree course devised and submitted by the Trust. He said that 'This degree course syllabus expresses the fundamentals of civilised life, which would still be valid in a hundred or even two hundred years, however much the approach towards certain aspects might differ from time to time.'

This is the real, living tribute to the pioneer founders of the National, and to Mrs Edith Clarke, which 'shall keep their memory green.'

Thus, is PHOENIX RISING.

COLOPHON

This book has grown from an anticipated hundred pages. It has
been produced at cost for the National Training College of
Domestic Subjects Trust in the Department of Printing in the
Faculty of Art and Design of Brighton Polytechnic (previously
Brighton College of Art). Typography by John Evans helped by
keyboard students Stephen Coleman, Alan Constable, David
Graimes, James Lawlor, Christopher Morris, Robert Ungless
and Richard Weaver. 'Monotype' Century Schoolbook is used
mainly in the 10 pt on 12 pt size with combined close-spacing in
the tradition of Leonard Jay of Birmingham, and proofed for
camera in twenty-galley batches. Process camera work, planning and platemaking by Peter Weedon (Technician). Printed
on Dickinson's Evensyde (106 gsm) by Ian Faux and his students
of lithographic printing on a Heidelberg KORA press. Frontispiece is printed letterpress by Morris Dixon and students of
letterpress printing and foil blocked on an Impress blocker by
David Igglesden (Technician) together with the cover. He also
bound the presentation copies. Examples of the National copper
were photographed in the Royal Pavilion by E. G. Phillippe
(Technician). Cover and final sections printed by Carmichael
and Company Limited in order to meet the dead-line.

*   *   *   *   *

Without the team effort of the teaching and technician staff
it could never have been completed within
the resources and time available

APPENDIX A

NATIONAL TRAINING SCHOOL FOR COOKERY

P R O S P E C T U S

At a meeting held at Grosvenor House, by permission of the Marquis of Westminster, on Thursday, 17 July 1873, it was unanimously resolved:

1. That the establishment of a Training School for Cookery, to be in alliance with the School Boards and Training Schools throughout the Country, is most desirable at the present time.
2. That the aim of the proposed School should be to teach the best methods of cooking articles of food in general consumption among all classes.
3. That an Association should be formed with the intention of making the School self-supporting.

And a Provisional Committee was formed,

Her Royal Highness the Princess Christian of Schleswig-Holstein,
Her Royal Highness the Princess Louise, Marchioness of Lorne,
and the following Ladies joining the Committee:

The Duchess of Buccleuch	The Hon. Mrs Armytage
The Marchioness of Westminster	Lady Barker
Maria, Marchioness of Ailesbury	Mrs H. Cole
The Countess of Bradford	Mrs F. Fowke
The Countess Spencer	Mrs H. Fulcher
The Countess Granville	Mrs Gladstone
Lady Arthur Russell	Miss Shaw Lefevre
Lady Marian Alford	Mrs Horne Payne
Lady Sophia Macnamara	Mrs H. Reeve
Lady Knightley	Mrs Synge

With power to add to their number.

An Executive Committee was appointed as follows:

THE HON. F. LEVESON-GOWER, M.P. (*Chairman*)

The Viscount Barrington, M.P.	Major E. F. Du Cane, C.B. R.E.
F. B. Alston, Esq	Captain Hans Busk, LL.D.
James Bateman, Esq, F.R.S.	J. MacGregor, Esq
Henry Cole, Esq, C.B.	W. W. Follett Synge, Esq

With power to add to their number.

1. It is proposed to commence the work of the National Training School of Cookery as soon as possible in Exhibition Road, South Kensington, in the building lately used for the International Exhibition School of Cookery, which the Commissioners for the International Exhibition have liberally placed at the disposal of the Executive Committee of the Training School for Cookery for a limited period.
2. In the MORNINGS of the days of instruction, Pupil Teachers and others engaged in public education will be instructed at fees as moderate as possible.
3. In the AFTERNOONS of the days of instruction, a Lecture and Demonstrations will be given, at which the public will be admitted upon payment for each Lecture, or for a course.
4. Every subscriber, in return for the subscriptions, will be entitled to receive tickets of a proportionate value for the courses of instruction open to teachers or for the public Lectures and Demonstrations.

5. Arrangements will be made, if possible, to give practical instruction to female cooks on certain days of the week.
6. The Executive Committee purpose to make arrangements for sending a Lecturer and a Staff of Instructors to such of the Colleges, or Training Schools for females throughout the Country, as may be willing to pay the necessary expenses. The Committee also hope that they may be able to send shortly one or more Lecturers with Teachers, to localities which may desire to have the instruction, and be ready to make the necessary arrangements.
7. The extent to which the foregoing intentions can be carried out will be regulated by the amount of funds which the public may place at the disposal of the Executive Committee. As soon as a sufficient sum has been subscribed, the various rates of fees for the courses of instruction will be published.
8. Donations are invited especially to cover the expenses of instruction for Training Schools and Teachers, and the amount of such donations will regulate the rate of the fees to be charged for such instruction.
9. Donations and subscriptions may be paid to the account of the National Training School for Cookery, at the London and Westminster Bank, 1 St James's Square, London.

The Committee appeal to the public to aid them with liberal donations and annual subscriptions in this national work, so necessary for the welfare, health, and comfort of all classes of the community, and especially the working classes. It is obvious that until the support of the public has been promised to an adequate extent, no effective steps can be taken.

The first list of donations and subscriptions will be published after 15 December 1873.

Temporary Offices
Kensington Gore   1 December 1873

APPENDIX B

OBJECTS OF THE SCHOOL
The National Training School of Cookery has been established to carry out the following objects:
1. To train and qualify persons to become Teachers in Cookery in Training Schools, School Board Schools, Poor Schools, and similar Institutions.
2. To instruct persons desirous of acquiring a knowledge of the principles of Cookery and paying the necessary fees.
3. To send Teachers and Lecturers, with the necessary apparatus for teaching the principles of Cookery, to localities and Institutions in the provinces willing to incur the attendant expense.

LOCALITY OF THE SCHOOL
The School has commenced its work in Exhibition Road, South Kensington, in a provisional building lately used for the International Exhibition School of Cookery, which the Commissioners for the Exhibition of 1851 have liberally placed at the disposal of the Executive Committee for a limited period.

MAINTENANCE OF THE SCHOOL
The School will be maintained by:
1. *Donations* which will be applied in fitting up the present temporary

buildings, and subsequently in providing and furnishing permanent school buildings.

2. *Annual Subscriptions* which will be applied in maintaining the School buildings and in training Instructors in Cookery. Donors and annual subscribers will have a proportionate right of nominating persons to be trained as Teachers.

3. *Fees* to be received from persons going through the various courses of instruction in the principles of Cookery, which will be applied in the same manner as the annual subscriptions.

REPORT OF THE EXECUTIVE COMMITTEE READ TO AND ADOPTED BY A PUBLIC MEETING HELD AT THE HOUSE OF THE SOCIETY OF ARTS ON 21 MAY 1874

A Public Meeting was held at Grosvenor House on Thursday, 17 July 1873 at which the following propositions were submitted for consideration:

1. That the establishment of a Training School for Cookery, to be in alliance with the School Boards and Training Schools throughout the country, is most desirable at the present time.

2. That the aim of the proposed School should be to teach the best methods of cooking articles of food in general consumption among all classes.

3. That an association should be formed with the intention of making the School self-supporting.

4. That it would be prudent to secure a capital, say £5,000, which might be raised by means of donations, giving the privilege of nominating students in the School, as well as by means of a Guarantee Fund; it is estimated that an expenditure of about £1,000 would be required to fit up a practical School or Laboratory.

APPENDIX C

Aims are as in Appendix A. The original subscribers, desirous of being formed into an Association, were:

Description of Subscribers	Amount Subscribed
EDWARD FREDERICK LEVESON GOWER, 14 South Audley Street	£100
NORTHAMPTON, 44 Lennox Gardens, S.W.	£100
W. P. TALBOT, 15 Cromwell Road, S.W.	£50
DANIEL COOPER, 6 De Vere Gardens, W.	£100
JNO. M. YORKE, 52 Rutland Gate, S.W.	£20
E. Y. W. HENDERSON, 4 Gledhow Gardens, South Kensington	£20
HY. WATSON PARKER, St Michael's Rectory, Cornhill, *Solicitor*	£50

NOTE: It has not been possible to record the Burnham Scale of salaries recommended for Training College staff as no official Authority has been able to supply us with any information before the end of the Second World War.

APPENDIX D

To THE EDITOR of *The Times*

Sir: Having watched the development of the National Training School for Cookery from the beginning, I think it may be generally useful to direct attention to the present state of the arrangements of the School, so that the country at large may take advantage of them. The School, which by the way is in vacation till the 13th September, is now fully organized for training Teachers to give instruction in localities varying with the circumstances of each place.

It has been demonstrated that any village school with 100 girls and upwards may have simple cookery suitable for artisans and labourers taught in the school, if the school will first send a girl to the Training School to be taught in the artisan class for three weeks at a fee of three guineas. The annual capital required by the village school ought not to reach £20. This includes the purchase of food, which is consumed by the children who are found in numbers able to pay twopence a head for their dinner which they help to cook in learning.

If the locality has several elementary schools and a population of about 3,000 or 4,000, including neighbouring villages, then an organization is possible which would teach cookery, not only in elementary schools, but to ladies of the middle classes who are or wish to be wives, and not to ladies only, but to domestic servants and artisans' wives. In this case, as in that of the elementary schools, the first want is to get a Teacher, but this is not difficult to meet. Let a locality feel the want of a School for Cookery, and its first work is to subscribe about £25 and to send a competent person to become a certificated teacher. Such person should be well educated – as well educated as a good elementary schoolmistress. She may well be the daughter of a clergyman, doctor, lawyer, or half-pay Army or Navy man, but she must have the desire to earn her own living and be content with an income of from £80 to £100 a year for giving, say, 40 weeks' instruction. So much the better if she has had any experience of teaching children in a Sunday or other school and has acted as a district visitor. She must have no defect in speaking, as she will have to address numbers in a class. Her age should be between twenty and thirty.

At the present time, when great numbers of the middle classes are away from their homes to get health at the seaside, much suffering from bad cookery is undergone, for every youthful drab is turned on to cookery. The cure is only to be found in local schools for cookery distributed over the country.

I am, Sir, Your obedient servant, HENRY COLE   17 August 1875

APPENDIX E

We are indebted to the Brighton Museums Department for information concerning the collection of copper cooking utensils presented by the Governors of the N.T.C.D.S. on the closure of the College in July 1962.

The provenance of the copper was discussed in August 1972 with the late Deputy Director of Brighton Museums, Mr H. F. Brazenor who in the course of a long and dedicated career had amassed an encyclopaedic knowledge of every type of antique which could conceivably be of interest to a museum. Mr Brazenor stated that some of the articles from the National Training College have no counterpart in the collections from Syon House and the Duke of Wellington's Estates already on display in the Royal Pavilion; of special interest in his view are the condiment sets.

Mr Brazenor unfortunately died before he could redeem his promise to compile a record of the age and probable origin of the National collection.

A senior member of the Brighton Museum staff has, however, been most helpful. He confirmed that in his view most of the pieces were acquired from London merchants, either new or secondhand, in the latter part of the nineteenth century. Some pieces however, particularly the bombe moulds, closely resemble pieces in the Wellington collection stamped with the date 1816.

The kitchen copperware prized by the National and so distinctive in the kitchens of great houses from the eighteenth century onwards to the end of the Edwardian era, fell into disuse in private houses after the First World War, when the staff to provide for its care and maintenance were no longer available, and joined other *objets d'art* in the antique market.

Many of the 177 pieces of copper listed at the Royal Pavilion as presented by the National bear the marks of London firms; for example W. S. Adams and Son of 57 Haymarket, Ironmongers to Her Majesty Queen Victoria; E. K. Wilson of 6 Sussex Place; Harrods Ltd; James Williams and Sons, London, S.W.1; Benham and Sons, Wigmore Street, London; Army and Navy Co-operative Society Ltd, Victoria Street; as well as Errington and Sons of Portsmouth; and Trottier, Paris.

The engraving reproduced in Chapter II of Mr J. C. Buckmaster delivering one of the series of lectures planned by the 1873 Exhibition Cookery Committee, shows copper utensils identifiable one hundred years later, as do other reproductions illustrating particularly the old condiment sets which have now become more rare.